The Cambridge Companion to the Spanish Novel

The Cambridge Companion to the Spanish Novel presents the development of the modern Spanish novel from 1600 to the present. Drawing on the combined legacies of *Don Quijote* and the traditions of the picaresque novel, these essays focus on the question of invention and experiment, on what constitutes the singular features, formal and cultural, of evolving fictional forms. They examine how the novel articulates the relationships between history and fiction, high and popular culture, art and ideology, and gender and society. Contributors highlight the role played by historical events and cultural contexts in the elaboration of the Spanish novel, which often takes a self-conscious stance toward literary tradition. Topics covered include the regional novel, women writers, and film and literature. This companionable survey, which includes a chronology and guides to further reading, conveys a vivid sense of the innovative techniques of the Spanish novel and of the debates surrounding it.

THE CAMBRIDGE COMPANION TO
THE SPANISH NOVEL
FROM 1600 TO THE PRESENT

EDITED BY

HARRIET TURNER

AND

ADELAIDA LÓPEZ DE MARTÍNEZ

University of Nebraska-Lincoln

PUBLISHED BY THE PRESS SYNDICATE OF THE UNIVERSITY OF CAMBRIDGE
The Pitt Building, Trumpington Street, Cambridge CB2 1RP, United Kingdom

CAMBRIDGE UNIVERSITY PRESS
The Edinburgh Building, Cambridge, CB2 2RU, UK
40 West 20th Street, New York, NY 10011–4211, USA
477 Williamstown Road, Port Melbourne, VIC 3207, Australia
Ruiz de Alarcón 13, 28014 Madrid, Spain
Dock House, The Waterfront, Cape Town 8001, South Africa

http://www.cambridge.org

First published 2003

Printed in the United Kingdom at the University Press, Cambridge

Typeface Sabon 10/13 pt. *System* LaTeX 2ε [TB]

A catalogue record for this book is available from the British Library

ISBN 0 521 77127 7 hardback
ISBN 0 521 77815 8 paperback

CONTENTS

CONTRIBUTORS

ISOLINA BALLESTEROS is Assistant Professor of Spanish at Barnard College/Columbia University. A specialist in contemporary Spanish literature and Spanish film, she has published essays on Spanish and Latin American women writers, the image of women in the post-Franco literature, and Spanish film after 1975, and two books: *Escritura femenina y discurso autobiográfico en la nueva novela española* (1994) and *Cine (Ins)urgente: textos fílmicos y contextos culturales de la España postfranquista* (2001). Currently she is working on a book entitled *"Undesirable" Otherness: Immigration, Xenophobia and Racism in European Film.*

LOU CHARNON-DEUTSCH is Professor of Hispanic Languages and Literature at the State University of New York, Stony Brook. She has served as President of Feministas Unidas (1992–4) and is currently the American Editor of the *Hispanic Research Journal*. She also serves on the editorial boards of *Letras Femeninas* and *Revista de Estudios Hispánicos*. Her recent books include *Gender and Representation: Women in Nineteenth-Century Spanish Realist Fiction* (1990); *Narratives of Desire: Nineteenth-Century Spanish Fiction by Women* (1994); *Culture and Gender in Nineteenth-Century Spain* (coedited with Jo Labanyi 1995); and *Fictions of the Feminine in the Nineteenth-Century Spanish Press* (2000). Her most recent work is entitled *A History of the Imaginary Spanish Gypsy.*

ANTHONY J. CLOSE is Reader in Spanish at the University of Cambridge, United Kingdom. He has published extensively on Cervantes and the Spanish Golden Age, specializing in the interpretation of *Don Quijote*, the history of its reception, and the relation between it and the comic genres of the time. His latest book is *Cervantes and the Comic Mode* (2000).

BRAD EPPS is Professor of Romance Languages and Literatures at Harvard University. He is the author of *Significant Violence: Oppression and Resistance in the Narrative of Juan Goytisolo* (1996) and of over fifty articles on Spanish, Latin American, French, and Catalan literature, film, art, and culture. He is currently preparing a book on gay, lesbian, bisexual, and transgendered issues in Spain, Latin America, and US Latino cultures (*Daring to Write*), a collection of essays, with Luis Fernández Cifuentes, on literary history (*Spain Beyond Spain*), and a collection of essays, with Keja Valens, on homosexuality and immigration (*Passing Lines*).

REBECCA HAIDT is Associate Professor of Spanish at Ohio State University. Her publications include *Embodying Enlightenment: Knowing the Body in Eighteenth-Century Spanish Literature and Culture* (1998), winner of the MLA's Katherine Singer Kovacs Prize for 1999, and *Seduction and Sacrilege: Rhetorical Power in Fray Gerundio de Campazas* (2002). She has served on several editorial boards including those of the *Revista de Estudios Hispánicos* and *Eighteenth-Century Studies*.

ROBERTA JOHNSON is Professor of Spanish and Portuguese at the University of Kansas, where she served as Department Chair from 1992 to 1997 and director of the Hall Center for the Humanities from 1997 to 2000. She has written numerous articles on twentieth-century prose and books: *Carmen Laforet* (1981), *El ser y la palabra en Gabriel Miró* (1983), *Crossfire: Philosophy and the Novel in Spain 1900–1934* (1993), *Las bibliotecas de Azorín* (1966), and *Gender and Nation: The Spanish Modernist Novel* (2003). She has received research grants from the Guggenheim Foundation and the National Endowment for the Humanities, among others, has held a Fulbright lectureship in Spain, and has served on a number of national and international committees and editorial boards.

ADELAIDA LÓPEZ DE MARTÍNEZ is Professor of Spanish and Women's Studies at the University of Nebraska-Lincoln. She has written widely on contemporary Spanish and Latin American literature, and has coordinated the publication of volumes such as *Sor Juana Inés de la Cruz: amor, poesía, soledumbre* (1985), *Voces femeninas en la literature de la guerra civil española: una valoración crítica al medio siglo de historia* (1986), *En honor de Victoria Urbano* (1993), *Discurso femenino actual* (1995), *A Ricardo Gullón: sus discípulos* (1995), *Dynamics of Change in Latin American Literature: Contemporary Women Writers* (1996), *Narradoras ecuatorianas de hoy: una antología crítica* (2001). From 1985 to 2001 she was the General Editor of *Letras Femeninas*, and continues to serve on the editorial boards of several scholarly journals. Her academic work has been honored with a number of citations, including the 1981 Southern Council on Latin American Studies annual award to the best publication in the humanities for her essay "'Las babas del diablo': teoría y práctica del cuento en Julio Cortázar."

ELISA MARTÍ-LÓPEZ is Associate Professor in the Department of Spanish and Portuguese at Northwestern University. She is the author of articles on publishing practices and the novel market in nineteenth-century Spain. She has also written on the *folletín* and the formation of the canon in relation to the popular novel. Her book *Borrowed Words: Translation, Imitation, and the Making of the Novel in Nineteenth-Century Spain* (2002) studies the emergence of the novel in Spain in the middle of the nineteenth century.

RANDOLPH POPE is Commonwealth Professor of Spanish at the University of Virginia. His field of specialization is the Peninsular novel and autobiography but he has also written extensively on other topics. He has taught at Barnard College, the University of Bonn in Germany, Dartmouth College, Vassar College, where he was Chair of Hispanic Studies, and Washington University in St. Louis, where he served as Chair of Comparative Literature for seven years. From 1991 to spring 2002 he was editor of the *Revista de Estudios Hispánicos*. He has published three books – on autobiography, the Spanish novel, and on Juan Goytisolo – and some ninety scholarly essays.

GEOFFREY RIBBANS was for fifteen years Gilmour Professor of Spanish and editor of the *Bulletin of Hispanic Studies* at the University of Liverpool. He was William R. Kenan, Jr., University Professor of Hispanic Studies at Brown University, Providence, RI, from 1978 until 1999, when he became emeritus. He is the author of numerous studies on the fiction, intellectual history and poetry of Spain (including Catalonia) in the nineteenth and twentieth centuries. His books include *Niebla y Soledad: Aspectos de Unamuno and Machado* (1971), *History and Fiction in Galdós's Narratives* (1993), and *Conflicts and Conciliations. The Evolution of Galdós's "Fortunata y Jacinta"* (1997).

ALISON SINCLAIR is Reader in Modern Spanish Literature and Intellectual History at the University of Cambridge, and Fellow of Clare College, Cambridge. She has taught and published on both the nineteenth and twentieth centuries, and in comparative studies. Among her books and essays are *The Deceived Husband* (1993), a comparative study ranging from the Middle Ages to the 1980s; a monograph on Valle-Inclán (1977); *Dislocations of Desire* (1998), a new and sustained psychoanalytic reading of Alas's late nineteenth-century novel *La Regenta*; and, most recently, *Uncovering the Mind* (2001), on Unamuno. Her current work, on cultural and intellectual life in Spain, examines the cultural exchanges through institutions, publishing houses, and individuals between Spain, Europe, and Latin America from 1900 to 1936.

GONZALO SOBEJANO, Professor of Spanish at Columbia University, is a member of the Order of Isabel la Católica, a recognition that honors a particularly distinguished career in teaching and scholarship in Spain, Germany, and the US. He is a specialist in Spanish poetry and prose of the sixteenth and seventeenth centuries, as well as the nineteenth and twentieth centuries. Among his editions, monographs, collections of essays, and scores of articles are *El epíteto en la lírica española* (1956, 1970); *Moderne spanische Erzähler* (1963); *Forma literaria y sensibilidad social* and *Nietzsche en España* (1967); *La novela española de nuestro tiempo* (1970, 1975), which won Spain's National Prize for Literature in 1971; and *Clarín en su obra ejemplar* (1985). His edition (1981, 1989) of *La Regenta* (1884–85) by Leopoldo Alas, now in its fifth printing, is widely cited in this volume.

AKIKO TSUCHIYA is Associate Professor of Spanish at Washington University in St. Louis and the Peninsular editor of the *Revista de Estudios Hispánicos*. She is the author of a book on Galdós and has published widely on nineteenth-century Spanish narrative, as well as on Spanish women's fiction of the post-Franco era. She is currently working on a book entitled *Women on the Margins: Gender and Deviance in Nineteenth-Century Spanish Literature*.

HARRIET TURNER is Professor of Hispanic Studies and Director of International Affairs at the University of Nebraska-Lincoln. Her publications include *Galdós, "Fortunata y Jacinta"* (1992); *Textos y contextos de Galdós* (coedited with J. Kronik, 1994); *Niebla* (coedited with R. Gullón, 1965); and a special issue of the journal *Letras Peninsulares* on the poetics of realism (2000), in addition to more than fifty articles and reviews. She has served as President of the International Association of Galdós Scholars (1985–88), as a member of several editorial boards, including the Nebraska Press, and as director of several international symposia and conferences.

NOËL VALIS is Professor of Spanish at Yale University. Among her publications are *The Decadent Vision in Leopoldo Alas*; *The Novels of Jacinto Octavio Picón*; and *In the Feminine Mode: Essays on Hispanic Women Writers* (coedited with Carol Maier), as well as editions of Carolina Coronado's

Poesías, Picón's *La hijastra del amor*, and Pereda's *Bocetos al temple*. She has also translated Pedro Salinas's *Víspera del gozo* as *Prelude to Pleasure* and Julia Uceda's poetry. In press are the second volume of *Leopoldo Alas (Clarín): An Annotated Bibliography* (2002); a book of poetry, *My House Remembers Me* (2002); and *The Culture of Cursilería: Bad Taste, Kitsch and Class in Modern Spain* (2002), which focuses on middle-class culture in nineteenth- and early twentieth-century Spain. She is working on a book entitled *Body Sacraments*, centering on Spanish and Latin-American narratives of confession, authority, and revelation.

TERESA M. VILARÓS is E. Blake Byrne Associate Professor of Romance Studies at Duke University. A cultural theorist with a strong interest in psychoanalysis, post-phenomenology, and material criticism, she works mainly on contemporary and modern cultural production. She is the author of *El mono del desencanto. Una crítica cultural de la transición española (1973–1993)* (1998) and of *Galdós: Invención de la mujer y poética de la sexualidad. Lectura parcial de "Fortunata y Jacinta"* (1995). She has edited the volume *Nuevas culturas metropolitanas* for the journal *Tropelias* (2000) and her essays have appeared in scholarly journals in the US, Chile, Germany, and Spain. She is currently working on a book-length study of Catalonia from the 1960s to the present. Teresa M. Vilarós is coeditor of the *Journal of Spanish Cultural Studies*.

CHRONOLOGY

1140	Anonymous, *Poema de Mío Cid.*
1455	Gutenberg prints the first Latin Bible (42 lines) at Mainz.
1492	Spanish conquest of Granada; expulsion of the Moors; the monarchy of Isabelle of Castile and Ferdinand of Aragon is consolidated. The Catholic Monarchs finance the voyage of Christopher Columbus that will lead to the discovery of the New World.
1499	Fernando de Rojas, *La Celestina.*
1508	Garci Ordoñez (Rodríguez de Montalvo), *Amadís de Gaula.*
1516	The future Holy Roman Emperor (Charles V of Germany) is crowned King Charles I of Spain at age sixteen.
1545	The Council of Trent convenes. Protestant Reformation and Catholic Counter Reformation are discussed until 1564.
1547	Miguel de Cervantes Saavedra (d. 1616) and Mateo Alemán (d. 1615) are born.
1554	Anonymous, *Vida de Lazarillo de Tormes y de sus fortunas y adversidades* (first picaresque novel).
1559	Jorge de Montemayor's *Diana*, the most important Spanish pastoral novel, is published.
1564	William Shakespeare (d. 1616) and Christopher Marlowe (d. 1593) are born.
1575	Torquato Tasso, *Jerusalem Delivered.*
1599	Diego Rodríguez de Silva y Velázquez (d. 1660) is born in Seville. Mateo Alemán, *Guzmán de Alfarache* Part I.
1603	Francisco Gómez de Quevedo, *La vida del buscón.* (Date of writing, presumed but not confirmed; first published 1626.)
1604	Mateo Alemán, *Guzmán de Alfarache* Part II.

1605	Cervantes, *Don Quijote*. Part I. Shakespeare, *King Lear*, *Macbeth*. Virginia Company of London, granted a royal charter, sends 120 colonists to Virginia. Galileo Galilei invents the proportional compass.
1612	Francisco de Quevedo, *El mundo por de dentro*.
1613	Cervantes, *El Coloquio de los perros*.
1614	Domenico Theotocopulos, "El Greco," moves to Toledo.
1615	Cervantes, *Don Quijote* Part II.
1617	Cervantes, *Los trabajos de Persiles y Segismunda*.
1618	Vicente Espinel, *Marcos de Obregón*.
1620	Pilgrims arrive in New Plymouth, Massachusetts, aboard the *Mayflower*. Velázquez, *The Water Seller of Seville*. Jacopo Sannazaro, *Arcadia*.
1623	Velázquez made court painter to Philip IV.
1624	Quevedo, *Sueños*. Rembrandt: *The Money Changer*. Rubens, *Mystic Marriage of St. Catherine*.
1628	Velázquez, *Cristo*.
1635	Pedro Calderón de la Barca, *La vida es sueño*.
1636	Calderón, *El mágico prodigioso*; Pierre Corneille, *Le Cid*.
1641	Luis Vélez de Guevara, *El diablo cojuelo*.
1656	Velázquez, *Las meninas*.
1667	John Milton, *Paradise Lost*.
1700	King Charles II of Spain dies. End of the Spanish Hapsburgs. Philip V, grandson of Louis XIV, declared heir to the Spanish throne. English take Gibraltar.
1712	Spanish National Library founded in Madrid.
1713	Royal Academy of the (Spanish) Language founded in Madrid.
1718	England declares war on Spain.
1719	France declares war on Spain. Ireland declared inseparable from England. Daniel Defoe, *Robinson Crusoe*.
1720	Spain occupies Texas. First serialization of novels in newspapers in France.
1721	Charles Montesquieu, *Persian Letters* (epistolary novel). Johann Sebastian Bach, *Brandenburg Concertos*.
1726	Benito Jerónimo Feijoo, *Teatro crítico universal* (1726–1740). Jonathan Swift, *Gulliver's Travels*.
1729	Bach, *Saint Matthew Passion*.
1730	Petrus van Musschenbroek, *Cours de physique experimentale et mathématique*.
1731	Abbé Prévost, *Manon Lescaut*.

1732	Covent Garden Opera House opens in London.
1733	French abolished in English courts.
1736–7	Diego de Torres Villarroel, *Los desahuciados del mundo.*
1737	Ignacio de Luzán, *Poetics* (prescriptive rules for writing neoclassic drama).
1741	George Frederick Handel, *Messiah.*
1743	Torres Villarroel, *Vida.* Handel's *Samson* given at Covent Garden Opera House.
1752	Treaty of Aranjuez between Spain and the Holy Roman Empire. Henry Fielding, *Amelia.* Charlotte Lennox, *The Female Quixote.*
1754	Etienne Bonnot de Condillac, *Traité des sensations.*
1758	José Francisco de Isla, *Historia del famoso predicador Fray Gerundio de Campazas.*
1759	Voltaire, *Candide* (philosophical novel).
1762	British capture Martinique, Grenada, Havana, and Manila. José Clavijo y Fajardo, *El pensador* (1762–67). Jean-Jacques Rousseau, *Social Contract.*
1765	Horace Walpole, *The Castle of Otranto* (Gothic novel).
1767	Laurence Sterne, *Tristram Shandy.*
1768	Sterne, *A Sentimental Journey Through France and Italy.*
1772	Judge William Murray decides that a slave is free as soon as he sets foot in England. Choderlos de Laclos, *Dangerous Liaisons.*
1773	Boston Tea Party in protest against tax on tea. Gaspar Melchor de Jovellanos, *El delincuente honrado.*
1774	Johann Wolfgang Goethe, *The Sorrows of Young Werther.*
1775	James Watt perfects his invention of the steam engine. The waltz is fashionable in Austria.
1776	The American colonies declare independence from the British Crown. F. M. von Klinger, *Sturm und Drang* (*Storm and Stress*).
1781	Diego Ventura Rejón y Lucas, *Aventuras de Juan Luis.*
1782	Spain conquers Florida.
1783	Wolfgang Amadeus Mozart, *Mass in C minor.*
1786	Pedro Montengón, *El Eusebio.* François Vernes, *Le voyageur sentimental, ou ma Promenade à Yverdun.*
1787	The Constitution of the United States is framed and signed. The US Federal Government is established, and the dollar is adopted as the official currency of the United States.

	Ignacio García Malo, *Flavio e Irene*, *La desventurada Margarita* in *Voz de la naturaleza.*
1788	Emmanuel Kant, *Critique of Practical Reason.* 1788–9: José Cadalso, *Cartas marruecas.*
1790	Washington, DC founded.
1791	Bernardo María de Calzada translates Vernes's *Le voyageur sentimental.*
1792	Vicente Martínez Colomer, *El Valdemaro.* Mary Wollstonecraft, *Vindication of the Rights of Women.*
1793	Marquis de Sade, *La philosophie dans le boudoir* (novel). Jacques Louis David, *The Death of Marat.* Francisco de Goya, *The Capricho Series.* Cadalso, *Cartas marruecas.*
1794	Goya, *Procession of the Flagellants.*
1795	Goya, *The Duchess of Alba.*
1797	Antonio Valladares de Sotomayor, *La Leandra.*
1798	José Mor de Fuentes, *La Serafina.* William Wordsworth and Samuel Taylor Coleridge, *Lyrical Ballads.* 1798–1801: *El ramillete, o los aguinaldos de Apolo.*
1799	Ludwig van Beethoven, *Symphony Number 1.* Josef Haydn, *The Creation.*
1800	Thomas Jefferson President of the United States. Schiller, *Maria Stuart.* Mme. De Staël, *On Literature.*
1801	François René de Chateaubriand, *Atala* (novel). Goya, *The Two Majas.* David, *Napoleon Crossing the Saint Bernard.*
1802	Jean Senebier, *Essai sur l'art d'observer et de faire des expériences.*
1803	The Louisiana Purchase.
1804	Louise Brayer de Saint-Léon, *Maclovie ou les mines du Tirol.*
1805	Admiral Lord Horatio Nelson defeats the Franco-Spanish fleets at Cape Trafalgar. Jerónimo Martín Bernardo, *El Emprendedor.* Chateaubriand, *René* (Romantic novel).
1806	Official abolition of the Holy Roman Empire.
1808	French Army occupies Madrid and Barcelona. Spanish royal family in exile. Joseph Bonaparte becomes king of Spain. Rebellion in Madrid. Joseph Bonaparte flees. Goya, *Execution of the Citizens of Madrid.* Chateaubriand, *The Adventures of the Last Avencerraje.* Beethoven, *Symphonies 5 and 6 (Pastoral).* Schiller, *William Tell.*
1810	Walter Scott, *The Lady of the Lake.* Goya, "The Disasters of War" (engravings).

1811	Duke of Wellington gains the upper hand in the Peninsular War. Jane Austen, *Sense and Sensibility.*
1812	Spain writes its Liberal Constitution in Cadiz. Napoleon invades Russia. Duke of Wellington arrives in Madrid. Beethoven, *Symphonies 7* and *8*. Goya, *Portrait of the Duke of Wellington.*
1813	Simón Bolívar President of Venezuela. Mexico declares independence from Spain. Jane Austen, *Pride and Prejudice.*
1814	Ferdinand VII returns to Spain and nullifies the Liberal Constitution of 1812. Jane Austen, *Mansfield Park.* Goya, *The Second of May 1808* and *The Third of May 1808.* Walter Scott, *Waverly. Maclovia y Federico o las minas del Tirol* (translated from the French of Louise Brayer de Saint-Léon).
1815	Napoleon defeated at Waterloo. Goya, *Tauromaquia* (etchings).
1816	Argentina declares independence. José Luis Munárriz translates Hugh Blair's *Lecciones sobre la retórica y las bellas letras.* Jane Austen, *Emma.* Goya, *The Duke of Osuna.*
1818	George Gordon, Lord Byron, *Don Juan.* Prado Museum founded in Madrid.
1820	Revolution in Spain. King Ferdinand VII forced to restore Constitution of 1812. José Marchena, *Lecciones de filosofía moral y elocuencia de los mejores autores castellanos.* Walter Scott, *Ivanhoe.* Shelley, *Prometheus Unbound.*
1825	Alessandro Manzoni, *The Betrothed.* Alexander Pushkin, *Boris Godunov.*
1826	James Fennimore Cooper, *The Last of the Mohicans.*
1828	Mariano José de Larra founds his newspaper *El duende satírico del día*, in which he publishes his first articles on the mores of the day.
1829	Washington Irving, *The Conquest of Granada* (best seller).
1830	Gaspar Melchor de Jovellanos, "Elogio fúnebre de Carlos III," *Colección de varias obras en prosa y verso.* Victor Hugo, *Hernani.* Stendhal, *Le Rouge et le Noir.*
1831	Charles Darwin sails on an expedition to the southern hemisphere. Honoré de Balzac, *La peau de chagrin.* Victor Hugo, *Notre Dame de Paris.*

1832	Larra founds his second newspaper, *El pobrecito hablador*, in which he continues to publish his articles on the mores of the day.
1833	Isabella II proclaimed Queen of Spain. Balzac, *Eugénie Grandet*. Pushkin, *The Bronze Horseman.*
1834	Spanish Inquisition abolished after 500 years of existence. Larra, *El doncel de don Enrique el doliente*. Balzac, *Le Père Goriot*. Edward Bulwer Lytton, *The Last Days of Pompeii.*
1835	*Lacock Abbey, Wiltshire*, first negative photograph, taken by William Henry Fox Talbot. The expression "l'art pour l'art," coined by the French Philospher Victor Cousin, comes into general use.
1836–42	Mesonero Romanos, *Escenas matritenses*. Charles Dickens, *Pickwick Papers* (serialized). Alfred de Musset, *Confessions d'un enfant du siècle*. Mendelssohn's *Saint Paul* premiered in Düsseldorf.
1837	Victoria becomes Queen of England. Balzac, *Illusions perdues*. Nathaniel Hawthorne, *Twice Told Tales*.
1838	Dickens, *Oliver Twist*. Auguste Comte gives the basic social science the name of Sociology. The Darrege–Niepce method of photography presented at the Academy of Science and the Academy of Art in Paris.
1839	Stendhal, *La chartreuse de Parme*. Edgar Allan Poe, *The Fall of the House of Usher*.
1840	Larra, *Macías*.
1841	Gertrudis Gómez de Avellaneda, *Sab*.
1842	Balzac begins publication of *La comédie humaine*. Eugène Sue, *Les mystères de Paris*. Nicolai Gogol, *Dead Souls*, Part I. Henry Wadsworth Longfellow, *Poems of Slavery*.
1844	José Zorrilla, *Don Juan Tenorio*. Alexandre Dumas, senior, *The Count of Monte Cristo*. Enrique Gil y Carrasco, *El señor de Bembibre*. Wenceslao Ayguals de Izco, *Ernestina*. Juan Martínez Villergas, *Los misterios de Madrid* (1844–5). José Nicasio Milá de la Roca, *Los misterios de Barcelona*. Anon., *Madrid y sus misterios*.
1845	Ayguals de Izco, *María, la hija de un jornalero* (1845–6). Anon., *Los misterios de Córdoba*.
1846	Prosper Mérimée, *Carmen*. George Sand, *La mare au diable*.

1847 Estébanez Calderón, *Escenas andaluzas*. Charlotte Brontë, *Jane Eyre*. Emily Brontë, *Wuthering Heights*. William Makepiece Thackeray, *Vanity Fair*.

1848 Karl Marx and Friedrich Engels, *Communist Manifesto*. John Stuart Mill, *Principles of Political Economy*. François-René de Chateaubriand, *Mémoires d'outretombe*. Alexander Dumas, junior, *La Dame aux camélias*.

1849 Fernán Caballero (Cecilia Böhl de Faber), *La gaviota*. Dickens, *David Copperfield*.

1850 Hawthorne, *The Scarlet Letter*. Richard Wagner, *Lohengrin*.

1851 Longfellow, *The Golden Legend*. Herman Melville, *Moby Dick*. Hawthorne, *The House of Seven Gables*. Giuseppi Verdi, *Rigoletto*.

1852 Fernán Caballero, *Clemencia*, *Cuadros de costumbres*. *Elia o la España treinta años ha*. Carmen Coronado, *Poesías*. Harriet Beecher Stowe, *Uncle Tom's Cabin*.

1855 Walt Whitman, *Leaves of Grass*.

1856 Fernán Caballero, *La familia de Alvareda*.

1857 Charles Baudelaire, *Les fleurs du mal*. Gustave Flaubert, *Madame Bovary*. Thackeray, *The Virginians*.

1858 Manuel Angelón y Broquetas, *El pendón de Santa Eulalia*. Dickens, *A Tale of Two Cities*. Alfred Tennyson, *Idylls of the King*. Charles Darwin, *On the Origin of Species by Natural Selection*. Mill, *Essay On Liberty*. Verdi, *Un Ballo in Maschera*.

1859 Rosalía de Castro, *La hija del mar*.

1860 Ceferino Tressera, *Los misterios del Saladero*.

1861 Outbreak of American Civil War. Dickens, *Great Expectations*. Fëodor Dostoevsky, *The House of the Dead*. Oliver Wendell Holmes, *Elsie Venner*.

1862 Rafael del Castillo, *Misterios catalanes o el obrero de Barcelona*. Ivan Turgenev, *Fathers and Sons*. Flaubert, *Salammbô*.

1863 María del Pilar Sinués de Marco, *Celeste*. Francisco Suárez, *Los demócratas o El ángel de la libertad*.

1864–9 Leo Tolstoi, *War and Peace*.

1865 Abraham Lincoln assassinated. American Civil War ends. Lewis Carroll, *Alice's Adventures in Wonderland*. Franz Peter Schubert, *Unfinished Symphony*. Wagner, *Tristan and Isolde*.

1866 Dostoevski, *Crime and Punishment.*

1867 Benito Pérez Galdós, *La fontana de oro.* Castro, *El caballero de las botas azules.*

1868 Revolution in Spain. Isabella II is deposed and flees the country. Dostoevski, *The Idiot.* Louisa May Alcott, *Little Women.*

1869 Flaubert, *Sentimental Education.* Mark Twain, *The Innocents Abroad.* Paul Verlaine, *Fêtes Galantes.*

1870 Assassination of General Juan Prim. Galdós, *La sombra,* "Observaciones sobre la novela contemporánea." Jules Verne, *Twenty Thousand Leagues Under the Sea.* Wagner, *The Valkyrie.*

1871 Galdós, *El audaz.* George Eliot, *Middlemarch.* Emile Zola, *La fortune des Rougon* (beginning Rougon-Macquart series). Giuseppe Verdi, *Aida.*

1872 Spanish Carlist Civil War. Jules Verne, *Around the World in 80 Days.*

1873 First Spanish Republic. Galdós, *Episodios nacionales* (beginning first series). Nicolai Andreyevich Rimsky-Korsakov, *Ivan the Terrible.* Peter Ilich Tchaikovsky, *Symphony number 2.* First color photographs developed.

1874–5 The Restoration: Alfonso XII king of Spain. Juan Valera, *Pepita Jiménez.* José Antonio de Alarcón, *El sombrero de tres picos.* Thomas Hardy, *Far from the Madding Crowd.* First Impressionist exhibition in Paris. "Impressionism" derived from name of Monet's painting *Impression: Sunrise.* Verdi, *Requiem.*

1875 Galdós, *Memorias de un cortesano de 1815.* Tolstoi, *Anna Karenina.* Mark Twain, *The Adventures of Tom Sawyer.*

1876 Galdós, *Doña Perfecta.* Giner de los Ríos founds the "Institución libre de enseñanza."

1877 Galdós, *Gloria, Los cien mil hijos de San Luis.* Henry James, *The American.*

1878 Thomas Hardy, *The Return of the Native.* René Sully-Prudhomme, *Justice.*

1879 Galdós, *Un faccioso más y algunos frailes menos.* Henrik Ibsen, *A Doll's House.* Henry James, *Daisy Miller.*

1880 Sinués de Marco, *Las sendas de la gloria.* Dostoevski, *The Brothers Karamazov.* Zola, *Nana.* Rodin, *The Thinker* (sculpture).

1881	Galdós, *La desheredada*. Henry James, *Portrait of a Lady*. Guy de Maupassant, *La Maison Tellier*.
1882	Galdós, *El amigo Manso*. Pardo Bazán, *La tribuna* José María de Pereda, *El sabor de la tierruca*.
1883	Pardo Bazán, *La cuestión palpitante*, essays on Naturalism. Pereda, *Pedro Sánchez*.
1884	Clarín, *La Regenta* (1884–5). Galdós, *La de Bringas*, *Tormento*. Pardo Bazán, *El cisne de Vilamorta*. Pereda, *Sotileza*. Narcís Oller, *Notas de color*. Mark Twain, *Huckleberry Finn*. Joris-Karl Huysmans, *A rebours*.
1885–1902	Regency of the Queen Mother, María Cristina. 1885: Friedrich Nietzsche, *Beyond Good and Evil*. Marx, *Das Kapital*. Van Gogh, *The Potato Eaters*.
1886	Galdós, *Fortunata y Jacinta* (1886–7). Pardo Bazán, *Los pazos de Ulloa*. Henry James, *The Bostonians*. Robert Louis Stevenson, *Dr. Jekyll and Mr. Hyde*. Statue of Liberty dedicated in New York. Auguste Rodin, *The Kiss*.
1887	Pardo Bazán, *La madre naturaleza*. Sir Arthur Conan Doyle, *A Study in Scarlet* (first Sherlock Holmes story).
1888	Rubén Darío, *Azul*. Galdós, *Miau*, *La incógnita* (1888–89). Valera, *Apuntes sobre el arte nuevo de escribir novelas*. Oscar Wilde, *The Happy Prince, and Other Tales*. Van Gogh, *The Yellow Chair*. Rimsky-Korsakov, *Sheherazade*. Zola, *Le rêve*.
1889	Galdós, *Realidad*. Zola, "The Experimental Novel."
1890	Galdós, *Angel Guerra*. Ibsen, *Hedda Gabler*.
1891	Clarín, *Su único hijo*. Pardo Bazán, *La piedra angular*. Oscar Wilde, *The Picture of Dorian Gray*. Conan Doyle, *The Adventures of Sherlock Holmes*.
1892	Narcís Oller, *Figura i paisatge*. Bernard Shaw, *Mrs. Warren's Profession*. Ibsen, *The Master Builder*. Henri Toulouse-Lautrec, *At the Moulin Rouge*. Première of Tchaikovski's *Nutcracker* ballet in St. Petersburg.
1893	Oller, *La febre d'or*. Wilde, *A Woman of No Importance*.
1895	Miguel de Unamuno, *En torno al casticismo*. Ramón del Valle Inclán, *Femeninas*. Valera, *Juanita la Larga*. Pereda, *Peñas arriba*. Vicente Blasco Ibáñez, *Flor de mayo*. Theodor Fontane, *Effi Briest*. Tchaikovski, *Swan Lake* ballet at St. Petersburg. Sigmund Freud, *Studies on Hysteria*. The Lumière brothers invent cinematography.

1896 Pereda, *Pachín González*. Rainer Maria Rilke, *Larenofer* (poems). Anton Chekov, *The Sea Gull*. Giacomo Puccini, *La Bohème*.

1897 Cánovas del Castillo, conservative Prime Minister of Spain, assassinated by an Italian anarchist. Unamuno, *Paz en la guerra*. Galdós, *Misericordia*.

1898 US declares war on Spain over Cuba. Spanish fleet in Manila is destroyed. Treaty of Paris whereby Spain cedes to the US Cuba, Puerto Rico, Guam, and the Philippines for twenty million dollars. Galdós, *Mendizábal*. Ganivet, *Los trabajos del infatigable creador Pío Cid*. Blasco Ibáñez, *La barraca*. Henry James, *The Turn of the Screw*. Oscar Wilde, *The Ballad of Reading Gaol*. Bernard Shaw, *Caesar and Cleopatra*.

1899 Galdós, *La estafeta romántica*, *Luchana*, *Vergara*. Oller, *La bogeria*. Tolstoi, *Resurrection*. Wilde, *The Importance of Being Earnest*. André Gide, *Le Prométhée mal enchaîné*.

1900 Pío Baroja, *Vidas sombrías*. Galdós, *Los ayacuchos*, *Bodas reales*. Joseph Conrad, *Lord Jim*. Maxim Gorky, *Three People*. Freud, *Interpretation of Dreams*. Pablo Picasso, *Le Moulin de la Galette*. Paul Cézanne, *Still Life with Onions*. Toulouse-Lautrec, *La Modiste*. R. A. Fessenden transmits human speech via radio waves.

1901 Thomas Mann, *Buddenbrooks*. First motorcycles.

1902 Unamuno, *Amor y pedagogía*. Baroja, *Camino de perfección*. Valle-Inclán, *Sonata de otoño*. Azorín, *La voluntad*. Galdós, *Las tormentas del 48*, *Narváez*. Joseph Conrad, *Youth*. Gide, *The Immoralist*. Conan Doyle, *The Hound of the Baskervilles*. Paul Gauguin, *Riders by the Sea*.

1903 Valle-Inclán, *Sonata de estío*. Galdós, *Los duendes de la camarilla*. James, *The Ambassadors*. Verdi's *Ernani*, first opera recorded.

1904 Picasso, *The Two Sisters* (blue period). Valle Inclán, *Sonata de primavera*. Galdós, *La revolución de julio*. Gabriel Miró, *Del vivir*. Puccini, *Madame Butterfly*.

1905 Albert Einstein formulates theory of relativity. Freud, *Three Contributions to the Theory of Sex*. Art exhibition under Matisse's leadership called the "Fauves." Valle-Inclán, *Sonata de invierno*. Pardo Bazán, *La quimera*. Edith Wharton, *House of Mirth*. E. M. Forster, *Where Angels Fear to Tread*.

1906 Galdós, *Prim*. Conrad, *The Secret Agent*.

1907 First Cubist exhibition in Paris. Picasso, *The Demoiselles of Avignon*. Marc Chagall, *Peasant Women*. Falla, *La vida breve*. Claude Debussy, *Iberia*. Galdós, *La de los tristes destinos, España sin rey*. Ramón Pérez de Ayala, *Tinieblas en las cumbres*.

1908 Valle-Inclán, *Los cruzados de la causa*. Blasco Ibánez, *Sangre y arena*. G. K. Chesterton, *The Man who Was Thursday*. Forster, *A Room with a View*. Anatole France, *The Island of the Penguins*. Gertrude Stein, *Three Lives*. Henri Matisse coins the term "Cubism." The Ford Motor Company produces the first "Model T."

1909 General strike in Barcelona. The army attacks the workers "Tragic Week." Filippo Tommaso Marinetti, first Futurist Manifesto. Matisse, *The Dance*. Frank Lloyd Wright, "Robie House" in Chicago. Valle Inclán, *El resplandor de la hoguera, Gerifaltes de antaño*. Galdós, *España trágica*.

1910 The Mexican Revolution breaks out. Baroja, *César o nada*. Galdós, *Amadeo I*. Gabriel Miró, *Las cerezas del cementerio*. Ramón Gómez de la Serna, *Greguerías* (1910–1960). Carmen de Burgos, *El veneno del arte*. Forster, *Howard's End*. Amedeo Modigliani, *The Cellist*. The "tango craze" is in full international swing.

1911 Mexican Civil War ends. General strike in Spain. The first National Commission of Workers is created in Barcelona. Baroja, *El árbol de la ciencia*. Galdós, *La primera República, De Cartago a Sagunto*. Pardo Bazán, *Dulce dueño*. Pérez de Ayala, *La pata de la raposa*. D. H. Lawrence, *The White Peacock*. Katherine Mansfield, *In a German Pension*. George Braque, *Man with a Guitar*. Paul Klee, *Self-portrait*.

1912 Canalejas, Prime Minister of Spain, is assassinated by an anarchist. Lenin takes over editorship of *Pravda*, with Stalin's approval. The *Titanic* sinks. Baroja, *El mundo es ansí*. Galdós, *Cánovas*. Somerset Maugham, *The Land of Promise* (play). Picasso, *The Violin*.

1913 Unamuno, *Del sentimiento trágico de la vida*. Baroja, *Memorias de un hombre de acción* (1913–34). Jacinto Benavente, *La malquerida* (play). Pérez de Ayala, *Troteras y*

	danzaderas. Willa Cather, *O Pioneers!* Lawrence, *Sons and Lovers*. Première of Bernard Shaw's *Pygmalion* in Vienna. Guillaume Apollinaire, *The Cubist Painters*.
1914	Outbreak of *First World War*. Millions of European immigrants begin to come to the US. Panama Canal opens. José Ortega y Gasset, *Meditaciones del Quijote*. Unamuno, *Niebla*. Miró, *El humo dormido*. Concha Espina, *La esfinge maragata*. Conrad, *Chance*. James Joyce, *Dubliners*. Robert Frost, *North of Boston*. Marcel Proust initiates publication of *Remembrance of Things Past* with *Du Côté de chez Swann*. Charles Chaplin, *Making a Living*.
1915	Marcel Duchamp, "The Large Glass Series" (1915–23). Carmen de Burgos, *El abogado*. Lawrence, *The Rainbow*. Somerset Maugham, *Of Human Bondage*.
1916	Galdós, "Memorias de un desmemoriado." Freud, *Introduction to Psychoanalysis*. Joyce, *Portrait of the Artist as a Young Man*.
1917	Bolshevik Revolution in Russia. Four suffragists arrested and sentenced to six months in prison for picketing the White House. Picasso designs surrealist sets and costumes for Satie's ballet *Parade*. C. G. Jung, *Psychology of the Unconscious*. Unamuno, *Abel Sánchez*. Carmen de Burgos, *La rampa*. Miró, *El libro de Sigüenza*.
1918	Allied victory ends the First World War. Ex-Czar Nicholas II and his family are executed. US Post Office burns instalments of James Joyce's *Ulysses* published in the *Little Review*. First exhibition of Miró's paintings. Tristan Tzara, *Dadaist Manifesto*. Cather, *My Ántonia*.
1919	Benito Mussolini founds Fascism. Third International is founded in Moscow. Race riots in Chicago. American steel strike, New York dock workers' strike. International Labor Conference in Washington endorses eight-hour workday. Gide, *La Symphonie pastorale*. Herman Hesse, *Demian*. Upton Sinclair, *Jimmy Higgins*. Klee, *Dream Birds*. Picasso, *Pierrot et Harlequin*, sets for Diaghilev's production of Manuel de Falla's ballet *The Three-Cornered Hat* performed in London.
1920	The Spanish Communist Party is founded. Galdós dies. Unamuno, *Tres novelas ejemplares y un prólogo*, *El Cristo de Velázquez* (poem). Valle Inclán, *Divinas palabras* (play).

Sherwood Anderson, *Poor White*. F. Scott Fitzgerald, *This Side of Paradise*. Franz Kafka, *A Country Doctor*. Sinclair Lewis, *Main Street*. *The Cabinet of Dr. Caligari* (film). Paul Valéry, *Le cimetière marin*. Edith Wharton, *The Age of Innocence*.

1921 Eduardo Dato, Spanish Prime Minister, assassinated. Unamuno, *La tía Tula*. José Ortega y Gasset, *España invertebrada*. Pérez de Ayala, *Belarmino y Apolonio*. Gómez de la Serna, *El secreto del acueducto*. Miró, *Nuestro padre San Daniel*. John Dos Passos, *Three Soldiers*. Aldous Huxley, *Chrome Yellow*. Lawrence, *Women in Love*. Luigi Pirandello, *Six Characters in Search of an Author* (play). Virginia Woolf, *Monday or Tuesday*. Braque, *Still Life with Guitar*. Picasso, *Three Musicians*.

1922 Benavente receives the Nobel Prize for Literature. Federico García Lorca and Manuel de Falla, *Cante Jondo*. Joyce, *Ulysses*. Sinclair Lewis, *Babbitt*. T. S. Eliot, *The Wasteland*.

1923 Miguel Primo de Rivera dictator of Spain. Lenin is succeeded by Stalin. José Ortega y Gasset founds *Revista de Occidente*. Pérez de Ayala, *A.M.G.D.* Gómez de la Serna, *El novelista*. Margarita Nelken, *La trampa del arenal*. e.e. cummings, *The Enormous Room*. Freud, *The Ego and the Id*.

1924 Baroja, *Las figuras de cera*. Carmen de Burgos, *La entrometida*. André Breton, *Surrealist Manifesto*. Thomas Mann, *The Magic Mountain*. Eugene O'Neill, *Desire Under the Elms*.

1925 Unamuno, *La agonía del cristianismo*. Ortega y Gasset, *La deshumanización del arte, Notas sobre la novela*. Dos Passos, *Manhattan Transfer*. Fitzgerald, *The Great Gatsby*. Kafka, *The Trial*. Gertrude Stein, *The Making of Americans*. Female fashion: waistline in dresses disappears, skirts above the knee.

1926 Valle-Inclán, *Tirano Banderas*. Azorín, *Doña Inés*. Pérez de Ayala, *Tigre Juan y el curandero de su honra*. Miró, *El obispo leproso*. Benjamín Jarnés, *El profesor inútil*. Pedro Salinas, *Vísperas del gozo* (poetry). Gide, *The Counterfeiters*. Ernest Hemingway, *The Sun Also Rises*. Kafka, *The Castle*. Duke Ellington's first record appears.

1927 The German economic system collapses. Trotsky expelled from Communist party. Martin Heidegger, *Being and Time.* García Lorca, *Romancero gitano* (poetry). Valle-Inclán, *La corte de los milagros.* Luis Buñuel, *El perro andaluz.* Cather, *Death Comes for the Archbishop.* Jean Cocteau, *Orpheus* and *La Machine infernale.* Marcel Proust, *Remembrance of Things Past* (completed; begin in 1914). Virginia Woolf, *To the Lighthouse.* Igor Stravinsky, *Oedipus Rex*, Paris.

1928 Valle Inclán, *Viva mi dueño.* Benjamín Jarnés, *El convidado de papel.* Miró, *Años y leguas.* Federica Montseny, *La indomable.* José Díaz Fernández, *El blocao.* Bertolt Brecht, *The Threepenny Opera.* Aldous Huxley, *Point Counterpoint.* Lawrence, *Lady Chatterley's Lover.* Virginia Woolf, *Orlando.* Maurice Ravel, *Bolero.* Walt Disney produces the first Mickey Mouse films. First scheduled television broadcast. First motion pictures with sound.

1929 Black Friday in New York. Stock Exchange collapses. World-wide economic crisis begins. Le Corbusier, *The City of Tomorrow.* Museum of Modern Art opens in New York. "Talkies" replace silent films. Lorca, *Poeta en Nueva York* (poems). Ortega, *La rebelión de las masas.* Francisco Ayala, *El boxeador y un ángel.* Díaz Fernández, *La Venus mecánica.* Jarnés, *Locura y muerte de nadie*, *Paula y Paulita.* William Faulkner, *The Sound and the Fury.* Ernest Hemingway, *A Farewell to Arms.* Woolf, *A Room of One's Own* (essays). Luis Buñuel and Salvador Dalí, *Un chien andalou.*

1930 Rosa Chacel, *Estación. Ida y vuelta.* Jarnés, *Teoría del zumbel.* Díaz Fernández, *El nuevo romanticismo.* Ramón Sender, *Imán.* William Faulkner, *As I Lay Dying.* Buñuel, *L'âge d'or.*

1931 Roosevelt's "New Deal Speech." Local elections in Spain. Proclamation of Second Spanish Republic. King Alfonso XIII goes into exile. Unamuno, *San Manuel Bueno, mártir.* Eugene O'Neill, *Mourning Becomes Electra.* Dos Passos, *1919.* Hemingway, *Death in the Afternoon.* Aldous Huxley, *Brave New World.*

1932 The Company of Jesus is dissolved. Hitler appointed Chancellor of Germany. Enabling Law grants him dictatorial powers. First concentration camps built. Valle Inclán, *Baza de espadas*. Miguel Angel Asturias, *El señor presidente*. Jarnés, *Lo rojo y lo azul*. Sender, *Siete domingos rojos*. Jung, *Psychology and Religion*. Matisse, *The Dance*, Expressionist painting.

1933 The Spanish Fascist movement known as "la Falange" is founded. Right-wing candidates win elections. García Lorca, *Bodas de sangre* (first in a trilogy of plays). André Malraux, *The Human Condition*.

1934 Left-wing uprisings in the northern regions of Spain. German plebiscite votes Hitler as Führer. Lorca, *Yerma* (second play in trilogy). Henry Miller, *Tropic of Cancer*. Fitzgerald, *Tender Is the Night*. Salvador Dalí, *William Tell* (surrealist painting).

1935 Sender, *Mr. Witt, en el cantón*. Eliot, *Murder in the Cathedral*. John Steinbeck, *Tortilla Flat*. Dalí, *Giraffe on Fire*.

1936 Germans vote 99% for Hitler. German troops occupy the Rhineland. Spanish elections won by Popular Front. Primo de Rivera executed. 18 July coup by Francisco Franco. Spanish Civil War begins. Foreign intellectuals support the Spanish Republic. Orwell, Malraux, Hemingway are in Spain. Olympic Games held in Berlin; Jesse Owens wins four gold medals. Lorca finishes writing *La casa de Bernarda Alba* (last play in trilogy). Unamuno and Valle Inclán die. Lorca is murdered. Margaret Mitchell, *Gone with the Wind*. Chaplin, *Modern Times*.

1937 Dos Passos, *U.S.A.* Hemingway, *To Have and Have Not*. Malraux, *Hope*. Steinbeck, *Of Mice and Men*. Jean-Paul Sartre, *Nausea*. Picasso, *Guernica*.

1938 John Huizinga, *Homo Ludens*.

1939 Spanish Civil War ends just as Second World War is breaking out. James Joyce, *Finnegan's Wake*. Steinbeck, *The Grapes of Wrath*.

1940 Franco and Hitler meet. Trotsky assassinated in Mexico. Scarcity and hunger mark the post-war years. Graham Greene, *The Power and the Glory*. Hemingway, *For Whom the Bell Tolls*. Hollywood Oscar for Alfred Hitchcock's *Rebecca*.

1941 Japanese attack on Pearl Harbor. Jorge Luis Borges, *Ficciones*.

1942 Spanish Parliament is created. Camilo José Cela, *La familia de Pascual Duarte*. Brecht, *Mother Courage*. Albert Camus, *The Stranger*. William Faulkner, *Go Down, Moses*. Sartre, *The Flies*.

1943 Mussolini is defeated. Gonzalo Torrente Ballester, *Javier Mariño*. Max Aub, *Campo cerrado* (first volume of the series of six novels published under the title *El laberinto mágico*). Roy Boulting, *Casablanca*.

1944 "D-Day." Allies land in Normandy. Carmen Laforet, *Nada*. Cela, *Pabellón de reposo*. Ignacio Agustí, *Mariona Rebull*. Max Aub, *Campo de sangre*. Tennessee Williams, *The Glass Menagerie*. Camus, *Caligula*.

1945 Second World War ends. US drops atomic bombs on Hiroshima and Nagasaki. Spain excluded from United Nations. Nuremberg trials of Nazi war criminals begin. Existentialism permeates culture. Gabriela Mistral wins Nobel Prize for Literature. Ignacio Agustí, *El viudo Rius*. Chacel, *Memorias de Leticia Valle*. George Orwell, *Animal Farm*.

1946 Churchill makes his "Iron Curtain" Speech in Missouri. Marc Chagall, *Cow with Umbrella*.

1947 Law of Succession ratifies Spain as a monarchy. Franco declares Juan Carlos de Borbón his heir. Pablo Casals pledges not to play in public as long as Franco remains in power. Rafael Gil, *Don Quijote de la Mancha* (film version). Camus, *The Plague*. Tennessee Williams, *A Street Car Named Desire*. Thomas Mann, *Dr. Faustus*.

1948 Gandhi assassinated. USA establishes Marshall Plan for Europe. Miguel Delibes, *La sombra del ciprés es alargada*. Ana María Matute, *Los Abel*. Cela, *Viaje a la Alcarria*. W. H. Auden, *Age of Anxiety* (poetry).

1949 North Atlantic Treaty signed in Washington. Borges, *El Aleph*. Orwell, *1984*. Arthur Miller, *Death of a Salesman*. Simone de Beauvoir, *The Second Sex*. Pedro Laín Entralgo, *España como problema*. Rafael Calvo Sotelo, *España sin problema*. Delibes, *El camino*. Francisco Ayala, *La cabeza del cordero, Los usurpadores*.

1950 José Suárez Carreño, *Las últimas horas*.

1951 Cela, *La colmena*. Rafael Sánchez Ferlosio, *Industrias y andanzas de Alfanhuí*. Aub, *Campo abierto*. J. D. Salinger, *The Catcher in the Rye*. Faulkner, *Requiem for a Nun*.

Dalí, *Christ of St. John of the Cross*. Color TV first introduced.

1952 Laforet, *La isla y los demonios*. Luis Romero, *La noria*. Hemingway, *The Old Man and the Sea*. Samuel Beckett, *Waiting for Godot*. Shaw, *Don Juan in Hell*.

1953 Spain signs economic and military agreements with the USA. Juan Benet, *Max*. José María Gironella, *Los cipreses creen en Dios*. Juan Rulfo, *El llano en llamas*.

1954 Juan Goytisolo, *Juegos de manos*. Ignacio Aldecoa, *El fulgor y la sangre*. Jesús Fernández Santos, *Los bravos*. Matute, *Pequeño teatro*. Françoise Sagan, *Bonjour Tristesse*.

1955 Spain becomes a member of the United Nations. Germany becomes a member of NATO. Universal Copyright Agreement is established. Delibes, *Diario de un cazador*. Carmen Martín Gaite, *El balneario*. Rulfo, *Pedro Páramo*. Vladimir Nabokov, *Lolita*. Salvador Dalí, *The Lord's Supper*. Picasso, *Don Quijote* (lithograph).

1956 Juan Ramón Jiménez awarded Nobel Prize for Literature. Brecht's Berliner ensemble performs in England. Sánchez Ferlosio, *El Jarama*. Ignacio Aldecoa, *Con el viento solano*. Rock and roll craze.

1957 Gore Vidal, *A Visit to a Small Planet*. Leonard Bernstein, *West Side Story* (musical, New York). Torrente Ballester, *Los gozos y las sombras* (1957–62), vol. 1, *El señor llega*. Aldecoa, *Gran Sol*. Ignacio Agustí, *Desiderio, 19 de julio*.

1958 European Common Market is formed. Guggenheim Museum, designed by Frank Lloyd Wright, is inaugurated. Van Cliburn wins the Tchaikovsky piano contest in Moscow. Cha-cha-cha craze. Juan Goytisolo, *La resaca*. Jesús López Pacheco, *Central eléctrica*. Martín Gaite, *Entre visillos*. Luis Goytisolo, *Las afueras*. Boris Pasternak, *Dr. Zhivago*. Truman Capote, *Breakfast at Tiffany's*.

1959 Fidel Castro succeeds in his revolution against Batista and becomes Premier of Cuba, expropriates US-owned sugar mills. Miró paints murals for UNESCO building in Paris. Juan García Hortelano, *Nuevas amistades*. Antonio Ferres, *La piqueta*. Delibes, *La hoja roja*. Federico Fellini, *La dolce vita*.

1960 Matute, *Primera memoria*. Goytisolo, *Campos de Níjar*. Armando López Salinas, *La mina*. John Updike, *Rabbit, Run*. Harper Lee, *To Kill a Mockingbird*. Gore Vidal, *The Best Man*. Alfred Hitchcock, *Psycho*. Laser device is fully developed.

1961 Berlin Wall is built. Freedom Riders attacked in Alabama. Benet, *Nunca llegarás a nada*. Alfonso Grosso, *La zanja*. Gironella, *Un millón de muertos*. Salinger, *Franny and Zooey*. Joseph Heller, *Catch-22*. Luis Buñuel, *Viridiana* (film). Rossen, *Judgment at Nuremberg* (film).

1962 Boom of Latin American novel begins. Mario Vargas Llosa, *La ciudad y los perros*. Martín Santos, *Tiempo de silencio*. Juan García Hortelano, *Tormenta de verano*. Alejo Carpentier, *El siglo de las luces*. Günter Grass, *The Tin Drum*. Aleksander Solzhenitsyn, *One Day in the Life of Ivan Denisovich*. Michel Butor, *Essays on the Novel*. Edward Albee, *Who's Afraid of Virginia Woolf*? Andy Warhol, *Marilyn Monroe*.

1963 Freedom Marchers demonstrate in Washington. President Kennedy assassinated in Dallas. Death of Pope John XXIII. Warhol exhibits at the Guggenheim Museum in New York. Torrente Ballester, *Don Juan*. Martín Gaite, *Ritmo lento*. Julio Cortázar, *Rayuela*. Aub, *Campo de moro*. Alain Robbe-Grillet, *For a New Novel*.

1965 Second Vatican Council ends. The Beatles. Op art craze. Aub, *Campo de los almendros*, *Campo francés*. Picasso, *Self-Portrait*. Eusebio Sempere, *Primavera* (*Las cuatro estaciones*). Benet, *La inspiración y el estilo*.

1966 Goytisolo, *Señas de identidad*. Delibes, *Cinco horas con Mario*. Juan Marsé, *Ultimas tardes con Teresa*. Gironella, *Ha estallado la paz*. Capote, *In Cold Blood*. Mitch Leigh, *Man of La Mancha* (musical).

1967 The peseta is devalued to attract foreign tourists. Pre-publication censorship abolished by law. Six-day War between Arab countries and Israel. Goytisolo, *El furgón de cola*. Delibes, *Cinco horas con Mario*. Benet, *Volverás a Región*. Gabriel García Márquez, *Cien años de soledad*. Guillermo Cabrera Infante, *Tres tristes tigres*. Gore Vidal, *Washington DC*. Buñuel, *Belle de Jour*. Arthur Penn, *Bonnie and Clyde* (film). Michelangelo Antonioni,

	Blow-Up (film). Barbara Streisand sings in Central Park for an audience of 135,000 people.
1968	Religious freedom is proclaimed in Spain. Cultural and social unrest in France. Riots and police brutality at the Democratic Convention in Chicago. Martin Luther King, American leader of civil rights movement, is assassinated. José María Guelbenzu, *El mercurio*. Ana María Moix, *Julia*. Updike, *Couples*. Arthur Hailey, *Airport*.
1969	Woodstock Music and Art Fair with over 300,000 people in attendance. The hippie movement at the core of culture. An American walks on the moon. Carlos Fuentes, *La nueva novela hispanoamericana*. Matute, *La trampa*. Cela, *San Camilo, 1936*. Angelino Fons, *Fortunata y Jacinta* (film). Nathalie Sarraute, *Between Life and Death*.
1970	Goytisolo, *Reivindicación del conde don Julián*. Benet, *Una meditación*. Chacel, *La sinrazón*.
1971	Pablo Neruda awarded Nobel Prize for Literature. Juan Antonio Mañas, *Historias del Kronen*. Updike, *Rabbit Redux*.
1972	President Nixon visits China. *All in the Family* most popular TV show in America. The Watergate Affair. Gonzalo Torrente Ballester, *La saga/fuga de J.B*. Benet, *Un viaje de invierno*. José María Vaz de Soto, *Diálogos del anochecer*. Francisco Umbral, *Memorias de un niño de derechas*. Buñuel, *The Discreet Charm of the Bourgeoisie* (film).
1973	Spiro T. Agnew, Vice-President of the US, resigns, accused of corruption. Embargo of oil shipments of Arab nations in retaliation for Western support of Israel. Energy crisis. Pablo Picasso, Pablo Casals, and Pablo Neruda die. Spanish Premier Luis Carrero Blanco assassinated in Madrid. Juan Marsé, *Si te dicen que caí*. Luis Goytisolo, *Recuento*.
1974	The Tower of London and the Houses of Parliament bombed by Irish terrorists. President Nixon resigns. First political kidnapping in the USA: Patricia Hearst. "Streaker" craze. Mercè Rodoreda, *Mirall trencat*. Sánchez Ferlosio, *Las semanas del jardín*. Manuel Vázquez Montalbán, *Tatuaje*. Martín Gaite, *Retahílas*. Carl Bernstein and Bob Woodward, *All the President's Men*. Solzhenitsyn, *The Gulag Archipelago: 1918–1956*.

1975 Francisco Franco dies. Juan Carlos de Borbón is sworn in as King Juan Carlos I. Museum of Contemporary Art opens in Madrid. Communist takeover of South Vietnam. US closes embassy in South Vietnam and evacuates last troops. First International Year of the Woman Conference takes place in Mexico City and adopts a ten-year plan to improve the status of women in the world. Anglican Church in Canada approves ordaining women into the priesthood. Juan Goytisolo, *Juan sin tierra*. Torrente Ballester, *El Quijote como juego*. Delibes, *Las guerras de nuestros antepasados*. Vázquez Montalbán, *La soledad del manager*. Carme Riera, *Te dejo el mar*. Carlos Barral, *Años de penitencia*. José Luis Borau, *Furtivos* (film).

1976 Spanish Sahara becomes independent. Lourdes Ortiz, *Luz de la memoria*. Chacel, *Barrio de Maravillas*. Antonio Ribas, *La ciutat cremada* (film).

1977 President Carter grants amnesty to all American draft evaders of the Vietnam War. National elections in Spain. Victory of the Central Democratic Party. Adolfo Suárez President of the National Government. All censorship is abolished by Royal Decree. The National Drama Center is created. Vicente Aleixandre awarded Nobel Prize for Literature. Torrente Ballester, *Fragmentos de Apocalipsis*. Barral, *Los años sin excusa*. Vaz de Soto, *Fabián*. Jorge Semprún, *Autobiografía de Federico Sánchez*. José Luis Castillo-Puche, *El libro de las visiones y las apariciones*. George Lucas, *Star Wars*.

1978 Karol Wojtila becomes Pope John Paul II. USA and China establish diplomatic relations. Test-tube baby born in England. New Spanish Constitution proclaims equal rights for women; homosexuality is decriminalized. Juan Goytisolo, *Libertad, libertad, libertad*. Martín Gaite, *El cuarto de atrás*. Marsé, *La muchacha de las bragas de oro*. Esther Tusquets, *El mismo mar de todos los veranos*.

1979 Direct elections to the European Parliament held for the first time. The "movida," which will last until the middle 1980s, begins in Madrid. Carmen Conde the first woman elected to the Spanish Royal Academy. Rosa Montero, *Crónica del desamor*. Vázquez Montalbán, *Los mares del sur*. Castillo-Puche, *El amargo sabor de la retama*. Kurt Vonnegut, *Jailbird*. Ricardo Franco, *La familia de Pacual Duarte* (film version). Josep Maria Forn, *Companys, procés a Catalunya* (film). Mario Camús, *Fortunata y Jacinta* (TV series).

1980 Shipyard workers strike in Gdansk. Lech Walesa becomes chairman of Solidarity. American Embassy employees are taken hostage in Iran. Oscar Romero, Archbishop of San Salvador, assassinated while celebrating mass. John Lennon shot in New York. *Dallas* TV show takes the world by storm. Benet, *El aire de un crimen*. J. Goytisolo, *Makbara*. Torrente Ballester, *La isla de los jacintos cortados*. Montserrat Roig, *L'hora violeta*. Cristina Fernández Cubas, *Mi hermana Elba*.

1981 Military coup at the Spanish Parliament thwarted by decisive action of King Juan Carlos I. Spain joins NATO. Divorce is legalized in Spain. The New York Museum of Modern Art donates Picasso's *Guernica* to the Prado Museum. Pope John Paul II is shot twice by Mehmet Ali Agca. Egyptian President Anwar Sadat is assassinated. Israel officially annexes the Golan Heights. Incredible success of *Cats*, musical based on T. S. Eliot's poems. AIDS is identified. Miguel Delibes, *Los santos inocentes*. Montero, *La función Delta*. Jesús Ferrero, *Belver-Yin*. Carme Riera, *Una primavera per a Domenico Guarini*. Carlos Saura, *Bodas de sangre* (film version).

1982 The Vietnam Veterans' War Memorial is dedicated in Washington DC with the inscription of more than 58,000 names. Video boom. Felipe González becomes Spain's first socialist Prime Minister. A new law is passed to support film production. Frances Betriu, *La Plaza del Diamante* (film version). Camús, *La colmena* (film version). Gabriel García Márquez awarded Nobel Prize for Literature. Juan Goytisolo, *Paisajes después de la batalla*. Álvaro Cunqueiro, *Alcancía*, *Ida y vuelta*. Miguel Espinosa, *Tribada. Theeologiae Tractatus*. Luis-Puche, *Conocerás el poso de la nada*. Vaz de Soto, *Fabián y Sabas*, *Diálogos de la alta noche*. Montserrat Roig, *L'opera quotidiana*. Marina Mayoral, *La única libertad*. Francisco Ayala, *Memorias y olvidos*. Updike, *Rabbit Is Rich*. Graham Greene, *Monsignor Quixote*.

1983 José Luis García's film *Volver a empezar*, receives Oscar for the best foreign film. The "Office of Women's Affairs" is created by the Ministry of Culture. Jaime Chávarri, *Las bicicletas son para el verano* (film version). Víctor Erice, *El sur* (film version). Juan Goytisolo, *La isla*. Carlos Barral, *Penúltimo castigo*. Fernández Cubas, *Los altillos de Brumal*. García Márquez, *Chronicle of A Death Foretold*. Alice Walker, *The Color Purple*.

1984 The Vatican issues "Theology of Liberation," a document warning against Marxism. Miró, Fernando Zóbel, Jorge Guillén, Vicente Aleixandre, Julio Cortázar die. Chacel, *Acrópolis*. Marguerite Duras, *The Lover*. Sandra Gilbert and Susan Gubar, *The Madwoman in the Attic*. Saul Bellow, *Him and His Foot in His Mouth*. Milan Kundera, *The Unbearable Lightness of Being*. Updike, *The Witches of Eastwick*. Camús, *Los santos inocentes* (film version).

1985 "La movida" rules Spanish high and low culture. Betriu, *Requiem por un campesino español* (film version). Juan Goytisolo, *Coto vedado*. Vázquez Montalbán, *El pianista*. Adelaida García Morales, *El Sur*.

1986 Spain and Portugal become members of the European Community. John Paul II, the first Pope to visit a synagogue, also leads one hundred world religious leaders in prayers for peace in Assisi. The space shuttle *Challenger* explodes on take-off. Horrible nuclear accident at Chernobyl Power Station. The D'Orsay Museum opens in Paris. The "Queen Sofia" Center for the Arts is inaugurated in Madrid. The musical *Les Misérables* wins eight Tony awards on Broadway. Juan Goytisolo, *En los reinos de taifa*. Antonio Muñoz Molina, *Beatus Ille*. Soledad Puértolas, *Burdeos*. Javier Marías, *El hombre sentimental*. Gironella, *Ha estallado la paz*. Pedro Almodóvar, *Matador* (film); Vicente Aranda, *Tiempo de silencio* (film version).

1987 Gorbachev campaigns for *glasnost* (openness) and *perestroika* (reconstruction). President Reagan calls on President Mikhail Gorbachev to tear down the Berlin Wall. "Black Monday": stock market share prices plunge all over the world. Camús, *La casa de Bernarda Alba* (film).

1988 Benazir Bhutto elected first female Prime Minister of Pakistan. Juan Goytisolo, *Las virtudes del pájaro solitario*. Montero, *Amado amo*. Bernardo Atxaga, *Obabakoak*.

Barral, *Cuando las horas veloces*. Chacel, *Ciencias naturales*. Toni Morrison, *Beloved*. Isabel Allende, *Eva Luna*. Salman Rushdie's novel *The Satanic Verses* is published and attacked by Muslims for blasphemy.

1989 Pro-democratic students take over Tianamen Square. Solidarity gains a landslide victory in Polish parliamentary elections. The Pope meets Gorbachev. Vicente Aranda, *Si te dicen que caí* (film version). Benet, *En la penumbra*. Javier Marías, *Todas las almas*. Riera, *Por persona interpuesta*. Soledad Puértolas, *Queda la noche*. Umberto Eco, *Foucault's Pendulum* (novel). Gore Vidal, *Hollywood*.

1990 Iraq invades Kuwait. Lech Walesa elected President of Poland. Mysterious circles appear in British fields. Octavio Paz awarded Nobel Prize for Literature. Luisa Castro, *El somier*. Cristina Fernández Cubas, *El ángulo del horror*. Arthur Hailey, *The Evening News*. Updike, *Rabbit at Rest*.

1991 Xosé Lluis Méndez-Ferrín, *Arraianos*.

1992 Spain celebrates the fifth centennial of the Discovery of America. World Fair in Seville. Madrid declared European Capital of Culture. Barcelona hosts Olympic Games. The Thyssen-Bornemisza Museum opens in Madrid. Luis Goytisolo, *Estatua con palomas*. Javier Marías, *Corazón tan blanco*.

1993 Juan Goytisolo, *La saga de los Marx*. Souso de Toro, *Tic Tac*. Arturo Pérez-Reverte, *El club Dumas*.

1994 Marina Mayoral, *Recóndita armonía*. Marías, *Mañana en la batalla piensa en mí*. Ray Loriga, *Días extraños*.

1995 Almódovar, *La flor de mi secreto*. Fernández Cubas, *El columpio*.

1996 Vázquez Montalbán, *El premio*. Mayoral, *Dar la vida y el alma*. Riera, *Dins el darer blau*. Luis Goytisolo, *Mzungo*.

1997 "Dolly" the sheep is cloned. Juan Goytisolo, *Las semanas del jardín*. Benet, *Cartografía personal*. Lucía Extebarria, *Amor, curiosidad, prozac y dudas*. Nuria Amat, *La intimidad*. Ana María Navales, *El laberinto del quetzal*.

1998 Riera, *Tiempo de espera*. Extebarria, *Beatriz y los cuerpos celestes*. Belén Gopegui, *La conquista del aire*. Laura Freixas, *Entre amigas*. Espido Freire, *Irlanda*. Souso de Toro, *Calzados Lola*. Jaime Camino, *El balcón abierto* (original 1930 film script by Federico García Lorca *Viaje a la luna*).

1999 Freire, *Melocotones helados*. Quim Monzó, *Vuitante-sis contes*.

2000 Delibes, *El hereje*. María Mayoral, *La sombra del ángel*. Lucía Extebarria, *Del todo lo visible y lo invisible*. Eduardo Mendoza, *La aventura del tocador de señoras*.

2001 Terrorists destroy World Trade Center in New York.

2002 The peseta is replaced by the euro.

I

ADELAIDA LÓPEZ DE MARTÍNEZ AND HARRIET TURNER

On the novel: mirror and text

Comparative in scope, this volume in the Cambridge Companion series presents the development of the modern Spanish novel from the seventeenth century to the present. Drawing on the legacies of *Don Quijote* and the traditions of the picaresque novel, the collected essays focus on the questions of invention and experiment, of what constitutes the singular features, formal and cultural, theoretical and philosophical, of the novel in Spain, and how the emergence of new fictional forms articulates the relationships between history and fiction, high and popular culture, art and ideology, gender and society, literature and film.

Three major concepts have guided the theme and structure of the volume: the role played by historical events and cultural contexts in the elaboration of the novel; the development of a reflexive, and at times parodic, stance toward writing and literary tradition; and the conviction, either expressed or implied, that ambiguity and the lived experience of time, filtered through memory, have defined human lives in transition, as scene and setting, characters and events become recreated through the diverse, dialogical modalities of the Spanish novel.

Regardless of the age, past or present, in the development of the Spanish novel we discern a fundamental element: the *quixotic* or what Nabokov has called "play in collusion with reality."[1] Here the accent falls not so much on the representation of the things of this world but rather, as Nabokov says, on the way "meaning gets into things and lives" (*Lectures*, p. xvi). Even when it appears that play is all, that there is no meaning, no message to take away from the novel, the imprint of the text, of the spectacle of verbal thinking, feeling, and imagining, creates meaning as it discloses collusion with a particular cultural moment. The depiction of things or ideas or actions or simply of dialogue, of the acts of reading, remembering, and

[1] V. Nabokov, *Lectures on "Don Quijote,"* ed. Fredson Bowers (San Diego: Harcourt, Brace, Jovanovich, 1983), p. xiv.

writing, evolves as various novelistic forms of enchantment in a disenchanted world.

These forms specify a tension between referentiality (manifested in "things" like furniture, fashion, modes of speech, and social codes) and textuality, the verbal web of discourse.[2] Such a tension generates fusions of the real and the fictional which, in turn, create a self-reflexive dimension that expands the concept of mimesis, informing the novel with an inner questioning about itself and its making. Questioning stems from the *Quijote,* as it does from the spectacle of painting in Velázquez's *Las meninas* (1656): each is a work of art that promotes the theme of its own identity as a fabrication, and each shapes basic aspects of the development of the Spanish novel. Thus Galdós, speaking in 1870 of the invention of the modern Spanish novel, cites Cervantes and Velázquez as masters of the art of illusion and of the generative power of disillusion,[3] of disenchantment, a power that nonetheless enchants, as Nabokov has observed of the *Quijote* (ibid.). Juan Goytisolo, a leading contemporary Spanish novelist and critic, in a recent interview (2001) also harks back to that mix of referentiality and textuality, arguing, on the one hand, for an understanding only granted through the specifics of place, gesture, and time, and, on the other, for the creative power of language. "I believe," he says, that "a writer is, above all, the language he writes." Goytisolo attributes the knowledge of this essential equivalence of the writer's craft to Cervantes: "When I was 25 years old, I read the *Quijote.* That says it all."[4]

The notion of the *quixotic*, then, marks the trajectory of the Spanish novel from the 1600s to the present. Once worked through the trope of the mirror, what is quixotic grows larger than the novel that contains it. Thus the time-honored image of the mirror may be taken as a central metaphor to illuminate the nature of the Spanish novel and its development through the centuries from the belief in the possibility of reflecting life, as in the eighteenth and nineteenth centuries, to the most daringly experimental novels of the twentieth century. For the mirror is a lie that tells the truth. The left and right sides interchange in a reflection, a perceptual action that the Spanish novel exploits not only to picture a hallucinated or self-hypnotic or inspired state of mind that seeks to reinterpret and remake "real life": mirror-like images

[2] The tension between referentiality and textuality is elegantly analyzed by Lilian R. Furst in her opening chapter "Truth to Tell," in *"All is True": The Claims and Strategies of Realist Fiction* (Durham, NC: Duke University Press, 1995), p. 12.

[3] B. Pérez Galdós, "Observaciones sobre la novela contemporánea" (1870), in *Ensayos de crítica literaria*, ed. L. Bonet (Barcelona: Ediciones Península, 1999).

[4] J. Goytisolo, "'Juan Goytisolo, escritor.' Entrevista con Arcadí Espada," *El País*, 10 June 2001, p. 13.

also question the role and identity of author, character, narrator, critic, and reader, as these re-creations imitate and reflect each other in a series of criss-crossing relations. Examples abound, from *Pepita Jiménez* (1874) and *El amigo Manso* (*Our Friend Manso*, 1882) to *Niebla* (*Mist*, 1914), *Cinco horas con Mario* (*Five Hours with Mario*, 1966) and *Beatriz y los cuerpos celestes* ('Beatriz and the Heavenly Bodies', 1998).

Thus one paradox of Spanish fiction is how the diverse images of the mirror act as a metaphor to articulate the defining coherence of a novelistic production that resists definition. For the ubiquitous mirror, in various guises, clarifies the evolving trajectory of a fundamentally quixotic, novelistic consciousness that characterizes the minds of author and character, narrator and reader. We move from the mirror of chivalry in the *Quijote* to the mimetic mirror and intertextuality of realist fiction; from the redoubled reflections of Unamuno's novels to the distortions of Valle-Inclán's concave mirror; from the "circus of mirrors" proposed by Azorín to Ortega's famous "window," a formalist frame through which a novel's plot must pass to achieve aesthetic integrity.[5] Finally we enter the dialogical reflections of the testimonial novel and the novel of memory, later to witness the "broken mirrors" of recent experimental fiction. However pictured, the image of the mirror expands across the centuries to encompass three interrelated concepts: mimesis, metafiction, and myth.

In the *Quijote* a mimetic focus on *menudencias* – the trifling things of life – acts as a kind of inset mirror that reflects those trifles within a nexus of relations that confers upon the ordinary an extraordinary range of meaning. An example is the brown, bristly mole in the middle of don Quijote's back: Sancho sees this bristly mole as the sign of a strong man, a token of virility like the abundant hair on his master's chest.[6] Don Quijote, however, takes the mole to be a mark of lineage, his affinity to chivalric heroes like Amadis de Gaula. Thus not only does the mole, like the barber's basin, provoke overlapping points of view and a belief in intersecting identities: the bristling hairs also denote a supra-textual vitality. That small sign of heroic, masculine identity will surface three hundred years later in the dainty little mole, bristling with three (no more, no less) copper-colored hairs, that enlivens the corner of the mouth of doña Lupe, a formidable domestic ruler in Galdós's *Fortunata y Jacinta* (*Fortunata and Jacinta*, 1886–7).

This particular bristly mole delineates the entrepreneurial spirit of a middle-class woman, a seasoned campaigner in the field. Doña Lupe, an

[5] A. Zamora Juárez, *El doble silencio del eunuco. Poéticas sexuales de la novela realista según Clarín* (Caracas: Editorial Fundamentos, 1998), p. 70.

[6] Nabokov, *Lectures*, p. 13.

expert in bargain hunting and the practice of usury, takes on transactions as seemingly impossible as don Quijote's windmills. One example is the reconcilation of Fortunata, a fallen woman, in marriage to her (Lupe's) nephew Maxi. Further, when the narrator counts the sprouting hairs as precisely three, refers to the years of her youth as "mocedades," and traces that shadow of an adolescent mustache over her upper lip, he parlays a tiny brown mole into a complex of qualities that hark back to literary tradition, one that had applied the term *mocedades*, meaning "adolescence," only to those early years of a male protagonist. In this way, those traits expose hidden characteristics such as doña Lupe's essentially masculine character, her acumen with numbers, and her capacity, like don Quijote's, for "heroic" deeds.

In the *Quijote*, something as ordinary as a brown bristly mole poses the problem of point of view, belief, and reality. In *Fortunata y Jacinta*, something as familiar as body hair creates inset stories: tiny bursts of action, scene, setting, and psychological insight. Examples are the black bunches of hair that bustle about the "balconies" of nose and ear of Nicolás Rubín, Maxi's incipient baldness, Fortunata's tumbling dark curls, or the treacherous Aurora's thinning hair. Trifling things – *menudencias* – and important political, social, and historical events collude to tell Galdós's two entwined stories of married women.

By the twentieth century, the motif of body hair takes on a temporal dimension, appearing in Rosa Montero's *Crónica del desamor* (*Absent Love*, 1979) as a sign of the passage of time and an improbable future, each bracketing, as it were, an acute recognition of the suffering caused by the traditional gender roles that a patriarchal society assigns to men and women. The narrator, Ana, and Javier, her lover, have played mind games with one another for ten years, unable to communicate true feelings. When Ana gives up on Javier, she confronts him with what she perceives to be his selfish, typically male behavior, only to discover that she – like Javier – had mistaken the clues that had shaped their relationship. During their last encounter, Ana intensely regrets those ten years of wasted opportunities, captured to her eye in the graying strands of her lover's pubic hair. Now *menudencia*s – those graying strands – function as a chronotopic image, depicting how the contemporary Spanish novel mirrors the space–time continuum while it embraces a more open approach to sexuality and a feminist imaginary.

As Michael Wood has observed, the mirror may be tilted, the slice of life taken at an angle.[7] In the twentieth century, Spanish novels like Luis Martín Santos's *Tiempo de silencio* (*Time of Silence*, 1962) or Juan Goytisolo's

[7] M. Wood, "The Art of Losing," *The New York Review of Books*, 18 February 1999, p. 7.

Reivindicación del conde don Julián (*Count Julian*, 1970) reposition the mirror to confront the text. Now that text, its genesis, literary tradition, critical and public reception, as well as the persona of writer and reader, stand encompassed by an all-inclusive mirror, which itself is part of the reality that the novel purposes to capture. The text, catching at the sleeve of author, narrator, character, critic, and reader, generates a series of mimetic transferences and exchanges to convert the novel into a metafictive mirror. This mirror "goes walking" to promote a series of simultaneous, kaleidoscopic perspectives, seeming to "break" as new writers discard linear plots, reliable narrators, and the unities of time and place, thereby questioning traditional authority. Novels like Esther Tusquets's *El mismo mar de todos los veranos* (*The Same Sea as Every Summer*, 1978) or Carme Riera's *Una primavera per a Domenico Guarini* (*Spring for Domenico Guarini*, 1984) dismantle the canon and replace vertical (masculine) concepts of rank and tradition by a horizontal network, even fusion, of entries and images. They also confound categories of high and low, gender and identity, and the role of author, character, narrator, and reader. *Amor, curiosidad, prozac y dudas* ('Love, Curiosity, Prozac, Doubts', 1997), Lucía Extebarria's title, brings together the broken pieces of the mirror in a gesture that only points up their dispersion in an electronic age.

Mythic reconfigurations also reverberate in the images reflected by mimetic, metafictive, or broken mirrors. As industrialization changed rural environments in the nineteenth century and as storytelling shifted from the written word to film and electronic images in the late twentieth century, space opens out to the unknown, communication proliferates through the Internet, and Spain becomes part of the global enterprise. Now the creation and consolation of myth articulate in the novel a resistance either to the recent past of the dictatorship or to capitalistic change itself. Spectacle engages the imagination, while the new historicism seeks times and settings untouched by consumerism and recent strife. Imitation, invention, experiment, rescue, and recovery: as the Spanish novel moves toward the condition of electronic media and cinematography, it retains in new forms the active principles of mimesis, metafiction, and myth.

These forms, old and new, stand reflected in the cover of this volume: the gnarled lines of Picasso's black and white lithograph *Don Quijote and Sancho*, set within the angles of the abstract rendition of spring by the contemporary Spanish painter Eusebio Sempere, depict the idea of the Cervantine "root" of the Spanish, and indeed of the European, novel. Sempere's background of geometric planes, bisected by light, provides an apt image of a "broken" mirror, communicating visually the idea of the "lites"/"lights" of the novel beyond modernity. Further, the juxtaposition of geometric shapes, lines, and colors projects the informing theme of mental and imaginative replay that takes place in the Spanish novel – in reading, writing, and in writing about writing.

This Cambridge Companion volume brings the most interesting, original, and difficult aspects of the Spanish novel to the attention of an informed reader, mainly (but by no means exclusively) in the English-speaking world. Samples of style and the analysis of tropes, imagery, idiolect, syntax, poetic diction, and other defining features, which are always related to a meaning that the reader can absorb and understand, display the distinctive qualities of this literature.

The volume opens with a chapter by Anthony Close that traces the legacy of *Don Quijote*, showing how Cervantes's great novel intersects with the genre of the picaresque. For the *Quijote* gives birth to the modern novel in Spain, the rest of Europe, and the Americas. As Close points out, the features of the picaresque and the Cervantine emphasis on the interplay of *menudencias* and idealizing fantasy, which shapes the inner life of an individual character, constitute not only the origin of nineteenth-century European realism but also mark the trajectory of the Spanish novel in the twentieth century.

In the third chapter, "The Enlightenment and Fictional Form," Rebecca Haidt argues the case for linking the concept of "enlightenment" and experimentation with fictional form. Taking as an example Cadalso's *Noches lúgubres* ('Dark Nights of Dejection', 1798) – not a novel and yet a text that struggles with fictional forms as it articulates certain concepts and trends of the Enlightenment – she presents several types of eighteenth-century fictional productions that fit the category of "novel."

In Chapter 4, "The Regional Novel: Evolution and Consolation," Alison Sinclair gives an overview of the ideas that produced the regional novel and the *costumbrismo* (attention to manners, dress, furnishings, local customs) that shaped a literary genre flourishing in the 1830s in Madrid and, by mid-century, also in the Spanish provinces. Following the legacies of the *Quijote*, the picaresque novel, and the Enlightenment, she focuses on the mix of evolution and consolation, tradition and innovation, in politics and culture that oriented the Spanish regional novel toward the realism of the 1880s.

Chapter 5, "The *Folletín*: Spain Looks to Europe," explores the question of what literary imitation meant for Spain in a time of rising nationalist sentiment. Elisa Martí-López analyzes the themes and narrative techniques of popular and salon fiction – the sentimental novel, derived from French and English models, the Romantic novel, and novels of social protest, which were published serially. She shows how the serial novel transformed publishing markets and how it informed, in part, the structural and stylistic innovations of realist writers like Benito Pérez Galdós.

Chapter 6, "The Realist Novel," concentrates on the art of creating a persistent belief in the reality of a fictional world, demonstrated to supreme and varied effect in *La Regenta* (1884–5) by Leopoldo Alas (Clarín) and Benito Pérez Galdós's *Fortunata y Jacinta* (1886–7). The analysis and interpretative details define the traditional and experimental nature of these and other novels, whose competing claims of referentiality and textuality hark back to Cervantes even as they foreshadow the invention of the modern existential novel, such as Unamuno's *Niebla* (*Mist*, 1914). This chapter also shows how Galdós's novels anticipate the narrative, dramatic, and cinematographic techniques that prefigure aspects of novel and film in contemporary Spain.

In Chapter 7, "History and Fiction," Geoffrey Ribbans elucidates the relations between history and fiction that, on the one hand, define the historicist vision of nineteenth-century Spain and, on the other, form the basis of a new type of novel: the forty-six *Episodios nacionales* written by Benito Pérez Galdós (1843–1920). He shows how Galdós established this genre at the same time as he created the contemporary social novel. Each series of novels served as a point of departure for the historical novels of Pío Baroja, Unamuno, Valle-Inclán, and Ramón Sender, all of whom articulated shifts in the concept of the genre. By dramatizing historical elements and situations through the subjectivity of their protagonists, these writers translate philosophy, melodrama, and romance into a uniquely existential mode of fiction. The historical novel, increasingly an element of popular culture, poses contested questions of the reconstruction of history, and of the relation of fiction to historiography, that will define the post-Civil War novel in Spain.

Chapter 8, "Gender and Beyond: Nineteenth-Century Spanish Women Writers," focuses on the question of gender and its consequence for writing practices in nineteenth-century Spain. Lou Charnon-Deutsch reevaluates fiction written by women within dominant realist discourses, interpreting the relevance of political, social, psychological, and religious factors to cultural assumptions bound up with the formation of the canon. Her chapter explores the contrapuntal dialogue between, on the one hand, the way nineteenth-century women wrote about themselves and their struggles, and, on the other, what that writing discloses about their stance vis à vis the working classes and the subjects of Spain's former colonies.

In Chapter 9, "Decadence and Innovation in *fin de siglo* Spain," Noël Valis probes the decadent mode in fiction: its distrust of surface representations, the desire to penetrate into a deeper reality, the perception of life as a charade, and the wish to evade the historical present, all of which gave rise to *modernismo*, symbolism, and the decadent movement, adumbrated in

La Regenta and brought to aesthetic fruition in the novels of Valle-Inclán. Her analysis centers on the stylized structures and forms of Valle-Inclán's novels, which, on the one hand, seek the cult of artificiality and distortion, while on the other hand displaying, as in *Tirano Banderas* (1926), bitter cynicism and an obsession with the perversities of political power.

Chapter 10, "From the Generation of 1898 to the Vanguard," illuminates the changing relations between narrative form and philosophical preoccupation which were taking place as the form of the novel evolved consequent upon the "disaster of 98" – the loss of Spain's last colonial possessions, Cuba, Puerto Rico, and the Philippines – in the Spanish American War of 1898. The stable structures of fiction yield to the predominance of ideas as ideological configurations come to shape character and action, scene and setting. Roberta Johnson shows how the year 1902 inaugurates the "Age of Silver" in Spanish letters, and how novels by an older generation of writers (Unamuno, Baroja, and "Azorín") and of the next generation (Pérez de Ayala, Miró, Chacel, Jarnés) display a confluence of fiction and philosophy, of theory as textual praxis. In their rejection of the staples of realism, they join the literary currents of European modernism.

In Chapter 11, "The Testimonial Novel and the Novel of Memory," Gonzalo Sobejano explores the novels that emerged from Spain's Civil War (1936–9). First he focuses on their biographical, social, and historical contexts, and then proceeds to discuss their formal innovations and obsession with the themes of war. Sobejano analyzes the themes of disillusion, loss, alienation, uncertainty, and evasion in novels by Cela, Delibes, Sender, Sánchez Ferlosio, Fernández Santos, and Martín Santos, and shows how the novel becomes a montage of narrative structures and modes of poetic diction that contest, by implication, with the coercive, "official" optimism of Francoist Spain. Sobejano explains how, after the death of the dictator, modalities of social realism shift to emphasize an alternate representation: the novel of memory, which evokes the past through remembering, writing, and reading. Just as the texts of popular culture (romances of chivalry) transformed, in Cervantes's great novel, the character and ordinary life of Alonso Quijano/Quijada/Quesada into the new, exalted persona of Don Quijote, so the texts of mass culture (romances, mystery stories, sentimental dance tunes known as *boleros* and folksongs styled as *coplas*) recapture the experience of the lost world of childhood before the war. Texts of mass culture thus allowed the roles of author/narrator/character and reader to merge and to speak as one multi-vocal participant.

Chapter 12, "Questioning the Text," analyzes the intertextuality, montage, and fragmentation that mark the novels by Benet, the Goytisolos, and Torrente Ballester in the 1970s. Promoting difference, crossing cultures, exploring sexual otherness, are thematic strands stemming from the interrelated approaches of feminism, psychoanalysis, film theory, and the visual arts. Brad Epps shows how linguistic experimentation, a renewed emphasis on subjectivity, the use of fantasy and the supernatural, and the parodic use of structuralist jargon take the resources of the imagination to extremes. Language itself turns into protagonist as the discourse of literary criticism turns into narrative.

In Chapter 13, "Women and Fiction in Post-Franco Spain," Akiko Tsuchiya concentrates on women's writings that defy the notion of fixed gender roles in life and literature. Incorporating concepts established by contemporary feminist thinkers, she examines how Spanish women writers create alternate patterns of communication, such as the disruption of gendered expectations, the construction of female utopian spaces, and the replacement of traditional rhetoric by discursive technique, that articulate the uniqueness of each writer's voice, vision, and ideology.

In Chapter 14, "Cultural Alliances: Film and Literature in the Socialist Period, 1982–1995," Isolina Ballesteros explores the intertextual relations between novel and film in contemporary Spain to show how these two forms of narrative pursue a common goal: the creation of belief in the reality of fiction. Responding to the cinematographic structures and textures of the modern Spanish novel, film-makers like Luis Buñuel, Víctor Érice, Carlos Saura, Mario Camús, Ricardo Franco, Vicente Aranda, and Francesc Betriu have recourse to narrative and drama, recasting themes that highlight in both novel and film how each genre operates within and across a semiotic system of meaning.

In Chapter 15, "The Novel Beyond Modernity," Teresa Vilarós traces new developments as today's writers return to the basic conventions of storytelling and popular genres, such as detective stories, adventures, and romance. She shows how this new fiction fuses roles, voices, and texts, and conflates culture and cult, art and fashion, historiography and legend, information and noise, pastiche and parody. She analyses techniques of fragmentation, pointing to the way an "encrypted" or "scarred" discourse attempts to mask or erase the notion of Spanish "difference" as Spain becomes part of the global enterprise. The notion of literature *lite* – brief, dazzling, cosmopolitan, oriented toward the consumer – combines with the "lights" of the transition from dictatorship to democracy during the 1980s. It refashions a genre that reflects, on the one hand, the uneven modernity of Spain and, on the other, the persistence of myth: writers engage in a distinctly Spanish mode of new historicism by creating medieval or pre-Columbian plots and settings. Once again myth reengages fiction, but now as a mode of erasure of the immediate past of the Francoist dictatorship.

In the concluding chapter, "Writing about Writing," Randolph Pope explores how Spanish novelists have textualized their theories about writing. From Cervantes to Goytisolo to Lucía Extebarria, writers have turned narrative into critical reflection and theory into story. He shows how, since Cervantes, novelists have conceived the process of writing as a central novelistic theme, amplifying the mimetic mirror with metafictive dimensions. The questions of parody, metafiction, and the polyphonic texture of narrative mark a thematic and artistic coherence, which, through the essays of this volume, becomes clearly discernible in the evolution of the modern Spanish novel.

Now a word about the process of editing: Each contributor was free to select the works, develop lines of argument, and propose an interpretation, directing the essay towards the general reader, undergraduate students, and specialists in Hispanic Studies. Thus each chapter refers to the historical moment, cultural context, and to the literary tradition in which particular novels arise, engaging theoretical concepts to illuminate text and context. Whether the contributors contemplate the writer as thinker, storyteller of plots, creator of character, theorist, or a mind as a mirror of his or her times, a concern for the use of language, structure, and point of view is always paramount. In every chapter, writing is thinking. Each contributor takes time to build arguments that are quite detailed and sometimes technical. At the same time, each takes care to use technical terms sparingly and to avoid jargon. Analytical sections, which focus on the novels most relevant to the chosen topic, show how these have affected the subsequent history of the genre in Spain.

Translations of the titles of novels appear parenthetically in the text of each chapter. If a translation has been published in English, we print the title in italics; otherwise the translated title appears in roman type. The volume includes a biographical note for each contributor, a chronology, bibliography, and index. The original dates of publication of the novels are given in the chronology. The publication date given in the bibliography normally refers to the edition cited by the relevant contributor. The chronology, providing more than a list of dates and works, frames the novels within salient historical and political events, social trends, artistic production, and popular fashions. In this way, the chronology instructs the reader about the complexity of the dynamics that have shaped the global context in which these novels were written and published. The bibliography consists of a comprehensive list of the novels cited in the volume, giving full references for translations published in English.

Preparing a volume in the Cambridge Companion series depends on collaboration. We thank our contributors for their skill and patience during the editorial process, and we gratefully acknowledge the help of three graduate students at the University of Nebraska-Lincoln: Irene Beibe, whose computer skills provided the initial lay-out for the book's cover; Lana Pashkevich, who assisted in compiling the index; and Carol Anne Tinkham, who collaborated on the translation of the essay by Gonzalo Sobejano and in the general process of editing. We deeply appreciate the guidance of our editors, Linda Bree and Rachel De Wachter, and our copy editor, Rosemary Williams, and we are pleased to recognize the Department of Modern Languages and Literatures and the Center for the Humanities at the University of Nebraska-Lincoln for grants in support of this project.

I

SINCE CERVANTES

2

ANTHONY J. CLOSE

The legacy of *Don Quijote* and the picaresque novel

This chapter is concerned with two aspects of *Don Quijote* and the picaresque: how the novels were intended and received in their historical context, and what posterity made of them.[1] Though modern criticism has tended to treat the *Quijote* and the picaresque novel as virtually opposed fictional worlds, they are much more closely related.[2] Indeed, in some ways, *Don Quijote* grows out of Alemán's picaresque classic *Guzmán de Alfarache* (1599). Thus we should consider first the picaresque before Cervantes.

The genre was born in 1554 with the publication of the anonymous *Lazarillo de Tormes*.[3] Five years later, *Lazarillo* was blacklisted on the first Spanish Index because of its irreverence towards the church, but was allowed to recirculate in expurgated form from 1573. The Inquisition's disapproval checked the development of the picaresque for the next forty years; but this genre, and comic/satiric writing in general, revived spectacularly with the publication in 1599 of the first part of Alemán's novel and its wildfire editorial success. A spate of robustly comic fiction followed in the immediate wake of *Guzmán de Alfarache*, including *Don Quijote*, Part I (1605), together with several picaresque sequels or successors to *Guzmán*, like Quevedo's *El Buscón* (written about 1605).

Thus the great formative period of Spanish fictional writing is concentrated in the space of just a few years, from 1599 to 1615, date of the publication of *Don Quijote*, Part II. This time span coincides with the zenith of the Spanish Golden Age: Góngora's major poems circulate in Madrid around 1612; the drama of Lope de Vega is in full spate; Quevedo writes his satiric *Sueños* (dreams of hell and the afterlife) from 1606, projecting an image of Spain as corrupted by avarice, hypocrisy, social climbing, the loss of sober ancestral

[1] M. de Cervantes Saavedra, *Don Quijote*, ed. L. A. Murillo, 2 vols. (Madrid: Castalia, 1978); M. Alemán, *Guzmán de Alfarache*, ed. S. Gili Gaya, 5 vols. (Madrid: Espasa Calpe, 1972).

[2] F. Lázaro Carreter, *"Lazarillo de Tormes" en la picaresca* (Barcelona: Ariel, 1972), pp. 226–8.

[3] Anon., *Lazarillo de Tormes*, ed. J. Cejador y Frauca (Madrid: Espasa Calpe, 1969).

virtues, and incompetent government. Despite the growing awareness of political decadence that is typified by Quevedo, most Spaniards still saw their nation as a mighty European power, defender of the Catholic faith against Islam to the south and east and Protestantism to the north, and possessor of an empire which extended from the rising to the setting sun.

Lazarillo fixed the formula that would be exploited and freely varied by subsequent picaresque novelists: that is, the autobiography of a disreputable drifter, who tells of his ignominious parentage and upbringing, his employment as servant with a succession of twisters or charlatans, his acquisition of street wisdom and a 'When in Rome...' philosophy, and his efforts to scramble up the social ladder to some kind of security and respectability. In *Lazarillo*, these efforts are presented by the hero, Lázaro, as the success story of the little man made good; however, this claim of honorable achievement proves risibly ironic, especially in view of the conclusion, which shows him as having sunk even deeper into the mire, in the moral sense, than when he started. He ends up married to the servant girl of an archpriest, turning a blind eye and a deaf ear to the evidence of her concubinage with his benefactor for the sake of the material perquisites of the situation. These add nicely to the percentage accruing from his job as Toledo's town crier, which includes crying – that is, advertising – its wines.

It is from this lowly position that Lázaro writes his memoirs, unfolding a career of ignominious mishaps, scrapes, and ruses: the public whipping of his black step-father and his mother as punishment for their immoral liaison and the step-father's thefts from his master's stable; the bashing of Lazarillo's ear against the stone bull of Salamanca by his first master, the blind man, as a lesson in the need for wariness; the boy's sadistic retaliation on the blind man for that trick and subsequent cruelties, which consists in making him run full tilt against a stone pillar; the subterfuges by which Lazarillo gets at the bread locked inside the chest of a stingy priest and covers up the theft. Most of the hoaxes and wisecracks that make up the action have a traditional ancestry – in proverbs, tales, comic theatre, and so on. Golden Age readers tended to see Lázaro's career as a loose assembly of this funny material, and Lázaro himself as more function than personality: tricksy agent of *burlas* or naive victim of them.

Now in that society, obsessed with honor and status, the flaunting of so lowly and dishonorable a career could only have a hilarious effect, which is accentuated by two factors. First, since no author's name appears on the title page, and since the writer of the prologue appears to be Lázaro himself, responding to the anonymous "Sir" ("Vuestra Merced") who has requested the story, *Lazarillo* exhibits an ambiguous similarity to real autobiography. Memoirs in that age, such as Columbus' accounts of his voyages, were customarily addressed to a noble patron; and Lázaro's relationship to "Vuestra Merced," resembling a letter writer's to an addressee, parodically evokes that literary form, particularly in the prologue, which strikes – tongue-in-cheek – an exemplary and self-justificatory pose. Secondly, the story's comicality is highlighted by the superbly droll and downbeat style in which it is told: understatement, euphemistic phrasing of shameful events, Biblical parody, plays on words and proverbs, mock-pathetic lamentation and other bogus solemnity.

We expect an autobiographer, exposing his intimate past before us, to speak fondly of parents, to narrate family catastrophes with due gravity, to show reverence for consecrated texts and values. Here is how Lázaro goes about it in the first section (*tratado*) of his story:

> When I was a boy of eight, they blamed my father for certain improper bleedings [*sangrías*] in the sacks of corn that people brought to the mill to be ground, on account of which he was arrested and confessed and denied not and suffered persecution for righteousness's sake. I trust to God that he is in paradise, for the Gospel calls such people blessed.[4]

The word *sangrías*, apart from its allusion to the slits through which Lázaro's father stole his clients' corn, puns cleverly on another sense of 'sangrías', water channels: i.e., those through which the water ran to turn the mill-wheel. The whole passage ironically borrows the language of the Gospels (John 1.20; Matthew 5.10) in order to dress up crime and its humiliating punishment as heroic Christian virtue. This flippant, casual, matter-of-fact wrongfooting of the reader's expectations is typical of the picaresque, and leaves a permanent imprint on the Spanish novel, particularly its brutal focus on life in its most drab and sordid aspects, which a later tradition of novelists – Galdós, Baroja, Cela, Juan Goytisolo – have recognized as their national brand of "realism." One perceives this kind of realism clearly in the way in which the hero of Camilo José Cela's *La familia de Pascual Duarte* (1942), writing his memoirs in the condemned cell, relates the uniformly ill-fated circumstances of his upbringing in a small village in Extremadura: his impulsive violence erupts for the first time when he shoots his own dog; his sister Rosario becomes a teenage prostitute; a pig chews off the ears of his mentally handicapped brother, who drowns in a vat of oil; his mother drinks; his father beats her and the children, dying eventually of the bite of a rabid dog. And all this is set forth with shoulder-shrugging resignation and laconic candor, in which the occasional gestures of polite attenuation merely intensify the macabre bathos.

4 Anon., *Lazarillo de Tormes*, ed. Julio Cejador y Frauca (Madrid: Espasa-Calpe, 1969), p. 66. My translation.

This cynical tone, reflecting a sleazy life and viewpoint, was a great novelistic discovery, and the author of *Lazarillo* made two further ones. What makes a suitable plot for a long comic novel, as distinct from a short funny story? Before *Lazarillo*, the answer to that problem eluded Western European writers, with one notable exception, Apuleius, whose novel *The Golden Ass*, written in Latin in the second century AD, tells of what happens to Lucius after he is transformed by witchcraft into an ass. He suffers a hectic series of misadventures in the service of various masters until the goddess Isis reveals to him in a dream how he can recover human form. The author of *Lazarillo* borrows from Apuleius' story the formula "wandering servant of many masters," suppresses the supernatural and macabre aspects, and accentuates the comedy and possibilities of satire. Thus was born an indefinitely adaptable framework for a long comic novel, which has triumphantly persisted for four hundred and fifty years in innumerable variations and metamorphoses, from Thackeray's *Vanity Fair* to Günther Grass's *The Tin Drum* to American road movies. I mean the story of a lowly, accident-prone character, whose travels, ups-and-downs, occupations, and acquaintances provide an endless kaleidoscope of adventures and characters, all unified by their relation to his or her unfolding destiny. Amongst modern Spanish novelists, Baroja, with his rootless, marginalized protagonists searching for a meaning for their lives in a decadent Spanish society, exploits it repeatedly. For example, Andrés, in *El árbol de la ciencia* (1911), is a thoughtful, critical, and morose descendant of Lázaro, and more particularly, of Guzmán. The same pedigree is shared by Pedro, the young scientist of Luis Martín Santos's *Tiempo de silencio* (1962), whose investigations into cancer-bearing mice bring him, directly or indirectly, into contact with the city's sordid shanty town, its dingy boarding houses, its brothels. Obviously, modern Spanish novelists, when harking back to the old picaresque models, recreate them in accord with contemporary concerns. The theme of the individual's quick-witted struggle for survival in an urban jungle, treated farcically in the picaresque classics, now acquires sombre, socially critical, and existentialist inflections.

Let me digress a moment to explain that word "existentialist," starting with the other revolutionary discovery made by *Lazarillo*. Its author found a convincing means of representing fictionally a fundamental truth about human experience: the individual's awareness, beginning in childhood, of his or her isolation in a hostile world, where adults are potential adversaries from whom insubordinate thoughts need to be concealed behind a polite face, and stratagems of survival must continually be improvised. The *pícaro* has, typically, a lonely and wary attitude to others; and, in *Lazarillo*, this is stylistically reflected in the frequency of passages consisting of the boy's unspoken thoughts. He spends as much time in critical observation of others as in active involvement; from this process, he picks up lessons and learns from past mistakes, ending triumphantly – or so he claims – in a safe haven.

The picaresque novel, then, presents a perverted educational process, in which the individual learns the appropriate means of coping with a nasty world; and the two most influential critics of the picaresque in modern times, Rico (1970) and Lázaro Carreter (1972), have interpreted this process in a way that aligns it with the modern novel's conception of the subject's relation to society.[5] For both these critics, each ingredient in the narrative of *Lazarillo* is designed by its narrator to explain, prefigure, and justify his present point of view, including his cynically marginalized outlook. The ragbag of traditional motifs that enters into the novel's construction is transformed and unified by the theme of the forging of a dropout's conscience, and by the perfect circular trajectory of a career whose conclusion returns us to the prologue and to the inception of the act of writing.

Despite its roots in primitive narrative forms, *Lazarillo* is strikingly modern by virtue of the realism, poised self-consciousness, and coherence of its conception of the subject. I quote Lázaro Carreter, who, in this context, treats *Lazarillo* as a shining exception to the kind of story that he has in mind: "The life of novelistic characters, however unusual and eventful, does not constitute a novel in the modern sense of the term unless those characters take conscious responsibility for their past life and act under its influence in each and every one of the decisive moments of their existence" ("*Lazarillo de Tormes*", p. 216). "Taking responsibility for one's life" is existentialist terminology. In Ortega y Gasset's philosophy, the individual, "shipwrecked" in a world for which traditional morality and religion offer no meaning, is thrown back on his or her own resources, forges a personal "life-program," and achieves authenticity by acting in accord with that individual set of beliefs. The novels of Azorín, Baroja, and Unamuno are full of "shipwrecked" survivors thrashing about in search of that kind of life-raft, a quest rendered more urgent by the decadence of the Spanish society in which they live. A more recent example of this existentialist perspective is Carmen Martín Gaite's *El cuarto de atrás* (1978), where the author, through the medium of fictional autobiography, narrates her struggle to create her own "Back Room," an escapist playroom of fantasy and rebellious impulse that offers a private refuge from the penny-pinching drabness and the asphyxiating ideology of Franco's regime. Whether the author of *Lazarillo* saw the hero in as heroically defiant a light as the critics do is doubtful, despite his attractive sympathy for the disadvantaged and his stinging ironies about the double standards of those higher up the social ladder. With Spanish Golden Age

5 F. Rico, *La novela picaresca y el punto de vista* (Barcelona: Seix Barral, 1970).

readers in general, he saw Lázaro essentially as a comic butt, whose acquiescence in his wife's protestations of virtue is a sign of crass credulity, not cynicism.

Alemán, in *Guzmán de Alfarache*, while preserving *Lazarillo*'s essential comicality, gives the picaresque theme a sombrely moralistic and censorious twist. In the preliminaries to Part I, he explains that this is the autobiography of a contrite criminal with a university background, condemned to the galleys for his crimes. His hero, Guzmán, writes his life story on the benches of the galleys, interleaving the misadventures of his youth with a penitent gloss, which presents him as a universally applicable example of how anyone is led into sin. The *pícaro*'s levelling sense of the brutish nastiness and self-delusion of the human condition goes together with a passionate attack – "left-wing" in modern terms – on the institutional forms of sin, such as society's respect for the "haves" rather than the "have-nots," its enslavement to honor and saving face, the cynical abuse of power masquerading as justice. Alemán's Christian and utopian objective, illustrated by negative examples, is nothing less than the building of the idea of a perfect man in a just, economically efficient society.

Guzmán's story, as well as giving new depth to the *pícaro*'s career, vastly expands its scope. Geographically and vocationally, in *Lazarillo*, such a career pursued a parochial itinerary, from Salamanca to Toledo, and from one menial job to the next. By contrast, the action of *Guzmán de Alfarache* shuttles between the great political and commercial centers of Spain and Italy. The hero's Protean vicissitudes justify the subtitle of the novel's second part, "Atalaya de la Vida Humana" ('Watch Tower of Human Life'), and lead him through a diverse range of occupations: inn servant, basket carrier, kitchen skivvy, thief, dandy, beggar, page, jester and go-between, confidence trickster, cardsharp, shady financial dealer, theology student, twice a husband, pimp of his own wife, majordomo, convict, and, of course, author of his own memoirs. The uniformly comic tonality of *Lazarillo* yields to a mix of jest and earnest, accentuated by Guzmán's variation of the narrative of his own adventures with romantic and tragic interpolations. Thus, the squalid farce of his adventures at inns on the road from Seville to Madrid, a road which also takes this Jewish pariah away from God and honorable society, contrasts with the heroic, poignant, and devout interpolation of Ozmín and Daraja at the end of Book I, culminating in the integration of the Moorish lovers in the Christian court of the Catholic Monarchs, Ferdinand and Isabel.

The expansion of *Lazarillo*'s range also includes the style. Alemán tones down its flippancy, and assumes a causticity, sombreness, and learned elegance to which the precursor did not aspire, including a whole repertoire of devices derived from Renaissance rhetoric and didactic literature.

Contemporaries of Alemán were dazzled by the ambitious sweep of the book and by its brilliantly paradoxical mingling of *burlas* and *veras*, jest and earnest. In a Latin epigram included in the preliminaries of *Guzmán de Alfarache* Part I, Vicente Espinel, author of the picaresque novel *Marcos de Obregón* (1618), asks Guzmán who has taught him to soar from dung to the stars, flit like a fly from clean food to putrid ulcers, teach and scold, heal and console, pass from the green groves of sacred Sophia to squalid and obscene jests. And Guzmán answers that these contradictions are explained by his function as an image of human life, encompassing its good and its misery.

Let us see how this mix of *burlas* and *veras* works in *Guzmán de Alfarache*. After running away from his home and his mother's care, Guzmán arrives at an inn, tired and famished after his first day's hike, seeing the place with the rose-tinted expectation with which Columbus first sighted the Indies (Part I, Book i, Chapter 3). The violent disillusion that he suffers is preceded by a distinction between two types of affliction: first, those sent by divine providence to test and temper the soul, "most precious jewels covered with a thin layer of dust" (i, 107) from which God retrieves the faithful, spiritually enriched; secondly, those brought upon the sinner by his own folly, which bring only material and spiritual harm. This topic of pulpit oratory elicits a cluster of commonplace images reminiscent of the same discourse: the second kind of affliction is like green fields full of poisonous vipers, deceptive jewels concealing scorpions, eternal death which deceives with brief life. The imagery is coextensive with the physical circumstances of the *burla* that Guzmán now suffers, in which a seemingly tasty omelette is replaced by jewels, and its revolting ingredients by scorpions. The innkeeperess, an aged hag with fetid breath, sits the boy at a table set with filthy and dilapidated accessories: an oven rag for a tablecloth, an egg crock for a water jar, the broken base of a water pitcher for a salt cellar, a loaf blacker than the rag. She then serves him an omelette which he wolfs down "like a pig rooting for acorns," undeterred by the bad taste and the splintering sensation of little bones between teeth and gums. Realization only dawns upon him when he has left the inn behind and vomits out all the contents of his stomach. In this adventure Alemán dramatizes a traditional joke, based on the diner's discovery that his eggs are half-hatched, transforming it into a religious emblem with profound thematic repercussions in the story.

From the early eighteenth century onwards, posterity – translators of *Guzmán de Alfarache*, editors and abridgers of it, literary critics – have tended to react with sharp disfavor to Guzmán's moralizing, treating it as an impertinently prolix intrusion into a racy comic story. In recent times, critics have given this historic tendency a new twist by interpreting the novel's didacticism as a symptom of rancorous and subversive motives implicitly hostile to the ideology that it appears to promote. However, despite the modern age's distaste for it, the kind of socially critical and philosophically reflective transformations of the picaresque that have been written in the modern age would be inconceivable without the precedent set by Alemán's novel. While it would be quite misleading to suggest that it and *Lazarillo* adequately represent the rest of the Spanish picaresque, these are the genre's two foundational novels and constitute the essence of its legacy.

Cervantes, though he never brings himself to say so, was as dazzled by Alemán's novel as his contemporaries. *Don Quijote*, Part I (though not so much Part II) and the best-known *novelas* are indebted to it, more or less deeply, even though they pursue very different directions. For example, in *Don Quijote* Part I its imprint can be discerned in the importance of inns as primordial theatres of conflict between the hero's illusions and base reality, the segregation of robust comedy from interpolated romance, the hero's alternation between lucid rationality and anarchic folly, and the choice of priests as beacons of charitable enlightenment. Yet despite these similarities, the two novels basically diverge, due to the distinct motivations of the protagonists: in Guzmán's case, an irresistible attraction to a hand-to-mouth life of cheating and scrounging; in Don Quijote's, a crazy urge to imitate a life of fabulous literary heroism in the world of here-and-now.

Don Quijote is a parody of Spanish romances of chivalry, launched by the immensely popular *Amadís de Gaula* (1508). This genre, an offshoot of the medieval *Lancelot* about King Arthur's Knights of the Round Table, presents an escapist version of the medieval code of chivalry, set in a remote era sometime after the death of Christ: a marvelous world of giants, enchanters, castles, forests, tourneys, battles, princesses, dwarfs, and dragons, through which heroic knights-errant roam in search of adventure and fame. Cervantes ridicules the genre primarily because of its implausibility, thus swelling a chorus of moralistic denunciations dating from the early sixteenth century. Yet his objections are more aesthetic than moral, being based on a neoclassical conception of what a prose epic should be, which is, in essence, that it should excite wonderment in the reader without infringing verisimilitude.[6] This view is expounded by his spokesman, the Canon of Toledo, in *Don Quijote*, Part I, Chapter 47.

That theoretical critique of the romances is followed in the very next chapter by a stinging censure of the theatre of the contemporary school of Lope de Vega; and the conjunction of the two passages gives us a clue as to why Cervantes should have been so bothered about a genre – i.e. chivalry books – virtually defunct as regards composition, though not consumption,

[6] E. C. Riley, *Cervantes's Theory of the Novel* (Oxford: Clarendon, 1962), Chapter 5.

in Spain around 1600. Formerly a successful dramatist, he found himself ousted from public favor in the 1590s by Lope de Vega and his followers; and he attributes the setback not to his own deficiencies but to the commercially motivated philistinism of the actor-managers and their pandering to vulgar taste. From that bitter experience he derived a lesson relevant to the kind of epic story of love and adventure which he planned to write, and which he eventually brought to realization in his posthumously published romance *Persiles y Segismunda* (1617). Indeed, within the briefer compass of the *novela* or interpolated interlude, such as those included in *Don Quijote* Part I, he wrote stories of that kind throughout his career. He inferred that since they were akin to chivalric romances in heroic and prodigious tone, public taste needed to be taught through parody how to discriminate good romance from bad; otherwise, the rebuff in the genre of theatre would be repeated in prose fiction.

Understanding Cervantes's artistic motives for writing *Don Quijote* helps us to appreciate how he managed to transform parody into something much less limited than what is normally meant by that term. Another motive that needs to be taken into account are his strong objections to the heavy didacticism of contemporary literature of entertainment, an offense, in his view, against the principle of decorum or fittingness. *Guzmán de Alfarache* is one of the examples that he has in mind. The objections are expressed with waspish wit in the prologue to *Don Quijote* Part I, which ends with the recommendations of Cervantes's friend as to how he should write his novel. The friend tells him that since his purpose is simply the comic demolition of chivalry books, "about which Aristotle never took note, St. Basil was silent, and no news reached Cicero," he has no need to go scrounging philosophical maxims, precepts of Holy Scripture, poetic fables, rhetorical orations, and miracles of saints; all he need do is write his story in a pleasing, plain, and merry style, concentrate on its argument, and observe verisimilitude, thus provoking the reader to sustained laughter. We might see this as a recipe for unremitting levity without the least concession to gravity or learning. This impression would be mistaken. In fact, since Cervantes shares his age's taste for the display of eloquence, erudition, and moral sententiousness, and since it is essential to his novel's design that the hero's constantly frustrated attempts to live on an authentically heroic and romantic plane should be contrasted with interpolations that show characters successfully doing just that, *Don Quijote* contains plenty of "philosophical maxims." However, Cervantes cannot be accused of incurring the faults that he condemns. This is because, in incorporating such material in his novel, he takes good care to ensure that it is genuinely integrated with the main comic theme by irony, thematic mirroring, idiosyncrasy of perspective, and other means.

A good example is Don Quijote's speech on the Golden Age, which is both a "poetic fable" and a "rhetorical oration," and forms a prelude to the pastoral episode of Grisóstomo and Marcela. This elegantly precious and learned rehearsal of a consecrated classical topos (Part I, Chapter 11), with echoes of scores of poets from Hesiod onwards, is presented as an aspect of Don Quijote's eccentrically bookish character and chivalric mania. He is moved to deliver the oration, oblivious of the incomprehension of his hosts, the goat-herds, merely because he has a full belly after supper, feels in an expansive mood, and holds a bunch of shrivelled acorns in his hand, which puts him in mind of that vegetarian age. Also, he treats the decline of the mythic age of gold into that of iron as the "historic" circumstance that brought about the genesis of knight-errantry, required to protect wandering damsels from sexual predators. The speech thus forms a natural introduction to the story of the chaste and independent shepherdess Marcela, subjected to the pestering of her many male admirers, chief of whom, until his demise, was the shepherd Grisóstomo.

The story of Grisóstomo's love for Marcela, and the drama of his burial and her eloquent intervention in it, are essentially treated seriously; yet they are harmonized with Don Quijote's doings, first by being initially presented from the parochial viewpoint of the goat-herd Pedro, which brings the literariness of the behavior of Grisóstomo and his friends and rivals down to earth with a satiric bump, and secondly by the excesses of their amatory lamentations, reminiscent of those of Don Quijote for Dulcinea. In essence, Cervantes proceeds in the same sort of way with all the grave matter that he introduces into his novel – the trials and tribulations of Cardenio and Dorotea in the Sierra Morena (I: 23–4, 27–9, 36), Don Quijote's counsels of government to Sancho (II: 42–3), and so on – and, in consequence, he endows it with a suggestive ambivalence. To what extent are Cardenio and Dorotea tarred with Don Quijote's brush? How seriously are we meant to take those counsels, commonplaces of the statecraft of the age? How do we discriminate good romance from bad, one level of fiction from another, 'inside' the fictional world from 'outside'?[7] For Cervantes and his contemporaries, steeped in cultural presuppositions that allowed them to make such distinctions instinctively, those problems did not exist. Yet for readers of later ages, unfamiliar with those presuppositions, the ambivalence would become ironically mesmerizing. Cervantes appears to present in his novel all the learned styles and topics, the authoritative discourses, and the forms of talk of his age, and to hold all this ironically at arm's length without taking sides. That

[7] Ibid., pp. 135–48.

at least is how his novel has been interpreted in the twentieth century, from Américo Castro to Leo Spitzer to Carlos Fuentes; and the interpretation has acquired a new lease on life in the post-modernist age, thanks to the pervasive influence of the 'dialogic' theory of Bakhtin.[8] It draws strength from the notorious "metafictionality" of *Don Quijote*: that is, Cervantes's practice of alluding within his novel to its own fictional status, which includes representing the process of creating, consuming, and criticizing fiction. We have an example of this in the Marcela/Grisóstomo episode. Don Quijote, the madman who believes he can live chivalric literature, hears from Pedro the story about the eccentric Grisóstomo and his party, who, for love of Marcela, live the life of literary shepherds. Then he observes Grisóstomo's burial, a solemn literary masquerade, with the mourners, the funeral bier, and ceremony dressed up like a scene from Sanazzaro's *Arcadia*. It is as though Don Quijote were reading a version of his own story.[9]

From the viewpoint of posterity, the same kind of ambivalence surrounds Don Quijote's motivation. In the early chapters of Part I, it is ridiculously unproblematic. He goes mad as a result of reading too many chivalry books, loses the distinction between them and true history, and resolves to becomes a knight-errant in the Spain of around 1600. His behavior from that point on, as Sancho aptly observes (II: 10), involves interpreting black as white – windmills as giants, sheep as armies, basins as helmets – with chaotically farcical results. While this black/white dichotomy is basic to a series of centrally significant contrasts through the novel, it is progressively refined by two factors in particular.

The first is Cervantes's peculiarly internal and empathetic relation to the object of his parody, due to the fact that he ridicules chivalry books from the perspective of an ideal alternative to them. Consequently, though Don Quijote's heroic conception of himself and of a consonantly prodigious world exists only in his fantasy, it stylishly and consistently replicates the original in many ways, while at the same time capriciously inflating, elaborating, and vulgarizing it. This continually improvised romance is made to absorb, with madly ingenious exuberance, a host of "purple" styles and learned topics, some more or less akin to the chivalric genre (pastoral, epic, history, ballads, Ariosto's heroic romance *Orlando furioso*), and others quite unrelated to it (the Golden Age, the Bible, poetic theory, statecraft, legal jargon, etcetera). Don Quijote does not merely play a chivalric role, but lives it, confusing

8 L. Spitzer, "Perspectivismo lingüístico en el *Quijote*," in *Lingüística e historia literaria* (Madrid: Gredos, 1955), pp. 161–225, and C. Johnson, "Cómo se lee hoy el *Quijote*," in *Cervantes* (Alcalá de Henares: Centro de Estudios Cervantinos, 1995), pp. 335–48.

9 E. C. Riley, *Don Quijote* (London: Allen and Unwin, 1986), pp. 124–32.

make-believe with reality; and the performance includes a thoroughgoing rationale of his vocation: its historical origins, its ethical principles, and so on. His enthusiastic and solemn immersion in a fictional world incites the reader, as Ortega y Gasset shrewdly pointed out,[10] to identify with him; and in this the modern reader is assisted by a tendency to overlook a distinction that Cervantes takes for granted: that is, the difference between mad make-believe and really doing or being. We can observe this tendency in Erich Auerbach's famous essay on "The Enchanted Dulcinea," a commentary on the adventure in which Sancho deceives his master into thinking that three uncouth wenches, met by chance outside El Toboso, are Dulcinea and two ladies-in-waiting (*Don Quijote*, Part II, Chapter 10).

Before setting forth on his third sally, Don Quijote rides to El Toboso to seek Dulcinea's blessing (II: 8); and Sancho is expected to lead his master to her palace, having supposedly gone there during the second sally to deliver a message to her. Sancho is put in a terrible pickle, for his account of his embassy to Dulcinea was all a pack of lies (I: 31). Quite apart from that, though Sancho is by now nitwittedly unclear on this point, the palace and Dulcinea's noble status are pure figments of the knight's imagination. After master and squire blunder fruitlessly about El Toboso in the dead of night (II: 9), Sancho is left to locate Dulcinea on his own, and he resolves on a ruse to get himself out of his jam. Reasoning that his master is mad, and habitually prone to take black for white, he decides to present to his master the first rustic wench that he meets, claiming that she is Dulcinea.

The encounter beween Don Quijote and the three girls is dramatically vivid in its oppositions of register, posture, and attitude, and the extremity of its irony. The knight, with bulging eyes and distraught gaze, confronts the moon-faced, snub-nosed "Dulcinea," one of whose companions delivers a coarsely rustic brush-off to Sancho, intermediary of the meeting. At this, Don Quijote delivers a preciously wordy entreaty to "Dulcinea" – "And thou, O limit of desirable worth, ultimate term of human courtesy, only remedy of this afflicted heart that adores thee!" (II: 110) – begging her to look gently and amorously upon him, unless he too has been made hideous in her eyes, just as she has been grotesquely transformed in his. Auerbach characterizes the speech as lofty, beautiful, grandly periodic, overlooking its stilted literariness and the ridiculous misapprehensions on which it is based.[11] Auerbach

[10] J. Ortega y Gasset, "Meditaciones del *Quijote*," in *Obras completas*, 7th edn, 9 vols. (Madrid: Revista de Occidente, 1966), vol. 1, pp. 380–1.

[11] E. Auerbach, "The Enchanted Dulcinea," reproduced in *Cervantes*, ed. Lowry Nelson Jr. (Englewood Cliffs, NJ: Prentice Hall, 1969), pp. 98–122. From *Mimesis: The Representation of Reality in Western Literature*, tr. Willard Trask (Princeton University Press, 1953).

is able to take this view because, although Don Quijote overdoes the language of lovers' adoration, he overdoes it marginally rather than crudely. For Cervantes, the speech's absurdity consists not so much in the style as in the grotesque mismatch between style and addressee, a failure of decorum which he would not have considered extrinsic to the dignity of expression.[12] Disregarding that, Auerbach assumes that the Don's hyperbolical rhetoric is as noble as that of other, seriously portrayed Cervantine lovers, and worthily continues "the great epico-rhetorical tradition," instead of degrading it. This assumption is facilitated by Cervantes's characteristic lack of comment on Don Quijote's motivation. Why, for example, does the knight fail to transform black into white in this scene, when in Part I, confronted by wenches quite as hideous as this one, his imagination invariably converts them into paragons of beauty? On this and other questions regarding his attitude to Dulcinea, Cervantes is silent. So the reader has to revert to Don Quijote's own explanations, which have a crazy inconsequentiality combined with an outwardly stylish and emotive form. Hence many modern readers substitute "sublime" for "crazy," including Auerbach, as the following quotation shows: "But Don Quijote's feelings are genuine and profound. Dulcinea is really the mistress of his thoughts; he is truly filled with the spirit of a mission which he regards as man's highest duty" ("The Enchanted Dulcinea," p. 107). From premises like these, a long succession of twentieth-century critics has read this adventure and the ensuing process of the knight's disillusionment as tragedy, not farce.

My purpose here is not to rebut them but to explain why, since about 1800, there has been a fundamental shift in readers' conception of Don Quijote's mania, which is no longer seen as a ridiculous, albeit amiable, aberration, but as a paradigm of the human imagination's struggle to transcend the pull of base reality, and thus to achieve some form of salvation, religious, artistic, or other. This, for Ortega y Gasset in his *Meditaciones del Quijote*, published in 1914, is the destiny of all human culture, and Don Quijote's transformation of the windmills on the plain of Montiel symbolizes it. Since, among works of fiction, *Don Quijote* has been the single most important influence upon the development of the European novel since 1800 (Close, *Don Quijote*, pp. 109–25), Quixotic figures abound in the genre – the heroine of Flaubert's *Madame Bovary*, Captain Ahab in Melville's *Moby Dick*, Dickens's Mr. Pickwick – and while their Quixotry is not always depicted in Ortega's grandiose terms, it tends to be seen as heroic, tragic, or at least, pathetic, rather than funny. In Spain, Galdós and Unamuno are the most heavily indebted to this model, with the former taking Don Quijote as a

[12] A. Close, *Don Quijote* (Cambridge University Press, 1990), pp. 96–7.

basic pattern for the delineation of his characters (e.g., Maxi in *Fortunata y Jacinta*, Don Francisco in *La de Bringas*), and the latter seeing him as the personification of all that is noblest in the Spanish soul, a Christ adapted to the modern age, like the protagonist of Unamuno's *San Manuel Bueno, mártir* (1931).

The second factor that refines the black/white dichotomy in *Don Quijote* is Cervantes's conception of the kind of reality that he juxtaposes to his hero's literary fantasies. Gray is often a more adequate symbol for it than black. One of the few chivalry books to be saved from the bonfire in the scrutiny of Don Quijote's library is *Tirant lo Blanc*, about which the priest says enthusiastically: "Here knights eat and sleep and die in their beds, and make their wills before dying, with other such things lacking in all the rest of the genre" (I: 6). Here the priest pinpoints the stuff of humdrum, everyday life, which Cervantes habitually designates by the term *menudencias*, trifles. In focusing on *menudencias*, he opened up a whole new zone of the real world as an object of fictional representation, distinctively different from the kind of "realism" in which picaresque novelists specialized, and in dramatizing the interplay between *menudencias* and idealizing fantasy, he discovered a major theme – some would say *the* great theme[13] – of the European novel from, shall we say, 1800 to 1930: *Madame Bovary*, George Eliot's *Middlemarch*, Clarín's *La Regenta*, Galdós's *Doña Perfecta*, Henry James's *The Ambassadors*, Unamuno's *Niebla*, Scott Fitzgerald's *The Great Gatsby*.

A good example of Cervantes's attention to *menudencias* is the last chapter of his novel, in which the priest's words about knights dying in bed and making wills before dying are explicitly recalled and literally come true. In this, one of the great death-bed scenes in literature, Don Quijote takes up an option which he has hitherto consistently rejected: fulfilling the social, personal, and religious obligations incumbent on him as the person he really is, Alonso Quijano el Bueno. He recants his chivalric delusions, which all fly out of his head as though they had never existed, save one: the promise of the island made to Sancho. Why does he remember this particular promise? The answer points to how Don Quijote's last will and testament specifically reflects the form and purpose of such documents in the Spain of Cervantes's age. By means of them, the author of the will could envisage departing this world with conscience clear and all debts settled, the latter being a prerequisite of the former. And so it was normal for testators to make bequests to faithful retainers in a form of words somewhat similar to the following:

[13] Harry Levin, "The Example of Cervantes," in *Contexts of Criticism* (Cambridge, MA: Harvard University Press, 1957), pp. 79–86.

> Item, it is my will that with regard to certain moneys held by Sancho Panza, treated by me in my madness as my squire, these moneys having been the subject of certain reckonings and argy-bargy between us, I do not want him to be held liable for them, nor asked to return any of them, but rather that if there should be any money left over after he has paid himself from what I owe him, and it can't be much, good luck to him; and, remembering how in my madness I was the means of giving him an island, if I could now, in my sanity, give him a whole kingdom, I would do it, because the innocence of his character and loyalty of his service deserve it. (II: 74)

These words nobly sum up the bond of affection between Don Quijote and Sancho; and they also mimic by their tortuous syntax the wording of real, historic wills. They match the substance too, with obvious differences, which reflect the partly burlesque nature of this testament. We could scarcely imagine a real scribe including in a legal document the idiosyncratic reference to madness and the concession of an island, still less using such colloquial, bread-and-butter expressions as "dares y tomares" ('argy-bargy'), "buen provecho le haga" ('good luck to him'). The whole passage typifies the constant tug in the novel between burlesque fantasy and fidelity to mundane particulars.

In the twentieth century, from Ortega's seminally influential *Meditaciones del Quijote* onwards, attention has shifted from Don Quijote to Cervantes, from the book or the hero as archetypal symbol to the individual system of thought expressed in that book and other writings. The seed that Ortega planted in the *Meditaciones* bore fruit in Américo Castro's *El pensamiento de Cervantes* (1925), whose influence, together with that of Castro's later essays on Cervantes, extends far beyond the borders of Cervantine criticism.[14] In that seminal book, reacting against the unproblematic image, encouraged by the great literary historian Menéndez Pelayo, of Cervantes as the artlessly inspired painter of nature, Castro gave an account of Cervantes's outlook that was thoroughly in tune with the times, in which Ortega y Gasset's vitalism and relativism were in the air, and the liberal Second Spanish Republic was in the offing.

Castro's Cervantes is a deeply ironic, self-conscious, and ambiguous writer, abreast of the most innovative currents of Renaissance thought, aloof from the oppressive ideology of the Spanish Counter-Reformation, and imbued with something like a pre-Ortegan concept of the moral subject, which he expresses in novelistic rather than philosophic form, artfully insinuated in muted asides and suggestive overtones. Later, Castro rejected the intellectual

[14] A. Castro. *El pensamiento de Cervantes*, 2nd edn, ed. J. Rodríguez-Puértolas (Madrid: Noguer, 1972), pp. 87–8, 243–4.

and European orientation that he attributed to Cervantes in 1925.[15] In the series of essays and books in which he developed his conception of Spanish history, expressed in *La realidad histórica de España* (1954), he identified its critical period as the sixteenth century, when the distinctive Spanish mindset took shape, formed through the interaction of the three castes which coexisted in the Spanish Peninsula after the Arab invasion: Jew, Moor, Christian. In that century, the Christians exerted repressive dominance over the other two races, seeking to destroy their cultures along with their religions and to assert their own caste-purity, without realizing how far they had assimilated the traits of their two neighbors. In *Cervantes y los casticismos españoles* (1966), Castro treats *Don Quijote* as a utopian political fable about how the tensions and insecurities of the Spanish life style can be overcome.[16] With or without these racial overtones, the conception of Cervantes as key to the enigma of Spanish identity and cure for its strife, crystallized by the writers of the Generation of 1898 and by Ortega, has remained a commonplace of intellectual discourse in twentieth-century Spain, and, after the mid-century, is reflected in such novels as Martín Santos's *Tiempo de silencio* (1962) and Juan Goytisolo's *Reivindicación del conde don Julián* (1970).

Guide to further reading

Close, A., *Cervantes and the Comic Mind of his Age* (Oxford University Press, 2000).

Dunn, P., *Spanish Picaresque Fiction: A New Literary History* (Ithaca: Cornell University Press, 1993).

Williamson, E. (ed.), *Cervantes and the Modernists: The Question of Influence* (London: Támesis, 1994).

15 A. J. Close, *The Romantic Approach to Don Quixote* (Cambridge University Press, 1978), pp. 228–39.

16 A. Castro, *Cervantes y los casticismos españoles* (Madrid: Alfguara, 1966).

3

REBECCA HAIDT

The Enlightenment and fictional form

Critical tradition holds that in Spain, the eighteenth century is one "without novels" in the sense of those produced by realist and naturalist authors; eighteenth-century novels have been characterized as didactic works lacking the stylistic interest and psychological depth of later narrative achievements, or as simply scarce presences in a century which in Europe saw the flourishing of the form. Yet recent scholarship has developed a more nuanced picture of the novel during the eighteenth century in Spain, a century that may no longer be accused of dearth in terms of either production or quality. In scores of original and translated or adapted works, eighteenth-century novelists gave readers access to "what was 'asked' of literature: observation of people, a realistic description of their lives, and a knowledge of their souls based on experience and their relation to society."[1]

Enlightenment fiction was the vehicle not only for moral instruction and lessons concerning virtue, but also for the observation of life and reality. Readers wanted fiction to represent experience as though it were happening before their eyes, and turned to novels for realist elements such as the portrayal of consciousness and the depiction of intense emotions, a key component of the most characteristic of Enlightenment fictional genres: the narrative of sensibility. Authors of fiction experimented with the possibilities of the form in many aspects, such as dialogical modalities and the narration of human experience in time. In fact, in the period of the Enlightenment the form was rehearsing crucial aspects of what later would serve as bases of the great Spanish literary movements which generated novels, realism and naturalism. How can we negotiate our way through didacticism and sensibility to the novel as conceived by writers such as Leopoldo Alas or Benito Pérez Galdós?

It will be useful first to review briefly some meanings of *novela* prior to the period under discussion, which for the purposes of this chapter extends over

[1] J. Álvarez Barrientos, *La novela del siglo XVIII* (Madrid: Ediciones Júcar), p. 16.

fifty years, from the middle of the 1770s to the end of the *trienio liberal* (The 'Liberal Triennium') in 1823. In the first half of the century the term *novela* designated not literary fiction but "lying, falsehood or calumny."[2] For much of the century novels, as works of fantasy appealing to the imagination, were decried by contemporary moralists as corruptors of youthful morals and as propagators of pernicious notions among women. Literary precepts adapted from Aristotle held that the novel, being a prose form, was not worthy of the esteem accorded genres such as tragedy or epic. The novel was theorized as more properly a variant of history; however, as it dealt in invented scenarios, it lacked that form's venerable claim to truth. The few poetics that addressed the form placed the novel as part of the field of rhetoric and not poetry; due to its persuasive nature, fiction was "invented to instruct by pleasing."[3]

Nevertheless, in the "Prólogo con morrión" to his novel *Historia del famoso predicador Fray Gerundio de Campazas* (*The History of the Famous Preacher Friar Gerund de Campazas; Otherwise Gerund Zofes*, 1758), José Francisco de Isla recognized that despite the prescription that authors produce "novelas útiles," anyone could create a novel:

> Well, what did I do? Only what the creators of useful novels and epic poems do. They propose a hero, either real or fictive, making him a perfect model of arms, letters, politics, or moral virtue [. . .]. From this, that or any other model they gather together whatever will serve to promote the perfection of their little idol, filling out the traits which they want him to exemplify. They apply a degree of inventiveness to the depiction of this figure, and with proportion and wit, imagine the adventures, incidents, and accidents they believe most natural so as to link story and action, deeds and history, and lo, you've got an epic poem, in prose or verse, exactly as required.[4]

As Isla points out, the rules for production of fiction were well established: develop a hero whose depiction "imitates nature in its universal aspect" (as Ignacio de Luzán put it in his 1737 version of Aristotle's *Poetics*);[5] exercise poetic invention so as to please the reader and attain verisimilitude; ensure unity of action. Yet Isla's vocabulary reflects the variability of terminology for description of fictional narratives: both *novelas* and *poemas épicos* refer to the novel; as would, changeably throughout the century, *romance*,

[2] L. Almanza, "Notas sobre la voz 'novela' en Feijoo y en la literatura de su época," in *II Simposio sobre el Padre Feijoo y su siglo* (Oviedo: Centro de Estudios del Siglo XVIII, 1981), p. 199.

[3] G. Mayans y Siscar, "Retórica," *Obras completas*, 5 vols., ed. Antonio Mestre Sanchís (Valencia: Ayuntamiento de Oliva, 1984), vol. III, p. 285.

[4] José Francisco de Isla, *Fray Gerundio de Campazas*, ed. Russell P. Sebold, 4 vols. (Madrid: Espasa-Calpe, 1969), vol. I, pp. 10–11.

[5] I. De Luzán, *La poética, o reglas de la poesía en general y de sus principales especies*, ed. Russell P. Sebold (Barcelona: Labor, 1977), p. 172.

fábula ('fable') *historia* ('story / history') *historia fingida* ('fictional history'), *anécdota* ('anecdote') and even *memoria* ('memoir').

The typology of fictional form also was flexible: the *abate* ('abbé') José Marchena, in the "Discurso preliminar" to his *Lecciones de filosofía moral y elocuencia* ('Lessons on Moral Philosophy and Eloquence', 1820), identified the novel's similarity to "tragedy or comedy";[6] and José Munárriz's translation of Blair's *Lecciones sobre la Retórica y las Bellas Letras* ('Lessons on Rhetoric and Belles-Lettres', 1789) grouped *romances* and *novelas* together in his section on prose fiction.[7] Brown observes that the term *novela* was not used to refer to the form in the modern sense until 1788;[8] until the end of the century, *historia* or *romance* frequently designated longer texts such as *Don Quijote* or *Fray Gerundio*, while *novela* often denoted shorter fictional works.[9] Experimentation in the shape of fiction drew on and enhanced the variability of period typology: for example, José Cadalso's *Cartas marruecas* ('Letters from Morocco'), an epistolary narrative, and *Noches lúgubres* ('Dark Nights of Dejection'), a prose dialogue (both produced in the middle of the 1770s), offered readers innovative structure and unusual narrative framing.

The form's pliability, along with the array of publications flooding the markets of Madrid and Valencia and stocking the import trade – adventures such as Jerónimo Martín Bernardo's *El Emprendedor* ('The Entrepreneur', 1805); satires such as Diego Ventura Rejón y Lucas's *Aventuras de Juan Luis* ('The Adventures of Juan Luis', 1781); Rousseauian considerations of love as in José Mor de Fuentes's *La Serafina* (1798); epistolary novels such as José Cadalso's *Cartas marruecas* (1788–9);[10] narratives of sensibility such as those collected in Ignacio García Malo's bestselling *Voz de la naturaleza* ('The Voice of Nature', 1787–92); parodies of the *Quijote* such as Bernardo María de Calzada's translation of Charlotte Lennox's *The Female Quijote* (1752) as *Don Quijote con faldas* (1808) – suggest that in the second half of the century the novel was a form of greater variety and availability to readers than traditionally acknowledged by criticism. Indeed, the 1780s and 1790s were a thriving period for production of the novel in Spain; one gauge of the genre's popularity – and profitability – is the dissemination of collections of both Peninsular and translated foreign novels, such as the *El ramillete o los*

6 J. Marchena, "Discurso preliminar," *Lecciones de filosofía moral y elocuencia . . . de los mejores autores castellanos*, 2 vols. (Bordeaux: Pedro Beaume, 1820), vol. I, p. xxvii.

7 H. Blair, *Lecciones sobre la retórica y las bellas letras*, tr. José Luis Munárriz, 4 vols. (Madrid: Ibarra, 1816–17), vol. III, pp. 291–9.

8 R. Brown, *La novela española 1700–1850* (Madrid: Dirección General de Archivos, Bibliotecas y Museos, 1953), p. 13.

9 Álvarez, *La novela del siglo XVIII*, pp. 16–29.

10 The *Cartas* were composed in the early 1770s but not published until much later.

aguinaldos de Apolo ('Apollo's Sweets and Soups', 1798–1801) to a public hungry for examples of the form. As Antonio Valladares de Sotomayor noted in the "Prólogo" to his novel *La Leandra* (1797), the 1790s produced an "amazing multitude of novels" for a booming readership.[11] Owing in part to publishers' and authors' financial motivations and in part to changing aesthetic standards, the novel was rehabilitated by century's end: as the prospectus for the *Colección universal de novelas y cuentos* ('Universal Collection of Novels and Stories', 1789–90) stated, "novels have the honor of being one of the first kinds of known literature and one to which the republic of letters owes a great measure of its progress."[12]

During the first half of the eighteenth century many types of literature, such as the essays of Benito Jerónimo Feijoo's *Teatro crítico universal* ('Universal Theatre of Criticism', 1726–40), cultivated readers' enjoyment of writings in prose.[13] Frequent reprintings of sixteenth- and seventeenth-century works such as novels by María de Zayas, Cervantes's *La Galatea*, picaresque narratives, and devotional texts indicate a steady market for the consumption of both fictional and non-fictional narratives in prose. In addition, as Hunter observes, characteristics of "the novel" – e.g. the depiction of everyday existence, language unfettered by privileged style, subjectivity, vicariousness[14] – were present and under development in a variety of prose texts popular in Europe in the first half of the century, such as saints' lives, accounts of marvels and wonders, or urban "guides." In Spain, Diego de Torres Villarroel's *Los desahuciados del mundo* ('The Hopeless of the World', 1736–7) employed everyday language within the genre of the satirical urban guide – a template for which in Spanish narrative was provided by Luis Vélez de Guevara's *El diablo cojuelo* ('The Devil Upon Two Sticks', 1641) and Francisco de Quevedo's *El mundo por de dentro* ('The World From Within', 1612) – to escort readers through the vice-ridden spaces and practices of the court; and Torres's hugely popular autobiographical *Vida* (*The Remarkable Life of Don Diego, Being the Autobiography of Diego Torres Villarroel*, 1743) inscribed the author's adventures as a dancing master, healer, astrologer and Salamancan professor, vicariously engaging readers in his exploits.[15] By the middle of the century the novel was further aided in development through print

[11] A. Valladares de Sotomayor, *La Leandra*, 2 vols. (Madrid: Antonio Ulloa, 1797), vol. 1, p. 16.

[12] Quoted in Álvarez, *La novela del siglo XVIII*, p. 222.

[13] Ibid., pp. 30–9.

[14] J. Paul Hunter, *Before Novels: The Cultural Contexts of Eighteenth Century English Fiction* (New York: Norton, 1990), pp. 23–4.

[15] The first four parts (what Torres termed "trozos") of the *Vida* were published in 1743; the fifth part appeared in 1750; the sixth in 1758; and all six parts were published together in an edition of 1799 (as volume 15 of Torres's complete works).

media such as journalism. In periodicals, such as José Clavijo y Fajardo's *El Pensador* ('The Thinker', 1762–7), the dialogic structuring of social criticism offered readers diverse psychological attitudes and narrative personalities.[16] By so variously supplementing the range of literary ideas available to the public in the popular theatres, writer and publishers of prose made it possible for readers to imagine themselves in dialogue with an author, undertake a personal reading of a text, and find rhythms and conventions not possible in verse.[17]

By the middle of the century the way was paved for the immense popularity of Isla's satirical *Fray Gerundio de Campazas* (1758).[18] *Fray Gerundio* depicts characters in everyday situations – dressing, taking a walk – and incorporates non-fictional texts, such as sermons, within the larger form of a moral tale concerning education, ambition and the dangers and pleasures of the imagination. Entwining invented episodes from the life of a young preacher with discussions of rhetorical theory, Isla trains the reader to shed ignorance of the differences between bad and good preaching and, thereby, to become a more thoughtful and less gullible Christian and citizen. Critics have faulted the characters' lack of psychological depth and the plot's episodic structure. Yet the eager reception of *Fray Gerundio* indicates that the text certainly offered mid-eighteenth-century readers key aspects of what they were looking for in fiction: fulfilling its didactic mission through a consistent presentation of the reform required in sacred oratory, the narrative complies with the dictates of precept in its combination of the useful and the pleasurable, and incorporates a variety of prose forms – e.g. sermons and rhetorical instruction – appealing to audiences of the period.[19]

After 1760, a good indicator of fictional form's post-Gerundian possibilities is found in a definition of the novel offered by Marchena in his "Discurso preliminar": the *abate* divides novels into pastoral and all others, which either "paint the origin and progress of a passion" or narrate the life of a hero, "linking it [the individual's life] with the events of a human life, gradually unfolding the character of the subject they depict."[20] Marchena identifies elements that readers would come to crave in fiction during the period of the

[16] I. Urzainqui, "Autocreación y formas autobiográficas en la prensa crítica del siglo XVIII", *Anales de literatura española* 11 (1995), pp. 194–5.

[17] Álvarez, *La novela del siglo XVIII*, p. 39.

[18] The first part of the novel appeared in 1758, its edition of 1500 copies selling out in three days; the second part was not published until 1768. The first complete Spanish edition with both parts appeared in 1787.

[19] The novel was prohibited in 1760 as a response to denunciations from outraged preachers and members of religious orders, which led to numerous pirated and foreign editions of the work.

[20] Marchena, "Discurso preliminar," vol. I, p. xxvi.

Enlightenment and afterward: the workings of emotions on the mind and body, and the growth of a character in tension and resonance with the society surrounding him or her. Gerundio is indeed a character of imagination and passion whose inclinations bring him both success and failure. Yet his depiction does not include the sharing of others' pain; he is rarely mindful of his own feelings; he is not, in other words, an aware, social being. One cannot lay Gerundio's characterization at the doorstep of the novel's didacticism, for even in one of the most didactic of novels produced during the eighteenth century, Pedro Montengón's *El Eusebio* (1786),[21] the protagonist exhibits a keen awareness of self: Eusebio is a thinking, reacting character through all his travails; he feels compassion for others, cries, worries, and is confused by conflicting thoughts and impulses; he imagines, remembers, and reflects upon his mistakes and his desires. Gerundio, on the other hand, is a character developed before a period in which readers increasingly sought contact with individual, immediate personal experience through fictional accounts. If earlier categorization of the novel as *romance* or *historia fingida* emphasized the shaping of the form within the dangerous domain of the unreal, later in the century the *novela* encoded concern with the "array of possibilities" inherent in real human existence.[22] From the 1770s onward, what Enlightenment readers began to appreciate was the novel's capacity to depict the complex mix of emotion, passion, desire, thought and circumstance that was the truth of human life.

Observation of the self was of prime importance to Enlightenment thought, which privileged the consciousness of the individual and taught the awareness of sensation as a source of knowledge of the truth. The Enlightenment cultivated a citizenry trained to be observers of "the real" as something that encompassed both the internal and the external, both underlying cause and surface appearance; the popularization of observation was an important factor informing what eighteenth-century readers and authors came to think of as "reality" in fictional characterization.

The eighteenth century saw the production of numerous and widely read works treating the role and methodology of "observation" and "experiment." In his 1730s treatise on observational method, Petrus van Musschenbroek advocated that above all the observer "must be persuaded that as a thing may be [*peut être*] in two different ways, ordinarily it will be so in the way most contrary to appearances."[23] Van Musschenbroek cautioned

[21] P. Montengón, *El Eusebio*, ed. Fernando García Lara (Madrid: Editora Nacional, 1984).

[22] Álvarez, *La novela del siglo XVIII*, p. 171.

[23] P. van Musschenbroek, "Discours sur la meilleure manière de faire les expériences," cited from *Cours de physique experimentale et mathématique*, 2 vols. (Leyden: Luchtmans, 1769), vol. I, p. 182.

the observing subject to avoid single-minded adherence to any one ideology, perspective or instrument so as to get beyond the surface of things and find the truth. In the 1770s Jean Senebier reminded readers that observation was integral to the lived self: "all moments of life impose upon men the obligation to survey themselves, to re-enter the past, to glance toward the future ... [and to] always have the senses alert"; the role of the observing self is that of a "reader of nature" who interprets the complexities of experience.[24] By the 1780s, enlightened Spanish readers were well acquainted with these and other works on experimental observation.

A more general audience was aware of the variety of public entertainments in urban theatres that featured visual and perceptual demonstrations with the camera obscura or electricity. Throughout the second half of the century, exhibitions of experiments in hydraulics, physics, and chemistry were advertised in *El Diario de Madrid*. Popularized science demonstrations played an important role in "the initiation of beholders into concealed causes,"[25] that is, the orientation of observers toward inquiry into the causes underlying the illusory, into that which lies below the exterior of things. In other words, a public increasingly comfortable with and trained to observe phenomena and recognize effects of "the real" and its relationship to inner or hidden experience was well under development by the end of the eighteenth century.

Enlightenment philosophy emphasized inquiry into links between feeling and morality; between the physical operations of sensing and their moral transcendence. These links could be traced through the concept of "sentiment" or "sensibility" (*sensibilidad*). Sensibility had as its intellectual basis the sensationalist philosophy of Locke and Condillac, in the assumption that the source of all knowledge is individual human experience as operative through the senses, such as sight. Sensibility was both a physiological condition and a moral practice. On the plane of morality, sensibility was engaged through sympathy or innate responsiveness to the sight of another's suffering or extremes of emotion. The notion of an innate human capacity to respond sympathetically to what is experienced by others was augmented during the eighteenth century by medical demonstrations of sensibility as a physiological process: the sense of self and of that self's relation to others in society was grounded in raw physical experience and the ideas of the mind arising from bodily impressions. In the concept of "sensibility," scientific and literary discourses converged in investigations of questions such as the

[24] J. Senebier, *Essai sur l'art d'observer et de faire des expériences*, 2 vols. (Geneva: J.J. Paschoud, 1802; earlier edition Geneva, 1775), pp. 3, 25.

[25] B. M. Stafford, *Artful Science: Enlightenment Entertainment and the Eclipse of Visual Education* (Cambridge, MA: MIT Press, 1994), p. 150.

function of sight in the links between mind and body, the moral grounding of physical impulses, and other aspects of what from the middle of the eighteenth century onward was termed "psychology." An immensely popular genre of fiction, the narrative of *sensibilidad*, provided readers with opportunities to imagine that they were observing the resonance of the experience of feeling. Sentimental fiction postulated the basis of the moral life in bodily feeling; narratives of sensibility demonstrated that in the "progress of a passion" (as Marchena put it), the workings of inner emotion are visible upon the bodies of characters and observable for evidence of moral relationships among members of society.

Readers of periodicals such as the 1780s *Correo literario de la Europa* ('Literary Courier of Europe') could learn of novels of sensibility along with the most recent foreign publications. As either imports or contraband the demand for such novels was high, as was the impact of such works in translation. Spanish readers embraced the literature of sensibility, thanks in part to publishers who commissioned translations of preponderantly French foreign novels as a means of capitalizing on a lucrative market, and in part to the work of numerous translators (such as Marchena himself, who rendered works by Montesquieu, Rousseau, and Voltaire), some of whom sought to bring important currents of European thought to Spanish audiences, and some of whom hoped to gain financially in the market for translated literature. Translations of foreign novels injected new prose styles and narrative techniques into the repertory of Spanish authors and introduced readers to a variety of characters, themes, and situations not available in native productions: for example, Bernardo María de Calzada's 1791 translation of François Vernes's *El viajador sensible* ('The Sympathetic Traveler', 1786) presented readers with a narrative voice imbued with Deist enthusiasm.[26] Reginald Brown observes that "the reading of translations [...] awakened the taste of the public at large and helped formulate the criterion by which the cultivated elites only a few years later would judge romantic literary productions."[27] Despite the Consejo de Castilla's 1799 prohibition of new licences for the publication of novels and a royal decree of 1805 that increased the difficulty of book publishing, readers were able to obtain copies of Spanish translations published in cities such as Bordeaux and Paris. Between the 1770s and the 1820s, some of the most popular and celebrated European fictional works by Chateaubriand, Richardson, Rousseau, Vernes and others, including many novels of sensibility, were made available in Spanish translations or adaptations.

[26] Vernes's original was published in 1786 as *Le voyageur sentimental, ou Ma promenade à Yverdun.*

[27] Brown, *La novela española*, p. 25.

By the 1780s, Spanish readers had cried with Richardson's heroines and experienced Rousseauian transports in considering nature and virtue.[28] While both *El Eusebio* and *Fray Gerundio* are didactic narratives of a protagonist's education, a crucial way in which their protagonists differ is signaled by the depiction of Eusebio's "ardent sensibility" (p. 277) – that is, of Eusebio as emblematic of the emotional nature of human perception of reality, which by century's end had become the novel's province. And though a wide variety of novels were produced during the latter part of the century, the narrative of sensibility is the Enlightenment fictional form par excellence for its encoding of preoccupation with the workings of the senses, the role of the feeling, imagining body in moral conduct, and the importance of observation to an individual's ability to reach his or her own conclusions about "the truth."

Indeed, the novel of sensibility claimed intense emotional agitation as the ground on which a moral character manifested itself. Within the culture of sensibility, the exhibition of extremes of affect when confronted by others' pain or joy was an important indicator of a person's virtue. In both autocthonous and translated foreign narratives of sensibility available to Spanish readers during the period of the Enlightenment, characters are overcome by feelings displayed through exterior signs of inner agitation, such as sighing, weeping, falling to one's knees, incoherent babbling, and fainting. When in Louise Brayer de Saint-Léon's *Maclovia y Federico* (1804; published in Spanish translation in 1814) the narrator informs the reader that Maclovia "tried to pronounce a few words, but fainted... succumbing to the force of the cruel sensations that she experienced,"[29] and when in Ignacio García Malo's 1787 *Flavio e Irene* Flavio "could find no words to express his pain" and so "took to weeping and sighing,"[30] the reader is provided an opportunity to learn that the feeling body evidences the person bound by social consequence.

Yet the novel of sensibility equally features scenes of emotional agitation as devices by which to illustrate the superiority of reason's capacity to distinguish and organize. As the protagonist of García Malo's *La desventurada Margarita* ('The Unfortunate Margarita', 1787) put it, "Passions are

[28] For example, Rousseau's *Emile* was well known in Spain by the 1780s and was a model for Montengón's *El Eusebio*; Gaspar Melchor de Jovellanos knew of (and had probably read) both Richardson's *Pamela* and his *Clarissa* by 1785 (cited in Álvarez, *La novela española del siglo XVIII*, p. 205). Both *Pamela* and *Clarissa* were available in Spanish from 1794.

[29] L. Brayer de Saint-Léon, *Maclovia y Federico y las minas del Tirol. Anécdota verdadera traducida del francés* (Valencia: Miguel Domingo, 1814), p. 55. The original French title was *Maclovie ou les mines du Tyrol*.

[30] I. García Malo, *Flavio e Irene*, in *Voz de la naturaleza*, ed. Guillermo Carnero (Madrid: Támesis, 1995), p. 256.

moderated by reason."[31] In Vicente Martínez Colomer's *El Valdemaro* (1792), the protagonist's mentor Ascanio counsels that the best man "imposes silence [...] upon his senses as he judges appropriate, and, delivered to himself through that silent repose, knows the essence of his being."[32] In Montengón's *El Eusebio*, the passions of the soul are "sinister" and are to be combatted by thoughful resistance. The ability to feel is the basis of moral existence in society; but a telling marker of virtue is found in the ability to harness human reason to convert the force of affect into orderly perception of the truth.

Providence is the benevolent guiding hand that must be acknowledged in order for a person to understand his or her place in the world: as the narrator of *El viajador sensible* states, "I was less confused by wondering where Divine Providence might place me, than I was by imagining how it had been able to find me" (p. 12). Yet although characters in these texts endure dishonor, disgrace, deception, and disasters such as war and shipwrecks, their resignation in the face of what they understand to be divine design provides moral underpinnings to plots dealing in what might seem to be merely episodic accidents. "Let yourselves be governed by Divine Providence," cautions Ascanio in *El Valdemaro*; "Nothing happens that does not owe recognition of its beginnings to the supreme and absolute Being that has created all" (p. 134). While in *El Eusebio* the protagonists Hardy and Eusebio embrace Senecan philosophy when faced with the rigors of destiny, paramount throughout narratives such as *La Eumenia* and *El Valdemaro* is the message that Providence guides friends toward the happiness and just rewards for which their virtuous conduct renders them worthy. In this respect, the Spanish novel of sensibility grounds what later will become one of the chief themes of Romantic fiction: the inevitability of the dictates of Fate.

"'All God's judgments are beyond the comprehension of man'," states the protagonist Termonio in *La Eumenia*, "affectionately taking the hand of the discouraged old man; 'but we must have faith in His compassion.'"[33] Termonio's outstretched hand exemplifies an important aspect of sensibility: it was conceived as a social virtue, a "kind virtue" among enlightened citizens, as Gaspar Melchor de Jovellanos phrased it in his 1788 "Elogio fúnebre de Carlos III" ('Funeral Elegy for Carlos III').[34] Sensibility was a state of

31 I. García Malo, *La desventurada Margarita*, in *Voz de la naturaleza*, p. 195.

32 V. Martínez Colomer, *El Valdemaro* (1792), ed. Guillermo Carnero (Alicante: Instituto de Estudios "Juan Gil-Albert," 1985), p. 61.

33 G. Zavala y Zamora, *La Eumenia*, *Obras narrativas*, ed. Guillermo Carnerod (Barcelona: Sirmio-Quaderns Crema, 1992), p. 69.

34 G. Melchor de Jovellanos, "Elogio fúnebre de Carlos III," in *Colección de varias obras en prosa y verso*, 6 vols. (Madrid: León Amarita, 1830), vol. II, p. 400.

social affections emanating favorably toward others, postulating a depth of connection among members of society. "How tender and gentle is the bond of friendship when formed by two sensitive and suffering hearts!" exclaims the narrator of *La Eumenia*; "How such feeling grows when it is based in love and virtue!" (p. 101). Scenes of suffering and joy encode the inextricable bond between moral goodness and the naturalness and complexity of feelings. The characters in narratives of sensibility exemplify the Enlightenment prizing of sociability as an ideal means by which persons might learn from and with one another and, in thinking about others' experiences, begin to think for themselves.

Within the Enlightenment discourse on sensibility, not only virtuous conduct, but also virtuous conduct *among others who feel*, is the basis of development of the moral compass. Thus the novel of sensibility predominantly features scenes in which several feeling persons are united, demonstrating emotion and sharing cognizance of one another's behavior. Often such scenes are staged around the simple occasion of suffering on someone's part; frequently the pretext is a re-encounter between family, friends, or lovers. As characters reveal themselves to one another or recount their tales of woe and hardship, their very grouping provides *tableaux* or living pictures of virtue and of the human capacity for sympathy. The *tableau* of the narrative of sensibility assembles persons in a scene of suffering or joy in such a way that the experience of each is detailed clearly for the reader's "eye," while the group's sympathy enhances depiction of pathos and conveys a moral message about the resonance of virtue.[35] In *Maclovia y Federico*, for example, "the agitation of the canoness, the tumult felt by Maclovia, and Federico's joy upon seeing his most beloved companion [...] offered a most interesting scene" (pp. 199–200). And in *El Valdemaro*, anagnorisis grounds a scene in which Valdemaro hears that a stranger on a ship is his sister: "Such an unexpected blow could not fail to overwhelm the most stalwart heart. Valdemaro fell in a faint, Rosendo stood stupefied, and the old man was hardly less than confused" (p. 114). The three men are grouped in mutual shock; the reaction of each is clearly detailed for the reader's imagination; and as his two companions share Valdemaro's agitation, the reader witnesses sympathy in the response of such virtuous sensibilities to distress.

Experimentation in poses and attitudes expressive of emotion was a constant in both theatrical (e.g. Gaspar Melchor de Jovellanos's 1773 *El delincuente honrado*, 'The Honorable Delinquent') and narrative (e.g. Laurence

35 The scenes described here differ from the eighteenth-century performance genre of the *tableau vivant*. See Kirsten Gram Homström, *Monodrama. Attitudes. Tableaux vivants. Studies on Some Trends of Theatrical Fashion 1770–1815* (Uppsala: Almquist & Wiksells, 1967).

Sterne's 1768 *A Sentimental Journey*) literature in the second half of the century across Europe, fueled by factors such as Addison's and Steele's critical appreciation of pantomimic style in acting, Diderot's enthusiasm for Richardson's sentimental scenes, and reappraisal of classical theories of gesture and persuasion such as those of Quintilian and Cicero, who in the *De oratore* instructed that as emotion "is often so confused as to be obscured and almost smothered out of sight," the person who would have the most impact on audiences will "dispel the things that obscure [emotion] and take up its prominent and striking points."[36] Sentimental fiction cultivated a rhetorical visuality designed to maximize the reaction of readers; techniques such as the *tableau* were crucial to sentimentalism's invocation of readers' emotional responsiveness to the illusion of observation.

Further engagement of Enlightenment interest in observation is achieved through depiction of the act of seeing. For example, the narrator of *El viajador sensible* describes the "easy violence" with which he feels compelled to observe a person (p. 78); in *Maclovia y Federico*, a character, "pierced by the compelling spectacle before her eyes, could not for a moment" remove herself from the scene she had witnessed (p. 114). In such scenes, the represented act of seeing functions as a means of enhancing the truthfulness of the character's experience. The importance of scenes of observation to developments in fictional form during the period of the Enlightenment and afterward cannot be overstated. In fact, the great nineteenth-century Spanish literary movements that focused on depiction of "the real" – *costumbrismo*, *realismo*, and *naturalismo* – have complex eighteenth-century origins in a wide-ranging public disposition to observe, which was stoked by the availability and popularity of narratives of sensibility.

As Russell Sebold has pointed out, the majority of Spanish poets and authors of the second half of the eighteenth century knew, from Locke, that ideas in the mind originate with sensations in the body:[37] with "such an impression or motion," as Locke put it, "made in some part of the body, as produces some perception in the understanding."[38] The role of sensationalist philosophy in the literary ideas of the Enlightenment laid the groundwork for later, Romantic thematics such as the dynamism of nature and the universality of pain and feeling. As early as the 1770s, José Cadalso harnessed the properties of sensationalism to render the reader witness to a

[36] Cicero, *De oratore*, tr. H. Rackham (Cambridge, MA: Harvard University Press, 1997), vol. III, I, vii, 215: 171–3.

[37] R. P. Sebold, "La filosofía de la Ilustración y el nacimiento del Romanticismo español," *Trayectoria del Romanticismo español* (Barcelona: Editorial Crítica, 1983), p. 94.

[38] J. Locke, *An Essay Concerning Human Understanding*, ed. John E. Yolton (London: J.M. Dent and Sons, 1990), vol. II, i, p. 117.

being awash with sensations that produce perceptions. The *Noches lúgubres* (which, through its numerous printings from 1789 onward, became one of the most popular and influential works of fiction produced during the Enlightenment) represent a character's cogitations as his physical being is stimulated by his sight and other senses. This brief and important text, in which the reader is made witness to not only the protagonist Tediato's manifestations of inward suffering but also his thoughts during every experienced sensation, is a meditation on the role of consciousness in the development of the sense of "self."

The *Noches* is centrally concerned with the depiction of a mind at work in its own consciousness of itself. Tediato is a character constructed through consciousness in the sense that Locke described: "Consciousness is the perception of what passes in a Man's own mind [...] and it cannot be less than revelation, that discovers to another, Thoughts in my mind, when I can find none there myself" (vol. II, i, p. 115). What passes through Tediato's mind – *every thought* that passes through Tediato's mind – is narrated in the course of the *Noches* as the constitution of his experience. But it is the discourse of sensation that engenders the succession of thoughts constitutive of the character's "self." "Self is that conscious thinking thing," observed Locke, "[...] which is sensible, or conscious of pleasure and pain, capable of happiness or misery, and is so concern'd for it*self*, as far as that consciousness extends" (II, xxvii, p. 341). Tediato has ideas of horror, of coldness, or of pain in connection with the data brought to his mind by what he sees, touches, hears, or feels upon his skin. Yet Tediato agonizes in his awareness: his universal suffering ("fastidio universal" as the poet Juan Meléndez Valdés would term it in 1794) is that of the sentient conscious self existing through time in a body whose sensations lead to ideas confounding reason.[39]

Cadalso's text inserts itself into a discourse on consciousness and self-awareness channeled through a variety of eighteenth-century European works, from Etienne Bonnot de Condillac's *Traité des sensations* (1754) to Laurence Sterne's *A Sentimental Journey Through France and Italy* (1768). In *El viajador sensible*, for example, the narrator minutely records his awareness of the sensations to which he is subject with each new experience: "Signs of pain attract me more strongly than those of pleasure," he avers (p. 62); "How many painful sensations I had to keep experiencing continously!" he exclaims during a dark passage on the return journey (p. 175). Enlightenment awareness of consciousness would later inform the agonized, ironic analyses penned by the *costumbrista* author Mariano José de Larra, who

39 R. P. Sebold, "Sobre el nombre español del dolor romántico," in *El rapto de la mente: poética y poesía dieciochescas* (Madrid: Prensa Española, 1979), pp. 133–4.

in essays such as "La Nochebuena de 1836" ('Christmas Eve 1836') and "El día de difuntos de 1836" ('All Souls Day 1836') narrated his perplexity and pain at "not understanding clearly all that I see" and at watching himself wander the streets "at the mercy of my thoughts."[40] The fiction of the period of the Enlightenment developed narrative techniques that permitted the reader-observer to have the impression of being "inside" the space of self, to see moral choices and struggles from within a character's perspective.

Experimentation with dialogic modalities generated new means of representing the experience of self. Epistolary narrative, for example, offered readers the illusion of access to a multitude of characters' intimate thoughts. In José Cadalso's *Cartas marruecas*, the interwoven letters of three distinct personalities function as interior monologues and provide "narrative immediacy" of individual experience.[41] Typographical markers, such as the alternation of italics and plain font, served to distinguish characters' voices and foreground individual utterances: in *El Valdemaro*, italics divide reported speech from a speaking character's first-person interventions (e.g., pp. 80–96, 131–5), enhancing the effect of that character's authentic persona or speaking self. The dialogue form of the *Noches lúgubres* alternates first-person, present-tense utterances as a means of representing the characters' awareness of experience in the very moment they live it. Yet another technique, used to advantage in novels of sensibility, is that of the narrator's sympathetic exclamations. In these instances, the narrator interjects what he or she imagines the character is feeling, but without encoding the information as either direct or indirect speech. In *Maclovia y Federico*, the narrator shifts abruptly from describing Maclovia's features to informing the reader "How she would have liked to remain alone until Bathilde returned . . . !" (p. 79); in *El viajador sensible*, when the narrator shifts from stating that a grieving man had to be pulled from the grave of his daughter to exclaiming "Ah! . . . What will never be again!" (p. 104), the emotional charge is not imputed to the character, but rather originates from within his or her consciousness.

The greatest impression of a character's interior experience is obtained through narratorial omniscience. The prevalence of an omniscient narrator is an eighteenth-century innovation that in nineteenth-century Spain became essential to realist depictions of characters' lived experience. Omniscience is grounded in narrative techniques such as free indirect discourse, which permits an apparently seamless transition from description to representation

[40] M. José de Larra, "El día de difuntos de 1836" and "La Nochebuena de 1836," in *Artículos varios*, ed. Evaristo Correa Calderón (Madrid: Castalia, 1976), pp. 543 and 553.

[41] S. Dale, *Novela innovadora en las "Cartas Marruecas" de Cadalso* (New York: Hispanic Institute, 1997), pp. 38–47.

of a character's inner state, and is identifiable when the narrator "places himself, when reporting the words or thoughts of a character, directly into the experiential field of the character, and adopts the latter's perspective in regard to both time and place."[42] Though with greater frequency narratives of the period aimed for the effect of an "experiential field" through techniques such as sympathetic exclamations, readers could encounter free indirect discourse in many texts, in particular in translated (French) novels of sensibility. For example, in *Maclovia y Federico*, the narrator both reports Maclovia's thoughts and represents her perspective:

> The events of the day arose reproduced in her tumultous imagination, and in that moment a torrent of tears sprang from her eyes and unburdened her oppressed heart. It was certain that the Emperor had decided her fate, how could she possibly resist complying with his high command; and above all, how could she renounce her beloved Federico . . . ? (pp. 56–7)

By directly entering Maclovia's thoughts, the narrator appears to have complete, unmediated commerce with her mind. Verbal tense is key to the transition into the character's experiential field, indicated by the introduction of the imperfect ("It was"). As Pascal says, the use of the imperfect tense in place of the preterite heightens listeners' or readers' "sympathetic self-identification with the subject of the verb concerned" (*The Dual Voice*, p. 11). Through the technique of free indirect discourse, the purveyor of such perfect access to a character's consciousness tempts readers with an eighteenth-century dream of the objective observer as the supremely sympathetic self.

In "The Experimental Novel" (1879), Emile Zola posits a novelist who would depict reality as an objective observer who can, in the mode of scientific experimentation, muster facts and data observed from "the body of man, as shown by his sensory and cerebral phenomena, both in their normal and pathological condition."[43] Zola's proposal of the union of scientific objectivity with both "cerebral" and "sensory" phenomena – that is, both mental and physical data – within the fictional experiment was augmented by Leopoldo Alas, who notes in his 1882 essay "On Naturalism" that depiction of "the real" must incorporate subtle and difficult combinations of cerebral and sensory phenomena, in such a way that characters are products of "natural action combined with prior forces, composed, received and assimilated over a long period of time, and in accordance with the individual

42 R. Pascal, *The Dual Voice: Free Indirect Speech and its Functioning in the Nineteenth-century European Novel* (Manchester University Press, 1977), p. 9.

43 E. Zola, "The Experimental Novel," in *The Experimental Novel and Other Essays*, tr. Belle M. Sherman (New York: Haskell House, 1964), p. 32.

character."[44] In other words, "observation" must take into account multiple, shifting, and even ephemeral factors such as time and memory, their repression and interpretation by characters, their uncertain meanings and complex effects. In the realist or naturalist novel, only the depiction of such messily mixed cerebral and bodily experiences will engage the reader-observer in recognition of the "real."

Enlightenment texts such as *Noches lúgubres* and narratives of sensibility equally aim to represent mixed cerebral and bodily experiences as "real" to the reader-observer. One key difference between these works and the novels of a century later is the absence of irony from many Enlightenment narratives engaged in the work of depiction of consciousness; another difference is suggested by the reliance of later novels on the imperfect tense in the free indirect discourse that became typical of nineteenth-century realism, corroborated by Alas's stipulation that to seem "real," characters must be the products of action developed over a long period of time. Nevertheless the Enlightenment opened the field of possibilities in literary representation of "natural action" (as Alas put it), generating fictional techniques and forms that permitted readers to engage in the practice of observation, crucial to the later realist project of representing complexities of character spanning memory and time.

Guide to further reading

Brissenden, R. F., *Virtue in Distress: Studies in the Novel of Sentiment from Richardson to Sade* (London: Macmillan, 1974).

Carnero, Guillermo, "Sensibilidad y exotismo en un novelista entre dos siglos: Gaspar Zavala y Zamora," *Romanticismo* 3–4: *Atti del IV Congresso sul Romanticismo spagnolo e ispanoamericano*, ed. Ermanno Caldera (Genoa: Biblioteca di Littere, 1988), pp. 23–9.

Haidt, Rebecca, *Embodying Enlightenment: Knowing the Body in Eighteenth-Century Spanish Literature and Culture* (New York: St. Martin's Press, 1998).

Pajares Infante, Eterio, "Sensibilidad y lacrimosidad en Cadalso: Sus fuentes extranjeras," *Boletín de la Biblioteca de Menéndez y Pelayo* 71 (1995), pp. 119–35.

Van Sant, Ann Jessie. *Eighteenth-Century Sensibility and the Novel: The Senses in Social Context* (New York: Cambridge University Press, 1933).

[44] L. Alas, "Del naturalismo," in *Leopoldo Alas: Teoría y crítica de la novela española*, ed. Sergio Beser (Barcelona: Laia, 1972), p. 141.

2

THE NINETEENTH CENTURY

4

ALISON SINCLAIR

The regional novel: evolution and consolation

For the intellectual historian of nineteenth-century Europe, certain words flag critical foci of interest: "revolution," "evolution," "nation," "travel," "industrialism." These words are no less important in the literature of the period, and in Spain they have a particular relationship with the regional novel. Of these words, "evolution," habitually associated with the ideas of Darwin, will be central to the discussion in this chapter. Common usage has accustomed us to apply it retrospectively and rather indiscriminately to areas of nineteenth-century life which, in their day, were innocent of such concepts. Yet the term "evolution" itself is one that has evolved. Coined by Haller in 1744, it initially indicated "preformationism," the gradual unfolding of a form of life already perfectly formed. In the course of the nineteenth century, "evolution" came to have the force of "transmutation" with which we associate it today.[1] Thus the shift was one from a consoling thought to a challenging one, from a position that maintained that change was, as it were, always and already foreseen, to the idea of evolution as a much more disturbing and challenging perspective, signaling that a change effected might become something new. The evolving concept of the term "evolution" thus moves from the idea of change as part of a pre-existing master plan (evolution as development) to the idea of change as a process lacking linear certainty (evolution as variation). When seen in the context of the regional novel, the other terms, such as "revolution," "nation," "travel," and "industrialism," are either symptomatic of "evolution" or act as stimuli to its discovery (in either of its two meanings – as development or variation).

While the term "regional novel," when applied to the literature of nineteenth-century Spain, is not precisely a misnomer, it does cover a variety of positions. For example, the term does not include literature from all the

[1] Stephen J. Gould, *Ontogeny and Phylogeny* (Cambridge, MA: Belknap Press of Harvard University Press, 1977), pp. 28–9.

regions but primarily refers to literature of the North (both Cantabria and Galicia) and of Andalucía. Its origins are generally held to be derived from a mixture of foreigners' travel writings, such as those of Ford (*Handbook for Travellers in Spain*, 1844) and Borrow (*The Bible in Spain*, 1842), and locally produced Romantic *costumbrista* vignettes of life and manners. The two best-known collections, those of Mariano José de Larra and Mesonero Romanos, depict Madrid.[2] Compared with the major novelistic productions associated with realism and naturalism, such as the *novelas contemporáneas* ('contemporary social novels') of Galdós or *La Regenta* by Leopoldo Alas ("Clarín"), the novels associated with regionalism in Spain run the risk of being sidelined for their political predictability and of being classed as inferior for their literary naivety. Such critical dismissals do not do them justice; examples such as Juan Valera's *Pepita Jiménez* (1874) and *Los pazos de Ulloa* (*The House of Ulloa*, 1886) by Emilia Pardo Bazán hold their own alongside the major works of realism.

The novels of regionalism do not, of course, habitually conform to the canons of realism, and if we read them according to expectations associated with realism, we are likely to be disappointed. If, however, we read these novels as examples of literary and political consciousness, viewing them as vehicles of cultural exchange, even if, at times, their enterprise turns out to be misdirected or failed, then their role in the history of the Spanish novel appears crucial. Furthermore, the positions adopted by the novels of regionalism, symptomatic of Spanish culture and politics at the time, extend far beyond the nineteenth century. Attitudes and ideologies will echo with a regularity as striking as it is chilling through the course of the twentieth century. For example, the return to the *pueblo* and the scrutiny of rural life to see whether it signals sickness or holds out hope of recovery to good health will be salient features in the writings of the Generation of 1898, essayists, novelists, and poets of the turn of the century whose concern was Spain's national identity and potential decadence. Subsequently, the appropriation during the Franco regime of the myth of rural idyll,[3] a prevalent theme in the novels of Goytisolo and Martín Santos, will come under attack in the 1960s and 1970s. In another rhythm of appropriation, Larra moves in and out of favor. His articles on Madrid life in the 1830s provided a biting satire of

[2] M. J. de Larra, *Artículos* ('Articles', 1830–7), ed. Seco Serrano, *Obras de D. Mariano José de Larra*, 4 vols. (Madrid: Biblioteca de autores españoles, 1960); Mesonero Romanos, *Escenas matritenses* ('Madrid Scenes', 1836–42), ed. María del Pilar Palomo (Barcelona: Planeta, 1987).

[3] Eduardo Sevilla-Guzmán, "The Peasantry and the Franco Régime," in *Spain in Crisis: The Evolution and Decline of the Franco Regime*, ed. Paul Preston (Cambridge University Press, 1976), pp. 101–24.

Spanish customs and a critique of bourgeois pretentiousness underpinned by his liberal political convictions. Echoed in the novels of Galdós and Clarín, Larra's critique and innovative narrative style[4] will be subsequently rediscovered by the Generation of 1898 and by Juan Goytisolo.

Literary history as a discipline encourages us to look longitudinally, seeking trends, causes, and effects. We are inclined to think of origins, influences, and developments. According to such a model, we might surmise that the regional novel in Spain grows "out of" *costumbrismo* and the literary products of Romanticism, grows "into" some other product labeled as the "regional novel."[5] This view is consistent with the fact that travel writings of foreigners were published in the 1840s, that *costumbrista* writing in the form of articles in the periodic press, notably by Larra, Estébanez Calderón, and Mesonero Romanos, was published through the 1830s and 1840s, and that the novels of regionalism were published from the middle of the century to the 1890s; examples are *La gaviota* ('The Seagull', 1849), by Fernán Caballero (Cecilia Böhl de Faber); Alarcón's *El sombrero de tres picos* (*The Three-Cornered Hat*, 1874); *Sotileza* (1886) and *Peñas arriba* ('Toward the Summit', 1895) by José María de Pereda, Juan Valera's *Pepita Jiménez* (1874) and Emilia Pardo Bazán's linked pair of novels *Los pazos de Ulloa* (1886) and *La madre naturaleza* ('Mother Nature', 1887). Seco Serrano emphasizes the close relationship between the tormented life of Larra (1809–37) and the turbulence of Spanish history.[6] This link is possibly the closest parallel between a writer and the context from which he comes. Nonetheless, a fundamental feature of the writing of regional novels is the context of history, philosophy, and politics that justifies, at least initially, a longitudinal approach.

The writing of travel books has frequently been the cultural response to periods of crisis and upheaval, particular examples being the writings of the Generation of 1898, such as Azorín's *Castilla* (1912). This response can be observed also in writing after the Civil War (1936–9), an example being *Viaje a la Alcarria* ('Journey to Alcarria') by Camilo José Cela. To some degree the writing of regional literature can be considered as constituting a similar response. These writings are, as it were, narratives of internal travel. Certainly the *costumbrista* sketches of Mesonero Romanos and the articles of Larra need to be framed in the context of the agitation following the

4 Susan Kirkpatrick, *Larra: el laberinto inextricable de un romántico liberal* (Madrid: Gredos, 1977), p. 7. Alma Amell, *La preocupación por España en Larra* (Madrid: Pliegos, 1990), pp. 10–11.

5 For example, see Derek Flitter, *Spanish Romantic Literary Theory and Criticism* (Cambridge University Press, 1992), pp. 151–3, on the influence of Romanticism on Fernán Caballero.

6 S. Serrano, "Edición y estudio preliminar," in *Obras de D. Mariano José de Larra*, 4 vols. (Madrid: Biblioteca de autores españoles, 1960), vol. 1, p. vii.

Napoleonic Wars, the brief period of the liberal constitution (1820–3), and the blow to liberalism formed by the restoration of Fernando VII to the throne first in 1814 and then in 1823. *La gaviota*, the first major example in Spain of a regional novel, can be seen as part of a Romantic reaction to that uncertainty as well as a search for the national soul. The remaining major examples of the regional novel, produced during the concluding three decades of the nineteenth century, have as their backcloth a divide between conservatives and liberals (*moderados/progresistas*), one stemming from the liberal revolution of 1868, the ensuing search for a suitable successor to Isabel II, the eventual, implausible choice of Amadeo of Savoy (1871–3), the First Republic (1873–5), and the years of the *turno pacífico*, a placid system of rotation in which liberals and conservatives took turns in and out of power, which characterized the Restoration (1874/75–97).

Within this historical context, a longitudinal view of the regional novel immediately becomes problematic. It would be as difficult to argue that the novel evolves (progresses) as it would be to assert that the history of nineteenth-century Spain does also. What the historical panorama reveals is that there is an alternating movement of national political development between conservative and liberal governments. The alternations characterizing the history of Spain in the nineteenth century (*pronunciamientos* [military coups]) followed by periods of relative calm, and then more *pronunciamientos*, finally resulting in the political *turno pacífico*, indicate patterns of repetition which have their parallels in the literature of the century.

If, however, we consider the actual form which regional writing takes through the century, there is little doubt that a longitudinal approach is valid. Thus the *costumbrista* articles of the 1830s and 1840s are followed by a novel, *La gaviota*. Although Eugenio de Ochoa's "Juicio crítico" at the time welcomed Fernán Caballero's novel as one that could compete with those of Cervantes, Fielding, and Scott,[7] a salient characteristic of *La gaviota* is the static impression given by its series of vignettes of Andalusian life. In her exemplary discussion of the novel, Susan Kirkpatrick shows how these *tableaux* or set pieces form a plot line through their sequence.[8] The actual action, however, and the sense of time as *durée* are relegated to the silences between chapters (a much-debated technique employed in 1884–5 by Leopoldo Alas, who places the final seduction of Ana Ozores in the silence between chapters 28 and 29 of *La Regenta*). Thus when we look at later novels of the genre, through the 1870s to the 1890s, narrative complexities

[7] E. de Ochoa, "Juicio crítico," reprinted in Fernán Caballero, *La gaviota*, ed. Julio Rodríguez Luis (Barcelona: Labor, 1972), p. 79.

[8] S. Kirkpatrick, "On the Threshold of the Realist Novel: Gender and Genre in *La gaviota*," *PMLA* 98/3 (1983), p. 335.

develop. Valera's *Pepita Jiménez* is a novel whose epistolary form lends a subtle, ironic focus to the narrative. *Peñas arriba* by Pereda contains multiple narrators and perspectives, resulting in an embedded narrative in which the protagonist, Marcelo, takes over the stories of others. Meanwhile Pardo Bazán's *Los pazos de Ulloa* and *La madre naturaleza*, reflecting a debt to the author's high regard for Zola and his narrative technique, contain high proportions of free indirect style and a narrative focused through characters of variable reliability.

When we look at regional novels laterally rather than longitudinally, and geographically and politically rather than chronologically, different patterns emerge. Particularly noticeable is a sense of continuity or repetition of political reaction within individual works. One of the most characteristic patterns evolves from a tension between the political views of the center and what the regions represent. The position of the center (Madrid) is commonly that of an advanced location in the Peninsula. But according to the politics of the regions – whether conservative, or questioning and critical as in the case of Pardo Bazán and Alas – the center and its possible influence on the periphery is regarded in a different light. Conservative writers see influence from the capital as threatening the life-affirming values of the regions. Liberal and critical writers see the center as a site of enlightened ideas in contrast to the backwardness and closed-mindedness of the regions. This second group nonetheless displays an attachment to the regions that motivates their novelistic elaborations of provincial life. Thus while it is important to perceive the distinction between the positions (political, cultural, religious) of the diverse literary works of regionalism, in one essential respect the various novels evince a unity based upon their concentration on the regions and their valuation of what is to be found there.

Regional novels communicate a type of cultural myopia that restricts the concept of viable life to regional boundaries. The novels commonly suffer from lack of farsightedness, of a perspective that might have permitted the concept of Spain as a whole to be entertained. Returning to the example of *La gaviota*, we find that the concept of nation – as inherited from Romantics who were enthused by Romantic nationalism elsewhere in Europe – is that of the *patria chica*, the homeland consisting of the immediate region, rather than one encompassing the whole of Spain. This emphasis contrasts with the national perspective offered by the novelistic corpus of Galdós, as shown in Geoffrey Ribbans's chapter on history and fiction in this volume. Regional novels always constitute a site of a tension, either explicit or implied: that of the contrast with other regions or with the world of any territory beyond the region, be it within the nation or outside it, a contrast experienced as conflict or the fear of conflict.

The geography of Spain as depicted in the novels of the nineteenth century is unevenly mapped. A preponderance of works focus on either North or South, in which the region in question is characteristically set in play against Madrid. Cantabria is the focus of Pereda, Galicia that of Pardo Bazán, and Asturias the region of Alas's novel *La Regenta*. Fernán Caballero, Alarcón, and Valera depict Andalucía. If we include the novels of Vicente Blasco Ibáñez, such as *Flor de mayo* (*The Mayflower*, 1895) and *La barraca* (*The Holding*, 1898), or the vignettes of customs such as *Notas de color* ('Notes of Color', 1884) and *Figura i paisatge* ('Figure and Landscape', 1892) by the Catalan novelist Narcís Oller, further areas of the map appear, firmly rooted in Valencia and Catalonia.

The political agenda of the novelists, however, presents this divide along a different axis. The writings of Alarcón, Fernán Caballero, Pereda, and Valera are traditionalist in contrast to the socially concerned writings of Alas, Galdós, and Pardo Bazán. Further, there is a difference of perspective: the first group works from imagination and faith, while the second works from the observation of social realities.[9] If we integrate the writers of *costumbrista* articles into this division of political focus, Larra takes his place with the second group, i.e. those who write inspired by a commitment to social realities and by dislike or despair at what they see, while Mesonero Romanos, in *Escenas matritenses*, and Estébanez Calderón, in *Escenas andaluzas* ('Andalusian Scenes', 1847), taking Madrid and Andalucía respectively as their focus to emphasize what was to be preserved, align with the conservative approach of the first group.

A related axis of difference may be inferred through the degree of openness towards Europe and its developments. According to her arguable inheritance of German Romanticism, Fernán Caballero (née Cecilia Böhl de Faber, a name revealing her German parentage) might be expected to be European in outlook. Caballero, however, with the enthusiasm of a convert, espouses the cause of Spanish nationhood, doing all she can to enshrine its customs in prose. Writing before her, Larra had evinced a much more radical awareness of the shortcomings of Spanish mores, viewing them through a prism formed by European civilization. Later in the century writers who continue in Larra's disenchanted vein – Galdós, Pardo Bazán, and Alas – will produce troubled narratives of the Spain of their times. They share with Larra awareness not only of gaps in Spanish life (in education, politics, and economics, when compared to life elsewhere in Europe), but also of currents of positivism, Naturalism, and Darwinism. Thus in *La cuestión palpitante* ('The Burning

[9] G. Gullón, "La novela de Alarcón y en envés de la narrativa decimonónica," *Insula* 535 (July 1991), p. 32.

Issue', 1883) Pardo Bazán gives a balanced account of Naturalism in Europe. Conversely, in his *Apuntes sobre el arte nuevo de escribir novelas* ('Notes on the New Art of Writing Novels', 1888), the conservative Valera not only held a view of the European novel as decadent and dangerous but disarmingly admitted that he had not read any Naturalist novels. He already knew enough of their underlying philosophy to be sure that they could in no way be good. Significantly, reflecting the metaphors of illness characteristic of Naturalist writing, Valera declared his essay to be an attack upon the malady of foreign culture. He noted "with distress" that "Civilization in its totality is suffering today from a grave malady that holds sway in France more than in any other part. It is against this malady, and so that someone at least may find its remedy, that I write these articles."[10]

Regional articles and novels claim on their own terms to be mimetic and to be devoted to a labor of preservation endowed with a moral value. The agenda of some early works of this nature is clearly that of preservation. Thus in her prologue to *La gaviota*, Fernán Caballero is at pains to emphasize the degree to which she is simply "copying" what is there (p. 63). The proclaimed intention of Estébanez Calderón in his *Escenas andaluzas* is to remind the reader of what he may have forgotten and to urge him to recreate as he reads. Estébanez narrates without hesitation "those unparalleled scenes, those Spanish features" (p. 136). In this connection Noël Valis makes a useful distinction between art and photography, pointing out how *costumbrismo* shares with physiognomy and physiology, and indeed with caricature, an interest in what is lasting, what endures of types and customs, whereas photography records the ephemeral variations.[11] The desire of the *costumbristas* like Mesonero Romanos, Estébanez Calderón, and Fernán Caballero, who wish to preserve for future generations types seen to be enduring examples of Spanishness, thus contrasts with the despairing snapshots of variation presented in Larra's articles.

Despite the agenda of preservation common to many regional writers, the perception of what is enduring leads also to idealization. This tendency is particularly characteristic of representations of Andalucía, presenting us with a fascinating phenomenon not restricted to the nineteenth century. In his dedication to the reader that precedes the *Escenas andaluzas*, Estébanez Calderón acknowledges and justifies the feature of *lo andaluz* as a feature

10 J. Valera, *Obras completas* (Madrid: Tello, 1888), vol. III, p. 146.

11 N. Valis, "Pereda y la mirada turística," *Insula* 547–8 (July–August 1992), p. 16; L. Fontanella, "Physiognomics in Romantic Spain," in *From Dante to García Márquez: Studies in Romance Literature and Linguistics. Presented to Anson C. Piper*, ed. Gene G. Bell-Villada, Antonio Giménez, and George Pistorius (Williamstown, MA: Williams College, 1987), p. 110.

both characteristic and problematic of *costumbrista* writing, namely that the recurrent interest of the *costumbristas* is in the marginal. This interest can take the form of "marginal" regions and "marginal" type. Indeed, one could extend his view of the value of the marginal as one which not only refers to the *andaluz* types and customs that he will portray, but to a more generalized valuation of regions within Spain that are not those of the geographical and administrative center. In a peninsula, what could be more marginal than the regions constituting the periphery? In contrast to the generation of 1898, which will view the peasant of Castile as the enduring type, the Romantics and *costumbristas* focus repeatedly on the peasant from Andalucía. Two interesting examples illustrate this emphasis. There is the idealization by Lorca and Falla in 1922 of Andalucía's *Cante jondo* ('Deep Song') as the heart of the most ancient music and poetry in Spain.[12] More controversial is Ortega y Gasset's essay "Teoría de Andalucía" ('Theory of Andalucía', 1927), in which, true to the tradition of the idle nobleman in the *Lazarillo de Tormes*, he singles out the *holgazanería* ('laziness') of the peasant as an indication of the physical lushness of a region that requires only minimal effort for the maintenance of life.[13] This point of view is shockingly at odds with the lived realities of the landless poor of the region.

While Estébanez Calderón focuses on the marginal, he presents his *cuadros* ('picturesque sketches') in a manner that makes Andalucía sound like Arcadia. In "La rifa andaluza" ("Andalusian raffle"), for example, he addresses specifically female readers ("beautiful subscribers, dear friends") and clearly intends a reading that will delight rather than shock. He sets the scene, and pulls no punches in his creation of a non-realist scenario: "imagine a clean and entirely picturesque hermitage, such as one finds at every turn in that land of poetry."[14] The keynote is magic: when, in "El bolero," he watches a dancer, he is instantly "borne away to another enchanted land" (p. 145). The embedded reaction of this writer to what he sees – being swept away into a world of perfection, which nonetheless is represented as the one of the fundamental realities of Spain – is typical of the *Escenas andaluzas*.

Uncertainties of tone and narrative approach in *La gaviota* present a contrast to *costumbrista* articles that convey a positive or idealized view of regional life. Instead of using a pen-character typical of *costumbrista*

12 F. García Lorca, "El cante jondo: primitivo canto andaluz," *Obras completas* (Madrid: Aguilar, 1954), pp. 1003–24; M. de Falla, *El cante jondo. Canto primitivo andaluz* (Granada: Urania, 1992).

13 J. Ortega y Gasset, "Teoría de Andalucía," *Obras completas*, vol. VI (Madrid: Revista de Occidente, 1957), pp. 111–20.

14 S. Estébañez Calderón, "Dedicatoria a quien quisiere," in *Escenas andaluzas*, ed. Jorge Campos (Madrid: Biblioteca de autores españoles, 1955), p. 139.

journalists like Larra, who writes as "Fígaro", or of Mesonero Romanos, who signs off as "El curioso parlante," *La gaviota* filters the narrative through the character of the young German doctor Fritz Stein, both narrator and observer. Just as we may discern the degree of influence that travel books of other Europeans exerted upon early nineteenth-century Spanish writing through being perceived by outsiders, something which arguably encouraged self-observation, so too in the regional novel the figure of the visitor becomes part of a necessary discovery of the terrain. We might also remain open to a facet of the novels highlighted by modern anthropology: the visitor is not without effect upon the community. Even as an observer or tourist, the visitor intervenes through his observation and does not leave untouched those whom he observes.[15] In *La gaviota*, the selection of a Germanic male protagonist, through whose eyes the vision of the region is initially focused, is simply a more extreme version of what we will find in other novels: Marcelo (*Peñas arriba*), Luis (*Pepita Jiménez*), and Julián (*Los pazos de Ulloa*) all act as surprised and impressionable newcomers to areas revealed to be rough diamonds of social models, or, in the case of Julián, a disturbing slough of decadence produced by isolation. In all cases, there is an element of some innocence in the visitor: whether simply a city lad (Marcelo), foreign doctor (Stein) or man of the church (Luis and Julián), each possesses a kind of civilized knowledge; each proves, however, to lack a knowledge of life and experience that come only as each makes contact with the region.

Set adrift in southern Spain, Stein "discovers" the rural idyll of an isolated community that harbors an even more isolated (and culturally neglected) young girl, known as *la gaviota* ('seagull') for the strength and quality of her voice. Although irony is almost unknown within the tone of this narrative, the characterization of an apparently beautiful singing voice as that of a seagull presents an interesting problem: either Fernán Caballero is being ironic about her rural subjects (they lack the discrimination to discern the raucous from the melodious) or she shares their lack of discernment. *La gaviota* turns on the motif of civilization and barbarism, offering a model of a rural life of virtue placed in danger by contact with the sophistication and pretentiousness of the city. This *beatus ille* plot, in which rural life is idealized, concerns a young girl, María, who is "rescued" from rural brutishness only to "fall" into immorality when removed to the city from her original environment. This plot is no more convincing than is the self-conscious *costumbrismo* of Fernán Caballero as writer. The text is littered with folkloric detail (not infrequently in footnote form) in a manner more suited to a Baedeker than to a work of fiction.

[15] Valis, "Pereda y la mirada turística," 16.

Of the novels under consideration in this chapter, *La gaviota* stands out for its strained idealization of chosen characters and its improbable plot; elements essential for credibility have been relegated to extra-textual silence. That the plot is somewhat strained and stilted is not due solely to this technicality. In contradistinction to the novels of realism, novels of regionalism tend to endow characters with a symbolic function, however ill defined, as evidenced by the plot of *La gaviota*. However, three features merit comment: the thematic relation to the idea of a *patria chica*, ambiguity of characterization, and symbolic connotations. The regions serve as a *patria chica*, a graspable experience of the national. They are places of value, the repository of what is enduring, representing all those features of the *pueblo* and its habitat later celebrated by Unamuno in *En torno al casticismo* (1895). In *La gaviota* the village of Marisalada, Villamar, is the *patria chica*, a place of innocence that contrasts with the pretentiousness and artificiality of city life in Seville. Concerning the ambiguity of the characterization of the female protagonist, Marisalada, we are given conflicting signals.[16] Apparently there is no doubt about her real musical talent; yet she has a type of moral frailty or shallowness that renders her fascination for Stein questionable – or at least questionable if she is to represent the Spanish *pueblo*. Kirkpatrick argues that this ambiguity of characterization stems from the female authorship of the novel: Fernán Caballero simultaneously desires to make her female character worthy while lacking the conviction to render her fully admirable. Her symbolic function appears to demonstrate the folly of moving outside the worthy regional home. Lastly there are the curious connotations of the seagull. Not only is its cry raucous, but it is also famed for its rapaciousness.

Part of the difficulty of *La gaviota* is the uneasy contact between the idealized world of the region and the artificial life of the town. In the case of two other novels of Andalucía, *El sombrero de tres picos* by Alarcón and Valera's *Pepita Jiménez*, this simplified contrast is avoided by two strategies. The novels are restricted entirely to the original location, and there is a decided literariness which pre-empts complications that might result from attentive social observation. In his preface to *El sombrero de tres picos*, Alarcón states that the novel constitutes the preservation not simply of custom, but rather of *literary* custom. Thus the tale of the miller, his beautiful wife, and the successful outwitting of her suitor, the *corregidor* (a law officer appointed by the Crown), is a traditional one, based on folklore. That this is a literary device is not in doubt, and one might observe that Alarcón deploys considerable skill in retelling traditional tales, endowing them with local color.

[16] Kirkpatrick, "On the Threshold," pp. 323–40.

The note struck by Alarcón contrasts with that of Estébanez Calderón. Indeed, one could posit a sliding scale that runs from evocations of Arcadia (Estébanez Calderón) through isolated innocence (Fernán Caballero) to a bucolic but decidedly Hispanic rustic setting (Alarcón). While local features – the *corregidor*, the nature of the miller, his wife, and their life together – represent a type of idealized rustic life, their robust vivaciousness is not unlike what we find in earlier literary tale-telling in Europe, notably in Boccaccio and Chaucer. Local custom is recounted in detail – chapter 2 is entitled "Of how people lived in that time"; the minutiae of daily diet are followed by the exclamation "Oh blessed time in which our land continued to be quietly and peacefully possessed by cobwebs [...]!"[17]; at the same time, pleasure is taken in storytelling, in contrast to the clarity of intention and resolution in *La gaviota*. *El sombrero de tres picos* is a narrative of consolation, like many conservative novels of regionalism. Even at the most dramatic moments there is no doubt of the eventual triumph of the quick-witted miller's wife over her adversary, in contrast with the troubling and uneven charting of Marisalada's fate in *La gaviota*. The difference may be that Alarcón takes pleasure in storytelling rather than being driven primarily by an agenda of regional worth.

The novels of Juan Valera are ostensibly set in the real world rather than the literary reality of folktale as revivified by Alarcón. But like the *patria chica* of *La gaviota*, Valera's "real" world of Andalucía is an isolated one. Repeated depictions of an implied Edenic innocence in the region convey the message that in isolation lie safety and comfort. A comparison of the plot of *Pepita Jiménez* with that of Pardo Bazán's *Los pazos de Ulloa* reveals the degree to which Valera's novels concentrate upon the creation of idyll rather than on the revelation of a less palatable world. In both novels, the arrival of a youthful cleric in a remote regional location sets in motion a sequence of events. While in *Los pazos de Ulloa* a priest faces the failure of his endeavors and a marriage ill conceived and catastrophic in outcome, in the case of *Pepita Jiménez* the cleric's arrival ultimately leads to the predictable happy end of marriage and children. This happy ending highlights the determination of Valera, not unlike that of Alarcón, to divert, to please, and to present literature for the reader's delectation.

There is initial titillation in the beginning of the novel. Just as Valera will add a layer of piquancy to *Juanita la Larga* (1895) by making his eponymous heroine of illegitimate birth, so in *Pepita Jiménez* he injects a dash of excitement by making his heroine a young widow and the young man who arrives

[17] P. de Alarcón, *El sombrero de tres picos* (1874), in *Novelas completas*. Prólogo de Jorge Campos (Madrid: Aguilar, 1974), p. 124.

on the scene, Luis, a seminarist, also illegitimate. Like *La gaviota*, Valera's novel is a narrative of growth and development. Valera, however, avoids the uneven and uncertain development of plot that characterized his earlier novel. In this case the heroine, Pepita, is exceptionally virtuous. By submitting, when in her teens, to marriage with an elderly man she proves herself an eminently acceptable female icon. In her widowhood she is both beautiful and cultured, and the narrative lets the reader understand that she awaits fulfilment through a more appropriate union. The more dramatic development is the arrival of the stranger Luis, on vacation from the seminary. His case represents growth from childish, untutored ways into mature masculine stature. He emerges from the avowedly innocent state of the seminarist into the man who will give comfort to his father's old age through marriage and the fathering of children.

This plot is one of sexual consolation for the masculine reader; key examples include Luis's transformation from one unable to ride to one who can manage a spirited horse. By simple sexual symbolism, in which horsemanship is equated with virility, an indication is thus given of his achieved masculinity and readiness for participation in a plot of marriage and procreation.[18] When viewed in terms of the regions and national vitality, we can see how this novel, like others by Valera, repeatedly insists upon the vitality, indeed the virility, of its masculine character, which will not only win him sexual prizes but will also win him, and all the others, the adoration of women who are as passionate and lovely as they are youthful. This kind of plot line represents a masculine myth of vitality, one of consolation in the face of aging and sexual waning. Just as the novels retain the reader in an idyllic form of Andalucía (evoked by the splendor of light and color rather than by the sombre qualities that Lorca will evoke in his essays on the *Cante jondo*), time is held in suspense, even within the plot. Further, Luis as future priest is far from blind to the pleasures and beauties of the material world. As he states in his letter of 4 April to his uncle, he does not want to be distracted from spirituality by the contemplation of natural beauty; yet his articulation of the delights of that beauty show him to be fully susceptible to it.

There is a clear contrast between *Pepita Jiménez* and *Los pazos de Ulloa* in the 'result' deriving from analogous initial plot situations. Why should one find such a clear North/South difference in Spain? Part of the answer lies in geography: the arid mountains of Andalucía, offset by fertile, lush *vegas* ('plains'), contrast with the rugged and difficult mountainous region of Galicia and Cantabria. Harsh winters and battles against the rigors of sea

[18] L. Charnon-Deutsch, *Gender and Representation: Women in Spanish Realist Fiction* (Amsterdam /Philadelphia: John Benjamins, 1990), pp. 21–40.

(*Sotileza*), land (*Peñas arriba*), or untamed wilderness (*Los pazos*) frame a hostile environment. In addition to these physical characteristics, two social distinctions are paramount: the degree of difference in the presence of the church and its institutions in North and South[19] and differing patterns of dependence/independence, mobility/immobility, arising from the markedly different systems of land-tenure in North and South. The relative sparseness of the clergy in Andalucía, contrasting with a more pronounced religious presence in Cantabria, is one factor of difference; even more significant is the fact that the priests of the mountainous North were habitually local to the area, while those of the South came from elsewhere. Within narratives dealing with the North the different land-tenure systems of Cantabria (family-held farms and cooperatives) and in Galicia, characterized by the wasting effects on property and wealth of *minifundismo*, in which land was divided between heirs instead of being inherited by a single family member, may have considerable bearing on the positive values given to Cantabria by Pereda and the negative vision of Galicia produced by Pardo Bazán.

The motif of isolation is arguably more significant in novels of the North than in those of the South. To understand the effects of isolation shown in regional novels, two models obtain. Conservative narratives, evidenced in those works celebrating Andalucía and the *patria chica*, extol the virtues of isolation: paradise untouched is paradise untainted; innocence can be preserved; beauty is 'natural', whether physical or moral. A similar approach to isolation characterizes the Cantabrian narratives of Pereda. By contrast, liberal (and hence negative) narratives of the North perceive the isolation of the regions as cases where entropy must inevitably ensue. The lack of exchange or contact with the outside world causes the internal and isolated social worlds depicted to fester and degenerate. The naturalism of Emile Zola, the late nineteenth-century French novelist, anticipated the theories of Max Nordau, author of the influential and widely translated work *Degeneration* (1892), and of Cesare Lombroso, the Italian criminologist who argued that physique and the tendency to crime were closely related. These writings exhibit all the case-material required in the depiction of rural degeneration by Pardo Bazán: reversion to "stock" is the consequence of inbreeding; it leads to atavism, criminality, and the eventual extinction of the race.

Two northern novelists, writing in the same period, construe questions of heredity in a completely divergent manner. In *Peñas arriba* Pereda opens his novel with a sort of surprise reminiscent of the opening of Calderón's classic Golden Age play *La vida es sueño* (*Life Is a Dream*, 1635). But in contrast to this play, where the unknown world of civilization leads Segismundo

[19] A. Shubert, *A Social History of Modern Spain* (London: Unwin Hyman, 1990), pp. 145–53.

to engage in the very monstrous behavior his father had sought to avoid by isolating him, Marcelo arrives at his uncle's estate from the supposed civilized world of Madrid, only to discover that the environment he initially perceived as rude and uncouth is in fact of sterling human worth: the individual has a real social place through the dictates of lineage (Marcelo will be chosen by his uncle as the rightful heir of the estate) and obligation (being lord of the estate is to have duties to fulfil, not privileges to be exercised in flagrant disregard of the human rights of the underclass).

Moreover, Marcelo has been diminished by city life. Initially his relationship to his physical environment is seen as impaired; he needs the restorative experience of direct contact with the natural world. The return to the earth and to physical life contrasts with the existence of superficiality and artifice in Madrid, a "civilized" life lacking direction. There is a strong teleological thrust to Pereda's narrative: life must lead to death, and that mortal end is kept firmly in view. Pereda puts dynamism into this mortal fate through the narrative of the bear-hunt. This "rural exercise" is part of Marcelo's initiation into the difficulties of mountain life. It is used to demonstrate simultaneously the bravery and sense of solidarity of the participants, and the physical strength of the priest don Sabas, a strength finally equated with moral strength.

Shadowing the narrative is the declared imminence of the death of Marcelo's uncle: this expected death is, after all, the motive for inviting Marcelo to stay, and the invitation itself should be read as an act of obligation and foresight. Continuity, lineage, and care of the community are not parts of life left to chance but are carefully predicted, motivating events. The necessity for forethought and planning responds, in extreme degree, to forces that determine life in the mountains – hazards of weather, vicissitudes of the natural cycles, and the risks of such an environment. Pereda proposes a social counter-balance to the elements that nature proposes as disruptive. Civilization itself must articulate the response to a *barbarie* that, in this case, is construed as that of the natural environment.

Pardo Bazán produces a different reading of the North. Her depiction of Galicia as a degenerate region, in contrast to Pereda's vision of Cantabria as demanding and rough but socially stable, relates in some degree to the greater impoverishment of the region, its soil leached by the weather and its population leached by emigration. *Los pazos de Ulloa* and its sequel, *La madre naturaleza*, are set deep in rural Galicia. They can be read as a pair of Naturalist novels that explore the dangerous results of an unhappy mix of heredity and environment. Hence the failure of the marriage between Pedro de la Lage, rural overlord but already over the cusp regarding his procreative capacity, running fast toward the fat of degeneration that will characterize him in *La madre*, and Nucha, a city-bred cousin, who is frail and ill-equipped by temperament and upbringing for the rigors of rural life.

The marriage of Nucha to Pedro is conceived (a word we shall later see to be significant in relation to Julián) as the solution to Pedro's immorality: his open living with his mistress Sabel, daughter of his steward. The role of go-between is carried out by Julián, a young, pale, "lymphatic" priest. *Los pazos* opens with his arrival at Ulloa, again a Calderonian surprise as Julián approaches the manor house while uncertainly mounted on his horse. The choice of Nucha is a preference over her sister Rita, a woman of outgoing temperament and ample hips – the obvious Naturalistic choice for the succession of the De la Lage family. There is an implicit (verging on the explicit) contrast between Nucha as an angelic figure and Rita, who, if not cast as whore (a role assigned to Sabel), is nonethless a potentially risky woman precisely because of that sensuality and fleshliness that fits her for the furthering of the race. It is with great difficulty that Nucha gives birth. Predictably enough, she produces a daughter, not a son, thereby proving her uselessness to her husband, and indeed his own folly, not only for having selected her as wife but for having allowed himself to take Julián's advice on the particular choice of wife to be made. Meanwhile Julián and Nucha are thrown together after the birth of Nucha's daughter, Manuela, forming a strange travesty of the Holy Family in which it is not clear whether Julián is to be read as father or replication of mother.

In *Los pazos de Ulloa* Julián and Nucha experience the region itself as hostile and as a place that fosters primitivism in its inhabitants, with whom, inevitably, they enter in conflict. Their ultimate fates contrast unhappily with the characters of positive regional texts. Whereas in *Pepita Jiménez* the seminarist is led, without loss of face, away from his priestly ambition towards marriage, and whereas don Sabas, the priest in *Peñas arriba*, acts as mentor to Marcelo, Julián reacts incompetently and disastrously in situations and in actions that he himself sets in motion. Nucha is weak, a hysteric, and an unfit match for the man she takes in marriage; she does not survive to bring her daughter to maturity. Meanwhile, those living in the region degenerate to the same level as the wild landscape around them.

In relation to twentieth-century Spain, Jo Labanyi argues that myths are there to console us. Such myths are almost inevitably regressive since they explain, round off, and offer a persuasively satisfying reading of the world.[20] For similar reasons, conservative regional novels of the nineteenth century

[20] Jo Labanyi, *Myth and History in the Contemporary Spanish Novel* (Cambridge University Press, 1989), pp. 5–34; "Nation, Narration, Naturalization: A Barthesian Critique of the 1898 Generation," in *New Hispanisms: Literature, Culture, Theory*, ed. Mark I. Millington and Paul Julian Smith (Ottawa: Dovehouse Editions Canada, 1994), pp. 127–49.

have much in common with these later, myth-creating Spanish narratives. All these narratives encode an awareness of change. Whereas Larra's essays encapsulate the struggle for reform in a society that rejects or only adopts change on a superficial level, and whereas the writings of Pardo Bazán and Leopoldo Alas represent an awareness of change through forms of degeneration and decay, in the conservative narratives of Pereda and Valera consciousness of cultural transitions takes the form of narratives of denial. Denial is inflected differently according to region and to a model that assigns the most positive value to Andalucía and a lesser, more problematic value to Cantabria, Asturias, and Galicia. The variation of inflection, exemplifying the second meaning of "evolution," largely characterizes many other aspects of writing in the nineteenth century, as will be evident from the following chapters in this volume.

Guide to further reading

Ferreras, Juan Ignacio, *La novela en el siglo XIX (desde 1868)* (Madrid: Taurus, 1988).

La novela en el siglo XIX (hasta 1868) (Madrid: Taurus, 1987).

Labanyi, Jo, *Gender and Modernization in the Spanish Realist Novel* (Oxford University Press, 2000).

Montesinos, José F., *Fernán Caballero: Ensayo de justificación* (Berkeley: University of California Press, 1961).

Zavala, Iris, *Ideología y política en la novela española del siglo XIX* (Salamanca: Anaya, 1971).

5

ELISA MARTÍ-LÓPEZ

The *folletín*: Spain looks to Europe

A critical approach to the nineteenth-century *folletín* must begin with an examination of this widely used term and with a revision of some of the prevalent ideas that frame our understanding of the literary and cultural nature of this novelistic production. The term *folletín* is not without problems. Based upon well-established critical notions, it has become a kind of critical steamroller that, while stressing some generally defined common traits, effectively cancels out all aesthetic differentiation among the texts included in this category. As we will see, some of these deep-rooted critical notions have to do with the poetics of the novel; others, with the Romantic understanding of literature as the highest expression of a nation's unique identity. Finally, the problematic nature of the term *folletín* is directly related to the highly influential distinction between High and Low forms of culture.

Folletín refers first of all to the form of publication of a novel. It describes the market-induced fragmentation a novel underwent when published in the *folletín* section of a newspaper. This section used to occupy the bottom part of one or more pages, or the last one, of a newspaper or journal, and was generally used to publish a miscellany of social news and recreational items. The practice was first introduced in France in 1836 by the editors of the newspapers *La Presse* and *Le Siècle* as a means to increase sales and, due to its great success, it was immediately adopted by most major newspapers and journals all around Europe and America: in Spain it was already a well-established practice in the 1840s. Describing a similar process of fragmentation, *folletín* is also often applied to novels that were published weekly or bi-weekly in serial form – *por entregas* – and sold to readers by subscription. But more often than not, *folletín* is used to describe not so much the method of publication of a novel, but rather its type – its content and style. In this sense, *folletín* is used to designate the tradition of melodramatic novel writing associated with popular and mostly female readership. More generally, *folletín* stands for commercial literature, that is, for novels created mechanically by the new publishing industry to secure a wide and immediate success among unsophisticated readers (*folletín* is thus often denounced as an example of the commodification of literature). Accordingly, *folletin*, *novela popular*, and *novela por entregas* are frequently used as synonymous terms and apply to an extensive novelistic production written from the 1840s to the early 1900s. In terms of number of writers and titles published, we can appropriately say that *folletín* designates most of the novel writing done in nineteenth-century Spain, and encompasses many of its dominant aesthetic forms. From the 1840s to the end of the century *folletinistas* such as Wenceslao Ayguals de Izco (1801–73), Manuel Angelón y Broquetas (1831–89), Angela Grassi de Cuenca (1826–83), Manuel Fernández y González (1821–88), Ramón Ortega y Frías (1825–83), Julio Nombela (1836–1919), and Enrique Pérez Escrich (1829–97), ruled over the new market of the Spanish novel. Most *folletinistas* were prolific writers who authored anything from dozens of titles to over 170, as in the case of Fernández y González.[1]

We have become used to referring to the *folletín* as "paraliterature" and "subliterature," thereby defining its existence as the product exclusively of the new market-oriented and mass-produced publishing policies of the nineteenth century, and to perceiving it as a writing that lacks aesthetic value. This is because our critical perception of the *folletín* still relies mostly on the cultural prestige assigned to realism and modernism – as the "artistic" forms of poetics – and, in particular, on their stand against the excess of imagination characteristic of the popular novel and other forms of Low culture. Recent important studies have explored the gender-and-class-based strategies used to establish the canon of the nineteenth-century novel, and, consequently, the criteria that support the exclusion of the *folletín* from it. These studies show the tactics of differentiation that have sustained the construction of the realist and modernist novel as mature male writing for a grown-up and select male audience in opposition to – and at the expense of – a supposedly feminine, childlike, and popular *folletín*.[2] Regardless of these contributions, however, the critical evaluation of the *folletín* novel by the realist writer Benito Pérez Galdós and the philosopher of modernism, José Ortega y Gasset, continue

[1] See Juan Ignacio Ferreras, *Catálogo de novelas y novelistas españoles del siglo XIX* (Madrid: Cátedra, 1979) and *La novela por entregas, 1840–1900: Concentración obrera y economía editorial* (Madrid: Taurus, 1972).

[2] See A. Blanco, "Gender and National Identity: The Novel in Nineteenth-Century Spanish Literary History," in *Culture and Gender in Nineteenth-Century Spain*, ed. Lou Charnon-Deutsch and Jo Labany (Oxford: Clarendon, 1995), pp. 120–36; C. Jagoe, "Disinheriting the Feminine: Galdós and the Rise of the Realist Novel in Spain," *Revista de Estudios Hispánicos* 27 (1993), pp. 203–8.

to dictate our evaluation of the genre.[3] We easily recognize in the critical approach of many contemporary critics Galdós's famous condemnation of the narrative naivety and imaginative excess of *folletín* novels, and his praise of verisimilitude – his insistence on observation over imagination – as the foundation of literariness and as key for the aesthetic construction of the novel. We also recognize Ortega y Gasset's contempt for popular forms of storytelling and their penchant for adventure and intrigue, as well as his idea that the novel, as a genre, evolves from aesthetically deficient early forms, in which pure narration dominates, to its modern and sophisticated version in which imagination has been definitively displaced by rigorous presentation.

Similarly, our understanding of the *folletín* is dominated by the politics of identity that define what constitutes a national literature. In Spanish literary historiography, *folletín* is associated with imitative practices and dismissed as a copy of the foreign writing of popular French authors such as Eugène Sue, Frédéric Soulié, Alexander Dumas *père*, and Victor Hugo. The rejection of *folletín* as imitative writing hardly comes as a surprise when we consider both the Romantic foundation and the nationalistic purpose of most histories of literature. As it is well known, the discipline of national literary history is a by-product of the notion of *Geist*, the belief in the unique spiritual configuration of a nation – the constant actualization of its *origin* in all its members. Imitations – perceived as lacking originality and authenticity – are said to stand for the voluntary resignation of a supposedly authentic expression (both personal and national) and the acceptance of an alien mask as true identity. The intrusion of foreign patterns of writing upon the sacred whole of native creativity is perceived as disruptive of the self-sufficient national tradition. This is particularly true for the history of the nineteenth-century Spanish novel, which, as Alda Blanco tells us, was written under "the obsessive fear of cultural invasion".[4] As imitations of foreign works, the *folletín* is said to perform a double shameful gesture – that of cultural submission and alienation; consequently, it is rejected as spurious literature and discarded as alien to Spanish processes of cultural formation and national construction. Critical awareness of the historical and ideological conditions that gave rise to the notion of *Geistesgeschichte* has not been able to forgo the nationalistic project of most literary histories. Thus excluded from the

[3] See Benito Pérez Galdós, "Observaciones sobre la novela contemporánea en España" (1870), in *Ensayos de crítica literaria*, ed. L. Bonet (Barcelona: Península, 1972), pp. 115–32, and José Ortega y Gasset, "Ideas sobre la novela" (1925), in *Teoría de la novela (Aproximaciones hispánicas)*, ed. Germán y Agnes Gullón (Madrid: Taurus, 1974), pp. 29–64.

[4] Blanco, "Gender and National Identity", p. 123.

prestige and authenticity associated with the notion of national uniqueness, the *folletín* is still constructed as aesthetically deficient, and its derivative writing (as a rewriting of a foreign text) is denied any legitimacy.

Consistent with the traditional understanding of national literature, *folletín* novels – as imitative and market-oriented writings – have been deprived of aesthetic qualities and cultural prestige and, consequently, have been said to lack individuality. In many studies, they become mere examples of a statistical category, multiple and repetitive samples of an identical negation of poetics itself: works with no style, examples of non-literary texts. Accordingly, no literary difference is acknowledged to exist between, for instance, the socio-historical imagination of a work such as *Los misterios de Barcelona* ('The Mysteries of Barcelona', 1844) by José Nicasio Milá de la Roca, the Romantic nationalism of a historical tale such as *El pendón de Santa Eulalia* ('The Banner of Saint Eulalia', 1858) by Manuel Angelón y Broquetas, or a domestic and recreational story written for the social instruction of women such as *Celeste* (1863) by María del Pilar Sinués de Marco. Similarly, the author of *folletines* is often described exclusively by his or her relation to the market and defined through production-oriented terms such as "workman" or "laborer." These definitions deprive the *folletinistas* of their own individual names and, consequently, of authorship, and, as Michel Foucault has pointed out, an author's name is precisely the signifier for both the existence and the status of a discourse within a society and culture: a discourse "that possesses an author's name is not to be immediately consumed and forgotten."[5] Indeed, most writers of *folletines* are unknown to us since the name *folletinista* stands precisely for the lack of individual originality. Widely encompassing terms, *folletinista* and *folletín* continue to signify the depreciated mode of existence, circulation, and functioning of numerous nineteenth-century novels within literary histories. But the fact that many of these novels had close ties to the market should not prevent us from analyzing them individually as aesthetic works. We should remember that most nineteenth-century novels, including the canonized realist and Naturalist works, shared the same publishing infrastructure as supported the *folletín*, since such works also were published in serial form.

More importantly, although it is accurate to say that many novels included in the term *folletín* did imitate foreign popular works, we need to approach the nature and necessity of imitation in nineteenth-century Spain as the result of new publishing conditions and policies and, more generally, the influence of hegemonic foreign forms of the novel in Spanish writers throughout the

5 M. Foucault, "What Is an Author?" in *Language, Counter-Memory, Practice: Selected Essays and Interviews* (Ithaca: Cornell University Press), p. 123.

century. When analyzing the imitative nature of many Spanish nineteenth-century novels we should remember that by the middle of the nineteenth century Spain had no novels but foreign ones. We should take into consideration the conditions created by the new publishing industry and how the new system of production and consumption of literature radically modified the practices of cultural exchange among different countries: for the first time in history, European literary processes were subjected to a ruthless centralization which effectively established the artistic dominance of Paris and London. These two cities dictated the succession of literary movements and, specifically, the mode of the novel, while their powerful publishing houses actively exported them to foreign cultural markets. The constitution of Paris and London as the hegemonic spaces of cultural creativity and production transformed most European book markets, whose functioning became progressively more dependent on French and English fashionable trends. The dependence of Spanish publishing houses on French literary production was not new; however, it is in the 1840s that we perceive the radical change that affected the middle and late nineteenth-century Spanish literary market.

From the 1840s on, Spain actively adopted the publishing practices that had already transformed the novel into a commodity in other European markets: first, the introduction of French – rather than English – bestsellers and fashionable authors (which allowed Spanish publishers to participate in European cultural and commercial trends); secondly, the adoption of the serial form of publication (and, consequently, the facilities of payment by subscription); and thirdly, the exponential increase both in the number of foreign titles published and in print runs. French bestsellers saturated the nineteenth-century Spanish book market and deeply transformed it, as the French novel became the focus of Spanish publishing activity: all commercial publishing resources were invested to promote the French novel, which eventually supplanted the Spanish novel in the national market and determined the habits and expectations of Spanish readers, thus depriving the incipient Spanish novel of the national resources that could have supported it. In these conditions, the urgency to satisfy the reading public's request for French novels redirected the creative energy of writers toward translation and imitation, and the close collaboration – both economic and artistic – between publisher and author that sustained the emergence of the novel as new hegemonic genre in nineteenth-century France and Britain was often replaced in Spain by a strictly economic transaction between publisher and translator and/or imitator.

Modern culture came to be identified with the events and artifacts produced by Paris and London and a new literary geography, highly hierarchical, was created: nations which were going through different narrative periods became contiguous literary markets. The interference of the prestigious nineteenth-century English and French models of novel writing in the literary life of other nations decisively modified the conditions for the production of autochthonous novels within those countries and radically limited their aesthetic options. As Franco Moretti explains in his *Atlas of the European Novel (1800–1900)*, "'diffusion'" was "the great conservative force": "One form; and an imported one [. . .] [I]n an integrated market – latecomers don't follow the same road as their predecessors, only later: they follow a different, a narrower road."[6] Thus to be a novelist in Spain at the time required the framing of one's work within the modes of writing dictated by the commercial success of the foreign novel. For the first time, to be a writer meant to have – or to aspire to have – a socially wide readership, and to imitate, to some degree, those foreign narratives whose commercial fortunes seemed closest to the social imaginary. In this context, imitation is no longer an individual, sporadic and shameful phenomenon (the influence of author A on author B), the characteristic of a particular genre (the *folletín* novel), or the sign of the alleged discrepancies between civilized nations and those other belated cultures that are continuously trying to catch up. It is rather a literary practice circumscribed by the narrowing of morphological freedom imposed by the conditions of dependency of the literary markets.

We need, then, to reconsider the imitative practices present in the *folletín* – and, in general, in all nineteenth-century novels – as part of the process of creation of autochthonous novel writing in Spain. Itamar Even-Zohar has commented that where a translated literature holds a central position – that is, when translations are "by and large an integral part of innovatory forces" – no clear-cut distinction is maintained between original and translated writings, and it is often the leading writers who author the translations.[7] Original writing, translation, and imitation often came to be one and the same thing in nineteenth-century Spain and numerous *folletín* novels attest to the blurred borderlines that supposedly separate imitation from original writing. There was no real alternative to translation and imitation in nineteenth-century Spanish literary and cultural practices. However, contrary to established critical views that reject those works that show signs of foreign writing, in the de-centered cultural consciousness of translation and imitation – in that hybrid voice both alien and indigenous – Spanish cultural and historical processes managed to find a voice. In this sense, under

6 F. Moretti, *Atlas of the European Novel (1800–1900)* (London and New York: Verso, 1998), pp. 190–1.

7 I. Even-Zohar, "The Position of Translated Literature within the Literary Polysystem," *Poetics Today* 11/1 (1990), p. 47.

a translator's name pokes out an incipient novelist, and under an imitation, the effort of whole generations to create an autochthonous writing for the novel.

As a depreciated form of literary writing, the *folletín* novel has become identified with a series of formal and thematic traits, a narrative uniformity that constitutes its well-known literary stereotype. Although the appropriateness of this typological description of *folletín* is questionable, we cannot ignore it: first, because it does describe certain literary traits of the works included in this extensive novelistic production; secondly, and more importantly, because it shows how much the narrative uniformity associated with these novels is, first of all, the result of the assumption of knowledge and the application of generalities that characterize our critical approach to the popular novel. The vocabulary and syntax of a *folletín* novel are said to be simple; the paragraphs, short; and the size of the letters, big. The fragmentation of the paragraphs is also due to the fact that writers were often paid by the line. The writing, dictated by the fragmentation in the publishing process of the work, is regarded as episodic; the story, as punctuated by multiple intrigues, constant surprises, and interruptions. In this generalization of the poetics of *folletín*, action predominates over description (and, consequently, dialogue over narration), imagination over reality, and stock characters over psychologically differentiated ones. In these novels good and evil are clearly differentiated, moral certainties conveyed, and happy endings secured. Thematically speaking, they encompass a wide range of subjects: sentimental novels, historical novels, detective stories, social novels, adventure novels, etc. As commercial literature, *folletín* is said to be an alienating fiction satisfying and promoting the escapist needs of both women and the working classes of the new industrial cities. Accordingly, the plot of these novels follow what Karl Marx, and later Umberto Eco, identified as the highly successful (as well as politically conservative) formula known as "literature of consolation": plots that create the illusion of breaking with the monotony and prosaic rhythms of modernity, and satisfy both readers' need for adventure and heroic deeds, and their belief in a transcendental (and paternalistic) justice.[8]

In a *folletín* plot, the figure of a helpless orphan (normally a beautiful and virtuous young woman) often represents the social cost and human suffering of industrialization as well as the alienation brought by the new cities – the loss of an individual sense of family and community. The orphans, being alienated from their families, are exposed to misery and the abuse of

[8] U. Eco, "Socialismo y consolación," in *Socialismo y consolación: Reflexiones en torno a "Los misterios de París" de Eugène Sue* (Barcelona: Tusquets, 1970), pp. 7–37.

unscrupulous and greedy men and women. Widows and honest workmen are also popular figures in the catalogue of victims. Stories about schemes to usurp someone's name and fortune proliferate, and adulterers, prostitutes, usurers, moneylenders and a diversity of criminals (thieves, murderers, forgers, etc.) often carry out the threats posed by unconstrained desire to the bourgeois patriarchal system. These characters (the villains) perform numerous assaults on the authority of the father (as citizen and proprietor) and the organization of society according to a hierarchy of class and gender. Against them, the *folletín* novel opposes compassionate figures of authority: kindhearted doctors, generous aristocrats, wealthy patrons, virtuous priests, etc. Murders, suicides, madness, vengeances, forged documents, and, in some cases, fantastic elements and events, organize the stories. The pure and chaste affection between young lovers is surrounded by numerous conspiracies; the marriage that normally signals the end of the story reconciles all opposites: love and duty, religion and politics, ambition and honor.

It is interesting to note that when we speak about *folletín* and *folletinistas* we often give the impression that we know our subject very well, that we know all there is to know. Yet we hardly read these works. With a few and important exceptions, especially the recent research on women's writing, we lack studies that analyze the literary mode and the individual literary practices of these texts.[9] We know very little about the system – or systems – of significations that underlies the numerous works encompassed by the term *folletín*, the textuality that sustained the pleasure of their reading, or the dominant forms melodrama adopted in Spanish fiction. Also, it is often said with regard to the *folletín* that the genre reached a crisis point during the revolutionary years (1868–72), that its stories and techniques became stagnant, and that the emergence of the literary realist novel definitively segregated Spanish readers. At the same time, and in contrast with the supposed decadence of the genre, the late 1880s saw the rise of Vicente Blasco Ibáñez (1867–1928), a very successful writer who captivated the imagination of Spanish readers and whose novels can be considered the culmination of the Spanish popular novel. Many questions and issues regarding the *folletín* novel need to be reconsidered. The fact is that we lack extensive and conclusive documentation about what titles were most popular, when, and why; the number of editions these novels had and the number of copies per edition; the forms in which they were published, and, in the case of *folletines* properly so defined, in which newspapers and magazines they appeared. We

9 See J.-F. Botrel, "Nationalisme et consolation dans la littérature populaire espagnole des années 1898," in *Nationalisme et littérature en Espagne et en Amérique latine aux XIXè siécle*, ed. Claude Dumas (Lille: Presse Universitaire de Lille, 1982), pp. 63–8. For studies on women's writing, see Lou Charnon-Deutsch's contribution to this volume.

have only a general knowledge about who were the most widely read foreign writers (and, presumably, the most imitated ones), but we do not know how the popularity of their titles changed during that long period. Neither do we have studies on the circuits of distribution and sale nor on lending libraries. In fact, we do not know exactly who read what.

We have only a little research on the specific – and changing – conditions of production that framed the writing of *folletines* over six decades. Thus basic questions that explain the market-oriented character of the *folletín* novel are still to be answered: what kind of contracts existed between publisher and writer? How much were the authors paid? How much did an *entrega* (a serial 'instalment') cost? What kind of creative control did the publisher have over the author? We lack studies that analyze the literary consequences of the interference of the new publishing conditions in the writing processes of a novel. How did authorship work, and what did collective authorship (when a novel was written by two or more authors) mean in terms of writing practices? We are also ignorant of the literary relationship that existed between a writer of popular novels and his or her public. We do not know when the *folletinistas* incorporated in their writing suggestions from their readers and, consequently, the kind of cultural and social processes to which this open writing (and its aesthetic forms) gave voice. Finally, we know very little about the control exerted by authorities (official and religious censorship) over publishers and writers. We do know, however, that those in power were always very concerned about popular literature and its destabilizing effect on social order, and that powerful people often moved to suppress particular titles such as *Madrid y sus misterios* ('Madrid and its Mysteries', 1844), *Los misterios de Córdoba* ('The Mysteries of Córdoba', 1845), or Francisco Suárez's *Los demócratas o El ángel de la libertad* ('Democrats or the Angel of Liberty', 1863). The truth is that, like Leonardo Romero Tobar twenty-five years ago, we are still struggling with the term – or terms – that will describe better the diverse aesthetic and cultural nature of the so-called *folletines*. Indeed, the extensive and varied body of nineteenth-century Spanish novels known as *folletines* is still a "confusing universe," and our knowledge of these works continues to be highly limited and quite muddled.[10]

To perceive the complex cultural processes and the diversity of literary practices sustaining *folletín* writing (and, consequently, the diversity of audiences these novels addressed), I will briefly examine the group of *folletines* known as the Spanish *Misterios*: novels written in imitation of Eugène Sue's *Les mystères de Paris* (*The Mysteries of Paris*, 1842–3). This group of novels

[10] L. Romero Tobar, *La novela popular española del siglo XIX* (Madrid: Fundación Juan March, 1976), p. 35.

is also known as *folletín social* since its melodramatic plots are set within contemporary social situations and often, but not always, convey the political message of progressive liberals or utopian socialists.[11] Specifically, I will comment on two works – Wenceslao Ayguals de Izco's *María o La hija de un jornalero* ('María or the Daughter of a Journeyman', 1845–6) and Ceferino Tressera's *Los misterios del Saladero* ('The Mysteries of the Prison-House', 1860). It is not my intention to take these novels as representatives of the group – rather the contrary. I would like to point out their distinctive writing among the diverse aesthetic configurations that constitute the Spanish *Misterios* and, more generally, the *folletín* novel.

The Spanish *Misterios*, mostly written between 1844 and 1870, belong to a cultural period when the new market-oriented literary practices were in full swing but the cultural denunciation of mass-produced popular culture – although in process of being conceptualized – was yet to be set in place. Only after *l'art pour l'art* emerged as the dominant aesthetic doctrine in Spain, during the revolutionary period beginning in 1868, was the question of the construction of a national literature framed by the distinction between High and Low cultures. Consequently, the writing of the mid-nineteenth-century *Misterios*, although constituted by many market-oriented narrative techniques, is characterized by the conspicuous absence of the strategies of cultural hierarchization so important later in the century. In this sense, the *Misterios* are both a commercially oriented narrative, since as imitation of Sue's works they reproduce some of his successful narrative formulas, and a literary enterprise undertaken by an educated elite, driven by the desire to create a modern Spanish novel while engaging in the aesthetics of that foreign and popular genre. As Juan Martínez Villergas stated, referring to his writing of *Los Misterios de Madrid* ('The Mysteries of Madrid', 1844–5), his novel was part of the aesthetic trials that were bringing forth the autochthonous Spanish novel: "Indeed I have the satisfaction," he said, "of having contributed to the cultivation of a national novel."[12]

The identification of the *folletín* with the unsophisticated and childlike reading habits said to be found in the working classes and women again proves to be far from accurate in the case of the *Misterios*. Studies on the social and economic conditions supporting readership in mid-nineteenth-century Spain have established the middle-class background of most readers of the early novel. In the case of the *Misterios*, the dense page composition, the use of footnotes, addenda, and small fonts – all distinctive traits of these

[11] We should remember here that the title of Eugène Sue's novel had a great impact and produced a wave of other works entitled *Misterios* whose content and form have nothing to do with the imitations discussed here.

[12] J. Martínez Villergas, *Los misterios de Madrid* (Madrid: Manini, 1844–5), pp. 316–17.

novels to a greater or lesser degree – seem to point to an audience with far more sophisticated reading skills than those of the barely literate working class. The proclaimed "extraordinary luxury" of the first editions of *María o La hija de un jornalero*, in addition to confirming the high cost of the book, seems also to be in agreement with the desires of a middle class anxious to acquire both social prestige and cultural capital. Similarly, and against the established idea of a mostly female readership for the *folletín* novel, the intended audience of the *Misterios* seems to have been male. The male readership of Sue's *Les Mystères de Paris* and its Spanish imitations is consistent not only with their often highly political nature but also with nineteenth-century printed and written records.[13] Rafael del Castillo, in the opening pages of his novel *Misterios catalanes o el obrero de Barcelona* ('Catalonian Mysteries or the Worker from Barcelona', 1862), not only identifies men as the appropriate readers of his text but, concerned with the serious matters undertaken in his novel, also warns off any possible female reader: "Our readers may go to the trouble of interpreting it in their own way. We abstain from any interference as we do not wish to offend the modesty of those few daughters of Eve who experience the delicious or fatal whim to read us." The social spectrum of the *Misterios* readership in Spain – male and middle class – is well exemplified by José María Álvarez (owner of a cake shop), who after his death in 1846 left a library consisting, among other unspecified books, of *Los misterios de París*, *Los misterios de Madrid*, *El Judío errante*, *Nuestra Señora de París*, *Hans de Islandia*, and *La vida de Espartero*.[14]

This does not mean, of course, that women did not read these novels. We need to remember that despite their intended male readership, various sources point also to a large female audience for the *Misterios* and other mid-nineteenth-century political novels: among them, the proliferation of the figure of the "bluestocking" (*la marisabidilla*) in the fictional and non-fictional writings of the time, and the numerous warnings by politicians and social commentators about the dangers of mixing political discourse and entertainment, precisely because it was creating a politicized female readership. In any case, the intended portrait of contemporary social issues by the *Misterios*, as well as their small font and dense page format, points to both an educated and socially aware national audience that enjoyed recognizing – or

[13] A male reader is depicted, for instance, in the caricature entitled "Lecture des *Mystères de Paris*" published in the magazine *Charivari* (22 November 1843). Similarly, the small library owned by Dussadier (the representative of the committed revolutionary low middle class in Flaubert's *L'Education sentimentale*) consists of three books and includes the novel by Sue.

[14] R. del Castillo, *Misterios catalanes o el obrero de Barcelona* (Madrid: Librería Española de E. Font, 1962), p. 169. See also J.-F. Botrel, "Narrativa y lecturas del pueblo en la España del siglo XIX," *Cuadernos Hispanoamericanos* 516 (1993), pp. 69–91.

expected to find – their own social concerns, political anxieties, and aspirations in fictional narratives.

The middle-class, mostly male and often politically progressive readership of the Spanish *Misterios* is coherent with the social base of Sue's extensive European readership: according to Antonio Gramsci, Sue was "widely read by the middle-class democrats."[15] The widespread use of the serial novel – in particular, the *Misterios* type of narratives – by politically minded liberals and, in some cases, utopian socialists also questions the preconception of an uneducated readership seeking plain escapist entertainment. Although it is accurate to affirm that these narratives reproduce the formula known as "literature of consolation," the *Misterios* are not alienating novels, nor are they all plainly conservative. The *Misterios* sanction basic forms of bourgeois authority and social order; however, we must remember that they also satisfied the symbolic needs of the political opposition to the *moderado* regime – progressive liberals, republicans, democrats, and utopian socialists. The ideological limitations of these political discourses (their ultimate alliance to bourgeois concepts of class and gender) should not prevent us from acknowledging the destabilizing role some of them had in mid-nineteenth-century Spain.

As the *Misterios* written by Ayguals de Izco and Ceferino Tressera show, mid-century writers, while using melodrama to express their social concerns and the consolatory formula to promote social reconciliation, questioned and pushed liberalism often to its limits before Marxist thought revealed the ideological shortcomings of their own critical discourses. These *Misterios* are definitively addressed to those social groups that made possible the 1868 Revolution and the First Republic, movements that stood for a social order that had little to do with the conservative regimes of the *Estatuto Real* (1833) or the Restoration (1874/75–1885). Thus, the *Misterios* locate themselves precisely at the center of the disparity between the rigid constitutional frame imposed by a system of representation based on strict property qualifications (*liberalismo censitario*) and the realities of a social opinion that, excluded from the system of representation, demanded its access to the new political system. Contrary to the perception of these novels as escapist and alienating literature, the emergence of the *Misterios* in the 1840s is related to the desire for political expression that gave rise to the daily press – a phenomenon inscribed in the process of raising the consciousness of an ever-wider reading public, set in motion by the middle class outside the boundaries of the prevailing constitutional system. In accordance with Raymond Carr's assertion

[15] A. Gramsci, "The Detective Novel, from 'Quaderni del carcere,'" in *Selections from Cultural Writings*, ed. David Forgacs and Geoffrey Nowell-Smith (Cambridge, MA: Harvard University Press, 1985), p. 370.

of the historical importance and political influence of the petty bourgeois sectors of Spanish society since the early 1850s, we can say that the *Misterios* are located at the center of the formal abundance, cultural complexity, and ideological contradictions experienced by the mid-nineteenth-century Spanish middle classes.[16]

Thus the imagination found in the novels by Wenceslao Ayguals de Izco and Ceferino Tressera is not detached from the historical conditions that gave rise to them, nor is it rigidly formulaic and meaningless. On the contrary, the novels by Ayguals and Tressera are the aesthetic response – the form that confers meaning – to the historical processes transforming Spain in the middle of the nineteenth century. *María* and *Los misterios del Saladero*, amplifying and multiplying Sue's use of footnotes in *Les Mystères de Paris*, are characterized by the merging of newspaper reporting and novel writing. In these narratives, romance is accompanied by long footnotes (some of them extending for several pages) in which the reader is provided with excerpts from public and statistical reports, scientific treatises, promulgated laws, newspaper articles, parliamentary speeches, and so on. Ceferino Tressera in *Los misterios del Saladero*, for instance, following in Ayguals's footsteps, uses statistics, maps, and salary and demographic tables to illustrate and support his political arguments. Furthermore, he not only discusses and quotes extensively from the political thought of utopian socialist authors, but also mentions Hegel and Darwin.

Ayguals's and Tressera's intensive resort to newspaper-like reports contributes decidedly to inserting their romances into specific socio-historical contexts: the journalistic reporting on current historical events gives a distinctive sense of a politically and socially motivated present to the *Misterios* narratives. The portrait of *folletines* as escapist fantasies is, in part, the result of the perceived ahistoricism of their plots. The notion of time organizing the events portrayed in the Spanish *Misterios* is often viewed through the historicist awareness of late-nineteenth-century novels and, consequently, perceived as lacking in historical consciousness and as falling into essentialist notions of time (an ahistorical notion of truth and reality). In fact, the journalistic writing found in the novels by Ayguals and Tressera (and other authors of *Misterios*), framed within a melodramatic representation of social evil and using strategies of consolation, plunges their readers into the calendrical time and familiar landscape that constitute national consciousness. They accomplish this by the appropriation of the journalistic purpose of recreating the present: its intent to give singular and current events a historical explanation and perspective, that is, a collective meaning. Ayguals had a name for this

[16] R. Carr, *Spain (1808–1939)* (Oxford University Press, 1966), p. 61.

special kind of journalistic retelling of Spain's transition from an absolutist monarchy to a liberal one – the story of those "great events that occurred in Madrid during the period of the *Estatuto Real*" – and its transformation into "contemporary chronicles": he called it a "history-novel."[17]

In the *Misterios* by Ayguals and Tressera, the fortunes and misfortunes of the characters are narratively inserted within recent and actual social events and connected to the political issues raised by them, extensively commented on in the newspaper-style digressions. In these novels, as has been observed apropos of the eruption of the political and the social into bourgeois sentimental novels, love affairs no longer face the opposition of hostile relatives or the prejudices of private morality, but instead the class and gender structure of society. Thus in these novels suicide attempts, seductions, love stories, plans of revenge, misappropriations, and restitutions of name and wealth are not only narratively framed by the profound economic transformations that characterized mid-nineteenth-century Spain (the proletarization of the work force, the first important migrations from rural areas to the cities, the introduction of steam engines, etc.). Their course also follows the political instability and intense social unrest in the Spanish liberal state during those mid-century years (the Carlist wars and the infighting among liberal groups). As one of the first representations of Spanish society struggling with modernization, these *Misterios* provide their own distinctive fictional answer to the disruption caused by historical processes in traditional forms of life, and reflect the anxieties and enthusiasm their readers themselves felt about the possibility of reinventing the country around a new modern state. In this sense, we can say that the romances written by Ayguals and Tressera show the ideological and aesthetic range – as well as the limitations – of melodramatic writing.

The last issue we must examine is the relation of the *folletín* to other nineteenth-century novel writing, specifically to realist and naturalist works. So far the few studies analyzing this question have focused on the impact of the *folletín* on the work of the realist writer Benito Pérez Galdós.[18] The literary and cultural relevance of the *folletín* in the history of the nineteenth-century Spanish novel has been mostly limited to its role in the development of the realist aesthetics of this particular writer. The importance the *folletín* had in his writing, as well as the complexity of the role it played in defining

17 W. Ayguals de Izco, *María o La hija de un jornalero*, 2 vols. (Madrid: Ayguals de Izco, 1845–6), p. 384.

18 On the influence of the *folletín* novel on Pérez Galdós's works, see Romero Tobar, *La novela popular*; F. Ynduráin, *Galdós entre la novela y el folletín* (Madrid: Taurus, 1970); A. Andreu, *Galdós y la literatura popular* (Madrid: Sociedad General Española de Librería, 1982). For a critical reformulation of Spanish Realism, see H. Gold, *The Reframing of Realism* (Durham, NC: Duke University Press, 1993).

his particular brand of realism, are generally acknowledged. Many critics have noticed the dependence of his novels and *Episodios nacionales* of the first period (1870–81) on *folletín* imagination and narrative techniques. At the same time, this dependence has often been denounced as a deplorable instance of literary contamination and explained as the result of the creative weaknesses of a young writer still unable to escape the corrupting effects of the *folletín*'s morbid aesthetics. The numerous references to the *folletín* – and *folletinistas* – that can be found in some of Galdós's later works, such as *La desheredada* (*The Disinherited Woman*, 1881) and *Tormento* (1884), have been analyzed as part of the mature writer's conscious parodying of the popular genre and regarded as one of the literary strategies that characterizes his own version of realist writing. But the relevance of the extensive production of *folletines* in the emergence of the modern Spanish novel – in the aesthetic trials that came to constitute the Spanish bourgeois novel in all its diversity – has hardly been explored. Of course, to acknowledge the presence of the *folletín* in the literary practices of the late nineteenth century would complicate the construction of cultural strategies of social distinction that characterizes the task of traditional literary history. It would also complicate the task of justifying the artistic legitimacy of the Spanish novel within the frame of modern European culture (as dictated by the prestigious French and English models). But it would allow us to understand fully what Stephanie Sieburth has identified as one of the characteristics of Spanish literary life: its "in-between" character, its participation in both High and Low forms of culture.[19]

New studies are approaching the *folletín* novel not as an alien form in the history of Spanish fiction but, on the contrary, as the result of different ways of appropriating a foreign and imported genre. Morever, the *folletín* is examined as a discursive solution to a crisis originated by the awareness of Spain's provincial separation from modern cultural processes, and the hybridity of the Spanish novel as related to the uneven modernization of Spain. Franco Moretti has rightly observed that the European popular novel does not represent a betrayal of literature but rather "the coming to light of the limits of Realism," that is, the dependency of realist poetics on the historical and social conditions of France and England and their middle classes.[20] In this sense, while pointing out the lasting and important influence popular novels had all over Europe, he has linked the emergence of mass literature in the nineteenth century to the representation of those European historical

19 S. Sieburth, *Inventing High and Low: Literature, Mass Culture, and Uneven Modernity in Spain* (Durham, NC: Duke University Press, 1994), p. 11.

20 F. Moretti, "Modern European Literature: A Geographical Sketch," *New Left Review* 206 (1994), p. 103.

conditions that were different from those experienced by its hegemonic centers, and to the social realities and imaginations that are obliterated by realist poetics. Moretti's understanding of popular culture gives a whole new relevance to the extensive and lasting production of the Spanish *folletín* novel. In this sense, we need to explore how the weakness of Spain's industrialization process, the violence of the civil wars, the unfinished character of its political revolution (the constant military uprisings), the well-rooted centrifugal forces of regionalism undermining the authority of the centralist state, the loss of the empire (when the most prosperous European nations were busy building new ones), and the repression and social stagnation of the Restoration period, found in the aesthetic diversity of *folletín* writing a distinctive vehicle of expression. In the successful narrative formulas of the popular novel – prone to unusual events and characters, to a clear-cut representation of conflicts and resolutions, and to the uncensored display of emotions – the off-center historical conditions of Spain with respect to the political and cultural hegemony of France and Britain, found a voice, or rather, many.

Guide to further reading

Botrel, Jean-François, *L'infralittérature en Espagne aux XIXe et XXe siècles* (Grenoble: Presses Universitaires de Grenoble, 1977).

"La novela por entregas: Unidad de creación y público," in *Creación y público en la literatura española*, ed. Jean-François Botrel and S. Dalaün (Madrid: Castalia, 1974), pp. 111–55.

Brooks, Peter, *The Melodramatic Imagination: Balzac, Henry James, Melodrama, and the Mode of Excess* (New York: Columbia University Press, 1985).

García Viñó, Manuel, "Notas sobre la novela popular en España," *Arbor* 399 (March 1979), pp. 59–69.

Lambert, José, "L'éternelle question des frontières: littératures nationales et systèmes littéraires," in *Langue, Dialecte, Littérature: Etudes romanes à la mémoire de Hugo Plomteux*, ed. C. Angelet, L. Melis, F. J. Merteens, and F. Nusarra (Leuven University Press, 1983), pp. 355–70.

Schwartz, Roberto, *Misplaced Ideas: Essays on Brazilian Culture* (London and New York: Verso, 1992).

6

HARRIET TURNER

The realist novel

When we think of realism in fiction, we think first of mimesis – the imitation of life – a concept that at once implies the existence of something outside the writer's own mind which he or she is trying to imitate. The imitation of this supposedly external "thing" undergirds the term "realism," whether applied to painting, philosophy, literature, or film. As Harry Levin reminds us, "Etymologically, realism is thing-ism. The adjective 'real' derives from the Latin *res* [meaning 'thing'] and finds an appropriate context in 'real estate'" – land, property, things.[1] The realist novel in Spain places a special emphasis on this primary engagement with the things of this world. In this emphasis, nineteenth-century Spanish realism harks back even to the epic *Poema de Mío Cid* (1140), in which a close-up focus on things – cages laid bare, emptied of hunting falcons, weeds growing on the threshold of an abandoned castle – participates vividly in telling the story of exile.

Writing in this realist tradition, Benito Pérez Galdós (1843–1920), in his 1870 essay on the art of the novel, first evokes the principle of mimesis. His stated aim is to *reproduce* life as objectively as possible, depicting things as they "really" are – houses, dress, furniture, gestures, and habits of speech. In a later essay (1897) he affirms that language itself constitutes the most telling sign of personal and national identity.[2] Similarly Leopoldo Alas (1852–1901), known by his pen name Clarín, advocates the idea of the novel as a "reproduction" based on close observation and documentary evidence, on "scrupulously examined details."[3] The trope of the mirror expresses the mimesis of this visible, external reality. Galdós speaks of the contemporary social novel

1 H. Levin, *The Gates of Horn. A Study of Five French Realists* (New York: Oxford University Press, 1963), p. 34.

2 B. Pérez Galdós, "La sociedad presente como materia novelable"(1897), in *Ensayos de crítica literaria*, ed. L. Bonet (Barcelona: Península, 1999), p. 220.

3 L. Alas, "Del naturalismo" (1882), in *Leopoldo Alas: Teoría y crítica de la novela española*, ed. Sergio Beser (Barcelona: Laia, 1972), p. 127.

as a "faithful mirror of the society in which we live."[4] Clarín reiterates the notion of the naturalist novel as "the exact reflection of life."[5]

These images recall Stendhal's famous definition (1830) of the novel as a mirror being walked along a road. On the one hand, the mirror reflects the dailiness of living, which is visible, constant, verifiable. On the other, that image is *moving* as the novelist carries his mirror the length of the road, and as a moving image it is subjective, variable, uncertain. As Michael Wood advises, "Stendhal's mirror on the road and the Naturalists' slice of life were gestures toward the neutral observation the nineteenth century thought it wanted and could have. But the gestures were full of other possibilities and the nineteenth century wanted other things as well. The mirror could be tilted and the slice taken at an angle."[6] Catching the tilt, espying the angle, are choices that establish, in the realist novel, a creative tension between part and whole. This tension stems, on the one hand, from the inclusiveness that writers sought (Galdós's emphasis, for example, on comprehensive lists, recurring characters, and a broad social, historical, and political canvas; Clarín's focus on an "omnicomprehensive form"[7]), and, on the other, from the imperatives of specificity. The aim was to achieve a depiction of the whole in a creative balance with the finiteness, and the lack implied by a focus on only of a specific part. This part stands for, intimates, or poses as the whole but is not, in and of itself, that whole. Yet in the realist novel that whole of something ought to persist, unnamed and inviolate, gesturing, as it were, at the margins or below the surfaces of things. For it is precisely this whole, the enacted *cosmovisión* or world view or wisdom so deftly secreted in the pieces and parts of the story and its structures, that realists like Galdós and Clarín aspired to communicate to their readers.

In the Spanish realist novel, tricking out that larger meaning through the interplay of part and whole called for experimentation with the tropology of image and motif. In telling, narrators keep associating one thing with another, digressing from plot to atmosphere to character, while objects become transformed into "synedochic 'close-ups' and metonymic 'set-ups'."[8] Examples in Clarín's *La Regenta* (1884–5) are the collusions of metaphor and motif in the development of the gaze, the image of the tower, of a ubiquitous mud-stained environment, slavering appetites, the hunt, and intertextual

4 B. Pérez Galdós, "Observaciones sobre la novela contemporánea" (1870), in *Ensayos de crítica literaria*, p. 124.

5 Alas, "Del naturalismo," p. 140.

6 M. Wood, "The Art of Losing," *The New York Review of Books* (19 February 1999), p. 7.

7 Alas, "Del naturalismo," p. 140.

8 R. Jakobson, "The Metaphoric and Metonymic Poles," in *Critical Theory Since Plato*, ed. H. Adams (Irvine: University of California Press, 1971), p. 1115.

allusions. In Galdós's *Fortunata y Jacinta* (1886–7), the bird-egg motif becomes a dynamic element of structure,[9] as do less visible *menudencias*, ordinary, trifling objects like buttons, the staff of Saint Joseph, or a pair of harnessed mules, homely origin of the mercantile fortunes of the Santa Cruz–Arnaiz alliance.

The interplay of part and whole also requires disguises: narrator as character and vice versa; the illusions of shadows, alter egos, or imagined personae; the interplay of voices through monologue, dialogue, and the free indirect style. These are linguistic strategies that construct the dialogic or polyphonic novel. We find also the themes of masks, play-acting, and inset stories that inhabit, and thus alter, the very story that the narrator tells. Even the phenomenon of intertextuality, the multiple ways in which one text reflects or echoes or alludes to another text, may operate at once as an instance of the mimetic mirror and as a mask. This convergence is brilliantly developed, as we shall see, in chapter 16 of *La Regenta* in which Zorrilla's famous play *Don Juan Tenorio* (1844) is performed. As Lilian Furst notes, Stendhal himself toys with his own "concoction," that mirror walked along the road: "[W]ith his usual love of disguises, [he] ascribes it in the epigraph to chapter 13 of *Le rouge et le noir* to a seventeenth-century historian, Saint-Réal (that is, the saint of the real)."[10] The mirror itself is a disguise for the rhetoric of the realists to represent life as it "really" is.

In the novels of Galdós and Clarín, the contradictory, unstable nature of mirror images, depicting at once what is constant and what is variable, also forms part of the process of change itself. In *La Regenta*, Ana Ozores, acclaimed by the city of Vetusta as "la Regenta," sits alone at the table and contemplates the "ruins" of dinner: a coffee urn of burnished tin, a glass emptied of anisette, and a half-smoked cigar lying "impregnated" (II: 10) on a saucer, "its ash forming a repulsive paste with the slopped-over cold coffee" (Rutherford translation, p. 351).[11] In these "ruins" she sees the world and her husband, a man "unable to go through with either the smoking of a cigar or the loving of a woman" (ibid.). She sees herself orphaned, alone, living an expropriated existence as la Regenta, the wife of a retired magistrate who is

9 A. Moncy, "The Bird Motif and the Introductory Motif: Structure in *Fortunata y Jacinta*," *Anales Galdosianos* 9 (1974), pp. 51–75.

10 L. Furst, *"All is True": The Claims and Strategies of Realist Fiction* (Durham, NC: Duke University Press, 1995), p. 8.

11 Quotations come from *La Regenta*, edited and with an introduction by G. Sobejano, 2 vols. (Madrid: Castalia, 1981). The translations are my own except in cases when I give John Rutherford's translation (Athens, GA: University of Georgia Press, 1984), as indicated in parenthetical references in the text. In the case of *Fortunata y Jacinta*, quotations come from the edition by Francisco Caudet (Madrid: Cátedra, 1983). The translations from this novel and others by Galdós are my own.

no longer a *regente* and, in truth, no longer a "real" husband: "She, too, was like the cigar – something which had proved not to be of use to one man and could no longer be of use to any other" (ibid.). Realism as thing-ism, as real estate, as property, surfaces ironically in this scene as Ana, in the manner of a realist writer, records as through a glass darkly her desolate existence as an expropriated person, one who is, nonetheless, "owned" as a piece of property. She is a household "good" like the coffee urn, the saucer, the glass emptied of anisette, the "impregnated" half-smoked cigar. All is reversed in these mirror images of Ana's own narrated and lived "realist" novel: household goods in Vetusta are bad, degraded things: the coffee urn is of tin, a base metal, not pure silver; an impregnated, half-smoked cigar foretells the barrenness consequent upon union with an aging, impotent husband.[12]

In Galdós's *Fortunata y Jacinta*, which bears the mirror-like imprint of intertextual allusions to *La Regenta*,[13] the unfaithful lover and philandering husband, Juanito Santa Cruz, talks to his reflection in the mirror. "*We're really something*," he declares (I: 282), aware of his reflection as a kind of companion (a good-looking, verifiable alter ego) and of himself as a potent, plural entity. At the same time, of course, he is unaware that in that moment he also appears in Galdós's mimetic mirror as a dual *image*, not only of his times but also as the novel's supreme emblem of the mirror-like metaphoric process of substitution and replacement. At the very beginning of the novel, Juanito had expounded his theory about real and imaginary pork chops – how much better, he says, to taste the real thing rather than experience it vicariously as a text, as a realistic story described in every detail.

This self-reflexive gesture toward a theory of the novel *in* the novel points up a special irony. For if Juanito, ostensibly at the center of things and a catalyst for action, discards mistress for wife and vice versa, thinking of them as texts to be read and reread, he also appears in the realist mirror as a textual artifact: the narrator compares the workings of his mind to a serial novel, a French *folletín*, a snippet of scripted speech and the speech of an amateur actor in a melodrama. From the moment, then, that Juanito propounds his theory about fiction and reality, comparing the idea of *novelas* to that of real and imagined pork chops, he gestures unknowingly toward himself as precisely that textual "pork chop." He also surfaces as the novel's richest repository of metaphor because, like a magician or prestidigitator, like the reversals of a mirror image itself, Juanito never is *really* what he appears or claims to be.

12 G. Sobejano, "La inadaptada (Leopoldo Alas: *La Regenta*, capítulo XVI)," in *El comentario de textos*, ed. André Amorós (Madrid: Castalia, 1973), pp. 136, 149.

13 S. Gilman, *Galdós and the Art of the European Novel: 1867–1887* (Princeton University Press, 1981), pp. 154–86.

Thus we recognize both the inner logic and the suspect reality of his non-being when, at the end, he, too, appears "discarded" – like the women he seduced. He is simply another "text, set aside as something already too well known" (1: 285), used up and old before his time. The italicized declaration "*We're really something*," so visible an image, thus decodes as "*We're really nothing*." Now thing-ism, material substance, becomes exchanged for an invisible textual sign of emptiness. In the Spanish realist novel of the 1880s, then, uncertainty is more than a constant. It is the very muse that inspires the artistic and intellectual fascination with the unstable nature of the mimetic mirror, on the part of the characters and the narrator, of course, but also of the text itself. As the above scenes illustrate, mirror images exhibit what Lilian Furst has identified as the tension between the claims of referentiality, on the one hand, and those of textuality on the other. This tension becomes "the distinctive hallmark of the realist novel."[14]

Américo Castro, singling out the common Spanish expression *pasarle a uno algo*, which expresses the idea of who or how you *are* in terms of having something *happen* to you – literally, having something *pass through* you – pin-points that frictive, intermediate space where changes take place in a character's thinking or feeling. Castro applies the concept to *Don Quijote*, showing how outer circumstance and surroundings – one's living conditions – become an inner action that the mind keeps making. The unanticipated shifts from naming to doing thereby present what is real as the living rub of thinking and feeling. This in-between action surfaces as a kind of dramatic scene or *tableau*, located *in* the mind and pictured at the very moment when that mind comes into play with reality, the one changing the other as events become *personned* and persons become *evented*.[15]

Thus, as Castro is quick to note, the *Quijote* was manifestly the origin for Stendhal's *Le rouge et le noir* as it was, later in the century, for Clarín's two novels, *La Regenta* and *Su único hijo* (*His Only Son*, 1891), as well as, among others, Galdós's *La desheredada* (*The Disinherited Lady*, 1881) and *Fortunata y Jacinta*. One example from the *Quijote*, the famous episode of the *baci-yelmo* (basin-helmet), pointedly illustrates the process that Galdós and Clarín develop in their realist novels of the 1880s. For don Quijote – the idealist – the barber's basin mutates into the glorious helmet of the giant Mambrino, while for Sancho – the skeptic – such a "helmet" stubbornly

14 Furst, "*All is True*," p. 12.

15 Quotations from Américo Castro's essay on the *Quijote* come from *An Idea of History. Selected Essays of Américo Castro*, tr. S. Gilman and E. King (Columbus: Ohio State University Press, 1977), pp. 77–139. The relations of Castro's analysis of the influence of *Don Quijote* to European realism and to the discussion of Galdós's particular theory of realism are developed further in my book *Galdós, "Fortunata y Jacinta"* (Cambridge University Press, 1992).

persists as a lowly basin. However, once "passed through" the exchange of minds in dialogue, the object becomes both "personned" and "evented" to produce an entirely new thing – a *baci-yelmo* – the living compromise of a basin-helmet.

This "inner doing" of two particular minds in dialogue is what renders the *Quijote* a touchstone for nineteenth-century realism. As Galdós declared in an early essay (1870), Cervantes and Velázquez (1599–1660), court painter to King Philip IV, are the direct precursors of the "modern" contemporary social novel in Spain: each locates what is real in that magical operation of a mirrored verisimilitude encoded in the verb *parecer*, "to seem like," "to appear as." Thus Galdós writes:

> When we see something amazing, anomalous, extraordinary, we say it *seems like* a novel [...] [my italics]. On the other hand, when we read the great works of art that Cervantes produced [in his time] and that today Charles Dickens is writing, we exclaim: "How true to life this is! It seems like life itself, that we have [intimately] known such characters." People in love with Velázquez find his characters so familiar that they feel they have known them, dealt with them.[16]

So astonishing is this impression of life-likeness, of the life-liveliness, of these novels and paintings that the idea of art and artifice appears erased: we are seeing the "real thing."

Erasure, however, is a function of metaphor, the invisible persuasion of its secret argument that art and life are one and the same. In effect, the "quasi-metaphorical dimension"[17] of the realist aesthetic forms an essential component of the rhetoric that Galdós and Clarín employ to create in fiction an illusion of reality so that the reader will confuse the two, applying to life outside the book the values imaged within. Thus while fiction stands recognized – even flaunted – as artifice, we may construe fiction as reality, the way life is, an "image of life" as Galdós told the members of the Spanish Royal Academy in 1897 ("La sociedad presente," p. 220). In that address Galdós reminded his colleagues that fiction is real and unreal at the same time. The job of the novelist is to keep the balance between art and life, he advised, for in the art of the novel, defined as the "modern," "veridical" social novel of manners, "there should always exist that perfect point of balance between the exactness [*exactitud*] and the beauty [*belleza*] of the reproduction" (p. 220).

Here, in his address to the Academy, Galdós sketches out a kind of "equation" for realism, positioning what is known or factual – *exactitud* – in

[16] Galdós, "Observaciones sobre la novela contemporánea," p. 126.
[17] Furst, "*All is True*," p. 16.

relation to beauty – *belleza*, that is, invention, aesthetic design. What is "real" *happens*. It is a process of exchange and transformation taking place in the mind of narrator, character, and reader, and thus this "real thing" eludes words. It is not always susceptible to naming. Rather the "real thing" precipitates, as it were, from the conjunction, the consequence, of one term and the other, establishing a dialectical structure that involves the roles of narrator, character, and reader. This concept of a dialectical realism reiterates, on another level, those triangular structures so prominently featured in the plots of the Spanish realist novel.

These plots, arising, in the main, from adulterous relationships, offer, as Ricardo Gullón has observed, the spectacle of changing love triangles.[18] For example, in *La Regenta*, the most salient triangular groupings are the following: Ana, her husband don Víctor, and her confessor, the Magistral; Ana, her seducer don Álvaro, and the unknowing, impotent don Víctor. Don Víctor, disconcertingly feminized in his vulnerability and passion for his friend Frígilis (who had arranged the marriage with Ana), cluckingly construes Frígilis as Ana's competitor; however, soon Víctor transfers his affections to the actor Perales and later to don Álvaro himself, who – ever the strategic plotter – imagines the offended husband as an enclosure, a "game preserve" ripe for poaching. In this ironic and predatory way (Víctor is himself a hunter, an expert marksman), Álvaro construes this husband as a passive, vulnerable feminine persona, one to be hunted as he, Víctor, inhabits a space akin to Ana's virginal garden.

Triangles proliferate: Don Víctor, enamored now of Álvaro – a shameless, almost mechanistically "electric" lover – is unfaithful in his mind to both Frígilis and Ana. Ana, in turn, reluctantly keeps company with a treacherous friend, Visitación, who is none other than a former lover of don Álvaro and who attempts to seduce *him* into seducing Ana in Ana's name, as if she, Visitación, *were* Ana – naked, moaning, tumbling among bedclothes. Meanwhile Álvaro engages the Magistral in a grim contest for the love of Ana, now the priest's own "daughter" of confession. After Ana's adultery with Álvaro is discovered, a duel ensues: Don Víctor pardons his rival at the moment that Álvaro's bullet pierces his bladder, which, the narrator darkly notes, "was full" (II: 518). Don Víctor dies face down, scrabbling and chewing dirt, in the end an honorable man poisoned by his body and by the best part of himself.

In *Su único hijo* these adulterous triangles criss-cross and blur further, configuring ever stranger alliances: the viciously imaginative and sensual Emma,

[18] R. Gullón, "Estructura y diseño *en Fortunata y Jacinta*," in *Técnicas de Galdós* (Madrid: Taurus, 1970), pp. 154–86.

her soulful, hapless husband Bonifacio, and Serafina, the English-Italianate opera diva, form the basic threesome. This group shifts to Serafina, Mochi (her manipulative impresario), and Bonis, and then mutates again into the triangle of Emma, Minghetti, a baritone in the traveling opera company, and Bonis. Finally, in an unexpected twist – what the narrator calls a kind of "contagion" – Serafina and Emma appear to fuse, trading roles, affections, and behaviors in the face of a discarded Bonis, while the "expropriated" Bonis, once in possession of his only begotton son, triumphs in his imagination as "virgin, father, and mother" within the "priesthood of parenting" as he forms a new family with Emma.[19]

Changing triangular relationships, dividing and combining in almost infinite permutations, also articulate the action of Galdós's great novel of adultery, *Fortunata y Jacinta.* Here we find, in kaleidoscopic combinations, Fortunata, a woman of the people, who is seduced by Juanito, the "dauphin" or bourgeois "prince," only son and heir to the mercantile fortune of the Santa Cruz family. Juan abandons Fortunata to marry his first cousin, the pretty, darting Jacinta. Given over to prostitution, Fortunata meets the deformed, idealistic little Maxi Rubín, a member of the petty bourgeoisie. Urged by him to spend time in Las Micaelas, a convent established for the reform of wayward women, she agrees to Rubín's proposal of marriage. Shadowing this incongruous pair of newlyweds is that compulsive, ubiquitous seducer Juanito Santa Cruz, who now repeatedly betrays both wife and former mistress.

In Galdós's novel, as in *La Regenta*, love triangles transgress the boundaries of family, age, social class, and gender. Barbarita, obsessed with her only son Juanito, plans an incestuous marriage to Jacinta, her niece, seeing this niece already as a daughter-in law. In this way Jacinta becomes programmed, as it were, to replace her aunt and mother-in-law as "mother" to the only son in what will prove to be an overtly sterile marriage. For her part, Jacinta imagines a love relationship with Moreno-Isla, a wealthy banker allied to the Santa Cruz family who, in pressing his suit, dies – literally – of heartbreak. Aurora, former lover of Moreno-Isla and new lover of Juanito, betrays Fortunata, while Fortunata, having conceived a child on purpose in order to achieve the status of her rival, Jacinta, the legitimate wife, comes into contact with the militant Catholic social worker Guillermina Pacheco, aunt to Moreno-Isla. As the "first mother" of the new child and heir, Fortunata imagines momentarily a new, "feminist" family: herself as "la mamá primera," Jacinta, and Guillermina as second and third in a radically new, "holy" and "Trinitarian" family of women. It is an inclusive family, resting

[19] J. Oleza, "Introducción" to *Su único hijo* (Madrid: Cátedra, 1998), pp. 46–56.

not on the Way to Egypt but on the great stone stair where the initial encounter between Fortunata and Juanito took place. Finally there are the changing triangles of reconciliation: Fortunata, Jacinta, and the newborn child, delivered upon Fortunata's death to Jacinta, who, in turn, imagines the child, the only legitimate heir of the Santa Cruz family, as belonging to the elegant, impassioned expatriate Moreno-Isla.

Tracing the branching pathways of these triangular relationships illuminates further the implications of Galdós's and Clarín's ideas about realism in the Spanish contemporary social novel. The basic "equation" as formulated by Galdós in his address to the Spanish Royal Academy accomplishes two, overlapping artistic objectives: the equation is *itself* a metaphor, picturing scales in balance, while it *operates*, as does metaphor, by joining two terms to engender a new figure. Thus the "equation" as metaphor creates an aesthetic of "birth" that reflects, on still another level, the motif of birth and hope of regeneration that impels the plot of *Fortunata y Jacinta* to its ambivalent conclusion and which, conversely, points up the absence of life-giving birth in *La Regenta*: in Clarín's novel, the metaphoric mode signals an "improper birth,"[20] a "monstrous birth"[21] – deprivation, orphaning, and absence. Absence arises pictured, for example, in the comparison of the beautiful but childless Ana to Raphael's painting of "La Virgen de la Silla": unlike the Virgin, Ana's sweet, shadowed face only tilts toward emptiness, toward the place in her arms where a newborn child should have been.

A further consequence of the duality or dialectic built into the theory and practice of the Spanish realist novel is the linguistic and literary articulation of a dynamics of movement and change. For example, as in the case of changing triangles in *Fortunata y Jacinta*, the terms or poles of Galdós's basic "equation" keep altering in nature or, at the least, keep being relocated at greater or lesser removes from the social or individual person, thing, or event that emerges as a live entity, captured and held, as it were, between the changing relations of one pole to the other. At the same time, the "thing" itself – the *res*, the real – keeps coming into being at the interface, the point of contact between two phases or two surfaces: external, visible signs and those inner beliefs or forces or mechanisms that keep operating below. Fortunata herself comes to recognize the dynamics of this deeper structure, picturing it in her mind as the face and inner clockwork of a watch. The narrator, taking his cue from *her* figure of speech, *realizes* through that self-same metaphor

20 N. Valis, "Aspects of an Improper Birth: Clarín's *La Regenta*," in *New Hispanisms: Literature, Culture, Theory*, ed. M. Millington and P. Julian Smith (Ottawa: Dovehouse Editions, 1994), pp. 96–126.

21 N. Valis, "On Monstrous Birth: Leopoldo Alas's *La Regenta*," in *Naturalism in the European Novel*, ed. Brian Nelson (New York: Bergo, 1992), pp. 191–209.

the conflictive fact of visible surfaces and invisible depths. Reflecting upon the spectacle of the exquisitely engineered, *real* event of the reconciliation of Fortunata's ill-fated marriage to Maxi, he slyly – ironically – confides to the reader: "It was one of those things that just happens, without anyone's knowing how or why [...]; for while one can sense these things coming, one simply can't see the hidden mechanisms that bring them to pass" (II: 162).

In several novels of the 1880s Galdós invents a kind of narrator-character who appears only to relate what he sees or hears, acting in the story as a reliable witness but in a somewhat distracted way. In *La de Bringas* (*That Bringas Woman*, 1884), as he, a small-time administrator, dozes during a gathering of friends, doña Cándida must rap him to attention, flicking his knee with the tip of her fan and repeating for his sluggish ear the words of a rather boring conversation. On other occasions, everything appears to pass through his mind effortlessly, and in this we discern, even in his distractions, a certain quality of transparency, a kind of porosity, about his sensibility. Galdós, recast as storyteller, seems to absorb vital essences and expel them as novels in the manner of a man breathing or, as Clarín once noted, of a man sipping a glass of water.[22] In his biographical essay on Galdós (1889), Clarín sums up the case: "Galdós is best at writing when he's not even aware of what he is doing and when the reader is no longer conscious of a presence mediating between the author's ideas and his own."[23] Clarín the critic has seized precisely on the parallel between the way Galdós writes a novel and the way his fictional characters cock an ear to gossip or whisper their stories as news, as *novelas*.

For his part, Clarín, a novelist possessed of an impassioned temperament and a fierce, biting intellect, also creates the *persona* of an ambivalent narrator but to very different effect. Apparently omniscient, focusing from on high, in *La Regenta* the narrator also steps into the story but in an oblique, shifting, winking manner. While ostensibly raised above the viscissitudes of Vetusta, a city contemplated as a blackened heap of stones sequestered in the rainy, dreary province of Asturias, the narrator not only moves into the minds of the characters: he jostles their elbows, peers into their dressing rooms, anticipates their speech, and cracks jokes at their expense. The very proteic nature of this narrator, at once reliable and controlling, at once absent and punishing, qualifies him as someone who participates in the suffering consciousness of his characters at the moment when he abandons them to that suffering.

[22] *Cartas a Galdós*, presentadas por Soledad Ortega (Madrid: Revista de Occidente, 1964), p. 249.

[23] L. Alas, *B. Pérez Galdós* (Madrid: Fernando Fe, 1889), p. 32.

Thus the *persona* of the narrator in *La Regenta* sketches out a disquieting resemblance to the very inhabitants of Vetusta who have become, from the outset, the target of his omniscient, critical, ironic gaze. Faced with such a mercurial, winking narrative presence, as readers we not only become "accomplices" in the telling of the story;[24] we are enjoined further to question the reliability of this apparently all-seeing narrator. To what degree is he, like the Magistral (Anna's confessor), or Don Álvaro (Ana's seducer), a voyeur and stage manager? Does he see too much, tell too often, and distort the outlines of characters' thought and behavior, enacting unawares a kind of betrayal of his own novelistic world? Does Clarinian irony become ironic about itself? Lou Charnon-Deutsch poses this troubling reassessment of the role and character of the voyeuristic narrator in *La Regenta*, arguing, in effect, that this narrator's all-seeing eye provides "a map of many men's fantasies."[25] The narrator's eye appears to participate in the very masculine machine of Vetusta that he himself so confidently criticizes.[26] At the same time Clarín, in this particular guise as author-narrator, keeps reflecting the action from an ever-widening range of perspectives. His is a singularly mobile, composite eye that *enacts in and of itself* the ironic interplay of satiric critique and confessional feeling that defines his point of view. His perspective as narrator alternately closes in and steps away, finally collapsing into the world view of his characters to shape one, interminably bleak, unredeemable image of perdition: the kiss that Ana, falling in a faint, feels smeared upon her lips as if that kiss were "the viscous belly of a toad" (II: 537).

In *La Regenta*, the spectacle of this errant collapse into one dissolving image of suffering and nausea reframes and expands the fundamental principle of mimesis upon which the Spanish realist novel is based. Within this expansion Clarín exploits further the literary strategies of mimetic realism while at the same time he illuminates that basic link, first established in Aristotle's *Poetics*, between imitation and knowledge. For in the case of *La Regenta*, the concept of imitation does not only refer to the ideas and practices of literary realism. In the story of Ana Ozores, imitation itself operates as a two-fold, defining mode of action, thought, and feeling. Corresponding to the division that Emilio Alarcos marks within the highly symmetrical structure of *La Regenta*,[27] forms of imitation may be said to be either "presentative"

24 J. Rutherford, *"La Regenta" y el lector cómplice* (Murcia: Universidad de Murcia, 1988).

25 L. Charnon-Deutsch, "Voyeurism, Pornography and *La Regenta*," *Modern Language Studies* 4 (Fall 1989), p. 101.

26 H. Turner, "From the Verbal to the Visual in *La Regenta*," in *"Malevolent Insemination" and Other Essays on Clarín*, ed. N. Valis (Ann Arbor: Michigan Romance Studies, 1990), p. 73.

27 E. Alarcos Llorach, "Notas a *La Regenta*," in *Clarín y La Regenta*, ed. S. Beser (Barcelona: Ariel, 1982), pp. 225–45.

(mirror-like posturings, servile, aping behaviors in dress, speech, or thought) or "active" (a performative mode that seeks to discover truth in representation). Chapter 16, the numerical mid-point of the novel, offers the spectacle of the convergence of these two forms of imitation, mimesis and mask, as, in turn, these occur within a metafictive, intertextual frame provided by Zorrilla's famous play *Don Juan Tenorio* (1844).

Chapter 16 opens, as we have seen, with Ana contemplating the "ruins" of her life. From this desolate reality, which she, in the manner of a realist writer, has represented to herself, Ana moves to the balcony at the moment that Don Álvaro appears below, riding a pirouetting white horse. A conversation ensues, Ana "falling into a well" of feeling as Álvaro plans his seduction, even an assault, proposing to take advantage of what he cynically construes as Ana's critical "fifteen minutes" of submission. The scene sketches an oblique allusion to the moment in *Don Juan Tenorio* when don Juan approaches the balcony of doña Ana de Pantoja. The mimetic imprint of this intertexual allusion frames and foretells the seduction that will take place also on a balcony – that ubiquitous, intermediate space – toward the close of Clarín's novel.

Now Ana, tagged by the narrator as "Doña Ana," attends the performance of *Don Juan Tenorio* and begins to participate in the play. She interprets – relives – character, scene, and setting as poetry, that is, as true-to-life images: the convent is her own cloistered existence; the cell, her empty house; the regimen, the rule of Vetusta; the Comendador, her aging, fatherly husband. Don Álvaro, seated behind her, is, of course, don Juan, although, at this very moment, even he, "el Tenorio vetustense" (II: 49), sees himself "debenched" by a powerful fictional rival. All he can do is strive for a fairly creditable "presentative" imitation, that is, to "play the part of the secret sentimentalist like the ones in Feuillet's plays and novels," thereby to conjure before Ana's impassioned eyes that indispensable "mirage of visionary enthusiasm" (Rutherford, p. 377). Most tellingly, however, Ana sees doña Inés as... none other than herself: "Ana shuddered when she saw Doña Inés in her cell. The novice looked so like her! As Ana noticed the resemblance so did the audience – there was a murmur of admiration, and many spectators ventured to take a look at Vegallana's box." (Rutherford, p. 376). Further, in still another convergence of the real and the poetic, the actress playing the part of doña Inés is, in real life, the wife of the actor Perales who plays the role of don Juan. Thus Doña Inés infuses her recitations with real feeling – "pasión cierta" – thereby achieving a "poetic realism" (II: 47) that, among actors and audience, only doña Ana and the narrator himself are capable of appreciating. Appreciating, in this context, means recognizing true value of a "poetic" realist art.

In this redoubled mimetic scene Ana, "drinking in" the poetry of *Don Juan Tenorio*, performs an act of imitation that allows her to come into knowledge. In that knowledge she enacts Aristotle's aesthetic concept of mimesis as a living event. It does not matter that Ana leaves the theater before the last act, or that she perceives the play's duel and pistol-shot as signs that foretell the eventual duel between her husband and don Álvaro. What matters in the scene is that Ana, through her imitative performance and dramatic moment of recognition, does not faint, does not lose her grip on reality, does not evade the "poetic" truth of what she sees. Upon returning home, she does not flee even from the impositions of another "incendiary letter" that recalls the famous "carta incentiva" of *Don Juan Tenorio*. This version of don Juan's letter is sent the next morning by Ana's confessor, the possessive don Fermín, who in this letter gestures as yet another donjuanesque figure. Within the convergence of the dual form of imitation, both "presentative" and "active" in expression, overt and covert, negative and positive in value, Ana and her story emerge as a living, tragic representation of a concept of mimesis both classical and modern, one that turns on the question of knowledge and its relation to the spectacle of literature lived as life and vice versa.

In this way, alert to that basic quixotic phenomenon of "enchantment," of transforming one person or thing into another, Galdós and Clarín exploit the possibilities of mimesis to question whether or not imitation leads to knowledge. Further, their novels question whether or not knowledge itself is possible, and, if so, how and why knowing takes place and whether what people know can reach beyond their own minds. The trajectory of their novelistic production articulates this increased focus on questioning. Galdós is the author of 77 novels, 26 plays, some short fiction and occasional pieces, essays, and journalistic writings. Clarín produced two major novels, with the second, *Su único hijo*, conceived as part of an unfinished *Sinfonía de dos novelas* ('Two Novels as a Symphony') that included "Una medianía" ('A Dull, Average Person'), consisting of seven chapters published serially in 1889. He also authored two chapters in a collaborative novel (*Las vírgenes locas* ['Crazy Virgins', 1886]), several volumes of short stories and novelettes, two plays (one published posthumously) and a biography of Galdós, as well as books of literary criticism and a voluminous quantity of essays and articles. Through this production, which established a lively dialogue between them, each author came to inquire more and more about the shaping or conditioning effects of "enchantment," of belief, perception, the will, and other invisible, "latent" presences, Clarín's word for the subconscious or the unconscious.

The term "unconscious" (*inconsciente*) began to appear with some frequency in the latter decades of the century and certainly before Freud. This term initiated the nineteenth-century reader into a perception of those unnamed, shadowy forces and fusions that gesticulate below the surfaces, as it were, of the realist novel. In consequence, recognition of the conscious and unconscious parts of the mind caused a readjustment in thinking about the nature and boundaries of texts and things. In Europe, nineteenth-century writers came to display this readjustment through a kind of self-reflexive perspectivism: the depiction, within a story or picture or novel or newspaper article, of the act of writing, painting, or creating that particular work. For example, Alexander Pushkin's narrative poem *The Bronze Horseman*, written in 1833 but published only posthumously in 1839, is manifestly based on fact. An advisory note carries this statement: "The incident described in this story is based on fact. The details of the flood are borrowed from newspapers of the time."[28] Yet when introducing the hero, "Young Evgeny," Pushkin breaks the mimetic mirror by inscribing a provocative instance of self-referentiality: "My rhyme / Selects this name to use in speaking of our young hero. It's a sound / I like; my pen has long been bound / in some way with it; further naming is not required [...]" (300). Pushkin's poem calls attention to itself as a linguistic artifact. This instance of self-reflexivity resembles similar moments in the *Quijote* or *Las meninas* (1656), in which the painter Velázquez paints himself painting at the same time as he reflects the dual subject of that painting – the little princess Margarita and her maids (*meninas*), facing the king and queen, whose "portrait" appears in the mirror on the back wall. Thus *Las meninas* takes a turn to reflect within itself the creative process of painting, as the *Quijote* does of writing, putting to question the idea of origins and of identity.

Such instances almost become an artistic norm in nineteenth-century Spain. As pointed up in the final chapter of this volume, the journalistic writings of Mariano José de Larra (1809–1837) are, in essence, self-reflexive compositions. In his guise as "Fígaro," Larra acts simultaneously as narrator and character, evolving through the dialogic structures of his texts simultaneously to picture, represent roles, and criticize those representations and performances. The slips and circularities of a regional novel like Valera's *Pepita Jiménez* (1874) eventually show how Valera's own omniscient narrative *persona* enacts unknowingly the Latin motto *Nescit labi virtus* ("Virtue ignores the possibility of sliding/gliding down"), which is meant to apply to his fictional character, the young, inexperienced don Luis de Vargas. In fact, this narrative *persona* also "slips down" to become subject to the same ironic critique that he has brought to bear on his protagonist. In this way, the author

[28] A. Pushkin, "The Bronze Horseman," in Wacław Lednicki, *Pushkin's Bronze Horseman. The Story of a Masterpiece* (Berkeley: University of California Press, 1955), p. 297.

as narrator invokes the kind of irony that had enlivened Fígaro's conduct in Larra's famous sketch "El castellano viejo" ('A Castillian of the Old Order', 1832). For in *Pepita Jiménez*, the "slips" of an omniscient narrator, one who declares himself to be "perfectly knowledgeable about everything,"[29] deconstruct mimesis and its link to secure knowledge. Further, the reflection of the narrator's preferences in those of the young, inexperienced Luis subverts the reliability of this narrator's omniscience, calling into question the validity of his own views, even of his identity as the teller of the tale.

Galdós and Clarín, dramatized variously in their novels as narrator-characters, also act out the impressive, confounded truths of their writings to depict on occasion when and how a novel comes into being. An intriguing case is that of Feijoo, a character in *Fortunata y Jacinta*, often perceived as an alter ego of Galdós. Feijoo's teachings in the ways of the world aim to reform Fortunata and thus offer, as an instance of the Pygmalion theme, a reflection of the act of artistic creation.[30] Another instance refers to the genesis of *Fortunata y Jacinta*. In his *Memorias* ('Memoirs', 1916), Galdós tells how, in the waning days of summer, he returns to Madrid, only to find at the door his friend and fellow novelist, don José Ido del Sagrario. Ido, bursting with the latest news, tells of the novel's characters, abandoned by their author over the summer. These characters appear to be reinvented by Ido, who is himself a fictional character and also a novelist, a hack writer of *folletines*. As such he "wanders" from novel to novel (his name literally means "gone from the sanctuary"). Now fictional people like Ido reflect the role of the novelist who carries his mirror to the streets. They move Galdós to action: *he* rambles through old Madrid, waving, talking, observing, listening, *copying*: here, Galdós says, is José Luengo, stall holder in the Plaza Mayor, a man who is the spitting image of parrot-faced Estupiña, a social type so faithfully rendered in *Fortunata y Jacinta* that no description is warranted. We have seen him already as the man really is.[31]

The scene presents Galdós and Ido – two friends, two novelists, two stories: each reflects the other not only to confound our notion of what is real but to make us relive the making of those stories. Galdós restarts a novel that contains Ido's own novel, patently false because it is both fictional and invented, about the child that Jacinta tries to adopt at the close of Part I. At the close of Part IV, however, that child has become a real, living person who reconciles Fortunata to Jacinta. Further, in the wake of Fortunata's funeral,

[29] J. Valera, *Pepita Jiménez*, ed. María del Pilar Palomo (Barcelona: Planeta, 1987), p. 79.

[30] J. W. Kronik, "Galdosian Reflections: Feijoo's Fabrication of Fortunata," *Modern Language Notes* 97 (1982), pp. 272–310.

[31] B. Pérez Galdós, "Memorias de un desmemoriado," in *Obras completas*, ed. F. Carlos Robles, 6 vols. (Madrid: Aguilar, 1966), vol. VI, p. 1652.

the pharmacist Ballester, who likes to talk about the realist aesthetic, proposes to his friend, the literary critic Ponce, that Fortunata's life be recreated as either a play or a novel. In this work the writer would mix, in appropriate measures, fact ("raw fruit") and fiction ("stewed fruit": II: 535).[32]

Such instances of self-referential perspectivism abound in Galdós's contemporary social novels as well as in his novels of historical fiction, the *Episodios nacionales*. For example, in his first novel, *La sombra* (*The Shadow*, 1870), Galdós as narrator-recorder leaves the scene half-persuaded of the reality of a hallucination suffered by the protagonist, don Anselmo, who has recounted to him, the narrator, in the manner of a confession, the various episodes that had determined his, Anselmo's, mental illness. The narrator becomes the shadow (*sombra*) of his own fictional character who, in turn, lives obsessed by *his* shadow, a multiple identity of Paris / Alejandro X***, pictured variously as the painting of the myth of Paris, Helen, and the Trojan War, and as a reenactment of another story: don Anselmo relives, as it were, the impertinence of the jealous husband Anselmo, protagonist of an interpolated story in the *Quijote* (*El curioso impertinente*). Don Anselmo also exists as a collective social construct: his jealousy and delusional behavior are driven by stories that a sick society maliciously fabricates to torment him. The version of the lover Paris in the person of Alejandro X*** is a gossipy tale cooked up to provoke Anselmo's fears about his wife Elena's – Helen's – infidelity.

Even an early, so-called "thesis" novel like *Doña Perfecta* (1876), which argues for progress in the face of religious fanaticism and social prejudice, offers the ambivalence of language usage as a theme. The narrator's attention to allegorical signs and speech, forms of word play and puns, lies and verbal "spin," and to intertextual references (e.g. *Don Juan Tenorio*) builds into the novel a self-referential critique of the written and spoken word. At the same time, the narrator keeps referring to allegory, image, and sign as indispensable tools for telling the story. Language as a means of communication is thrown into doubt, causing the enterprise of novel making to become the instrument of its own meditation.

La desheredada (1881), which initiates Galdós's "second style," is manifestly the most Quixotic of his novels. The story of Isidora Rufete, who in the manner of a popular serial novel sees herself as a changeling and rightful heiress to the fortunes and title of the Marquise of Aransis, dramatically reenacts the conflict between fact and fiction. Intertextual allusions to the *Quijote* and to the process of making a novel propel the plot forward as a kind of detective story aimed at discovering who or what is responsible for

[32] Moncy, "The Bird Motif and the Introductory Motif," p. 53.

Isidora's delusions. Now the literary technique of constructing a palimpsest of texts expands the horizons of the novel. The story of noble birth concocted by Isidora's father has contaminated the imagination of her Quixotic uncle, don Santiago Quijano, a rural priest from Tomelloso, a place somewhere in La Mancha; thus do Isidora's origins echo obliquely the famous opening words of *Don Quijote*. Santiago Quijano, in a series of letters and documents, writes up fiction as truth, laying the ground for Isidora's "novel" of noble birth. At the same time, that very fiction (a "deplorable comedy": VI: 1141) is actually powered by a vital truth: a person's desire "to be somebody" in a reified world, even "if only for ten minutes. We who are nothing fall prey to such dangers" (VI: 1150), murmurs Isidora's godfather, now an alcoholic, half-mad for her attentions, and who pathetically – incestuously – proposes marriage to save her from prostitution.

In the telling of the palimpsest of Isidora's story, scientific views appear to prevail over illusion, reason over passion, and the claims of modest obscurity, sanctioned feminine roles, and household thrift over romance, beauty, artistic insight and its degraded form as a brilliant kind of consumerism. And yet Isidora's extraordinary, even insane powers of imagination on occasion almost "de-bench" masculine reason, exercised in the person of the doctor, Augusto Miquis – fittingly, a name denoting things both large and small – and in the authorial control of the narrator. Miquis comes from Toboso, the town of Dulcinea in the *Quijote*, and at times he inadvertently plays the role of Sancho to Isidora's Quixotic illusions. Yet both Miquis and the narrator fall under Isidora's spell, registering loss and missed opportunities even as they show how Isidora, gripped by her conviction that she *is* somebody, inevitably slips into degradation. *La desheredada* becomes both a referential and textual enigma of disenchantment and disinheritance, at the same time gesturing as a realistic symbol of the Spanish state itself.

Autobiographical eyewitness narration in *El amigo Manso* (*Our Friend Manso*, 1882) represents another experiment in the riddles of literary self-reflexivity. Galdós depicts himself as a hack writer who "buys" a story from his character, Máximo Manso. Thus the act of telling that story evolves through a re-framed narrative structure, a metafictive set-up in which Manso's interpolated story alternates with his declaration that he doesn't exist, that he is a fictional being, born from an inkwell. He himself brings meaning into being as he weaves and unweaves the text, reminding us that he, too, is a reader, inside and outside his own story. In this exchange of roles, identities, and destinies of author, character, and reader, *El amigo Manso* anticipates Unamuno's *Niebla* (*Mist*, 1914), an almost post-modern narrative experiment that blurs the boundaries between fiction and reality.

Later novels like *La incógnita* (*The Unknown*, 1888–9) and *Realidad* (*Reality*, 1889) capture an interrelated series of letters and dialogue, both veridical and illusory as Galdós construes the reader–writer relationship as part of the plot. *Realidad* does not only represent the reworking of the text of *La incógnita*.[33] The epistolary relationship of the enigmatic Equis, a quasi-parental figure, and Manuel Infante, a younger man, even child-like in his flawed use of words (*infante*, from *infans*, "without speech"), together "raise up" a new "family" member – a pair of novels that, like Siamese twins, depend vitally upon each other for existence. In turn, their complementarity sketches a metafictive model for the acts of reading and writing as Equis ("X"), the internal reader, completes the verbal potentiality of Infante's text by filling in its gaps – the *incógnitas*.[34] In their symbiotic relationship, *La incógnita* and *Realidad* actually reinvent the staples of realism: the focus on family alliances, recurring characters, physical and psychological clues, and the gaps produced by unconscious motivations as these become *passed through* the structures and plots of detective fiction, newspaper articles, and popular serial novels.

In this way, as Linda Willem notes, Galdós accomplishes the transformation of a part into a whole, that is, a "half" of something into whole, living thing ("el ser completo y vivo"), a whole at once more than and different from the sum of its parts ("Turning *La incógnita*," 389). *Misericordia* (*Compassion*, 1897), seen as Galdós's "last word" for realism, is a novel in which social documentation underlies the theme of charity.[35] *Misericordia* also records the experience of one Benina who dreams up a fictional character who becomes real. Her creation of a character shadows Galdós's creation of herself as the protagonist of the novel. At the same time, as Nicholas Round argues, "in the dialogue which Galdós as maker and shaper of his text carries on with his readers, one ever-present element is a questioning of the simpler perspectives on offer: do we really know what we think we know? Can we safely judge as we think ourselves entitled to judge?" ("*Misericordia*," p. 156).

Such basic questions inhere, as we have seen, in Clarín's artistic expansion and critique of the concept of mimesis, which, in *La Regenta*, encompasses glancing hints of self-referentiality. One example occurs toward the end of the novel. Shocked by the scandal that the city's own gossip and strategic plotting have so viciously concocted, Vetusta reflects upon Ana's adultery,

33 Willem, "Turning *La incógnita* into *Realidad*: Galdós's Metafictional Magic Trick," *Modern Language Notes* 105 (1990), p. 389.

34 Ibid., p. 389.

35 N. Round, "*Misericordia*: Galdosian Realism's 'Last Word'," in *A Sesquicentennial Tribute to Galdós 1843–1993*, ed. L. Willem (Newark, DE: Juan de la Cuesta, 1993), p. 156.

the duel and death of Víctor, the evasion of don Álvaro, the murderous rage of the Magistral "as if [such a scandal] were a novel" (II: 535). The interplay of imaginative and physical acts of procreation in *Su único hijo* further tilt Clarín's realist and naturalist novel toward modernism. As author he passes the phenomenon of self-referentiality through the fitfully exalted but meticulously realized paradoxes of tradition, perversity, and the reality of willed belief. These converging and diverging mixtures articulate the "family romance" of Emma, Bonis, and the newborn child.[36] Thus the shadowed, quasi-visible figures of the late Spanish realist novel, as illustrated by *La incógnita*, *Realidad*, and *Su único hijo*, come also to resemble, in their way, the "spectra" inhabiting James's famous story *The Turn of the Screw* (1898) or the "ghost" that haunts Fontane's novel of adultery, *Effi Briest* (1895).

Américo Castro's seminal insight (1960) about the basic shift in artistic representation in *Don Quijote* provides the key to understanding how the realists created and maintained the art of illusion in a reified world. All told, this is a deeply disquieting, unstable world of things, old and new, arising within the flux of civil and foreign wars and radical economic, social, and political changes. Rapid change, ushering in the fear of the unknown, as well as a nascent confidence in progress, redefined nineteenth-century daily life, especially in Spain, given the context of her uneven, imperfect transition to modernity.[37] Further, Jo Labanyi argues that the shift from a mimesis of things to a mimesis of perception is "linked inextricably to the rise of mercantilism," to paper money and credit.[38] Now what is real is merely (really) a representation, a piece of fiction in a manner similar to the relationship of paper money to coins and bars of gold. She suggests also that "this major shift in the European world view had its origins in the sixteenth-century Spanish discourse on inflation" (*Gender and Modernization*, p. 390), for inflation destroyed the notion that signs have a stable referent (p. 387).

There is little doubt that mercantile, monetary links between the 1600s and the 1800s do form another, albeit elusive, parallel between, on the one hand, the works of Cervantes and Velázquez and, on the other, the nineteenth-century Spanish realist novel. The parallel pivots, in part, upon self-reflexivity. In Part II of the *Quijote*, don Quijote and Sancho read about their adventures in a published version of Part I. They reflect and comment upon the truth-value of those images in fiction. Further, the very genesis of their story, arising from the translation by a Morisco of a manuscript

36 Oleza, "Introducción," pp. 46–56.

37 S. Sieburth, *Inventing High and Low. Literature, Mass Culture, and Uneven Modernity in Spain* (Durham, NC: Duke University Press, 1994).

38 J. Labanyi, *Gender and Modernization in the Spanish Realist Novel* (Oxford University Press, 2000), p. 390.

in Arabic by a certain shadowy Cide Hamete Benengeli, a punning name that combines the notion of Castilian epic valor (*Poema del Cid*) and Arabic horticulture ("eggplant"), establishes from the outset how the *Quijote*, like *Hamlet*, contains concocted mirror images of itself. Similarly, as we have seen in *Las meninas*, Velázquez's mirror contains the image of himself painting as it does the apparent subject of that painting – the faces of the king and queen. At the same time, the picture we see most vividly is of the little princess Margarita, at play with *las meninas*. Thus the painting proposes intersecting images of subject and object that blur the boundaries, spatial and pictorial, between art and life.

The works of these masters, visibly accessible not merely as influences but as active agents of the artistic imagination, engaged nineteenth-century writers in Spain to exploit the metafictive phenomenon of self-reflexivity. They fused, in a single text, social critique, a theory of representation, and a reproduction, faithfully mirrored, of the mores, costumes, objects, actions, beliefs, and rites of their times. Jo Labanyi finds such self-reflexivity to be the defining feature of the Spanish realist novel. Self-reflexive perspectivism, already built into the fundamental dualities of realism, leads to an expanded definition of realism as "the representation of a reality constituted by exchange relations" (*Gender and Modernization*, p. 392). These relations have responded to the impact of complex forms of monetary and political representation upon which consumer capitalism and a liberal democracy depended in nineteenth-century Spain (p. 386).

In this way, the concept of the mimetic mirror once again bridges the gap between reality and representation by collapsing, in Labanyi's words, "the two into a single entity; that is, a reality constituted by representation" (p. 385). What is real is *passed through* a national or individual consciousness to become represented in the abstractions and instabilities of paper money and political agendas. Thus we find, particularly in the novels of Galdós and Clarín, a reinvented notion of the Quixotic: people inevitably become, in part, the images they make for themselves. It is this perception about human behavior that each writer captures as they mirror the uncertainties of the economic, political, and social life of their times. While the question of dualism, of image and reality persists unresolved in theory, it is ever alive in the mediation that takes place between text and world in the nineteenth-century Spanish realist novel.

Guide to further reading

Gold, Hazel, *Reframing Realism* (Durham, NC: Duke University Press, 1993).

Ribbans, Geoffrey, *Conflicts and Conciliations. The Evolution of Galdós's "Fortunata y Jacinta"* (Lafayette: Purdue University Press, 1997).

Rutherford, John, *Leopoldo Alas, "La Regenta."* Critical Guides to Spanish Texts (London: Grant and Cutler, 1974).
Sieburth, Stephanie, *Reading "La Regenta." Duplicitous Discourse and the Entropy of Structure* (Amsterdam: John Benjamins, 1990).
Sobejano, Gonzalo, *Clarín en su obra ejemplar* (Madrid: Castalia, 1985).
Urey, Diane, *Galdós and the Irony of Language* (New York: Cambridge University Press, 1982).
Valis, Noël M., *The Decadent Vision in Leopoldo Alas* (Baton Rouge: Louisiana State University Press, 1981).
Willem, Linda. *Galdós's Segunda Manera* (Chapel Hill: North Carolina Studies in the Romance Languages and Literatures, 1998).

7

GEOFFREY RIBBANS

History and fiction

The nineteenth-century realist novel is in general founded on a bedrock of history. The status of history as the modern scientifically based humanism was largely unchallenged at the middle of the century and little doubt was entertained about the finality and accuracy of historical knowledge, "as it actually happened," in Leopold von Ranke's words. Similarly, the accuracy and reliability of the mimetic procedures of fiction tended to be taken for granted: the novel's purpose, it was thought, was to reflect objective reality precisely, and it was to be judged by its success in accomplishing this aim. Clearly, there are important reservations to be made concerning this forthright and confident approach. First, it is evidently not shared by modern theorists like Hayden White, who react sharply against concepts of historical certainty and even against the relevance of history in general (Roland Barthes).[1] Second, in their practice novelists were by no means fully observant of these norms.

It follows, nonetheless, that history – viewed as the objective reality of the past – plays, from the socially based novels of Balzac onwards, a vital role in the portrayal of the present in the contemporary novel. Lukács is correct in establishing a direct link between Sir Walter Scott's historical novels and Balzac's *Comédie humaine*.[2] In fact, in Spain it would be broadly true to say that imitation of Scott's much-admired model divided into two divergent directions, corresponding to the Romantic, exotic, or *costumbrista* side and the realist side of his achievement respectively. The first gave rise to the proliferation of Romantic historical novels like *El doncel de don Enrique el doliente* ('Henry the Infirm's Page', 1834) and *El señor de Bembibre* ('The Lord of Bembibre', 1844), the second to the near-contemporary realistic

[1] See, for example, Hayden White, *The Content of the Form: Narrative Discourse and Historical Representation* (Baltimore: Johns Hopkins University Press, 1987) and Roland Barthes, "The Discourse of History," in *Comparative Criticism: A Yearbook*, vol. III, ed. E. S. Schaffer (Cambridge University Press, 1981), pp. 3–20.

[2] G. Lukács, *The Historical Novel* (Harmondsworth: Penguin, 1969), pp. 34–5.

development in Balzac, which entered, or reentered, Spain with Benito Pérez Galdós (1843–1920) and his contemporaries. In one of the most substantial of his rather meager pieces of critical writing, his prologue to Clarín's *La Regenta*, Galdós links naturalism, a substantial bone of contention at the time, with the Spanish picaresque and Cervantine tradition of a "humorous quality which was perhaps the race's most brilliant attribute." He sees the course of the novel as "a circular current like the gulf-stream [which] brought more heat and less delicacy and wit" as it makes its way onward, incorporating English humor and French analytical skill. The revived Spanish novel has regained, he declares, the "art of being natural with a felicitous harmony between the serious and the comic."[3] Such an emphasis on indigenous humor (a sly type of humor: *socarronería*), attenuates, we should observe, the solemn note of the historical realism we are discussing.

Historicity in its broadest sense is, then, intrinsic to the realist novel as formulated and practiced by Galdós, the pivotal figure in any discussion of the issue. The type of historical narrative he is concerned with deals with events not too distant from the present. In speaking of historical novels, in fact, it is important to distinguish between those concerned, like *Salammbô* or *The Last Days of Pompeii*, with the remote, potentially exotic, past, which have little direct relevance to the contemporary situation, and those which treat of the immediate past. "'Tis Sixty Years," the subtitle of Scott's *Waverley*, provides an excellent example of an effort to assess in fictional form the lasting influence of a decisive event two generations earlier – the Jacobite defeat – on contemporary Scotland.

Thus Galdós commenced his novelistic career with historical novels of immediate relevance (*La fontana de oro* [*The Golden Fountain Café*, 1867–8], *El audaz* ['A Daring Man', 1871] even though an enduring note of fantasy is struck up in *La sombra* [*The Shadow*, 1870]). At the same time, this approach also embraces a concern with continuous social development and mobility, with the result that, in his programmatic "Observations on the Contemporary Novel in Spain" (1870), he singles out the rising urban middle class as "the great model, the inexhaustible source" for fiction.[4]

In establishing around 1870 his criteria for an analysis of past and present, Galdós seems to have felt a need to separate two somewhat disparate objectives. One is to trace in detail events of the not too distant but not immediate past, "memory at one remove," in Tillotson's phrase,[5] in order to explain

[3] B. Pérez Galdós, *Ensayos de crítica literaria*, ed. L. Bonet, 2nd edn (Barcelona: Península, 1990), pp. 198–9.

[4] Ibid., p. 112.

[5] K. Tillotson, *Novels of the Eighteen-Forties* (Oxford University Press, 1954), p. 99.

present circumstances; the other to take near-contemporary subjects, of more direct relevance, and show the inherent social conflicts within them. Hence, the creation of a new form, the *episodio nacional* ('national episode') to tackle the first, and the writing of the *novelas contemporáneas de la primera época* ('contemporary novels of the first period') for the second. While the first impulse, which quickly gained him popularity and income, gave rise to a rapid production of twenty narratives covering the periods 1805 to 1824 (first series) and 1824 to 1834 (second series), the second conception yielded, at the same time as the initial undertaking of writing historical chronicles was completed, to the more complex and objective representation found, from 1881 onwards, in the full *novelas contemporáneas*.

Later, at a time when the essential thrust of his great contemporary novels was spent, in 1898, came a renewal of the writing of *episodios nacionales*, giving rise to three more series (the fifth incomplete, with only six narrations, the last one in 1912), chronicling the events from the First Carlist War (1834–40), through the reign of Isabella II and the revolutionary period (1868–74) until the Restoration of 1874/75. The *episodios nacionales* and the *novelas contemporáneas*, though obviously closely interrelated, have very different points of emphasis, and should by no means be taken, as they sometimes are, to be identical. As we shall see in what follows, the differences between them cast light on their divergent objectives.

In the novels individual historical events are used, frequently but not in any systematic fashion, to provide a kind of factual stiffening – which is more than just background – for selected fictional occurrences, to indicate parallels between private and public behavior, and to broaden characterization. Political figures and events from both the present and the immediate past are utilized in a shorthand fashion; moreover, the fictional characters are normally firmly locked into the overall political and social context. Thus Auerbach's remark on Stendhal's *Le rouge et le noir* that its characters are "embedded in a total reality, political, social, economic, which is concrete and constantly evolving,"[6] applies no less to Galdós. Not all the major events of the time of action are included, as is required in the *episodios*; nor are those that are necessarily treated in more than a partial and limited way. What is conveyed, rather, is the immediate impact of certain crucial events and an acute awareness of the continuity of past and present: in Peter Bly's words, they are "stepping-stones of historical data which lead to the novel's overall historical dimension."[7] Thus, while it is inappropriate to classify

[6] E. Auerbach, *Mimesis: The Representation of Reality in Western Literature* (Princeton University Press, 1968), p. 462.

[7] P. A. Bly, *Galdós' Novel of the Historical Imagination* (Liverpool: Francis Cairns, 1988), p. 5.

Galdós's fittingly named "contemporary novels" as historical novels, just as it is regarding Balzac's *Comédie humaine*, there is no doubt that they are historically conscious novels. The term used by Bly in his thorough and perceptive study, the "novel of historical imagination," is perhaps the most suitable.

Broad parallels are on occasion established between characters and major historical developments. Two of the most notable examples are the dishonorable course, parallel to that of Spain, pursued by Isidora in *La desheredada* (*The Disinherited Lady*, 1881), as she accepts a moral degradation consonant with that suffered by the country through the murder of the principal revolutionary general Juan Prim, and the parallel between Spain's public life veering between law and disorder and the private life of Juanito Santa Cruz in *Fortunata y Jacinta* (1886–7): "There occurred in him what don Baldomero [his father] had said about the country: he suffered from alternating fevers of freedom and peace" (II: 56).[8] Some fictitious characters are grafted into historical situations: the Bringas couple, deeply implicated, within the Royal Palace, in the fall of Isabella II, and Villalonga, the opportunistic parliamentary deputy who in a masterly scene describes in parallel fashion General Pavía's *coup d'état* in Congress in 1874 and Fortunata's return to Madrid. Torquemada, the sordid moneylender turned banker and *nouveau riche*, serves as the barometer of economic developments throughout the period, as Villaamil does of the vicissitudes of a redundant civil servant's (*cesante*) existence in *Miau* (1888). Manuel Infante (*La incógnita* [*The Unknown*, 1888–9]) represents the somnolent parliamentarism and *caciquismo* ('local boss-ism') of the full Restoration period.

Another type of historical reference characteristic of the novels consists of historical recapitulations in no way integrated into the plot. Characters are chosen to provide a rapid and purely superficial listing of the salient events of recent history, thus inducing a broader awareness of the past or simply jogging the memory. The best examples are two characters from *Fortunata y Jacinta*: Plácido Estupiñá, whose historical memory goes back to politicians declaiming histrionically from a balcony from the time of Napoleon's brother, Joseph I, onwards, and doña Isabel Cordero, whose many children are born on key historical dates and who herself dies on the same day as Prim is assassinated. The same function is fulfilled by Beramendi's children in the *episodio La de los tristes destinos* ('A Woman of Ill Fortune', 1907), which describes the expulsion of Isabella II. Normally, however, this recourse is not required, given the historical continuity of the genre.

[8] B. Pérez Galdós, *Fortunata y Jacinta*, ed. Francisco Caudet, 2 vols. (Madrid: Cátedra, 1983), vol. II, p. 56.

Similarly, consecrated historical figures or incidents from the past, which no longer form part of the ongoing historical process, are evoked in the novels as models, warnings or justifications of some current action. Prim is frequently recalled in this way, but the outstanding example is the harrowing memory Ángel Guerra has of the horrendous public execution of sixty-six sergeants from the San Gil barracks twenty years before, in 1866. Another device is to indicate the physical likeness between a character and an eminent historical figure, normally foreign, usually with ironic intent. Notable examples are the stingy and blinkered bureaucrat Francisco Bringas, consistently identified physically with the French economist and statesman Thiers; the pompous Basilio Andrés de la Caña's resemblance to the Italian statesman Cavour; and the constantly evolving iconographical comparisons made between Mauricia *la dura* ('Tough Mauricia') and Napoleon in *Fortunata y Jacinta*.

History is not, however, treated in fact as a fixed series of great events, and the absolute confidence of nineteenth-century historical determinism is accordingly mitigated. While Galdós frequently flirts with the suppositions of the deterministic approach to history, he never accepts them fully. Perhaps a striking sentence from *La desheredada*, in which Fate, Chance, and the army all play their part, most clearly expresses his viewpoint: "Fate and Chance play chess about Spain, which has always been a board with squares [but also barracks] of blood and silver."[9] An essential method by which diversity and flexibility, and at times ambiguity, is established is by the extensive use of everyday illustrations of social evolution, what has been called "la historia chica" ('minor history') as opposed to "la historia grande" ('major history'). The *historia chica* not only includes the largely unrecorded undercurrent of steady yet unobtrusive historical change – what Unamuno later termed "intrahistoria"[10] – but also embraces fictional invention which is itself historically representative. In these more domestic issues the fictional story lends life and credibility to the historical process. The essential thing is that both major and minor happenings must interact constantly and consistently in close metonymic relation. Galdós's talent in this respect is one of his outstanding qualities. In the novels *la historia chica* or the fictional story is the predominant factor, whereas in the *episodios* the situation is to some extent reversed: while *la historia grande* gains in importance, *la historia chica*, even if no longer fully autonomous, remains essential, coordinated and intertwined as it is, in a highly effective way, with the major events.

9 B. Pérez Galdós, *Obras completas*, ed. Federico Carlos Robles, 6 vols. (Madrid: Aguilar, 1968–71), vol. IV, p. 1067.

10 M. de Unamuno, "En torno al casticismo," in *Obras completas*, ed. M. García Blanco, 9 vols. (Madrid: Escelicer, 1966–71), pp. 795–8.

Both forms of narrative use recurring characters, but Galdós does not utilize the device to the same degree as Balzac and does no rearranging of previously published material. Recurrence evidently enhances the plausibility and coherence of the mimetic world of fiction, and thus lends it a greater historical verisimilitude, but while in contemporary novels the device is optative and selective, in the *episodios* it is organically required. Once firm relationships have been established between fictional characters and real-life historical personages or situations, the former have become part of the structure and cannot be realistically abandoned in subsequent volumes; they can only be gradually modified or replaced.

The quantity of historical data which has to be accommodated in the *episodios* is far larger than in conventional novels and more extensive, too, than in standard historical novels. The *episodio nacional* therefore needs to be treated as a highly individualized type of historical novel, a subgenre that makes special demands, like an overall factual exactness in its historical content and an easily intelligible chronology. It has a characteristic structure of ten narratives per series and is relatively short. Unlike the novels, the distance between the time of the action ("story time") and the time of the narration ("discourse time")[11] is invariably and inevitably very great, with a time scale lasting as much as sixty years. In most of them "discourse time" is not allowed to intrude upon "story time" and readers are induced to view events as contemporaneous. While the narratee is closely involved in the situation, the implied reader is very remote from the events taking place, though he may identify imaginatively with them. What is present, but without breaking the immediacy of the presentation, is what Lukács (*The Historical Novel*, p. 68) calls the "necessary anachronism" associated with any reconstruction of the past.

The *episodio nacional* also professes an evident if secondary didactic aim of providing information and stimulating thought about the issues of the immediate past. As Galdós himself declared in 1885, his work is "free from any purpose other than to present in a pleasant form the main military and political actions of the most dramatic period of the century, with the aim of entertaining *and also of teaching, though not a great deal* those people who are fond of this type of reading" (my italics).[12] The very titles adopted for the *episodios* makes their sustained purpose abundantly clear: every one of the forty-six refers explicitly to a historical event, date, or personage, while not a single title of the contemporary novels after *La fontana de oro* contains any

[11] I use the terms employed by Seymour Chatman in *Story and Discourse: Narrative Structure in Fiction and Film* (Ithaca: Cornell University Press, 1978), p. 62.

[12] B. Pérez Galdós, *Los Prólogos de Galdós*, ed. E. H. Shoemaker (Urbana/Mexico City: University of Illinois Press/Ediciones de Andrea, 1962), p. 56.

direct historical or political allusion. In every *episodio* some major historical figure or development, from Godoy to Cánovas, from the Napoleonic period to the Restoration settlement, is shown in action, even though the historical figure, in accordance with Lukács' dictum (*The Historical Novel*, p. 33), is never the protagonist of the work.

The priority necessarily given to political history over the fictional story does not make these narratives real contributions to historiography, for the content is entirely second-hand. What it does do is to give the form of the *episodio* a more inflexible and unmodifiable structure. As Galdós himself says in a discarded comment in 1875, "the action and plot are made up *by a multitude of events* which must not be altered by whim" (my italics).[13] It appears that the story was normally added subsequently: "Now I am preparing the canvas, that is, the historical set-up [...] Once the historical and political background has been sketched in, I shall invent the intrigue," Galdós declared in July 1910.[14]

This scheme is, however, merely the starting point. It does not indicate a lack of concern for the fictional story, on which the effect and quality of the work must essentially depend. Thus the narratives are two-pronged: "the novelesque genre with a historical base."[15] The panoramic and comprehensive view embraces society as well as politics, and for this the *episodios* depend on their fictional scaffolding. Nor is any absolute predominance of large political issues implied. Unrecorded or overlooked personal events – *la historia chica* once more, and as such mostly fictional – form a large and indispensable part of the totality of history:

> The personal tangles and incidents between individuals who make no claim on the judgment of posterity are branches of the same tree that produces the historic timber with which we put together the external structure by which countries and their princes operate, with their convulsions, statutes, wars, and peace treaties. With timber of one sort or the other, joined together as best one can, we raise up the tall scaffolding from which we see, in luminous perspective, the soul, body, and humors of the nation.[16]

The protagonist Pepe Fajardo, on returning from Italy to chronicle Isabeline Spain, characterizes the role of the individual and his impact in a most effective metaphor:

[13] A. Smith, "El epílogo a la primera edición de *La Batalla de los Arapiles*," *Anales Galdosianos* 17 (1982), p. 106.

[14] H. Hinterhäuser, *Los "Episodios nacionales" de Benito Pérez Galdós* (Madrid: Gredos, 1963), p. 223.

[15] Galdós, *Los Prólogos de Galdós*, p. 58.

[16] B. Pérez Galdós, *España sin rey*, in *Obras completas*, vol. III, p. 785.

> History is the continuous process of the birth of some events in the womb of others. It is the daughter of Yesterday, the sister of Today and the mother of Tomorrow. All men make unrecorded history; everyone living is continually creating ideal volumes that are not printed or even written. Anyone who in some way leaves the trace of his/her existence on passing through the world will be worthy of Clio's praise, like snails which as they slowly move along leave behind a thread of slime imprinted on the stones. This I shall do, a snail with a long trail still ahead of me; and don't tell me that the trace of slime that I am leaving doesn't deserve to be seen by those who come after.[17]

The progress of *intrahistoria* may not be much – the image of the snail's track is a very modest one – but it is continuous and accumulative.

Initially, in the first series, Galdós adopted a technique of autobiographical reminiscence, with Gabriel Araceli describing events from his old age. Despite the advantages of continuity, this procedure suffered from inevitable limitations, and by 1875 Galdós was inveighing vehemently against the rigidity of narrating for so long from the viewpoint of just one person. First-person narration is therefore abandoned for "free narration" and relatively autonomous development in the second series. A major exception is *Memorias de un cortesano de 1815* ('Memoirs of a Courtier of 1815', 1875), narrated by the sycophantic Juan Bragas, which casts an ironic light on the reign of Ferdinand VII. Galdós also indicates a second change, which emphasizes the novelistic qualities of the works: "as the action passes in them from battlefields and besieged garrison towns to political jousts and the great theatre of common life, the result is more movement, more novel, and therefore, greater interest. *The historical novel thus becomes confused with the novel of everyday living*" (my italics).[18] The shifting balance between the two constituent elements – history, fiction – of the *episodio nacional* is thus clearly established.

Moreover, the successive volumes are accumulative and interdependent to a remarkable degree: "linked between themselves, but without undue effort."[19] Various techniques are used to provide a thread of continuity between individual *episodios* and even across series. One is the use of key figures. An outstanding example is Jenara Baraona, so conspicuous in the second series through her unhappy marriage to Carlos Navarro and her amorous entanglement with the series' protagonist Salvador Monsalud, among others, and as narrator – the only woman so employed, a remarkable fact in itself – of *Los cien mil hijos de San Luis* ('The Hundred Thousand

[17] B. Pérez Galdós, *Las tormentas del '48*, in *Obras completas*, vol. II, p. 1428.
[18] Galdós, *Los Prólogos*, p. 58.
[19] A. Smith, "El epílogo a la primera edición de *La Batalla de los Arapiles*," *Anales Galdosianos* 17 (1982), p. 107.

Sons of Saint Louis', 1877). She thus plays the crucial role of linking public and private events, with much greater personal involvement than characterized Estupiñá, from Joseph Bonaparte's time right up to Espartero's regency (1841–3) and beyond.

On returning to the subgenre with the third series in 1898, Galdós tackles the First Carlist War, which, with its pointless cruelties and frequent executions, lasted until the 1839 Peace of Vergara agreed between Espartero and Marote. The events of the war alternate with attempts at economic reform (*Mendizábal*, 1898) and descriptions of Romanticism (*La estafeta romántica* ['The Romantic Mail', 1899]). Largely third-person narrators continue to be used: the priest, José Fago, for the first narrative; the Carlist hero Zumalacárregui, and Fernando Calpena subsequently. On several occasions, however, seeking greater immediacy, Galdós introduces a modified first-person form: the epistolary mode, already used in the novel *La incógnita*. Letters, from some dozen correspondents, constitute the entire structure of *La estafeta romántica* and play a considerable part in *Luchana* (1899), *Vergara* (1899) and *Los ayacuchos* (1900), – *ayacuchos* were soldiers who supported Espartero. Such structural devices militate against pure historicism. So does the degree of selection exercised. The first sentence of the last *episodio* of the third series, *Bodas reales* ('Royal Weddings', 1900), already concerned with the young queen Isabella II, makes an important distinction between History, which fixes and retains all human occurrences, great and small, and Time, which is memoryless.[20] By indicating the inexhaustible abundance of historical reference available, this statement demonstrates, not the rejection of History, but the variety of evidence that needs sifting and selecting to provide specific significant examples – to offer, in other words, "stepping-stones," in Bly's apt phrase, in the inexorable course of undifferentiated Time.

The fourth series, devoted to Isabella's reign and her fall, uses a mixed narrative technique, providing maximum flexibility, of roughly alternating first- and third-person narrative. It commences with Fajardo's first-person memoirs in the twin narratives *Las tormentas del '48* ('The Tempests of '48', 1902) and *Narváez* (1902). Then comes an intercalated third-person narration for *Los duendes de la camarilla* ('The Goblins of the Antechamber', 1903) before we return to Fajardo's memoirs in *La revolución de julio* ('The July Revolution', 1904). What is now sought is an adequate method of conveying a contemporaneous situation: a historical reconstruction of the past that occurs before our eyes. Diachronic time or consecutive time yields, at intervals at least, to synchronic time, or past events viewed simultaneously. Historical and fictional figures are seen in the process of playing their role

[20] B. Pérez Galdós, *Bodas reales*, in *Obras completas*, vol. II, p. 1307.

in the present – their present – and are therefore subject to the pressures and uncertainties of the moment. The narrator and the story, and so the narratee, are thus extremely close, but are remote in time from the implied author and implied reader. By this alternation convincing immersion in an earlier contemporary reality is achieved. The third-person narration, used in the last three narratives, allows, by extensive use of "summary," a faster narrative pace than the memoir and establishes a certain distance in time and space from the events while still mirroring the attitude of the leading characters, with whom the reader is already acquainted.

Similar techniques continue into the fifth series, dealing with the revolutionary period from 1868 to 1875. The first volume, *España sin rey* ('Spain without a King', 1907–8) has an anonymous personal narrator, as amid lively fictional incidents the extended search for a constitutional monarch is undertaken. The second, *España trágica* ('Tragic Spain', 1809), on Prim's murder, is centered on Vicente Halconero and includes lengthy extracts from his diary. A break comes, however, in the last four volumes, from *Amadeo I* (1910) onwards. These are concerned with particularly important issues for later generations: the failed experiments of the Savoyan monarchy and the First Republic and Cánovas's problematical success in restoring the Bourbon dynasty. At the same time they are characterized by a radically new first-person technique. They are narrated directly by the extravagant figure of Tito Liviano, from the narrator's present, that is, "discourse time," now deliberately acknowledged, at a great chronological distance from the events narrated, and are laced with much explicit commentary. The earlier balance, by which "story time" prevailed over "discourse time," is thus destroyed. Instead, there is bitter, unmediated denunciation of traditional politicians and of the church, culminating in a famous defense of Revolution at the end of the last *episodio*, *Cánovas*. The dialogic structure of previous narratives has been lost.

To return to the second batch of *episodios* as a whole: in all of them procedures aimed at providing continuity remain important. Thus a few families exercise a tentacular hold over the structure of several volumes. The most evident is the extended Ansúrez family, to a large extent a repository of primitive Celtiberian values and fierce independence, in the fourth series. Although the symbolism may at times be rather wooden, such figures have an essentially representational function. The most important is Lucila, the Celtiberian beauty who entranced Beramendi and Santiuste, became Bartolomé Gracián's lover, made two middle-class marriages and was the mother of Vicente Halconero. Also symbolic in name and character are the two Santiago Iberos, father and son. Coming from the "Rioja alavesa" – a mixture therefore of Castilian and Basque – they exemplify for Galdós the honesty and tenacity of the primitive Iberian race. Another family example, of a more adaptable sort, are the Fajardos, to which the key figure of Beramendi belonged. All these groups and many others are interlocked by ties of personal relationships or marriage or political affiliation. Links are also provided with earlier series and between generations. In all the intricate web of fictional relationships historical underpinning is never lacking.

Historical involvement on this scale evidently poses problems for modern theorists hostile to conventional history. Purist writers like Henry James have always objected to what appeared to be a hybrid form. Structuralists and deconstructionists decry the presence in a work of creation of such extraneous features as history and politics. Diane Urey adopts the interesting criterion of minimizing the effect of the historical structure and extolling the fictional story to which Derridean concepts can be applied: "Derrida's critique of history is applicable to the *Episodios nacionales* overall because it questions any form of representation and the indissolubility of the linguistic sign."[21] Accordingly, Urey's work has the merit of paying overdue attention to the story and narrative structure, rightly discerning in them "an amazing artistic virtuosity" (*Novel Histories*, p. 10) and a "brilliant manipulation of language [that] could surely only be achieved by a keen perception of its intrinsic and inseparable role in every aspect of life, including what is called history" (pp. 11–12). She is also fully conscious of the open-ended quality of Galdós's presentation of historical events, in which an extraordinarily broad spectrum of contemporary opinions is assembled, whether the event is the *Ministerio Relámpago* ('Lightning Ministry,' 1849), when the Liberal prime minister was accused of coercing the young queen, or the assassination of Prim (1870).

Undoubtedly the most daring and imaginative experiment of the later period is the transformation in *Prim* of the character of Juan Santiuste, now known as "Confusio," into the creator of an imaginary "Logical-Natural History of the Spaniards of the Two Worlds in the Nineteenth Century." Under the patronage of Beramendi, who shares his profound dissatisfaction with the course of Spanish history, "Confusio" constructs an idealized historical frame in which what occurs is what ought to happen, not what did actually happen. Thus, Ferdinand VII, instead of being rescued by a French invasion, is shot by the patriots at Cadiz, and the civil war that followed is turned into another war of independence, after which Isabella II (transformed into the daughter of the earlier queen Isabel de Braganza) marries a Ferdinand of Aragon. Under these new Catholic Monarchs the military opponents, represented by Serrano and Prim, are reconciled, and eventually

[21] D. F. Urey, *The Novel Histories of Galdós* (Princeton University Press, 1989), p. 166.

Alfonso XII leads Spain into a long period of peace and prosperity that lasts well into the twentieth century. These extravagant notions have met with much criticism as being the outpourings of a madman, but we should bear in mind the utterly desolate character of Spanish history before and up to the time when Galdós was writing. The purpose of the "Logical-Natural History" may well be to demonstrate how arbitrary the course of national life had been, to offer a sort of antidote against the pessimism and despair engendered by the true history of the period, and to confound a rigorously deterministic interpretation of Spain's failures. Moreover, in creating such an imaginative stimulus to meditation on recent Spanish history, Galdós is also making clear the limitations of the narrowly scientific concept of history with which we started.

Another flirtation with a certain type of historical novel is found in *La tribuna* (*Tribune of the People*, 1883) by Emilia Pardo-Bazán (1851–1921), centered around the key event of the recent past, the "Glorious" Revolution of 1868 and its consequences. Among the novel's many innovatory merits is its creation, in an age of social unrest that purported to offer promise of social equality, of a major female protagonist within a working-class setting, at the cigarette factory at La Coruña. Amparo, naively believing in the slogans of the Revolution, becomes a "tribune" of the people, and at the same time allows herself to be seduced by a prosperous middle-class youth who promises to marry her. By ending the novel with two simultaneous events, the birth of Amparo's son (with a notable physical description of such a previously untouchable subject as child-birth) and the euphoric triumph of the proclamation of the ill-fated Federal Republic (11 February 1873), the prospects of both the child and the country are left poised in a parallel uncertain future.

José María de Pereda (1833–1906), untypically, also tried his hand at a novel with strong historical implications, *Pedro Sánchez* (1883), in which the July Revolution of 1854 is powerfully evoked. The most effective moments are those in which Pereda's ingrained hatred of urban laxity and corruption is expressed before the inevitable return of his hero to the moral tranquility of the country. The Catalan novelist Narcís Oller (1845–1930), a realist with a sentimental streak (Zola writes accurately of his "étude de personnages légèrement idéalisés et traversant un milieu très exact"[22]), has some works with near-contemporary historical themes. The extensive novel *La febre d'or* ('Gold Fever', 1893) is an impressive analysis of the fever for investment, which inevitably led to a market collapse, in an industrializing Barcelona during the early Restoration period (1875–85). In one of his best, a

[22] In the letter-prologue to the French translation of *La papillona* (*Le papillon* ['The Butterfly'], 1885), quoted in Sergio Beser (ed.), Narcís Oller, "Pròleg 8," *La societat catalana de la restauració* (Barcelona: Edicions 62, 1965).

short novel entitled *La bogeria* ('Madness', 1899), the deranged protagonist, Daniel Serrallonga, is an unconditional supporter of Prim and assiduously collects pictures of his hero. The character's delusions are skilfully intertwined with references to a politician of special significance for Catalonia, whose accomplishments and defects are directly enumerated by the narrator.

The thrust of the major work of Miguel de Unamuno (1864–1936) is radically opposed to the historicist tradition, but he has one substantial early novel that broadly fits into that tradition. Significantly enough, his *Paz en la guerra* (*Peace in War*, 1897) is closely related to Galdós. Unamuno sent him a copy and rather persistently sought his support. The novel is an unwieldy study of the Third Carlist War, but with considerable reaching back to the first, known as the "guerra de los siete años" ('seven years' war': 1833–40), in which his subject overlaps with Galdós's third series of *episodios nacionales*. In fact, Unamuno took great pride in his unproven belief that *Paz en la guerra* influenced the *episodios*, notably in the treatment of the battle of Luchana and the Peace of Vergara.[23]

Unamuno's purpose, however, is to examine the struggle within the Basque community between the millennial rural tradition and the liberal affiliations of Bilbao. It is a conflict between country and town, rural barter and modern commerce, local rights (*fueros*) and centralizing policies, Basque and Castilian, clerical intransigence and religious tolerance. Such disputes are viewed with deep sympathy for both sides involved, as for example in the profoundly felt scenes of the country wedding attended by Ignacio, where he experiences for the first time the strengths of rural tradition and its expression in Basque; in the traditionalist *tertulia* (a gathering to discuss philosophy, politics, art) of Pedro Antonio, which embraces the varied opinions of characters like those of *el tío* ('old') Pascual, don Braulio, don Eustaquio, etc.; in the mercantile atmosphere of the Arena family; and in Pachico's political indifference. The crisis of a society in turbulent evolution is presented, no doubt in excessive detail, as Unamuno himself later came to feel. This presentation alternates with a series of fluctuating personal problems, which correspond to certain phases of the author's spiritual anguish.

What could have been, with a bit more selection, a coherent *Bildungsroman* is confused by having the reader's attention divided between three key characters, even though each represents a different facet of the conflict: Pedro Antonio standing for underlying historical continuity (*intrahistoria*, already

[23] Unamuno writes to Clarín on 9 May 1900: "Do you know what has given me the greatest private satisfaction? Well, it is to see, without my experiencing any doubt about it, the influence my novel has had on Galdos's *Luchana* and other of the last *episodios*," *Epistolario a Clarín. Menéndez y Pelayo, Unamuno, Palacio Valdés. Prólogo y notas de Adolfo Alas* (Madrid: Ediciones Escorial, 1941), p. 99.

discussed), Ignacio for an ideological-spiritual conflict resolved in death, and Pachico, a survivor who seeks, in an idiosyncratic fashion, peace from within war. The peace (reflected in the title) that Pachico so precariously constructs in the ending to the novel is of purely personal dimensions, political considerations having vanished from his consciousness. In all this we have an example of the extremely fragile conjuring trick with which Unamuno is seeking to satisfy his own spiritual yearnings. The Tolstoyan aspiration for resolution of conflict is very different from Galdós's, for it depends not on conciliation or fusion, but on the maintenance of tension between two irreconcilable objectives, a sort of truncated dialectic that never resolves into a synthesis. *Paz en la guerra* is a work of transition and an anomaly. As Nicholas Round has indicated, it both continues and concludes the realist novel, without leaving any descendants.[24]

The major novelist of a slightly later generation who retains an interest in the historical novel in a way comparable with the realist tradition is Pío Baroja (1872–1952). At the same time his concept of history is very different from that of Galdós, as he himself indicated in a well-known passage: "Galdós has turned to history through affection for it; I have turned to history through curiosity toward a type of person; Galdós has sought out the most brilliant moments to chronicle them; I have insisted on those moments given me by the protagonist."[25] Even if Baroja's characterization of Galdós's *episodios* is not entirely accurate – his undoubted affection for history is tempered by agonized frustration at its failure to achieve progress and he hardly pursues "the most brilliant moments" where few exist – it is clear that Galdós has a concern for elucidating the major events of his time, even when, as they usually did, they ended in futility. By contrast, Baroja is concerned, as he notes, with individual biography, treated in an informal, unchronological and unsystematic fashion, without any integration into a broader framework: a sort of demythification of history, as Marsha Collins put it.[26]

In writing his major historical sequence, the twenty-two-volume series on the political intriguer Eugenio de Aviraneta entitled *Memorias de un hombre de acción* ('Memoirs of a Man of Action', 1913–34), Baroja clearly – even obsessively – has Galdós, as author of the *episodios nacionales*, in mind. It is evident, for example, that at times Baroja is concerned to put Galdós right.

[24] N. G. Round, "'Without a City Wall': *Paz en la guerra* and the End of Realism," in *Re-Reading Unamuno*, ed. N. G. Round, Glasgow Colloquium Papers I (Glasgow: The University, 1989), pp. 101–20.

[25] P. Baroja, *Memorias*: "La intuición y el estilo," in *Obras completas*, 8 vols. (Madrid: Biblioteca Nueva, 1948), vol. VIII, p. 1077.

[26] M. S. Collins, *Pío Baroja's "Memorias de un hombre de acción" and the Ironic Mode: The Search for Order and Meaning* (London: Támesis, 1986), pp. 81–104.

This is particularly evident in his urge to rectify Galdós's somewhat low opinion of Baroja's hero Aviraneta, described in *Un faccioso más y algunos frailes menos* ('One More Rebel and Fewer Friars', 1879) as "a colossal genius of intrigue and an inimitable showman."[27] Baroja is also concerned to confront his senior rival's concept of Juan Martín *el empecinado* ('the stubborn warrior'), the guerrilla leader of the Peninsular War. Their respective attitudes pinpoint an interesting contrast between the two writers. As Carlos Longhurst indicates in his excellent study of Baroja's historical novels, *El empecinado* is one of the very few historical figures whom Baroja praises unconditionally and treats as "a symbol of early Spanish liberalism."[28] For Galdós, on the other hand, *El empecinado* scarcely enters the mainstream of the historical process. Baroja also seeks to cover the campaign in El Maestrazgo by Ramón Cabrera during the First Carlist War more thoroughly and with greater vehemence against the bloodthirsty Carlist general than Galdós had done.

The most important coincidence of subject matter concerns the murder of police chief Pedro Chico during the 1854 revolution. Baroja's brief description of the spectacular apprehension of this official coincides with Galdós's in such features as the white shirt, the red cap, the action of fanning himself. Pereda also has a similar description in *Pedro Sánchez*. As we would expect from its author, Baroja's narrative is more vivid and direct, with a great deal of emphasis on physical and sartorial details: "he went along half naked, covered with a white shirt and a handkerchief round his neck, a red cap on his head and carried a fan in his hand with which he calmly fanned himself. The expression on his face was sullen, bitter, and almost mocking."[29]

Where Baroja differs markedly from Galdós is in ignoring the social and political background. Baroja attributes the murder almost exclusively to a personal rivalry between Chico and a certain brigadier Castelo for the favors of one Paca Dávalos. It was Castelo who instigated the stirring up of the people by a bullfighter nicknamed Pucheta. Baroja is not concerned with Chico's own record, but takes his execution as a fine example of stoic equanimity in the face of death. His only comment on the motivation for the uprising speaks of "that simplistic feeling of the crowd" which imagines that by getting rid of Chico they will get rid of injustice.

[27] B. Pérez Galdós, *Un faccioso más y algunos frailes menos*, in *Obras completas*, vol. II, p. 316.

[28] Carlos Longhurst, *Las novelas históricas de Pío Baroja* (Madrid: Ediciones Guadarrama, 1974), pp. 98–99. See also Pedro Ortiz Armengol, *Aviraneta y diez más* (Madrid: Prensa Española, 1979), pp. 5–34.

[29] Baroja, *El sabor de la venganza*, vol. III, p. 1155.

It is a good example of Baroja's refusal to countenance any cause and effect factor in history, and his preference for seeking examples of human conduct in isolation. He is not at all worried by questions of political morality affecting his hero Aviraneta in his relations with the queen mother María Cristina and her morganatic husband Fernando Muñoz, Duke of Riánsares. The issue for Baroja is a personal one, to such an extent that he links *Pucheta* with Riánsares on the quite arbitrary grounds that they share the same surname, Muñoz: "So we had a Muñoz above [Cristina's husband] and a Muñoz below [Pucheta]. The revolution of '54 was a conflict between two Muñozes."[30] One might as well say that the American War of Independence was a war between two Georges!

Baroja takes great pride in his research and his visits to historic places, and these no doubt help give his writing a personal authenticity. He cherishes an almost superstitious respect for factual documentation, and chides Galdós for his failure to gain similar personal experience. His essential interest therefore is to follow the course of Aviraneta's individual intrigues and adventures. He is resolutely opposed to a purely scientific view of history, claiming that subjectivity plays an important part in any historical judgment, and that complete objectivity is impossible.[31] By failing to conceive of the interaction of forces and persons on more than an individual level, he adopts a purely casual criterion that concedes supreme importance to chance: "History for Baroja is a succession of events occurring by chance, without order or concord."[32] Evidently, too, it has no didactic role.

Since he is from a younger generation than Galdós's and clearly influenced by Nietzsche, Baroja's concept of time is more cyclical than linear, and he thinks of it in terms of flowing water, with frequent references to Heraclitus: "Becoming is an eternal game which has its objective and its justification in itself... it seems that this theory of the closed circle and of periodical cataclysm contains some truth."[33] His conception still has something of the nineteenth century about it. Perhaps the closest comparison is with Thomas Hardy, who conceived of History as a stream rather than a tree, its directions not determined by any law but casually, by mediocre individuals. Baroja shares this concept of the randomness of history, but thinks rather of men of action and intrigue determining events against the odds, within a context of historical inconclusiveness.

In the lively conversation Baroja sets up between Aviraneta and Leguía in the Prologue to "Las figuras de cera" ('Wax Figures', 1924), the former

30 Ibid.

31 Baroja, *Memorias*: "La historia," in *Obras completas*, vol. v, pp. 1124–8.

32 Longhurst, *Las novelas históricas de Pío Baroja*, p. 143.

33 Baroja, "La historia," p. 1106.

represents a factual, more historical, criterion against Leguía's insistence on imaginative freedom: "Aviraneta was dogmatic, a supporter of realism, and he believed that sooner or later truth shone forth, like the sun among the clouds. Leguía thought that in the cemetery of History, full of bones, ashes and knicknacks, each investigator chooses what he wants and puts it together as he pleases."[34] Here the question is left open, but when he speaks with his own voice, Baroja, under the influence of Schopenhauer (as Longhurst notes, *Las novelas históricas*, pp. 148–54), argues for the superiority of literature: "A good novel is more exact in reflecting a social environment than an excellent historical work."[35] At the same time, he equates history and fiction in a parallel formlessness: "The novel, in general, is like the flow of History: it has no beginning or end; it begins and finishes where one wants it to."[36] As a result, Baroja takes pride in rejecting any unity of action or structure, for fiction as well as history, "a novel is possible without an argument, without architecture and without composition,"[37] in taking a strong interventionist line as far as the narrator is concerned, leaving entirely out of account any balance between the historical and fictional plots, which in fact vary enormously throughout the series. In compensation, his concern is always for the thrust toward capturing the vital spirit of his subject. His merits lie in his lively penetration into individual eccentricity, his capacity to treat such individuals with dignity, his hatred of cruelty, and his consistent sense of the arbitrariness of human destiny that leads to an idiosyncratic type of existentialism. All his novels are full of the most varied and often highly concentrated incidents, expressed with great narrative verve and sense of melodrama, with an engagingly naive openness to new experience.

One of the most creative writers of the early twentieth century, Ramón del Valle-Inclán (1866–1936), takes a very different view of the historical novel. Immersed in his early work in a decadent esthetic akin to *modernismo*[38] and professing scant respect for detailed description or realist chronology, Valle-Inclán early became fascinated by heroic figures of the immediate past. In a first trilogy of historical novels (1908–9) entitled *La guerra carlista* ('The Carlist War'), comprising *Los cruzados de la causa* ('The Crusaders of the Cause'), *El resplandor de la hoguera* ('The Glow of the Bonfire'), and *Gerifaltes de antaño* ('The Bigwigs of Yesteryear'), set during the ill-fated

34 Baroja, "Las figuras de cera," vol. IV, p. 174.

35 Baroja, "La objetividad de la historia," vol. VIII, p. 957.

36 Baroja, "Sobre la novela realista," vol. VIII, p. 973.

37 Baroja, "La nave de los locos," Prologue to vol. IV, p. 326.

38 An aesthetic movement of Hispano-American origin prevalent around the turn of the century.

Federal Republic (1873–4), he is concerned with the dissolving of old traditionalist values, which he treats with a certain ironic sympathy and sardonic detachment. His most original work in this genre, however, is the unfinished series entitled *Ruedo ibérico*, which consists of two completed novels, *La corte de los milagros* ('The Court of Miracles', 1927), *Viva mi dueño* ('Long Live My Master', 1928), and a considerable portion of a third, *Baza de espadas* ('Trump in Spades' or 'Sword Trick,' posthumously published in 1958), all of which deal with the last year (1868) of Isabella II's reign. Valle-Inclán has by now developed, in both drama and narrative, a highly original technique known as the *esperpento* ('grotesque farce'), consisting of the systematic distortion of classical models. Drawing on popular satire and intercalated official documents, the distortion lies more in the expression than the content: a joy in the incongruous, in juggling chronology, and in a devastating iconoclasm which delights in "mocking, mocking everything and everyone."[39] Valle-Inclán develops a bewilderingly rapid set of visual impressions full of theatrical elan, forming a circular structure, the effect of which is appropriately compared by Valle-Inclán himself to *pointillisme*.[40] He concentrates on a few well-chosen themes: the ludicrous honoring for her virtue of the notoriously promiscuous *reina castiza* ('the Ultra-Spanish Queen') by the Pope with the *Rosa de oro* ('Golden Rose'); the death of her strong-arm protector Narváez; the intrigues and maneuvers of Prim, toward whom Valle shows special animosity; the scurrilous love-life of the queen herself, all expressed in the most lively and impressionistic language.

Later developments of the historical novel also connect, not surprisingly, with Galdós. The most conspicuous example is Ramón J. Sender (1902–82), who before the Civil War cultivated fictionalized history of the relatively recent past, particularly in his recreation, in *Míster Witt, en el cantón* ('Mr. Witt in the Canton', 1935), of the revolutionary canton of Cartagena in 1870, the subject of two of Galdós's later *episodios*, *La primera República* ('The First Republic') and *De Cartago a Sagunto* ('From Carthage to Saguntum', both 1911). It is a remarkable novel that combines in equal proportions a notable density of historical reference and a substantial fictional story of the vacillations and treachery of the English engineer of the title, the husband of Milagritos, a local patriot.

The key figure, for Sender as for Galdós, is one of the historical leaders of the insurrection, Antonete Gálvez, who combines a genuine compassion

39 L. Schiavo, *Historia y novela en Valle-Inclán: Para leer "El ruedo ibérico"* (Madrid: Castalia, 1987), p. 55.

40 Ibid., p. 53.

toward the underprivileged with a capacity for command. Another important figure, Colau, whom Sender decisively relates to an earlier revolutionary, Froilán Carvajal, provides the link with the fictional story, since Carvajal was Milagritos's admirer and was killed through Mr. Witt's deceit, as is gradually revealed in the course of the action. A second act of treachery concerns Colau when the ship *El Tetuán* is blown up, apparently but falsely claiming Colau as its most prominent victim. Mr. Witt personifies all that is at odds with a revolutionary stance like Gálvez's or Colau's: indifference versus active engagement; cold calculation versus spontaneity; hypocrisy, resentment, and jealousy versus serene confidence; cowardice versus resolution. The culmination comes when he explicitly recognizes that he deserves the label *canalla* (swine) rather than his preferred pose of an honorable lack of involvement. The opposite applies to Milagritos, whose suppressed tears when the Canton falls express grief for all those implicated in the tragic events – Carvajal, Colau, the Canton and herself – and who, while heroically staying with her husband in the hope of having a child, continues to represent the spirit and lost hope of an impossible dream.[41]

The Spanish Civil War (1936–9), the historical circumstances that occasioned it, and its long repressive aftermath could not fail to trouble the consciences of contemporary novelists. Some historical novels still reminiscent of the realist tradition, but with little innovation, were produced, the most notable being Ignacio Agustí's Barcelona-based series entitled *La ceniza que fue árbol* ('Tree into Ashes') comprising *Mariona Rebull* (1941), *El viudo Rius* ('The Widower Rius', 1945), *Desiderio* (1957), *19 de julio* ('The Nineteenth of July'), and José María Gironella's massive trilogy, beginning with *Los cipreses creen en Dios* (*The Cypresses Believe in God*), followed by *Un millón de muertos* ('A Million Dead', 1961), and *Ha estallado la paz* ('Peace Has Broken Out', 1966). Max Aub's multi-volumed *Laberinto mágico* ('Magic Labyrinth', 1943–68) and Sender's post-war novels maintain an effective balance between a continuing debt to Galdós and more modern techniques. Other fine novelists, writing from abroad or within Spain (Francisco Ayala, Camilo José Cela, Miguel Delibes, Mercè Rodoreda, Ana María Matute, Rafael Sánchez Ferlosio, Carmen Martín Gaite, Juan Goytisolo, among others) thoroughly assimilate echoes of those traumatic years into wider narrative or structural perspectives very different from those we have been discussing. In them diachronic time gives way decisively to synchronic time.

[41] For further discussion see my "El cantón de Cartagena en Sender y Galdós," in *El lugar de Sender: Actas del I Congreso sobre Ramón J. Sender* (Huesca: Instituto de Estudios Altoaragoneses/Zaragoza: Institución Fernando el Católico, 1997), pp. 627–33.

Guide to further reading

Bly, Peter A. (ed.), *Galdós y la historia*, Ottawa Hispanic Series 1 (Ottawa: Dovehouse, 1988).

Carrasquer, Francisco, *'Imán' y la novela histórica de Sender* (London: Támesis, 1970).

Fletcher, Madeleine de Gogorza, *The Spanish Historical Novel 1870–1970* (London: Támesis, 1974).

Regalado García, Antonio, *Benito Pérez Galdós y la novela histórica española, 1868–1912* (Madrid: Ínsula, 1966).

Ribbans, Geoffrey, *History and Fiction in Galdós's Narratives* (Oxford: Clarendon Press, 1993).

8

LOU CHARNON-DEUTSCH

Gender and beyond: nineteenth-century Spanish women writers

Accounts of the evolution of narrative forms in Spanish literature often hinge on an unacknowledged notion of progress in which expressions of pride accompany resentment at the world's failure to recognize national achievements. A glorious start (Cervantes, the picaresque novel) was followed by a period of decline (the unpatriotic eighteenth century, the underdeveloped local-color piece, the contemptible serialized novel), then a reawakening (to use Menéndez Pelayo's term) during the nineteenth century with the emergence of the great masters of realism, notably Pérez Galdós. As Alda Blanco has argued, this trajectory is often narrated as a sexualized competition, in which "feminine" forms, linked with mass culture, are despised or ignored, while more "virile" forms are held up to compete with the work of celebrities such as Balzac or Zola. In describing this narrative trajectory as a response to anxiety over legitimacy, both sexual and national, feminists today are engaged in a healthy critique of literary standards and the evaluative rhetoric of evolution that implies literary perfectibility.[1]

The process of reassessing a feminine tradition begins with a search, discovery, reediting and reevaluation of what has been excluded from the predominantly male canon. In the case of Spain this process is still in its initial phase, although considerable impetus has come recently from the collection of women writers edited by Castalia in conjunction with the Instituto de la Mujer ('Institute for Women's Affairs'). The goal of this series, explained on the Castalia website, is to "recover women's literary contributions" and "recover a lost memory." In addition to important poetry collections by Concepción Arenal, Carolina Coronado, and others, the series has begun recovering neglected works of prose fiction such as Emilia Pardo Bazán's *Dulce dueño* ('Gentle Master') and Angela Grassi's *El copo de nieve* ('Snowflake').

[1] These statements summarize Blanco's "Gender and National Identity: The Novel in Nineteenth-Century Spanish Literary History," in *Culture and Gender in Nineteenth-Century Spain*, ed. Lou Charnon-Deutsch and Jo Labanyi (New York: Oxford University Press, 1995), pp. 120–36.

Similarly the publishers horas y HORAS, in conjunction with Dirección General de la Mujer de la Comunidad de Madrid ('City of Madrid General Office for Women') has embarked on an ambitious project, outlined on their book jackets, to "show, with scientific rigor and elegance, the authentic contribution of women throughout human hisbory." Finally Cátedra, in cooperation with the University of Valencia's Instituto de la Mujer, has translated important works of feminist literary criticism. With a focus on archive work, this series is bringing to light long-forgotten documents essential for the reassessment of Madrid's urban feminine culture.[2]

Coinciding with the publication of recovered texts and documents there has been a more refined critical evaluation of women's writing. Styles formerly judged negatively, such as lachrymose sentimentality or melodrama, are vindicated or at least reinterpreted. Themes that before seemed pedestrian or unimaginative – religious education, domesticity, feminine intuition, rewards for perseverance, devotion, obedience, maternity – are being reassessed either as evidence of alternative social values and cultural practices or for their role in shaping those values and practices. Traditionally, women writers were either categorized as "exceptional brains,"[3] like Emilia Pardo Bazán and Rosalía de Castro who are often held up to compete with a male standard, or grouped among the minions or lesser luminaries whose flaws justifiably excluded them from established canons. Now, however, it has become important to investigate the politics of canon formation; "to study not just how power relations are embedded in texts, but also the social and political institutions and processes through which aesthetic standards are established."[4] In other words, now that the "archaeological labor"[5] of uncovering actual writers and texts has begun, it is time to problematize the text called "literary history."

It is also important to understand not only what political and ideological pressures prevented these lesser women writers from competing with

[2] Archive research is keeping apace with these publishing ventures, although much work remains to be done. Important stimulus has come also from Giuliana Di Febo's often-cited article "Orígenes del debate feminista en España" and Geraldine Scanlon's *La polémica feminista en la España contemporánea (1864–1974)*. The recently published *La mujer en los discursos de género: Textos y contextos del siglo XIX*, ed. Catherine Jagoe, Alda Blanco and Cristina Enríquez de Salamanca (Barcelona: Icaria, 1998) offers the most comprehensive set of documents to facilitate the study of gender in nineteenth-century culture.

[3] E. Martín, *Tres mujeres gallegas del siglo XIX. Concepción Arenal, Rosalía de Castro, Emilia Pardo Bazán* (Barcelona: Editorial Aedos, 1977), p. 211.

[4] J. Sinnigen, "Symbolic Struggles: Literary Study, Social History, Value Judgments," *Revista de Estudios Hispánicos* 27 (1993), p. 445.

[5] A. Blanco, "Escritora, feminidad y escritura en la España de medio siglo," *Breve historia feminista de la literatura española (en lengua castellana)*, vol. v, *La literatura escrita por mujer (Del s. XIX a la actualidad)* (Barcelona: Anthropos, 1998), p. 10.

their male counterparts, but also to assess the considerable appeal that such novelists as María del Pilar Sinués de Marco (with her 73 books one of the most prolific of women authors), Concepción Gimeno de Flaquer, Faustina Sáez de Melgar, and Angela Grassi held for their now forgotten readers. The 1990s saw a rise in the publication of criticism resituating the work of women writers in its proper literary context: Marina Mayoral's *Escritoras románticas españolas*, followed by Susan Kirkpatrick's *Las románticas* and Íñigo Sánchez Llama's *Galería de escritoras isabelinas*; Alda Blanco's essays on, among others, Sinués de Marco and Sáez de Melgar; Maryellen Bieder on Gimeno de Flaquer and Emilia Pardo Bazán; John Sinnigen on Catherine MacPherson, and my survey of women novelists, *Narratives of Desire*.[6]

In reevaluating women's fiction, critics in the US and abroad have relied heavily on Anglo-American as well as non-Spanish continental theory, compensating for a void in critical work on gender and representation in Spain. Anglo-American criticism has been particularly useful for the analysis of nineteenth-century texts. One of the reasons for this is the conviction that the pressures on women writers of the Victorian era mirrored those experienced by women in a very Catholic nineteenth-century Spain that had constructed a religion out of family values. Although applying this theory to Spanish women writers can be problematic, certain texts have contributed greatly to the understanding of Spanish domestic fiction. Denise Riley's *Am I That Name?*, Nancy Armstrong's *Desire and Domestic Fiction*, and Sandra Gilbert and Susan Gubar's *Madwoman in the Attic* are but three of the works that have influenced the way that we approach nineteenth-century Spanish women's texts.[7]

Another trend in Anglo-feminist criticism may also prove useful as the examination of women's writings enters a new stage. Victorian women writers are coming under scrutiny for their unrecognized role in the ends of empire and in the class stratification that have been the subject of numerous critiques by male writers. As victims of a repressive patriarchy, women writers had somehow constituted themselves as a class apart, immune to accusations

[6] M. Mayoral, *Escritoras románticas españolas* (Madrid: Fundación Banco Exterior, 1990); S. Kirkpatrick, *Las románticas: escritoras y subjetividad en España, 1835–1850* (Madrid: Cátedra, 1989); I. Sánchez Llama, *Galería de escritoras isabelinas. La prensa periódica entre 1833 y 1895* (Madrid: Cátedra, 2000); L. Charnon-Deutsch, *Narratives of Desire: Nineteenth-Century Spanish Fiction by Women* (University Park: Pennsylvania State Press, 1994), pp. 58–77.

[7] D. Riley, *Am I that Name? Feminism and the Category of Women in History* (Minneapolis: University of Minnesota Press, 1988); N. Armstrong, *Desire in Domestic Fiction: A Political History of the Novel* (New York: Oxford University Press, 1987); S. Gilbert and S. Gubar, *The Madwoman in the Attic. The Woman Writer and the Nineteenth-Century Literary Imagination* (New Haven: Yale University Press, 1984).

of class bias, imperialism, and racism since they did not finance or fight in wars, determine factory wages and working conditions, or enforce repressive laws. Increasingly, an awakened consciousness of the hidden scenes of collaboration, a vital concern of third wave feminist critics, has shifted the focus away from women's marginalization and victimization towards women's participation in various imperialist projects and in the forging of the modern capitalist state.

It would seem at first that this criticism is not particularly useful to critics of Spanish women writers: Spain's imperial star was in decline by the time Britannia ruled the waves, and its bourgeois class less entrenched. While England was relocating itself "within a much larger circle of the world map,"[8] Spain was focusing attention on ever-smaller circles of influence and power, not only among its colonies, but among nations like France and England, formerly regarded as equals. However, a brief sampling of texts shows the degree to which Spanish women writers constructed their narratives of feminine victimization and self-sacrifice on unchallenged differences of class, race, and ethnicity. Although any number of works would serve to illustrate these issues that complicate the study of gender in novel and narrative, in what follows I focus on four representative samples: Gertrudis Gómez de Avellaneda's *Sab* (1841), María del Pilar Sinués de Marco's *La senda de la Gloria* ('The Path to Glory', 1880), Rosalía de Castro's *El caballero de las botas azules* ('The Gentleman in the Blue Boots', 1867), and Emilia Pardo Bazán's *Los pazos de Ulloa* (*The House of Ulloa*, 1886).[9] My purpose is not to heap blame on writers who were blind to their class bias or racism, but rather to suggest a contrapuntal dialogue between the way nineteenth-century women wrote about themselves and their struggles, and, on the other hand, their patterns of writing about the working classes and the subjects of Spain's former colonies.

Heralded as the first Hispanic anti-slavery novel, Avellaneda's *Sab* is also notable for anticipating the explicitly feminist argument of Pardo Bazán's *Los pazos de Ulloa*, in which the danger for women lies not in books or the public sphere, as writers of domestic fiction feared, but behind the doors of the family home. A domestic drama tending towards the Gothic, *Sab* narrates the trials of an *ingenue* who marries her true love only to discover

[8] E. Said, "Jane Austen and Empire," in *Contemporary Marxist Literary Criticism*, ed. Francis Mulhern (London: Longman, 1992), p. 100. Rpr. from *Raymond Williams: Critical Perspectives*, ed. Terry Eagleton (Oxford: Polity, 1989), pp. 150–64.

[9] G. Gómez de Avellaneda, *Sab*, ed. José Servera (Madrid: Cátedra, 1997); M. del Pilar Sinués de Marco, *La senda de la gloria*, 2nd edn (Madrid: La Moda Elegante Ilustrada, 1880); R. de Castro, *El caballero de las botas azules*, ed. Ana Rodríguez-Fisher (Madrid: Cátedra, 1995); E. Pardo Bazán, *Los pazos de Ulloa*, ed. Marina Mayoral (Madrid: Clásicos Castalia, 1987).

that her husband is a mean-spirited tyrant. This anti-marriage plot, borrowed from George Sand,[10] is infrequent or at least disguised until the latter decades of the nineteenth century. Carlota's post-marriage dilemma represents a departure from conventional women's fiction that championed the ideal of the home as women's socially assigned place.[11] On the other hand, the point of many women's texts, especially those in the decades following *Sab* when the popularity of the domestic novel peaked, is that domestic bliss is rarely achieved or at best can only be earned through great personal sacrifice, a kind of strategic masochism that has its rewards. Undeniably *Sab*'s anti-slavery rhetoric is a departure from mid-century fictions in which a pro-slavery rhetoric (as far as women's slavery is concerned) predominated. What it shares with conventional women's fiction of its day, however, is the conviction that the reward for suffering feminine slavery can only come in the next life, and a recognition of the inextricable relationship between a woman's marketability and her dowry.

Following the model of Mary Wollstonecraft's *Vindication of the Rights of Women* (1792), Avellaneda negotiated the pressure points and limits of ideal femininity by associating the marriage contract with the notion of feminine subjugation. Appropriating the handy colonial rhetoric of freedom and slavery, she constructed her heroine as a slave in the guise of a wealthy and spoiled white Cuban creole. Sab, Carlota, and to an extent Teresa, the other woman slave of the novel, are endowed with superior sensitivity and capacity for altruism and passion; all wear the "chains" that bind them to the world of a ruthless, white male mercantilism. On her deathbed Teresa offers Carlota, suffering under the yoke of her avaricious and indifferent husband, a world of consolation through shared suffering: unloved slave, unloved nun, and unloved wife create a "secret fellowship of superior souls as a way of mitigating the isolation of the feeling subject in an alien world."[12] All three are forced into submission to a new and ruthless order linked to a British colonialism that curiously evades the issue of Spanish exploitation. All three will have to await their rewards in another world where, as the Biblical phrase quoted in the text predicts (*Sab*, p. 212), they will at last be enfolded into the arms of the Lord and relieved of all burdens and cares.

By closely intertwining their destinies, Avellaneda insured that for any one of the three slaves to be truly understood, the oppressed conditions of

[10] See Kirkpatrick, *Las románticas*, p. 142, for Avellaneda's debt to George Sand. For a study of the similarities to Sand's Indiana, who also depicts herself as a slave to men's will, see S. Beyer and F. Kluck, "George Sand and Gertrudis Gómez de Avellaneda," *Nineteenth-Century French Studies* 19.2 (Winter 1991), pp. 203–9.

[11] Kirkpatrick, *Las románticas*, p. 150.

[12] Ibid., p. 153.

all three must come into play. Sab is enslaved by the needs and desires of a white man of means but he is penniless and dependent like Teresa. His love of beauty, justice, and knowledge is a useless and involuntary attribute given his status. But he is a slave not just for the chains that bind him (he is in fact never chained) but because he has no country or family and is unloved by Carlota. Carlota is a slave not just because she married a man incapable of love but because she must, as a dutiful wife, serve interests and ideals that are abhorrent to her. Sab complains that Carlota's husband has purchased her just as one would a slave: "like a piece of merchandise, through calculation, convenience... engaging in a shameful speculation on the most holy tie, the most solemn undertaking. She, who would give him her soul!" (p. 222). A squalid and hateful pack of regrets pursues women when once they wed, the wise slave continues; "like slaves, they patiently drag their chains and lower their head beneath the yoke of human laws. With no other guide but their credulous and ignorant hearts they select a master for life" (pp. 270–1). Sab's melodramatic diatribe reveals that the seemingly anti-slavery stance of the novel is a form of colonization of the mulatto slave's subjectivity and that "the issue of slavery was from the start secondary to that of women."[13] A slave can buy his freedom, suggests Sab, while a woman can only be freed by death; hers is an "enslaved freedom" (p. 261) while "the slave at least can change masters, he can hope that by saving his gold he will some day gain his freedom" (p. 271). This act of staking a claim for a more authentic status as victim, implausibly spoken by a true slave who describes his status as circumstantial since it can be terminated, if nothing else, invites readers to ignore the unenviable conditions of the freed slave in societies where slavery was still legal. As Jerome Branche has demonstrated, *Sab* is not a true abolitionist text; its insistence on the ambivalence of Sab, and its failure to vindicate black women, demonstrates Avellaneda's allegiance to the dominant order.[14]

Reminiscent of the anti-slavery rhetoric of *Sab* or the poetry of Carolina Coronado,[15] fledgling feminist novelists of the mid-century such as María

[13] Ibid., p. 156.

[14] J. Blanche, "Ennobling Savagery? Sentimentalism and the Subaltern in *Sab*," *Afro-Hispanic Review* 17.2 (Fall 1998), pp. 12–23.

[15] See Carolina Coronado's poems in *Water Lilies. An Anthology of Spanish Women Writers from the Fifteenth Through the Nineteenth Century*, ed. Amy Katz Kaminsky (Minneapolis and London: University of Minnesota Press, 1997), pp. 438–47. Avellaneda's analogy between the bitter plight of the black Cuban slave and the woman enslaved by patriarchy found echo in the poet Coronado, who, like Avellaneda, was a confirmed abolitionist. In her poem "To the Abolition of Slavery in Cuba" (1863), she castigates Spain for not freeing her slaves when even the "mighty eagle" (America) had seen fit to do so. On the contrary, in "To Spain" Coronado imagines Spain not as a cruel master but as a slave in order to

del Pilar Sinués de Marco enlisted oppressed classes to redefine what they perceived as the general oppression of even the most elite classes of women in a patriarchal society. In keeping with their bourgeois myopia, however, they often cordoned themselves from the working classes at the same time as they claimed an equally oppressive enslavement. An award-winning work of art by the heroine of Sinués's *La senda de la gloria* graphically illustrates this point. After she has been abused and beaten by her worthless husband, Julia, her husband's "slave," produces her most ambitious work. In "Egoism" she juxtaposes the greed and indifference of the wealthy towards the working classes with the cruelty and indifference of a husband faced with the suffering of his family.

In the background of the painting a storm rages, fishermen struggle with their sails, and a stricken sailor lies across the bow of his boat, blood gushing from his chest. In the center a corpulent man sits on a veranda beneath a canopy of vines, suggesting he is on holiday. He raises a fork to his mouth with a piece of fowl on it, while before him spreads a sumptuous dinner that he alone is enjoying. He is equally oblivious of the agonized visages of the fishermen, the emaciated dog begging a crust of bread at his feet, and his delicate and beautiful wife holding a sickly child to her breast. The bond uniting the neglected wife and child and the floundering fishermen in the background is forged by the couple's servant, who stares in horror at the stricken fisherman while at the same time holding the sick child's hand with a gentle and intimate gesture: "to signal that the state of the child also caused a great part of her pain" (p. 209). Beyond the horror of the struggling fishermen, the desperation of the abused wife, the servant's tender gesture, the suffering

draw attention to her country's diminished position among the great European nations: her enslaved woman-nation languishes in wait for a Cid or Pelayo to rescue her from humiliation – "thus from black slave woman that she is now / will she become Lady Spain" (*Water Lilies*, p. 441). Elsewhere in Coronado's poetry, the category of slave is reserved for women suffering under the yoke of patriarchy. In the 1849 poem "In the Salvatierra Castle" she complains bitterly that since the tearful women enslaved by Goths and Arabs rent their veils and consumed themselves in senseless suffering, very little has improved the lot of women: "not one link has time chipped off from our ancient and barbarous chains" (p. 445).

Emilia Pardo Bazán exploited the same dichotomy of progress versus stasis later in the century. Echoing Coronado, she complained that worldwide progress for men was widening the gulf that existed between the sexes: "Imagine two people standing in the same place; make one advance and the other remain immobile: as much as the first advances, the other remains behind. Each new conquest for man in the area of political freedoms deepens the moral abyss that separates him from woman, and renders her role more passive and enigmatic. Freedom of education, freedom of religion, the right to assembly, suffrage, parliamentarism, all allow half of society (the masculine half) to acquire strength and activities at the expense of the feminine half" (*La mujer española y otros artículos feministas*, ed. Leda Schiavo, Madrid: Editora Nacional, 1976, p. 33).

of the sickly child and the "cruel egoism" of the rich bourgeois, however, Julia's painting also carries the equalizing message of an earlier generation of women writers who confounded the exploitation of the domestic angel (whether rich or poor) with that of the servants, housekeepers, wet-nurses, and other victims of class disparity with whom the domestic angel shared her bondage.

Just as it is possible to read *Sab* as domestic fiction, Rosalía de Castro's *El caballero de las botas azules* can be read as an anti-slavery novel. On the back cover of the novel, Ana Rodríguez-Fisher asks readers to discard any notion of Castro as a fragile, sweet poet. *El caballero*, she suggests, is "urbane, social, satirical, Cervantine, realist and fantastic, rupturist and protean. A novel that foregoes the plaintive and launches a message of protest and liberty." In her introduction, Rodríguez-Fisher complains that Castro has been mischaracterized as a romantic voice forever bound to her "feminine condition" (p. 11). Implied is her conviction that *El caballero* has been unjustly overlooked by critics like Menéndez y Pelayo, who classified novels written before 1870 as "drivel and monstrosities,"[16] when in fact it competes with the more energetic prose that characterizes the realist novel. It is not difficult to see why this corrective is warranted when we compare this novel with the works of Castro's contemporaries or even with her other productions such as *La hija del mar* (*Daughter of the Sea*, 1859). This is all the more reason, however, to subject it to the same critical scrutiny usually reserved for authors whose works have generated the most critical acclaim and attention.

In *El caballero de las botas azules*, a desperate author conjures up a muse named Novelty to guide him to literary fame. Novelty transforms the erstwhile author into the Duque de la Gloria (Duke of Glory), who makes a stunning entrance into Madrid society wearing blue boots and a bizarre eaglet-feather cravat and brandishing a wand studded with diamonds and bells. Rumors abound that the Duke has come to Madrid to publish the "book of books" that will surpass every work of literature previously published. He is so handsome, seductive, and novel that everyone rushes to copy his dress and seek out his company. As one by one women fall under his spell, the Duke relentlessly unmasks their frivolous desires, alienation, and materialism. Censuring women's failure to distinguish between fiction and reality, he admonishes them "to be resistant readers, to read critically the fantasies scripted for them."[17] Meanwhile, implementing what Kirkpatrick calls a "supremely

[16] Blanco, "Gender and National Identity," p. 122.

[17] S. Kirkpatrick, "Fantasy, Seduction, and the Woman Reader: Rosalía de Castro's Novels," in *Culture and Gender in Nineteenth-Century Spain*, p. 88.

successful marketing strategy," he makes men sense their mediocrity and shortcomings, until the very mention of his "book of books" makes them cringe with envy. Finally, when everyone is convinced that Spanish literature and society are worthless, the Duke orders a great pit dug and has every book but his own thrown into it. With all the women gathered around him dressed as his slaves, he delivers a sermon about bondage, arguing that women have been slaves to fashion and crass materialism, bad reading habits, unbridled passions, and inappropriate class aspirations. Having completed his mission of "belling the cat," he then mysteriously disappears, leaving behind a great stock of his "book of books."

Generally disliked and misunderstood, *El caballero* is now finally garnering attention for its subtle problematizing of feminine desire and the cultural production of gender. For example, Kirkpatrick has analyzed its critique of women's reading habits and the nefarious consequences of a public manipulated by a market-driven press. However, as far as women's roles are concerned, we are still some distance from understanding the precise relationship between patriarchy and capitalism and perhaps still under the influence of the celebratory phase of feminist recovery of a lost tradition, and thus have not adequately scrutinized the class bias implied in Castro's text. For example, several questions remain to be explored: What contradictions are implied when, on one hand, women are exhorted to become better readers but are only ever pictured, and only imagine themselves, as morally and sexually degraded slaves of the Duke? What does it mean that the Duke encourages only wealthy women like Vinca Rúa to become better readers, while he exhorts underprivileged women to find and keep their humbler place in a society of non-readers? Finally, are the novel's complex mechanics of desire a recognition of social manipulation or evidence of desire's ontological origin, or both?

A focus on feminine desire reveals *El caballero* to be one of the most fertile texts of Spanish literature, a catalogue of the many dissatisfactions and demands attributable to a decadent society in which the pursuit of pleasure never results in satisfaction or the abatement of desire no matter what other advantages (money, beauty, or class) a woman possesses. It can be argued, then, that the mechanics of desire reveal primary as well as social processes. One of the Duke's principal missions is to enthrall women sexually and then exploit their obsession in order to ridicule their reading habits, social customs, and lack of productivity. Yet in the process he also reveals important information about the psychological mechanics of desire. Beyond admonitions regarding feminine excess and vanity, *El caballero* explores the dissatisfactions that define women as subjects *because* they desire, regardless of the appropriateness of the desired object. For this reason a combined materialist-psychoanalytic analysis of this novel would best explore both its false consciousness and processes of alienation. These themes converge precisely in the description of the goals and production of desire. While a materialist view centers on the economic and political interests implied in the production of desire, psychoanalysis discloses the way material interests depend on the emotional necessities of those driven by impossible desires.

A useful step in analyzing desire as it relates to gender stratification in *El caballero* is to ascertain its affinity with capitalist exploitation. The Duke demonstrates that women's desire to identify with him, thus exploiting their creative and sensual nature, is impossible: their romantic fantasies are unrealizable and they mistake sexual degradation for freedom. The parallel with Marxist descriptions of the worker under capitalism is evident: the fundamental capitalist contract implies only two possibilities regarding the buying and selling of labor power, either "selling oneself into bondage or purchasing a slave."[18] On the one hand, the Duke's boots unchain a feminine passion for spending; there is no end to women's desire to purchase the precious articles or associate themselves with those who possess such objects. On the other, like Avellaneda's Sab, the Duke reveals that women themselves are also merchandise, mere slaves who mistakenly imagine themselves to be free. Their slavery highlights the lack of reciprocity between men and women: the longed-for romantic hero turns out to be a slaver instead of a poet come to rescue them from boredom. The Duke is a master teacher but uninterested in overseeing the conditions of his reformed slaves.

The publishing industry banks on the desire of modern societies for the new, which is why Castro appropriately called the Duke's muse 'Novelty.' The reason everyone will always desire her, she explains, is that whatever she becomes for them, whether a steam engine in the present or air travel in the future, will never be enough to satisfy human curiosity. In other words, the muse personifies desire, who, she claims, was her mother. Novelty attires the Duke so bizarrely that his grand entrance into Madrid has much the same effect as queen consort María Cristina's entrance had on her subjects in 1829. And much like the queen's admired blue dress and supple leather gloves, the Duke's blue boots exert a strange, mesmerizing effect over everyone who sees them. The glow of the smooth, unseamed leather boots increases in proportion to the passion with which the Duke is contemplated. For example, when he visits one lady's boudoir, "the boots discharged a glow that disturbed eyes and thoughts ... Perhaps they had never looked so handsome" (pp. 698–9).

[18] E. Victor Wolfenstein, *Psychoanalytic Marxism. Groundwork* (New York: Guilford, 1993), p. 308.

While psychoanalytic theory leads us to see the desire for these precious commodities as a form of expression of repressed desire,[19] a materialist analysis is needed to articulate exactly how the quest to satisfy desire always implies a slave–master relation and how the social and sexual relations of *El caballero* function within Spanish cultural institutions such as the publishing industry at the time the novel was written. The transactions between the Duke (or the market where he is on sale) and women involve situations of surrender (of sex, money, and labor) and domination that structurally mirror capitalist relationships of domination invoked in Marx's notion of commodity fetishism. The Duke's clothes have both a symbolic and a material value; the author casts the craving for them as something universal and natural, an ontological desire to possess secret knowledge, and, beyond that, to repossess the plenitude that is lost to the child at the dawn of subjectivity. But we also need to understand craving as something unnatural, the effect of market strategies creating a demand for inappropriate or impractical material goods. Thus the lack that creates an insatiable desire for what can never be recaptured helps to explain the importance of establishing difference and distinction, especially the class distinctions that are at the core of the novel's didacticism.

The protagonist's desire to be a great writer unmasks Spanish society's frivolous obsession with fashion, novelty, and technological progress – exemplified here as a flying machine – at the expense of social progress. In their quest for the exotic aristocratic women have forgotten how to be of use to society. Middle-class women, instead of helping ends meet by knitting stocking caps, dream of dressing like the queen: "the better off dream and discuss how they can dress like princesses, while the poorer rant about silk and lace" (p. 675). Although the response to them is intensely personal, the blue boots are a collective social object: they produce highly charged emotional responses which the Duke uses to criticize the pervasive decadence of Spanish society. The various forms of obsession, occasioned by the boots, are linked to a desire for something incommensurate with what the Duke poses as healthy social, sexual, and cultural values.

While critics usually focus on Spain's consumerism and decadence during the period of the Restoration of the Bourbon monarchy (1874–85), already in 1867 Castro condemns the ills of excessive consumerism and novelty-seeking and their link to cultural and sexual malaise, arguing for a more moral and productive society: women should sew and write instead of going to dances; become producers of cultural and material objects instead of mere pawns in the endless exchange of women and goods in a capitalist market. Her

[19] Charnon-Deutsch, *Narratives of Desire*, pp. 87–8.

critique of these social and sexual ills led her to the brilliant choice of an exotic male figure whose play of masks and precious clothing dazzles every sector of Madrid society. The symbolic complexity of the boots demonstrates Castro's awareness of both the economic and non-economic (sexual, cultural) processes involved in the working of desire; both are constituent factors in the determination of subjectivity.

The libidinous investment in the Duke's blue boots qualifies them as a fetish object in both the psychoanalytic and materialist sense. Like fetish objects in mercantile exchanges with Africa and other "exotic" lands in the sixteenth and seventeenth centuries, they are a cross-cultural object. The narrator emphasizes the fact that the raw materials for the boots and feather cravat come from the mysterious banks of the Jordan. Together with the Arab servant Zuma, the boots symbolize the increasing Spanish obsession with exotic locales and fashions that the magazine *Correo de la moda* described in 1851 as the height of fashion: "jackets bordered and festooned like those of Turkish and Armenian women, babuchas embroidered with gold, pearls and multi-colored silk."[20]

The boots also serve as a cross-class interaction or commerce, an overdetermined signifier of class ascension that the text explicitly condemns as dangerous and debilitating. To the beleaguered bureaucrat, they represent his womenfolk's unbridled drive to consume and, through the purchase of certain commodities, to indulge in futile attempts to attract men and thereby enhance their exchange value on the marriage market. The narrator condemns this extravagant display as a class-debilitating expenditure: "At the cost of such sacrifices and humiliations, the middle class supports the apparent luxury that debilitates it in its death throes" (p. 732). Castro clearly wants middle-class women to recognize that the blue boots and other accessories, examples of extravagantly expensive clothing, are valued falsely. Belonging to the middle class carries with it the responsibility to be frugal, productive members of society, and to relinquish aspirations of class mobility.

Finally, in classical Freudian terms the blue boots are a phallic fetish. For their would-be possessor they advertise a tantalizing plenitude while at the same time designating a lack, since what they symbolize ultimately cannot be had. The Duke is a walking phallic symbol, a mirage that, like all fetishes, simultaneously negates lack and stands in for what is lacking. The blue boots, feather cravat, and diamond-studded wand the Duke waves in front of everyone's nose mask emptiness, represented in *El caballero* as Spain's lack of an aesthetic sublime. The Duke masquerades as the possessor of something beyond par, deploying beauty, seductiveness, and genius as

[20] *Correo de la moda*, 1.1 (1 November 1851), p. 127.

projections of his sublime book of books whose content he never reveals. As an aesthetic signifier, his clothes symbolize for the men who emulate them what they lack: the chance to gain professional autonomy, a way of distinguishing themselves from the mundane by acquiring an outstanding literary style that is unreproducible or achieving some other professional distinction. Both men and women project onto the boots and cravat the power of realizing repressed desires, even while, as Marxists argue about the drive to possess money, the ultimate object of desire "remains perpetually and tantalizingly out of reach."[21]

Conceptualizing the various attributes of the fetish helps to underscore the fact that material, cultural, and sexual needs interlock in *El caballero de las botas azules*. Above all the Duke shows his slaves that they are enthralled by a simulacrum, a substitute for what society can no longer recognize: truth, aesthetic beauty, duty, and enduring love. At the same time, by casting the boots as a commodity of priceless value, Castro forces readers to recognize that the production, value, and purchase of the boots are linked to specific relations of class, ethnicity, and gender. That is, the novel enjoins us to study more closely the relationship between aesthetic production and consumerism in nineteenth-century Spain.

In addition to the rhetoric of slavery that problematized women's duties in the domestic sphere, the canon of women's texts in nineteenth-century Spain offers another perspective: the viewpoint of those who toiled at the heroine's leisure yet who never gained the rhetorical category of "slave" reserved for more spiritual heroines. Household servants in Spanish literature were despised or demonized by even the most feminist of authors, such as Emilia Pardo Bazán, whose stellar career would not have been possible without the contingent of household servants that catered for her needs. The bourgeois mythology championed in the writing of Sinués de Marco, Grassi, Gimeno de Flaquer, Böhl de Faber, and others advocated middle-class motherhood as a loftier aspiration than literary fame. This stance complicated notions of public and private gender roles and made for odd justifications of the restrictions on women's activities and movement. Whereas cultural dogma held that children belonged to their fathers even while mothers were supposed to provide their environment, nourishment, and early religious training, women authors, most of whom were also mothers, problematized this Rousseauian notion in a variety of ways.

Rather than directly challenge male supremacy in the family or diminishing women's material importance, writers like Pardo Bazán exaggerated women's spiritual role or split women into two classes: those who bore and

[21] Wolfenstein, *Psycholanalytic Marxism*, p. 3–4.

gave physical nourishment to children, such as Sabel in *Los pazos* or María Pepa in *La quimera* ('The Chimera', 1905), and those for whom maternity entailed complicated and contradictory aspirations, traumas, spiritual and physical dangers, usually upper middle-class and aristocratic women who stood in sharp contrast to their healthier but less educated counterparts. Setting aside exceptions such as Amparo of *La tribuna* (*Tribune of the People*, 1882) or Antonia in *La piedra angular* ('The Cornerstone', 1891), the working-class women whom Pardo Bazán occasionally praised in her feminist essays were not the mothers she chose to feature in her novels. As a result, the ideal of the nurturing, tender, conserving mother figure depends more on class than on gender.[22] Only women with leisure time, a stable living environment, and steady male companionship have the luxury and inclination to be good mothers, even though tragedy or ill health may strike and break the mother–child bond. Poor mothers, like Leocadia in *El cisne de Vilamorta* (*The Swan of Vilamorta*, 1884), have to make impossible choices that turn them into bad mothers if they are not already *naturally* inclined to neglectfulness by virtue of their class status.

This double vision of motherhood in Pardo Bazán's novels reminds us how myopic educated women can be when portraying themselves as victims. Only by acknowledging this can we understand what else is at stake in Pardo Bazán's concept of feminine subjectivity. For example, in *Los pazos*, our understanding of Nucha as an outsider who erroneously stumbles in on a cultural wasteland only gains contour by contrast with the native version of the mother, Sabel, who is the most conspicuous outsider in this fiction of the saintly mother. For modern feminist readers such as Gayatri Spivak, Sabel would represent the excluded other woman more than Nucha since her role is to allow the good female subject to emerge as the one worthy of admiration and pity. As one of Nucha's victimizers, the text marginalizes Sabel to the border where animal and human species are barely distinguishable. By sacrificing Sabel's subjectivity to the other maternal figure of the novel, Pardo Bazán does more than unmask the category of the natural by revealing the brutality of uncivilized country life; she relegates the servant to the dim field of vision within which members of one class could justify their feelings of superiority over others. Elevating Sabel to a position of power in the Ulloa household does not make readers hope for a rise in her fortunes. Since Sabel is the *bad* mother, we can only hope that eventually she will be confined to the kitchen with the cook, scullery maids, and the village witch.

[22] See Geraldine Scanlon's notes in *La polémica feminista* on the complex interplay of class and gender in *La Tribuna*. As Scanlon states, Pardo Bazán's attitude towards Amparo's role was ambivalent: she was sympathetic to her gender struggle and aspirations while condemnatory and condescending toward her political goals.

As defined by Julia Kristeva, motherhood is associated with the primitive semiotic, prior to the acquisition of speech when the dyadic relation with the mother is seamless. This description is from the point of view of the adult, whose unconscious memory of the early maternal bond keeps threatening the male subject with collapse. At times Pardo Bazán's representations of motherhood connect to this psychological narrative, especially during the first, most materialistic stage of her fiction. However, even in early works such as *Los pazos*, we can distinguish two divergent conceptions of mother, one taken from the child's perspective and the other from a mother's point of view. For the child, Mother Nature represents the primitive maternal, a remembered maternal presence threatening pre-symbolic non-differentiation and, by extension, the collapse of the civilized. She belongs to the realm of the masculine imaginary rather than representing motherhood as a lived experience. The woman who embodies this fear in Pardo Bazán's fiction is a woman of inferior caring instincts and often inferior class to which Pardo Bazán feels comfortable assigning the negative category of the mind–body and nature – culture dichotomies. The second and prevalent representation of motherhood, taken from the perspective of those adults who give themselves over to mothering, represents society's "civilizing" feminine element that fosters a sense of community and intersubjectivity, checking sexual appetites. This is the maternal ideal or imaginary that Pardo Bazán wove into her fictions of motherhood. Women who do not readily accept the responsibility of this type of motherhood – usually poorer or uneducated women in Pardo Bazán's view – bring death to their children and chaos to their households; they are not, in other words, true mothers.

In the above examples I have argued for a more critical view of feminine production that reflects shifts in late twentieth-century feminist thinking among eminent Hispanists (e.g. M. Bieder, C. Jagoe, H. Gold) who have shared their reflections in private communications. The shift is not the result of a subsiding interest in women writers or gender studies but a response to an uncomfortable feeling about pursuing the "woman-as-victim-of-phallocentrism" (Bieder) line of earlier images-of-women criticism and a general wariness of "theory that isn't grounded in history" (Jagoe).[23] It is clearly no longer sufficient merely to argue that women have been disadvantaged within patriarchy: this truism should be "a point of departure for our research rather than a conclusion" (Gold). Several are turning their attention to issues relating to the "wider spectrum including race and nation" (Jagoe), recognizing especially that "class is fundamental to any study of

[23] The comments of Beider, Gold, Jagoe, and Blanco, quoted in this concluding paragraph, are from personal communications with the authors.

nineteenth-century women" (Bieder). Rather than teach courses or write books on an individual or even a group of women writers, many now choose to frame gender as "one aspect of a larger theme" (Gold), for example, the role of literature in the construction of national identity or regional ethnicity, the alienated writer or reader and the urban setting, the intermixing of mass culture and elite culture, the presence (or absence) of the colonial figure in realist fiction. Yet a word of caution is in order. Perhaps, suggests Alda Blanco, "in other national literatures, work on women writers has run its course, but this is sadly not the case in our field." The move in the most recent decade from feminist literary criticism to gender studies to cultural studies and now post-colonial studies has left the pre-twentieth-century Spanish canon largely intact.

Guide to further reading

Di Febo, Giuliana, "Orígenes del debate feminista en España. La escuela krausista y la Institución Libre de Enseñanza (1870–1890)," *Sistema* 12 (1976), pp. 49–82.

Rivière Gómez, Aurora, *La educación de la mujer en el Madrid de Isabel II* (Madrid: horas y HORAS, 1993).

Ruíz Guerrero, Cristina, *Panorama de escritoras españolas*, vol. II (Cádiz: Universidad de Cádiz, 1997).

Scanlon, Geraldine, *La polémica feminista en la España contemporánea (1864–1974)* (Madrid: Siglo XXI, 1976).

Simón Palmer, María del Carmen, *Escritoras españolas del siglo XIX: manual bio-bibliográfico* (Madrid: Castalia, 1991).

Zavala, Iris M. (ed.), *Breve historia feminista de la literatura española (en lengua castellana)*, vol. III (Barcelona: Anthropos, 1996).

9

NOËL VALIS

Decadence and innovation in *fin de siglo* Spain

By the end of the nineteenth century, a deep sense of disillusionment and exhaustion had settled over Spain. While the perception of decay and lost opportunities was generally felt throughout Europe, in Spain the circumstances were particularly striking. Despite a century of enormous progress and changes, the Old World was ill at ease with itself, a feeling of crisis at hand. Somewhat belatedly, Spain, too, had participated in the economic and social advances of the period, but always with the awareness of having once been an empire. Indeed, by 1898 the loss of empire was almost total after the disastrous war with the United States in Cuba. The sense of having come undone nationally, however, coexisted paradoxically with another feeling: the growing suspicion that the nation had never really coalesced ideologically or historically. Both regionalistic and political differences became more pronounced at the same time, as elsewhere secularization signaled a crisis of spiritual and moral values. On a personal level, Unamuno expressed Spanish isolationism thus: "Every soul lives alone among other souls alone, in a naked, sterile desert, where they twist and turn like the poor spirits of skeletons shut inside their anemic skins."[1]

This inwardness suggests both atomization and the *fin de siglo* desire to evade unpleasant historical realities. Similarly, narrative tends to break down into smaller fragments, thus on the one hand mimicking the perceived instabilities of the period and on the other problematizing an uneasy relationship with the present. In this essay, I shall use the texts of Ramón del Valle-Inclán as exemplary of decadent writing in *fin de siglo* Spain, placing his work within his native Galician, Spanish, and European contexts of historical decline, local nationalism, and pan-European aesthetic movements. On the local and national levels, Valle's early work *Femeninas* ('Feminine Portraits') and the *Sonatas* can be seen as heavily committed to a cultural and literary

[1] Miguel de Unamuno, "Sobre el marasmo actual de España," in *En torno al casticismo*, 7th edn. (Madrid: Espasa-Calpe, 1968), p. 140.

genealogical imperative. Here, through the figure of his creation of the Marqués de Bradomín, Valle invents his own new "lineage" of the self through writing, thus accomplishing two things: the establishment of his own originality and the legitimatization of a renascent Galician culture. Paradoxically, he does so ideologically on the basis of Galician and Spanish historical decadence. Even more paradoxically, he creates this new, peculiarly Galician-Spanish lineage by inventive borrowings from the European tradition of aestheticism, which begins with Baudelaire. Decadence as a generative metaphor produces artistically a genealogy of the literary imagination. This notion of lineage is often literally part of the narration itself in the form of decaying aristocracies and enfeebled *anciens régimes*. Such characters and their family histories symbolically serve as figures of a socio-historical crisis, the crisis of a decadent society faced with the arrival of the modern. These figures function in a positive sense as a way of working around the problem of decline, because as tropes they also represent a new style, a new vision of things, albeit fragmented and unstable. This genealogy of the writing self is, in the final analysis, anti-genealogical in nature.

An obsessive preoccupation with decadence defines the last years of the century throughout Europe. But decadence is not simply a central theme: it becomes the explanatory metaphor, closely related to the way degeneracy theory in clinical medicine, science, politics, and religion seemed to explain why societies did not work properly and therefore did not conform to the expected scheme of things. As Stuart Gilman points out, a generative metaphor like degeneration (or decadence) occurs "in situations where there are dilemmas – social circumstances where there are stubborn conflicts of perspective."[2] At the same time, he adds, the "closeness of 'fit' [of degeneracy theory] with accepted perceptions of reality makes it acceptable, and, in a sense, makes it generative."[3] Thus, for example, inequalities between the sexes or domination over colonized peoples could be "explained" without having to deal seriously with the problems and conflicts engendered by such relationships.

Decadence as a generative, or explanatory, metaphor could be used, like degeneracy theory, to justify cultural or historical decline, scientific alarmism (the end of the universe, as revealed in the second law of thermodynamics), or moral corruption, among other things. By the same token, decadence,

[2] Stuart C. Gilman, "Political Theory and Degeneration: From Left to Right, From Up to Down," in *Degeneration: The Dark Side of Progress*, ed. Edward Chamberlin and Sander L. Gilman (New York: Columbia University Press, 1985), pp. 167, 173.

[3] Stuart Gilman takes the term from Donald Schön's "Generative Metaphor: A Perspective on Problem-Setting in Social Policy," in *Metaphor and Thought*, ed. Andrew Ortony (Cambridge University Press, 1979), p. 255.

which can only be understood in relation to such normative concepts as progress, health, and nature, is implicitly an unstable idea, subject to differing interpretations and dependent on a range of shaded meanings. Why, for example, did there persist a feeling of decline in post-1870 France, despite the country's rapid recovery from the Franco-Prussian War? Clearly, subjective understandings of decay come into play here. Decadence suggests, etymologically and historically, a falling away; and temporally points backward to the past. The relation between the past and the present becomes fraught with dissonance and disjunction. Preoccupation with decadence is only partially about the past, and has more to do with the present, with dissatisfaction over present realities, which are viewed through the prism of pastness.

In this sense, decadence, which is a pan-European preoccupation, contains within it both a backward and a forward movement, making it difficult to assess precisely the standpoint from which the phenomenon is being viewed. Marx, for example, perceived the bourgeoisie as decadent. Yet cultural refinement and aesthetic sensibility, which are characteristic of decadence in the arts and literature (Oscar Wilde, the symbolist painter Gustave Moreau, the Naturalist turned decadentist writer Huysmans, Valle-Inclán), spring, ultimately, from that very same bourgeoisie. Decadence is usually seen in opposition to progress; yet some nineteenth-century observers considered progress itself, such as the intensive industrialization of England, a sign of decadence. As David Weir points out, "the paradoxical nature of decadence and its resistance to definition are among the most important elements of its meaning."[4]

In the realm of aesthetics, decadence as style and as aesthetic creed emerges from the ashes of Romanticism, turning into the phoenix of modernism. Literary and artistic decadence is not only transitional in nature, but paradoxically innovative. Indeed, David Weir suggests that decadence "is less a period of transition than a dynamics of transition" (*Decadence*, p. 15). In narrative, decadent writing wavers between the mimetic drive toward realism and an anti-realistic impulse away from the present, away from coherent, linear plot and character developments. What realist and decadent writings have in common is a profound dissatisfaction with the material world of the historical present. Hence, a realist-Naturalist novel like Clarín/Leopoldo Alas's *La Regenta* ('The Judge's Wife', 1884–5) is deeply absorbed in the presentation of everyday realities – the backbiting provincial world of Vetusta, the physical and psychological illnesses of the protagonist, Ana Ozores – as signs of cultural, historical and moral decadence without forsaking causality

[4] David Weir, *Decadence and the Making of Modernism* (Amherst: University of Massachusetts Press, 1995), p. 2. In my discussion of the meanings of decadence, I am indebted to Weir's invaluable study.

or the fiction of mimesis. Yet, like Zola and Huysmans, who were steeped in realism and Naturalism, Clarín drifted into another transitional mode of writing, clearly foreshadowed in the pervasive decadent motifs of his masterpiece and brilliantly developed in his second novel, *Su único hijo* (*His Only Son*, 1891), in which he deploys heavy doses of decadence, hysteria, and reverie. One could fruitfully read this later novel alongside narratives like Huysmans's *A rebours* (*Against Nature*, 1884), the key text of decadent writing, and Zola's *Le Rêve* (*The Dream*, 1888), drenched in symbolism and escapism.

In Spain, one of the best literary examples of decadence as both innovative art form and a generative metaphor is the early work of Ramón del Valle-Inclán, in particular *Femeninas* (1895) and the *Sonatas* (1902–5). Valle-Inclán's first book, *Femeninas*, drew the notice of fellow Galician Manuel Murguía, a key figure of the Galician literary renaissance. In his prologue to *Femeninas*, Murguía hails the newness of Valle's work: "Such is its merit that it speaks to us of what is always eternal, always young, in a new form, under a different style and with an original charm."[5] He adds, however, that the newness of *Femeninas* is relative, being new only in the place of its publication (the province of Galicia). Murguía's argument joins originality to local nationalistic concerns, claiming Valle as a native son whose style and vision are intrinsically Galician (hence, original). The privileging of feeling, the lightly ironic tone, the fluid style, he says, are Galician, while the derivative character of *Femeninas* arises from the *modernista* mold (or decadent style).

Murguía also insists on an implicit realism in Valle's text, suggesting that these exotic tales of love are based on actual experiences, not mere inventions ("Prólogo," p. 47). Using Naturalist language, he refers to both the adventures and the women of these stories as "human documents" and the product of "experimentation" (p. 48). He considers the stories "confessional" as well. It is hard to judge how much Murguía really took seriously the "documental" or "confessional" nature of *Femeninas*. But the "nouveau frisson" (his words), or new thrill, he sees in Valle's book, which he relates to the prose-poem form, is consistent with his insistence on the experimentation he finds in *Femeninas* (p. 51). Murguía slides over any possible conflicting understandings of the term "experimentation," which suggests both Naturalistic and modernistic meanings in his prologue. This is important, because it provides us with a fascinating glimpse into one reader's reaction to Valle's early work. Murguía has captured the transitional form of the work, seeing it as "romantic, and yet quite new" (p. 50).

[5] Manuel Murguía, "Prólogo" to *Femeninas. Epitalamio* by Ramón del Valle-Inclán (Madrid: Espasa-Calpe, 1978), p. 45.

The prologue is illuminating in another way, as it is structured through an implicit contrast between the feminine and the masculine in *Femeninas*. The style of Valle's text, he says, is "feminine," possessing "a feminine, nearly sinuous, grace" (p. 47); it is feminine, too, in feeling and subject matter (p. 50). In contrast, Murguía places the author and the notion of authorship within a male context. I remember Valle's father well, he exclaims; the son bears the same name and follows the same path of glory. He concludes on this note: "And in the name of his father, I say to him: Son, fulfill your destiny, and may the future awaiting you be good to you!" (p. 53).

In this manner, the paternal order is passed on, not only personally but collectively since it is also part of a Galician tradition ("the pride and glory of this poor Galicia", p. 53). Murguía links Valle-Inclán as author biologically and culturally to a genealogy, which is not only familial but textual. His prologue inscribes the text and writing as feminine, while authorship, though male-centered, becomes equally internalized, made textual as it were, by being linked in a cultural genealogy to a line of Galician "fathers." Murguía makes note of Valle's forebears, who were great captains and notable men of science and literature. It is for this that Galicia is remembered. Ironically, we remember Manuel Murguía today mainly for being the husband of the poet and novelist Rosalía de Castro, one of those proverbially strong-minded Galician women of whom Emilia Pardo Bazán spoke so forcefully in *La mujer española.*

An exquisite verbal *bibelot* or decorative object, *Femeninas* may strike us today as hopelessly dated and derivative writing. Nonetheless, Murguía's intuition was essentially correct. *Femeninas* is Valle-Inclán's first significant experiment in what has variously been called *modernismo*, *decadentismo*, or simply aestheticism. As such, the stories of *Femeninas* anticipate the novelist's more mature writing of the *Sonatas* and later works. As decadent style, content and form, both *Femeninas* and especially the *Sonatas* are supremely narcissistic texts, reflecting a heightened artistic self-consciousness which insists on writing as verbal artifact, privileges the superiority of art and artifice over nature, explores new sensations, presents a fragmented sense of reality, and evades the present.

Like other decadent writers, Valle-Inclán deliberately exploits what Max Nordau, author of the influential study *Degeneration* (1895), and others harshly criticized as decadent, weak, or immoral as a way of simultaneously glorifying the artist and artistic originality *and* of criticizing what Valle, Huysmans, Wilde, Rachilde, and others considered truly decadent: the dull middle-class spirit of conformity and cowardice. Valle-Inclán found an alternative world in the recreation of an idealized, aristocratic Galician past, an invented genealogy of quasi-biological and cultural significance. Yet the really fundamental genealogy created here is more textual than literal or biographical: textual in the sense that what Valle legitimizes as his true "lineage" is writing itself, symbolized in the melancholy posturing of the Marqués de Bradomín, a don Juan whose greatest conquest is not of women (with whom he more often than not fails) but of language (his memoirs, or the *Sonatas*). Brad Epps has argued that in Valle's *Sonata de otoño* (*Autumn Sonata*, 1902) "genealogy, and the generative force it implies, is at once deadened and melancholily preserved in and as autobiography, itself repeatedly posed, and posing, as a not so distant relative of fiction."[6] Epps's helpful insight encourages us to examine further what the "autobiographical" might mean and what place it holds within a literary frame of highly self-conscious writing. I would suggest that Valle's constant recreation of himself through writing and through the mask of the Marqués de Bradomín is not literally autobiographical (as Epps also sees), but a symbolic genealogical impulse which ultimately deconstructs itself into something else. That something else is writing itself.

Murguía unconsciously saw the link between genealogy and writing, when he spoke in the same breath of Valle's new style and his family history. Valle's texts are indeed about families. But as with many other decadent texts, such realist/Naturalist rootedness, which appears ideologically and causally determined, is an illusion. The classic work of this kind is Huysmans's *Against Nature*, which begins with these lines: "Judging by the few portraits that have been preserved in the Château de Lourps, the line of the Floressas des Esseintes consisted, in bygone days, of muscular warriors and grim-looking mercenaries."[7] The first sentence of Alas's *Su único hijo* is: "Emma Valcárcel was an only child, and spoiled."[8] Emma's family tree, like that of des Esseintes, is long and illustrious but decayed, having begun to retrogress atavistically back to the tribal state. She, too, is the last of her line.

In contrast, *The Picture of Dorian Gray* (1891) appears to swerve from the same kind of opening: "The studio was filled with the rich odour of roses, and when the light summer wind stirred amidst the trees of the garden there came through the open door the heavy scent of the lilac, or the more delicate perfume of the pink-flowering thorn."[9] Then Wilde moves on, first to a painterly, distanced description of nature as seen from within the studio, and next to a full-length portrait of a young man. Similarly, Rachilde

6 Brad Epps, "Recalling the Self: Autobiography, Genealogy, and Death in *Sonata de Otoño*," *Journal of Interdisciplinary Literary Studies* 5.1 (1993), p. 152.

7 Joris-Karl Huysmans, *Against Nature* (*A Rebours*), ed. Nicholas White, tr. Margaret Mauldon (Oxford University Press, 1998), p. 3.

8 Leopoldo Alas (Clarín), *Su único hijo*, ed. Carolyn Richmond, 2nd edn. (Madrid: Espasa-Calpe, 1990), p. 51.

9 Oscar Wilde, *The Picture of Dorian Gray*, ed. Isobel Murray (Oxford University Press, 1998), p. 1.

in *Monsieur Venus* (1884) begins with the realistic setting of a tenement in which she places a young aristocratic woman, Mlle Raoule de Vénérande: "In the dark, narrow passage that the concierge had pointed out, Mlle de Vénérande was groping for a door."[10] But the differences are only apparent, for like Huysmans and Clarín, both Rachilde and Wilde rely on genealogy as the literal and symbolic generative metaphor for their narratives. Dorian Gray is the last grandson of Lord Kelso, and an orphan with "an interesting background. It posed the lad, made him more perfect as it were" (p. 35). His mother, carried away by "a mad passion," married unsuitably. Mlle de Vénérande is also orphaned, with a blue-blooded debauché for a father and a mother with "the most natural and violent appetite" (p. 282). Joining this decayed aristocracy is Valle-Inclán's Marqués de Bradomín, whose inveterate don Juanism brings him to the brink of commiting incest in *Sonata de invierno* (*Winter Sonata*).

In all of these decadent narratives, something has gone wildly wrong with the family histories contained therein. These stories are not about the biological imperative to reproduce or generate a family (or text). They are framed by artifice. It is the "frame" of art that is really the focus of these texts. Thus, Dorian Gray's picture becomes more central than Dorian Gray himself, who is "simply a motive in art" to the painter Basil Hallward (p. 11). Prefacing the novel are a series of aphorisms about art, beginning with: "The artist is the creator of beautiful things" (p. xxiii). *Against Nature* privileges art over story with an opening series of family portraits in the prologue. As Nicholas White suggests in his introduction, Huysmans is writing against (*à rebours*, literally the wrong, or opposite, way) plot, against conventional storytelling as represented by family history (*Against Nature*, pp. xiv–xv). Clarín also underplays plot in *Su único hijo*, centering instead on the dreamy character of Bonifacio Reyes, whose initial presentation seems like a portrait from the Romantic era: "He was good-looking in a romantic sort of way, regular stature, pale very *oval* face [...]" (p. 51). The only thing exceptional about Bonifacio, says the narrator, is his handwriting, which is fantastic and capricious, that is, artistic. For Bonifacio, like des Esseintes, Dorian Gray, Raoule de Vénérande, and, of course, the Marqués de Bradomín, possesses an artist's soul – or at least he, like they, likes to think he does. In all these texts, one could say that the portrait, or the pose, takes over, in the guise of the archetypal decadent figure, that of the dandy. (Even Mlle de Vénérande is a cross-dressing dandy.) The dandy, as Baudelaire saw in one of the key texts to decadence, "The Painter of Modern Life," glorifies the self and

[10] Rachilde, *Monsieur Venus*, in *The Decadent Reader*, ed. Asti Hustvedt (New York: Zone Books, 1998), p. 274.

individuality, being "in love with *distinction* above all things." In dandyism, he continues, there "is first and foremost the burning need to create for oneself a personal originality."[11] To be decadent is not simply to cultivate but to create the self as though it were a work of art. The decadent places artifice and the artificial above nature. Decadence, then, is a peculiar form of heroism for Baudelaire, because the dandy must strive for the perfection of distinction, of singularity, set apart not only from the deadening conformism of middle-class life but from the apparent formlessness of nature itself.

The dandy, or the decadent, I would suggest, represents the figure of art itself in texts like *Against Nature*, *The Picture of Dorian Gray*, and the *Sonatas*, in which the trick is to convert life into art. The cult of personality which the Marqués de Bradomín espouses in Valle's narratives moves us away from the weight of biological heredity (family histories), and thereby mimetic representation of the "real," and toward art as autonomous verbal artifact, toward a "poetics of the real," in which language begins to efface the traces of representational writing. Thus there is a continuous line connecting such decadentist texts as the *Sonatas*, *Against Nature*, and *The Picture of Dorian Gray* to modernism, in which all of the characteristics noted above are fully realized, in this sense incorporating the achievement of decadent writing (Virginia Woolf, Joyce, Azorín, Miró, etc.).

If decadent writing innovatively looks forward to modernism and the avant-garde, it also looks backward, to decline and the past. The styles and concept of decadence are, ultimately, inseparable in this sense. One can only understand decadent style in the light of what such writers felt they were missing. Decline is conceivable only because of what came before, a presumably more glorious and splendid time. The loss of empire, among other things, becomes a key image in decadent writing. Huysmans not only incorporates the fall of the Roman Empire into the more essayistic portions of *Against Nature*, but discursively exploits the development of Late Latin, partly as a way of illustrating des Esseintes's love of things deliquescent, including linguistic decomposition.

What Huysmans really does is to *make* the fall of the Roman Empire an actual part of his narrative (in chapter 3) and, indirectly, to suggest as a consequence the historic importance of philology as a kind of narrative. He writes: "The Western Empire crumbled under the impact [of the Barbarians] [...] the end of the universe seemed to be at hand [...] Years went by; the Barbarian tongues began to systematize themselves, to emerge from their sclerosis, to develop into true languages [...]" (p. 31). In other words, language in *Against*

[11] Charles Baudelaire, *The Painter of Modern Life and Other Essays*, tr. and ed. Jonathan Mayne (London: Phaidon Press, 1995), p. 27.

Nature not only takes center stage but does so as a consequence of historical decline, of loss. Language takes an active role in constructing itself, according to this view. Philology in Huysmans's text does what Edward Said says it does in another context: "Philology taught one how culture is a construct, an *articulation* [...] even a creation, but [nothing more than] a quasi-organic structure."[12] The construction of philology, like that of decadent writing, is built on the remains of something lost, whether it be a common unifying language, the unity of empire, or the wholeness of the individual personality. This sense of loss produces feelings of ambivalence, because what is yearned for is often perceived as decayed, fragmented, or dissolving into thin air.

This same contradictory impulse, which in moving simultaneously backward and forward remains unresolved in the end, is also visible in Valle-Inclán's *Sonatas*. The Marqués de Bradomín's memoirs are shot through with ironically tinged nostalgia for a decayed Galician nobility, for a largely ceremonial *ancien régime*, for a vanished Spanish Empire. And yet, Bradomín laces gesture toward the past with the self-awareness that this past is a dream, impossible to experience though perhaps possible to recover through and as language. Language in the *Sonatas* turns Valle's regressive, haunted narratives into a dream of decadence, akin to the darkly shimmering images of Gustave Moreau's paintings, which give pale, intense life to figures reminiscent of the dead or of ghosts. The generative metaphor of decadence insists on decay but attributes a morbid specialness, a strange vitality, to it. Decay, in turn, is predicated on loss and fragmentation. We expect ruin. We expect ghostly presences. Valle gives us plenty of both.

The most spectral of the four narratives is *Sonata de otoño*. Appropriately, it begins and ends with a dying body. More significantly, Valle presents memory itself as the ruins of experience. The Marqués de Bradomín receives a letter from a dying woman, who is also his cousin and former mistress, Concha. "I had always believed," he says, "in the resurrection of our love. It was a vague nostalgic hope which filled my life with the scent of faith: It was the chimera of the future, the sweet chimera asleep in the bottom of blue lakes, where destiny's stars are reflected."[13] One might easily mistake this passage for Romantic prose, except for the subtle traces of irony present in the self-conscious use of words and phrases like *resurrección* and *indecisa y nostálgica*. "Resurrection" is a term more appropriately found in religious texts, while Bradomín's "vague, nostalgic hope" suggests not a wildly romantic passion but rather the mere memory of an old love, which of course is what he is really resurrecting in this opening passage. Likewise, the "scent

[12] Edward Said, *Orientalism* (New York: Penguin, 1978), p. 148.
[13] Ramón del Valle-Inclán, *Sonata de otoño* (Madrid: Espasa-Calpe, 1985), p. 7.

of faith" is already a contradiction in terms, especially when juxtaposed to what immediately comes after: the "chimera of the future." Already on the first page Valle has deftly turned the sharp point of his highly self-conscious writing into the remains of romantic feeling expressed here. How fitting that this faint hope of a revived love be "vague" and "nostalgic," for such terms express ambivalence toward the object of desire: not simply Concha, but the narcissistic yearning to be once more in the position of being loved and adored.

Stylistically, this moment, like many others in the *Sonata*, resonates with echoes of self-reflecting imagery. Thus, the chimera that sleeps at the bottom of blue lakes is an elusive image of the depths that invokes its opposite image, the reflection of stars on the surface of the waters. Valle repeats this image of specularity, of self-reflecting surfaces, throughout *Sonata de otoño*, creating multiple framing effects of images within images. Similarly, the settings he creates for this particular *Sonata* are labyrinthine, filled with garden mazes, endlessly long corridors, proliferating hallways of mirrors, and receding interiors. Mirror imagery abounds and is often associated with death.

Indeed, death is at the heart of this and all the *Sonatas*. One of the most haunting and yet grotesque images of death comes as Bradomín, in a panic to avoid scandal, stumbles through dark corridors, carrying Concha's dead body back to her own room. Her long hair becomes entangled in a door, and he is forced to pull brutally at the strands:

> I groped in the dark to loosen her hair. I couldn't. It was getting more entangled by the minute [. . .]. With horror I saw it was almost daylight. I grew dizzy and pulled . . . Concha's body seemed to want to escape my arms. Anguished, I held on to her in desperation [. . .]. [H]er waxy eyelids began to half-open. I closed her eyes, and holding Concha's body in my arms with an iron grip, I fled. I had to yank brutally until those perfumed strands of hair I loved so much broke loose . . . (p. 83)

This is an extraordinary passage. It upsets all our expectations as readers of Romantic texts. Concha has died, and instead of the sadly dignified treatment we are waiting for, she is broken up, metaphorically speaking, like this scene, into individual body parts. Indeed, there is a fetishistic obsession with body parts in all these texts. In the passage just cited, Valle's first-person narrator-protagonist focuses first on Concha's hair, literally attempting to separate the snarled strands from the door, then on her half-opened eyelids and eyes. Her body appears detached, indeed even seeming "to want to escape [Bradomín's] arms." In another passage, he describes her in these terms: "Concha's neck flowered from her shoulders like a wan lily, her breasts were two white roses perfuming an altar, and her arms, with their delicate and fragile slenderness, seemed like the handles of an amphora circling her head" (p. 26). Elsewhere, I have noted how this breaking up of the female body into individual parts (evident in all the *Sonatas*) miniaturizes Concha's presence, turning her into a kind of *bibelot* or decorative object. This is a good example of the highly self-conscious writing of decadence in which language creates figuratively and linguistically objects of art, verbal artifice. Images taken from nature, such as the lily and roses, are deliberately made artificial by association with cultural artifacts like the altar/amphora comparison in the passage just quoted.

Significantly, Valle symbolically connects this concentration on fetishistic images, such as body parts, with death, for in all these texts the metonymic parts singled out refer to a "whole," which is either dying or, in fact, dead. In *Sonata de otoño* Concha's body is simply the spectral remains of a dead love. More importantly, her death signals yet another end, Bradomín's own future death, symbolically figured in fetishistic imagery in the last line of the text: "I wept like an ancient god upon seeing his cult extinguished!" (p. 86). In *Sonata de primavera* (*Spring Sonata*), a literal idol in the hex shape of a small wax figure bears a grotesque resemblance to Bradomín.[14] Other decadent writers also stressed the connection between the imagistic fragmentation of the body and death. Dorian Gray's picture clearly takes on a spectral life of its own, worshipped as a kind of idol of the self. But this strange vitality of the portrait also points to the death of a soul. Rachilde turns the dead body of Raoule's lover/husband into a wax figure, made up of artificial and natural parts taken from the corpse and possessing a hidden spring which "connects with the mouth and brings it to life" (p. 366). Villiers de l'Isle-Adam simply bypasses the human altogether and creates a completely artificial automaton in *The Future Eve* (1886).

Asti Hustvedt has suggested that the decadent aesthetic "disavows the natural and with it the body. The truly beautiful body is dead, because it is empty."[15] Yet the body, even fragmented, is never entirely empty in these texts, for this void points to an absence, a loss, which not even irony and self-parody, key components of decadent literature, can completely efface. Nor is it simply the human body that undergoes this fracturing process. In *Sonata de invierno*, for example, it is the politically lost Carlist cause, which, like the female body, has been emptied of its fullest significance. Bradomín has defended the Cause all his life in part because it is so closely identified with his family history and with Galician traditionalism. But near the end of

[14] Ramón del Valle-Inclán, *Sonata de primavera* (Madrid: Espasa-Calpe, 1984), p. 66.
[15] Hustvedt (ed.), *The Decadent Reader*, p. 26.

the *Sonata*, he says to Brother Ambrosio: "I don't mind saying I'm glad that the Cause is a lost one." Seriously? asks Brother Ambrosio, and Bradomín replies yes: "And it was true. I've always found majesty fallen more beautiful than enthroned, and I defended tradition out of a sense of aesthetics. Carlism for me has the solemn charm of great cathedrals, and even in the days of the war, I would have been content had it been declared a national monument."[16] Seriously? Well, yes and no. As with all such decadent texts, the aesthetic pose is paramount here, meaning that irony forms the very core of Bradomín's stance. Only an ironist could conceive of an unstable political movement of limited appeal like the ultra-traditionalist Carlism as a kind of "national monument."

Carlism, like the Galician aristocracy that Bradomín represents, was, by the time Valle-Inclán wrote the *Sonatas*, largely a dead issue, having deteriorated through poor leadership and petty squabbling within the ranks. Yet the very decay of ideology and class appealed enormously to Valle, for like other decadent writers he saw an aura of specialness, of uniqueness, in both. Hence, the image of Carlism as a national monument possesses, like all things imbued with nostalgic feelings, traces of an earlier significance.

Similarly, the imperial shadow of Spain in the New World plays an analogous role in *Sonata de estío* (*Summer Sonata*), as well as in its earlier version, "La niña Chole" ('Mistress Chole,' from *Femeninas*). Bradomín embarks on a journey to the New World, where he has come to claim properties from an inheritance. He is filled with nostalgia remembering the history of the Conquest:

> I recalled nearly forgotten books of my childhood that had made me dream of that land, daughter of the sun: stories that were half fiction, half history, in which men with copper skins, sad and silent as is expected of defeated heroes, were depicted.

He continues:

> As it is not possible to renounce one's own country, I, a Spaniard and a gentleman, felt my heart swell with enthusiasm, and my mind teeming with glorious visions, and my memory filled with historical memories. I felt the noble stirrings of History rising in my adventurous, Christian gentleman's soul.[17]

The highly literary, bookish reminiscences of "history" in this passage suggest, once again, a narrative and aesthetic self-awareness that is ironically confirmed in the less than heroic but fictionally exotic adventure Bradomín has with "la Niña Chole" later in *Sonata de estío*. The Marqués struts his

[16] Ramón del Valle-Inclán, *Sonata de invierno* (Madrid: Espasa-Calpe, 1985), p. 163.
[17] Ramón del Valle-Inclán, *Sonata de estío* (Madrid: Espasa-Calpe, 1984), p. 98.

stuff like "a Conquistador of old" before la Niña Chole (p. 105). She is the "the captive princess" to his Conquistador (p. 141). Through Bradomín's Western eyes, la Niña Chole incarnates everything exotic in the New World. She *is* the exotic. Exploiting a stereotype of the period, Valle draws a close parallel between the feminine (la Niña Chole) and the land:

> la Niña Chole possessed that beautiful presence of an idol, that ecstatic, sacred quietness of the Mayan race, a race which was so old, so noble, so mysterious that it appeared to have emigrated from the depths of India [...] My God! It seemed to me that from that body bronzed by the burning Yucatan sun came languid emanations, and that I was breathing them in, I was drinking them down, I was intoxicated with them. (p. 89)

The protagonist then says: "When she turned toward me, my heart stopped. She had the same smile as Lili. My Lili, so loved, so reviled!" (p. 89).

The exotic figure of la Niña Chole, it turns out, is not so exotic after all. What Bradomín discovers in the New World is the inescapable presence of the Old World. While in the Iberian peninsula, the novelist Maurice Barrès looked out at the Atlantic, seeing "nothing in front of us, but the limitless Ocean. We heard some cries out to sea. It was, in the evening mist, the signal of ships doubling the cape and leaving for over there [*là-bas*]. But *over there* no longer has any unknown lands, nothing but repetitions of our Europe."[18] La Niña Chole not only reminds Bradomín of the Old World (Lili). She, like this entire episode of *Sonata de estío*, is conceived in the highly literary imagery of the West, which is to say, as Edward Said, Chris Bongie, and others have noted in general, that the New World, like the Orient, is an invention of the Old.[19] The historical realities are one thing. But the *image* of the New World – as an exotic Other – is a creation, meant to supplement or to substitute for something that is missing from the Old World. Thus, Bradomín sets out for Tierra Caliente: "like an adventurer of old, I was going to lose myself in the vastness of the ancient Aztec Empire. An Empire with an unknown history, buried forever with the mummies of its kings, among the cyclopean remains that speak of civilizations, of cults, of races that once were, and can only be compared to the mysterious, remote Orient" (p. 84).

The repeated parallels between the New World and India or the Orient simply reinforce to what degree Valle/Bradomín finds mirror images in the

[18] From *Du sang, de la volonté et de la mort* (1894), quoted in Chris Bongie, *Exotic Memories. Literature, Colonialism, and the Fin de Siècle* (Stanford University Press, 1991), p. 19.

[19] See Jesús Torrecilla, "Exotismo y nacionalismo en la *Sonata de estío*," *Hispanic Review* 66 (1998), pp. 35–56.

Old and New Worlds. The idea of the "Orient" – the mysterious, the exotic – says much more about the Old World than the New. Bradomín, on the one hand, seeks to *lose himself* in the vastnesses of a former empire. On the other hand, it is clear that he has also come to find himself, or at least a role – that of Conquistador – which will serve to define him. But the posing, like the highly wrought, artificial rhetoric of the writing itself, is a half-confessed sign of inauthenticity. They are, like Dorian Gray, a "motive in art." From our standpoint, they are also symbolic of an absence, what Chris Bongie in his discussion of exoticism has called "the sign of an aporia – of a constitutional absence at the heart of what had been projected as a possible alternative to modernity." The exotic, he says, is "a space of absence, a dream already given over to the past. This is one half of the decadentist intuition that provides so much of fin de siècle writing with its largely unheard resonance. That such dreams can be followed up on, and traced back, albeit posthumously, is the second half of this intuition."[20]

Remarkably, the dream of recovering what has been lost, or perhaps never existed – the dream, for example, of a common language, of a strong national or personal identity – is given extraordinary expression in one of Valle's last works, not normally associated with decadence or aestheticism, the vanguardist *Tirano Banderas* (*The Tyrant*, 1926).[21] In the *Sonatas*, Valle counterbalances the tendency toward fragmentation by the unifying rhetorical vision incarnated in the narcissistic personality and narrating voice of the Marqués de Bradomín. Bradomín may be an empty tomb of dated *modernismo*. But he *covers up* his emptiness with the seductive flow of words, with the comfort of art.

This illusion of a unifying personality vanishes completely in *Tirano Banderas*. For one thing, there is no longer a unifying voice or presence in the text. For another, everything tends toward dissolution, toward the rending of body parts, in a brilliant series of metonymically conceived images, starting with the literal decomposition of human remains in the horrifying episode of the Indian Zacarías's baby (who is devoured by pigs) and ending with the mutilated corpse of the tyrant being strewn about in pieces from one end of the country to the other. More significantly, the very language of *Tirano Banderas* consists of pure fragments. Fragments of the debris of empire, which is what is left in the mythical country of Tierra Caliente. Fragments of language. For what Valle does is to incorporate a multitude of idioms, words, and expressions taken from several different Latin American countries,

20 Bongie, *Exotic memories*, p. 22.

21 See Dru Dougherty's *Guía para caminantes en Santa Fe de Tierra Firme: Estudio sistémico de "Tirano Banderas"*(Valencia: Pre-Textos, 1999), for a thorough treatment of the reception of *Tirano Banderas*.

Spain and, in addition, invented by Valle himself. Language ruptures, breaks down, in *Tirano Banderas*. But one could also argue that underneath the disintegration, the decay, there persists the utopian dream of a common language, reminding us as well of Huysmans's narrative of philology and lost empire in *Against Nature*. As in Huysmans, Valle's imaginative construction of language turns linguistic invention into a structural component of his narrative, a narrative in which is implied the veiled desire to rediscover through words (or philology) a vanished unity of individual and collective identity.

Language reigns supreme in *Tirano Banderas*. In a curious way, this brings our trajectory full circle, back to Valle's original decadent texts, *Femeninas* and above all the *Sonatas*. For what Valle created in the *Sonatas* and in the persona of Bradomín was a dream of language. Bradomín's outer trappings and history – his Galician aristocratic roots, his conquests – are the external manifestations of a textual transformation. His genealogy – the family history to which he returns obsessively in the *Sonatas* – is a figure of another genealogy at work: the process of creating from scratch as it were, from the force of imagination and personality itself, one's *own* history as text, as language. In this, the innovation of Valle's style and vision, from the *Sonatas* to *Tirano Banderas*, remains undisputed.

Guide to further reading

Allegra, Giovanni, *El reino interior: premisas y semblanzas del modernismo en España* (Madrid: Encuentro, 1986).

Cardwell, Richard A. and Bernard McGuirk (eds.), *¿Qué es el modernismo? Nueva encuesta, nuevas lecturas* (Boulder: Society of Spanish and Spanish-American Studies, 1993).

Grass, Roland and William R. Risley (eds.), *Waiting for Pegasus. Studies of the Presence of Symbolism and Decadence in Hispanic Letters* (Macomb: Western Illinois University, 1979).

Litvak, Lily. "Temática de la decadencia en la literatura española a fines del siglo XIX. 1880–1913," *Kentucky Romance Quarterly* 33 (1986), pp. 201–10.

Maier, Carol and Roberta L. Salper (eds.), *Ramón María del Valle-Inclán: Questions of Gender* (Lewisburg: Bucknell University Press, 1994).

3

THE TWENTIETH CENTURY

10

ROBERTA JOHNSON

From the Generation of 1898 to the vanguard

The period from about 1900 until the Spanish Civil War (1936–9) is often considered a second Renaissance in Spanish culture, a "Silver Age," as José Carlos Mainer calls it. The novel of this period was particularly precocious, showing early signs of the artistic innovations that came to be called modernism in other European literatures. From 1870 onwards the novel had come into its own as a major cultural form in Spain for its ability to mirror a bourgeois society anxious to read portraits of itself. By the turn of the century, however, a growing intelligentsia was losing patience with middle-class values and their political and artistic manifestations. The Restoration government, which replaced the revolutionary initiatives of 1868–74, had created a peace and stability that Spain had not enjoyed during most of the earlier nineteenth century; at the same time, intellectuals were disgusted with its corrupt politics and support of conservative Spanish institutions such as the church hierarchy and the landed aristocracy. Modern philosophy and ideologies gave the intellectuals and writers the impetus they needed to seek new social and cultural forms.

"¡Adentro!" ("Turn inward") exhorted Miguel de Unamuno in 1900, arguing for a reorientation of the collective psyche away from the material, scientific, technological aspects of life to the internal and spiritual.[1] Writers of Unamuno's era, who came to be known as the Generation of '98, were born at the same time as Spain somewhat belatedly entered the modern age. Modernity was arriving in Spain in the guise of a more vigorous industrial-technological revolution, philosophical iconoclasm (Schopenhauer, Kierkegaard, Nietzsche), and social liberalism (democratic political ideas and workers' movements). The writers were modernists in the European sense of the word, concerned with the effects of modern life on

[1] M. de Unamuno, "¡Adentro!" in *Obras completas*, ed. Manuel García Blanco (Barcelona: Vergara, 1958), vol. III, pp. 418–27.

society and the individual, and they found in the novel a means to express their anxieties. Miguel de Unamuno (1864–1936), Ramón del Valle-Inclán (1866–1936), Pío Baroja (1872–1956), and José Martínez Ruiz ("Azorín," 1873–1967), the principal novel-writers associated with the Generation of '98, all shared themes and forms with the major European and American modernists – Marcel Proust, James Joyce, Thomas Mann, Virginia Woolf, William Faulkner. They privileged individual consciousness over the detailed studies of social contexts we associate with the realist and Naturalist novel of the end of the nineteenth century, and thus they experimented with new novelistic forms that reveal the contents of the individual consciousness.

The modernist novel in Spain arose somewhat earlier than in the rest of Europe (around 1902 rather than with the onset of the First World War), a phenomenon perhaps explained by an earlier existential crisis in Spain. If the First World War was a culminating event in the European collective consciousness, in Spain intellectual ferment was occasioned in the 1890s by a corrupt government and stagnant social forms that appeared completely out of tune with the progressive socialist ideas and iconoclastic philosophies arriving from outside Spain. This ferment was exacerbated by Spain's ignominious war with the United States in 1898 in which it lost the last vestiges of its colonial empire – Puerto Rico, Cuba, and the Philippines. The label "Generation of '98" derives from this event, although, as many critics of the label point out, the group of writers collected under the rubric was diverse and did not necessarily coalesce around this one single historical moment.

Each of the novelists usually considered "members" of the Generation of '98 had his own personal history that intersected with modern life in a unique way, and each was conscious of creating new art forms in order to distinguish himself from the realist-Naturalist mode that preceded him. Unamuno called his original version of the novel *nivola*, in which he eliminated external descriptions to emphasize dialogue and internal monologue. His characters are more concerned with existential problems (Do I exist? How do I know I exist? Is there life after death?) than with "real world" issues, although the existential dilemmas are always embedded in concrete situations such as love and marriage. The same year as Unamuno published *Paz en la guerra* (*Peace in War*, 1897), a more conventional novel with realistic descriptions and historically recognizable events, he suffered a religious crisis and began writing intense, personal essays about his desire to reconcile the rational and the spiritual sides of life. He desperately wished to rediscover the innocent religious faith of his childhood that had been destroyed through his intellectual development and contacts with scientific thinking, especially positivism.

In 1902 he devised a form of narration that dramatized his personal anguish. Avito Carrascal, the main character of *Amor y pedagogía* (*Love and Pedagogy*, 1902), is an unapologetic positivist, who proposes to marry and raise a child in a completely scientific and predictable manner. His wife Marina is, on the other hand, an intensely religious woman, who attempts to introduce spirituality into their son Apolodoro's life. Apolodoro eventually commits suicide over unrequited love, a sad ending to Avito's experiment in unsentimental education. Many critics consider *Amor y pedagogía* Unamuno's first *nivola*, although he did not articulate his theory for a new kind of novel until 1914 when he published his third, full-length novel *Niebla* (*Mist*). In the case of *Niebla*, not only did he strip his novel of external descriptions and depictions of social ills and institutions, but he also introduced a metafictional element: the characters discuss the process of novel-writing, specifically the kind of novel we are reading. Víctor Goti, friend of the main character Augusto Pérez, is writing a *nivola*, which he defines as having a great deal of dialogue and no plot or a plot that makes itself up as it goes along, just as life is lived: "whatever comes out.... makes itself."[2] Unamuno called this kind of spontaneous novel a "viviparous" narration (born alive), which he contrasted to the carefully structured "oviparous" novel (born from an egg).

Unamuno introduced yet another metafictional element in *Niebla*. The author himself appears as a character who engages in an important conversation with Augusto. The wealthy Augusto has fallen in love with Eugenia, who already has a boyfriend named Mauricio. Eugenia, disgusted with Mauricio's suggestion that she marry Augusto but continue their relationship on the side, breaks with him and finally agrees to marry Augusto. At the last minute, however, she elopes with Mauricio and writes Augusto a devastating farewell letter. In despair Augusto decides to commit suicide, but before doing so, he travels to Salamanca to consult with Unamuno, who tells him that he cannot kill himself because he is a fictional entity. Augusto, up to this point a passive character, begins to assert himself. He determines to prove his existence by committing suicide; he eats too much for dinner and dies, leaving the reader to decide whether it was Unamuno who killed him or if he killed himself. Other metafictional or self-conscious elements in the novel include a series of interpolated stories that mirror Augusto's love dilemma in one way or another and an epilogue – Augusto's funeral oration – spoken by his dog Orfeo.

Niebla is a ground-breaking work that points the way to the playful vanguard novel initiated by Pedro Salinas's *Víspera del gozo* (*Prelude to Pleasure*)

[2] Unamuno, *Obras completas*, vol. II, pp. 894–6.

and Benjamín Jarnés's *El profesor inútil* ('The Useless Professor') in 1926. The comic elements, especially the narrative irony present in *Amor y pedagogía* and *Niebla*, disappear in Unamuno's later novels – intense stories of existential anguish. *Abel Sánchez* (1917) is a reworking of the Cain and Abel myth in which Cain becomes a modern hero for his struggle with envy. *La tía Tula* ('Aunt Tula', 1920), Unamuno's only novel with a female protagonist, focuses on Tula's overwhelming desire for motherhood and her reluctance to accept marriage or sex. As a surrogate mother to her dead sister's children, she hovers between saint and monster, the two types into which many of Unamuno's female characters fall. *San Manuel Bueno, mártir* ('Saint Manuel The Good, Martyr', 1933), Unamuno's last novel, chronicles the despair of a priest who does not believe in everlasting life, but keeps up appearances for the sake of his congregation.

Religion is also central to Ramón del Valle-Inclán's modern thematics. The Marqués de Bradomín, protagonist-narrator of his four *Sonatas* (*Sonata de otoño* [*Autumn Sonata*, 1902] *Sonata de estío* [*Summer Sonata*, 1903], *Sonata de primavera* [*Spring Sonata*, 1904], *Sonata de invierno* [*Winter Sonata*, 1905]) is "ugly, Catholic, and sentimental,"[3] but his religion is of a modern variety that worships at the altar of sex and beauty more than at the cross. Valle-Inclán's language is charged with religious references within a context of physical pleasure: "Concha had the delicate, sickly pallor of a mourning Mary, and she was so beautiful in that weakened, emaciated state that my eyes, lips, and hands found all their pleasure in the very thing that saddened me."[4]

Like Unamuno, Valle-Inclán was aware that he was creating a new kind of literature, and by 1920 he was calling both his plays and his narratives *esperpentos* ('scarecrows'), art forms in which he held up a distorting mirror to Spanish society in order to reveal its corruption and inequities. The grotesque images that result from Valle-Inclán's inventive use of language and narrative techniques can fruitfully be compared to German Expressionist paintings filled with twisted, fragmented bodies often integrated with mechanical parts. *Tirano Banderas* (*The Tyrant*, 1926) is set in a Latin American country reminiscent of Mexico, where Valle-Inclán had spent time in his formative years. The progress of a dictatorship is narrated in staccato, stylized language that transforms real horror into an artistically rendered nightmare. The tyrant Banderas is often referred to as a mummy whose face wears a

3 Leda Schiavo, "Introducción" to Ramón del Valle-Inclán, *Sonata de otoño* (Madrid: Espasa-Calpe, 1989), p. 13, quotes the "Nota" appended to the first edition in which the Marqués de Bradomín is thus described. Although the note was dropped in subsequent editions, this description is widely known and cited.

4 Valle-Inclán, *Sonata de otoño*, p. 50.

"green grimace."[5] Some critics argue that Valle-Inclán does not belong to the Generation of '98, especially in his early works that seem to favor artistic elaboration over socio-political themes or existential angst. Such arguments indicate the futility of categories with rigid boundaries; all of Valle-Inclán's narratives share with those of his contemporaries a modern view of life that finds artistic means to question the efficacy of traditional power structures (religion, aristocracy, political forms).

Pío Baroja also relied on artistic language, especially in his early novels, to convey a sense of anxiety about the modern world. His first important novel *Camino de perfección* ('Way to Perfection', 1902) established his idea of what a novel should be, a new conception of narrative that endured throughout his long career. He believed novels should be "porous" (loosely structured) and thus conform more to life's unstructured path than to the traditional pattern of beginning, middle, and end. (Although Unamuno insisted that his novels were unfettered by a preordained structure, they are actually organized along lines more carefully planned than are Baroja's.) To this end Baroja borrowed liberally from the picaresque tradition in which one central character, moving through the world, encounters other characters from various walks of life; these secondary characters rarely reappear in the novel. *Camino de perfección*'s Fernando Ossorio, like so many modern "heroes," suffers a crisis and sets out on a journey of self-discovery that takes him to several important Spanish locales such as Toledo, saturated with religious history, and the verdantly natural Valencia where his story ends. Fernando begins as a painter, extolling the virtues of nature transformed by art, but ends up rejecting art (artifice) for unmediated nature.

Baroja was Spain's most prolific novelist of the pre-Civil War period; he published some eighty full-length narratives. Most critics consider his best to be those written between 1902 and 1912. Concluding this productive decade are *El árbol de la ciencia* (*The Tree of Knowledge*, 1911) and *El mundo es ansí* ('The Way of the World', 1912), which represent his interest in the role of science in the modern world and the relationship of writing to life, respectively. Baroja, who had a medical degree and was a practicing doctor for a short time, explored through Andrés Hurtado, the protagonist of *El árbol de la ciencia*, the limitations of science and philosophy in dealing effectively with the basic problems of humanity – poverty, disease, immorality, and loneliness. *El mundo es ansí* employs a variety of narrative techniques (witness narrator, letters, diary) to chronicle the life of Sacha, an intelligent Russian woman who marries a Spaniard. As Carlos Longhurst points out,

[5] Ramón del Valle-Inclán, *Tirano Banderas. Novela de tierra caliente* (Madrid: Espasa-Calpe, 1987), p. 62.

the novel "is an exploration of the relationship between art and life, between an individual consciousness and the objective world, between an author and his work."[6]

El mundo es ansí contains a number of references to feminism, a social movement that has not usually been taken into account in discussions of Spanish modernist or Generation of '98 fiction. Feminism in Spain was less organized and militant than in the United States or England, but there were Spanish feminists who advocated greater social liberty for women (including equal educational opportunities, legal rights, and divorce). Carmen de Burgos (1867–1932) and Concha Espina (1869–1955), two women writers born about the same time as the "members" of the Generation of '98, nonetheless are not included in that group of writers. Because novels written by women during the first thirty years of the century do not incorporate the kinds of narrative innovation and exploration of individual (male) consciousness that we have seen in the male modernist novel, women writers have been left out of literary history and the canon. Although perhaps only Carmen de Burgos considered herself a feminist, both women wrote about women's lives in a way that depicted Spanish society as out of step with modernity in the way it educated and socialized women.

Carmen de Burgos's fiction was published primarily in series of novelettes (*La Novela Corta* ['The Short Novel'], *La Novela Semanal* ['The Weekly Novel'], *Los Contemporáneos* ['Contemporaries']) that became very popular and widely read in the first decade of the twentieth century. Burgos used this popular venue to argue against unfair laws that condemned women for adultery but exonerated men (*El artículo 438*, 1921); that prevented divorce in situations abusive to women (*El hombre negro* ['The Black Man', 1912]); and that absolved men from responsibility for children born out of wedlock (*El abogado* ['The Lawyer', 1915]). A number of her novellas have now been collected in the volume entitled *La flor de la playa y otras novelas cortas* ('Beach Flower and Other Novellas').[7] One novel in that collection, *El veneno del arte* ('The Poison of Art', 1910) satirically portrays the false pretensions of would-be artists and writers in early twentieth-century Spain. The parody of Madrid's artistic circles forms the backdrop for several long monologues by a female artist whose sincerity and authenticity contrast sharply with other characters' hypocrisy. Burgos also introduces alternative sexualities (homosexuality, lesbianism, transvestitism) in this and other novellas, a surprising thematic innovation for Spain at that time.

[6] C. Longhurst, *Pío Baroja. El mundo es ansí* (London: Grant & Cutler, 1977), pp. 100–1.

[7] Carmen de Burgos, *La flor de la playa y otras novelas cortas*, ed. Concepción Nuñez Rey (Madrid: Castalia, 1989). Other novellas by women writers of the period 1900–36 are collected in *Novelas breves de escritoras españolas 1900–1936* (Madrid: Castalia, 1989).

Although more conservative and religious than Burgos, Concha Espina also exposed the vulnerability and suffering of Spanish women. Her best novel *La esfinge Maragata* (*Mariflor*, 1914) chronicles the life of Mariflor, an intelligent, well-educated girl; when her mother dies and her father goes to the new world to seek his fortune, she is sent to live with impoverished relatives in the Maragata region. Most of the men of the Maragata region have also emigrated to America because of dire economic conditions in that part of Spain. The women are left to support themselves by working long hours in the fields and coping with heartless moneylenders to tide them over when the land is unyielding. Aside from the sharp contrast between male modernist narrative techniques and women's more realistic style, it is interesting to note that male writers' protagonists rarely have economic problems. They are supplied with a private income that allows them to concentrate on their personal development.

Azorín's narratives offer a sharp contrast to Concha Espina's depiction of independent women. Azorín, primarily a journalist who wrote seven novels, began his novelistic career in that all-important year 1902 with *La voluntad* ('Will Power'), a companion novel to his friend Pío Baroja's *Camino de perfección*. The protagonist of Azorín's novel is, like Fernando Ossorio, an intellectual in existential limbo, unable to find his way either in the Spanish provincial setting where he grew up or in the modern city. He ends up married to a domineering woman in a provincial town, his career as a writer and intellectual overpowered by these domesticating forces. The novel's structure, like that of *Camino de perfección*, eschews traditional plot development and relies on parallel episodes that pair scenes of traditional Spanish society (church, family) with modern intellectual free-thinking. Azorín is credited with initiating in this novel and subsequent works a spare, luminous style that breaks with the tendency of the nineteenth century to construct dense sentences and weighty paragraphs: "In the distance, a slow, deliberate, melancholy bell rings. The sky begins to lighten indecisively. The fog extends over the fields in a long white brushstroke."[8]

Azorín addressed feminism and women's roles in a number of his newspaper articles, and in *Doña Inés* (1925), written in a period when feminism was gaining a firmer foothold in Spain, he created a strong independent female protagonist who does not appear to desire marriage. The wealthy Inés is somewhat beyond the bloom of youth and has had a series of unsatisfying love affairs. The last of these is a brief flirtation with a young poet in Segovia, where she has extensive property holdings. Inés provokes a scandal in the provincial town when she is seen kissing the poet in the cathedral.

[8] J. Martínez Ruíz, Azorín, *La voluntad*, ed. E. Inman Fox (Madrid: Castalia, 1982), p. 61.

Subsequently, she divides her fortune among friends and relatives and moves to Argentina, where she founds a school for orphans and lives out her days in lonely self-imposed exile. Her story is complicated by the fact that her uncle is writing the biography of one of their female ancestors, who had a tragic love affair with a troubadour. The style of *Doña Inés*, as is typical with modernist narrative, is as important as its thematics, which center on the problem of time (human aging and the possibility of historical recurrence). Azorín incorporates many cinematic techniques (scenic juxtaposition, close-up, panning, cropping, fade-out) into the structure of the novel and employs an elliptical, poetic phrasing in many passages. The novel was published in the same year as the novels that are considered the beginning of a vanguard narrative in Spain. Azorín's work of this period should be considered in the context of vanguard aesthetics, of which he, as a cultural critic, was keenly aware.

Gabriel Miró (1879–1930) and Ramón Pérez de Ayala (1881–1962) are somewhat younger than the authors who are counted as members of the Generation of '98, but they are often included in it. They are also sometimes linked with a group called the Generation of 1914, whose intellectual leader was the philosopher José Ortega y Gasset. In his *Meditaciones del Quijote* ('Meditations on the Quijote', 1914), Ortega introduced Spain to phenomenology, a philosophy that emphasizes the way humans perceive the world around them. Ortega's *Notas sobre la novela* (*Notes on the Novel*, 1925) argued against novelistic realism and in favor of narratives that encapsulate the reader in their own artistic world. The novelistic art of both Miró and Pérez de Ayala reflects these interests; they seek complex linguistic and structural means to represent human perception of and interaction with the world. They play with time and space in ways that attempt to destroy traditional temporal linearity and project the human experience of memory and simultaneity.

Miró, who has often been compared to Proust for his slow-moving, exceptionally dense prose, wrote fiction that is sometimes hard to define as a novel. His *Del vivir* ('Of Living', 1904), *El humo dormido* ('Slumbering Smoke', 1914), *Libro de Sigüenza* ('The Book of Sigüenza', 1917), and *Años y leguas* (*The Years and the Leagues*, 1928) are series of vignettes in a rich and labored style that evoke the sensual experiences of his native Alicante. Like many Generation of '98 fictions, they also have an important philosophical content, although Miró preferred to explore the nature of perception and the relationship of language to memory and lived experience. His full-length novels are concerned with the same issues of language and consciousness. *Las cerezas del cementerio* ('The Cherries of the Cemetery', 1910), like James Joyce's *Ulysses*, intertwines intricate references to classic mythology and Biblical stories with actions of contemporary characters within a specific geographical location (Dublin or Alicante). Like Joyce, Miró also calls on regional and unusual linguistic forms to create a thick prose that requires a great deal of attention on the reader's part. His best-known novels, *Nuestro padre San Daniel* (*Our Father San Daniel*, 1921) and *El obispo leproso* ('The Leprous Bishop', 1926) chronicle Spain's laborious entry into the modern secular, technological world. In these novels, the conservative forces of the past (political reactionaries and dogmatic members of the Catholic church) are pitted against enlightened people from the city who wish to bring modernity to a provincial Spanish town. In each case, the story unfolds through the eyes of two highly sensitive characters – Paulina, the focus of *Nuestro Padre San Daniel*, and her son Pablo, the main character of *El obispo leproso*. The sensuality of these figures and others is both artistic and sexual, creating the opportunity for language and literary references that evoke numerous levels of meaning. Paulina's and Pablo's sensual and sexual awakenings parallel the rise of modernity in Spain in a covert way that allows the reader to experience the agony and frustrations involved in both.

Ramón Pérez de Ayala likewise masterfully combines a commentary on Spain's backward institutions with a rich and complex prose style. His tetralogy, which includes *Tinieblas en las cumbres* ('Darkness at the Summit', 1907), *A.M.G.D* (1910), *La pata de la raposa* (*The Fox's Paw*, 1911), and *Troteras y danzaderas* ('Mummers and Dancers', 1913) is reminiscent of Azorín's *La voluntad* and Baroja's *Camino de perfección* in that the protagonist Alberto Díaz de Guzmán, a budding artist and writer, searches for a meaningful life path in a stagnant, early twentieth-century Spain. Pérez de Ayala's dense layering of Biblical and classical references coincides with Miró's, and foreshadows the kind of modernist emphasis on linguistic pyrotechnics and literary allusion often first attributed to James Joyce in *A Portrait of the Artist as a Young Man* (1916). Pérez de Ayala's verbal wit and irony carry a much sharper edge than Joyce's, however.

Pérez de Ayala's masterpieces *Belarmino y Apolonio* (1921) and *Tigre Juan* and *El curandero de su honra* ('Tiger Juan' and 'The Healer of His Honor', 1926) are the work of a mature writer who has found a truly original voice. He unabashedly incorporates elements of nineteenth-century realism (ironic portraits of members of specific institutions and classes) with an elliptical, lyrical style that draws on references to a wide array of literary sources. These works portray life – love, death, disillusionment, and renewal – in provincial Spanish towns through memorable characters, such as the two shoemaker-protagonists Belarmino and Apolonio or Tigre Juan, the misogynist herb vendor with a heart of gold.

Disaffection from the Restoration monarchy reached crisis proportions by 1923 after a series of disastrous military campaigns in North Africa. To quell the unrest, King Alfonso XIII ceded governing power to General Primo de Rivera, and Spain was ruled as a military dictatorship from 1923 to 1930. As is evident in the mature work of Gabriel Miró and Ramón Pérez de Ayala, the arts flourished in Spain in the 1920s despite Primo de Rivera's repressive regime, a dictatorship with fascist leanings (though hardly to the extent of a Mussolini or Hitler). In retrospect, the genre of the novel may have been overshadowed by the brilliant poetic creations of Jorge Guillén, Pedro Salinas, Federico García Lorca, and Rafael Alberti (a group known as the Generation of '27), but novels certainly shared in the creative wealth. Unamuno published his *La tía Tula* in 1921; Azorín's *Doña Inés* appeared in 1925; Baroja continued to produce about two novels a year, including a series of historical novels; and Valle-Inclán produced his masterpiece *Tirano Banderas* (1926). It is worth noting that two of these older writers created – a rarity for them – female protagonists during this period when feminism had finally gotten a foothold in Spain in the wake of the First World War. Both Tía Tula and Doña Inés are strong, independent women who refuse to marry and both end rather badly, perhaps a commentary on the fate of women who tried to live outside the accepted boundaries of Spanish tradition even in the third decade of the twentieth century.

The 1920s saw greater cosmopolitanism in Spain, and Spanish literary production began to adhere chronologically more closely to artistic currents in the rest of Europe. Ramón Gómez de la Serna (1888–1963) had published a Spanish translation of the Futurist Manifesto in his journal *Prometeo* ('Prometheus') in 1909. José Ortega y Gasset devoted himself from the first decade of the century onward to importing European ideas into Spain, and in 1923 he founded the journal *Revista de Occidente* with the express purpose of making European (especially German) thought better known in his native country. Ortega also founded a novel series, *Nova Novorum*, in 1926 to create an outlet for new kinds of fiction writing. His essay *La deshumanización del arte* (*The Dehumanization of Art*, 1925) did much to vindicate the new art, an art of ideas designed to be understood by a select minority rather than by the masses to which realism appealed.

The novels of Ramón del Valle-Inclán, Miguel de Unamuno, Pío Baroja, Azorín, Miró, and Pérez de Ayala broke new narrative and thematic ground and prepared the way for a significant, albeit brief, flowering of the vanguard novel in Spain from 1926 until about 1934. If the earlier modernist novel in Spain emphasized elliptical plots, individual consciousness, lyrical language, and dense literary references, the vanguard novel pushed linguistic virtuosity to its narrative limits. These novels also introduce a playful element that was not present in the earlier modernist novel; the serious philosophical and mythological themes disappear and are replaced by what Gustavo Pérez Firmat terms a "pneumatic" quality – a light, airy tone.[9] In high vanguard novels the influence of film techniques often creates a fragmented (scenically centered) narrative that also draws on the spatial innovations of cubism and futurism in painting.

Ramón Gómez de la Serna, who spent a great deal of time in Paris, the capital of the avant-garde and its several "isms," was a key figure in the introduction of vanguard aesthetics into Spain through his journal, *Prometeo*, and the *tertulia Pombo*, a literary group. He was interested in things and their relation to human beings (his Madrid apartment was a veritable museum). This preoccupation, which coincides with the attempts of impressionism, cubism, and surrealism to render human perception artistically, led to his development of linguistic means to explore the psychology of the interrelation of things and people. His invention of the *greguería* ('aphorism') around 1910 is central to this project of linking words, mental processes, and visual perception. For example, in the *greguería* "La 'q' es la 'p' que vuelve de paseo" ("'q' is a 'p' returning from a walk"),[10] the visual form of the letters suggests a person first going one way and then another. The inventiveness of the expression both surprises and delights. The wit and emphasis on visual perception of the *greguería*, which Gómez de la Serna defined as a cross between metaphor and humor, became an important verbal vehicle for practitioners of the vanguard novel.

Gómez de la Serna's *El secreto del acueducto* ('The Aqueduct's Secret', 1921) narrates a man's obsession with the aqueduct of Segovia. His fascination with this great work of Roman architecture blinds him to his young wife's adultery. Like many vanguard novels, what in a more traditional novel would lead to a tragic denouement (a jealous husband discovers his wife's unfaithfulness), is converted into a voyeuristic situation as the husband resigns himself to observing his wife's liaison with another, while he himself continues to have an "affair" with the aqueduct. *El novelista* ('The Novelist', 1923) is a highly self-conscious novel in which an author proposes a variety of plot possibilities, many of them ludicrous and clearly mocking traditional novel-writing. *El novelista* even parodies recent novelistic innovations such as Unamuno's confrontation of author and character in *Niebla*. A Gómez de la Serna character who visits his author comes not to learn of his existential situation but to complain that he lost his job because of the denouement

9 G. Pérez Firmat, *Idle Fictions: The Hispanic Vanguard Novel, 1926–1934* (Durham, NC: Duke University Press, 1982), pp. 40–63.

10 R. Gómez de la Serna, *Greguerías. Selección 1910–1960* (Madrid: Espasa-Calpe, 1968), p. 143.

of the novel; he demands that the novelist use his connections to find him another position.

In 1926 Ortega y Gasset's *Nova Novorum* series published *Víspera del gozo* by Pedro Salinas (1891–1951) and *El profesor inútil* by Benjamín Jarnés (1888–1950), two works often singled out as the initiation of the vanguard novel in Spain. *Víspera del gozo* and *El profesor inútil* are similar in structure and theme. The novel's chapters are discrete units that defy the integrative plots of the traditional novel. In *Víspera del gozo* the protagonist of each chapter is a different man, but the experiences of each are similar. In each case the man is looking forward to an assignation with a woman (the expectation of pleasure), but the consummation of the love act is thwarted. These scenes, rather than focusing on the tragic nature of an unfulfilled love, are opportunities to explore the way human consciousness and perception work and how these processes can be expressed in language.

The first chapter of *Víspera del gozo*, titled "Mundo cerrado" ('Closed World'), finds a young man on a train traveling to see a recently married woman with whom he was intimate years ago. He attempts to read a book, but his attention is drawn to the scenery outside the train window. Reading and the sights and sounds of the train and landscape intermingle in his experience:

> And then, something ill-timed and fatal like those sudden distractions that assault us in the middle of reading without our knowing where they come from, as if an inner breath of air propelled them, thrusts between our concentration and the printed word a strange and impenetrable ingredient: unexpectedly, the locomotive would throw out here, toward our side and aided by the wind – coming from outside this time – billows of thick gray smoke, behind which perhaps the most exhilarating scene of the book was vertiginously fleeing, hopelessly expiring before our eyes.[11]

The idyll he had imagined with his former lover, whose name he has been imaginatively reconstructing during his train journey, is dashed when at the end of the train ride he learns from her husband that she has recently died.

In Benjamín Jarnés's *El profesor inútil*, a schoolteacher on summer vacation takes a series of pupils for tutoring, but in each case his lessons are subverted by romantic temptations. These diversions give Jarnés the opportunity to transform sensual experience into startling linguistic effects. Unlike Salinas, who was primarily a poet and only wrote three narrative works, Jarnés wrote a series of novels in the late 1920s and early 1930s. His other major novels, *El convidado de papel* ('The Paper Guest', 1928), *Locura y*

[11] Noël Valis (tr.) P. Salinas, "*Prelude to Pleasure*". *A Bilingual Edition of "Víspera del gozo*." (Lewisburg: Bucknell University Press, 1993), p. 24.

muerte de nadie ('Madness and the Death of a Nobody', 1929), *Paula y Paulita* (1929), *Teoría del zumbel* ('Theory of the Top', 1930), and *Lo rojo y lo azul* ('The Red and the Blue', 1932) have more developed plots than *El profesor inútil* without giving up Jarnés's trademark linguistic innovation. Some of his novels (especially *Locura y muerte de nadie*, *Paula y Paulita*, and *Teoría del zumbel*) also recall the existential themes of Unamuno's and Baroja's novels, but Jarnés gives Unamuno's existential angst a flippant twist that inscribes it with the vanguards' desire to undermine the icons of Western culture (compare Dadaist Marcel Duchamps's bearded "Mona Lisa" or surrealist Salvador Dalí's melting watches).

Women's novelistic production in the 1920s takes a decidedly different path from that of the male vanguard novel. Many women writers were deeply engaged in the feminist movement during this decade, and in the Republican political movement that promised the kinds of social reforms that progressive women advocated. Carmen de Burgos, even though she was Ramón Gómez de la Serna's companion for some twenty years, does not appear to have been influenced by his aesthetics. In addition to the novelettes mentioned above, in 1924 – just two years before the date usually assigned to the beginning of the vanguard novel – Burgos published *La entrometida* ('The Busybody'), a highly amusing portrait of a feminist's attempts to make a living in Spain. The novelette contains much of the wit and humor of a vanguard novel, but with a less lyrical style. It also bears a serious social message that we do not normally associate with the novels of Gómez de la Serna or Jarnés.

Similarly, Margarita Nelken (1896–1968) and Federica Montseny (1905–), both feminists and Republican activists, employed fiction to a socio-political purpose in the 1920s. Margarita Nelken's *La trampa del arenal* ('The Sandtrap', 1923) introduces into the superficial materialism of traditional bourgeois life a "new woman," appropriately named Libertad. Libertad lives alone and supports herself by means of a career in translating. Luis, married to a woman who thinks only of the external trappings of bourgeois society, is attracted to Libertad's class-free and unpretentious values. Their budding relationship ends, however, when Libertad moves to Paris to accept a new job. Luis is left mired in his loveless marriage and unrewarding bureaucratic work – "la trampa del arenal."

The same attention to class distinctions and to freedom from social constraints is also the focus of Federica Montseny's autobiographical novel *La indomable* ('The Indomitable Woman', 1928). The novel centers on the difficulties that Vida, an intelligent, politically active woman, has in finding an appropriate mate. Although she has many feminine traits (she cooks, sews, cleans house, and has a nurturing personality), she is too strong for the men she meets, even those who are politically militant like her. Vida's philosophically sophisticated ideas about the self focus on the social, rather than the individual; for her, society is a union of individuals who are interrelated. Her view of the self differs significantly from that displayed in the male-authored novels of the period, in which the protagonists are usually lovers. Unfortunately, neither Vida's philosophy nor any of her fine personal qualities garner her the male companionship she seeks. Her activism and intellectual qualities are too threatening even to the enlightened men who are accustomed to more passive, less educated Spanish women.

Rosa Chacel (1898–1992), also a pro-Republic woman writer, did write a narrative with similarities to the male-authored vanguard novel, although with significant differences. Chacel, perhaps twentieth-century Spain's most accomplished female novelist, had a closer relationship to José Ortega y Gasset's circle than other women writers; those contacts induced her to attempt the kind of novel that she believed Ortega was theorizing in *La deshumanización del arte* and *Notas sobre la novela*. Despite similarities in plot structure and linguistic virtuosity to male vanguard novels, her effort, entitled *Estación. Ida y vuelta* ('Station. Round Trip', 1930), bears a more serious message about moral values. A young man, unofficially engaged to one woman in his apartment building, has an affair with another residing in the same edifice. When his fiancée becomes pregnant, he travels to Paris, but returns to his paternal responsibilities when the child is born. As in other vanguard novels, this simple set of circumstances is overshadowed by long moments of visual perception in which the protagonist paints verbal pictures of objects upon which his attention focuses. At the end of the novel, he is contemplating writing a movie script and proposes several alternative scenarios, suggesting the metafictional mode we associate with modernist and vanguard fiction.

Like that of so many of the artists and intellectuals associated with Spain's "Silver Age," Chacel's contact with Ortega's circle and the vibrant artistic life of Madrid in the 1920s and 1930s was interrupted by the Spanish Civil War (1936–9). Chacel continued to write in exile in South America, but her production was slow and intermittent. In 1945 she published *Memorias de Leticia Valle* (*Memoirs of Leticia Valle*), a psychological study of the battle of wits and sensuality between an eleven-year-old girl and her much older tutor. Traces of Chacel's vanguard beginnings are apparent in the novel's elliptical style, but she had found her own voice with her move to the new world. Her masterpiece, *La sinrazón* ('Unreason', 1960), consummates her development of a complex style that reveals an individual consciousness's engagement with its surroundings. Chacel had learned much from her apprenticeship in the Spanish vanguard and from European modernists, such as James Joyce (whom she read in Spanish translation in the 1920s); however, she moved beyond those models to incorporate a philosophical concept of the individual as a social as well as a metaphysical being.

Other writers of the pre-Civil War vanguard period whose careers continued in exile during the post-war period include Ramón Sender (1902–82) and Francisco Ayala (1906–). By the late 1920s, when these writers began publishing fiction, Spain's political stability was collapsing. Primo de Rivera's dictatorship ended and King Alfonso XIII went into exile, opening the way for the Second Republic proclaimed in 1931. The Republic suffered wild swings between leftist radicalism and conservative backlash that led to the Civil War in 1936. Both Sender's and Ayala's novelistic careers began in the vanguard style that emphasizes linguistic virtuosity over social thematics, but their interests shifted to incorporate contemporary political concerns within the growing social consciousness of the 1930s.

In his essays in *El nuevo romanticismo* ('The New Romanticism', 1930), José Díaz Fernández articulated a vanguard aesthetic that retained stylistic innovations but incorporated socio-political content. Díaz Fernández exemplified his aesthetics in two novels: *El blocao* ('The Blockade', 1928) and *La Venus mecánica* ('The Mechanical Venus', 1929). While not officially subscribing to any stated aesthetics, the narratives of Sender and Ayala are excellent examples of how the formal innovations of modernism and vanguardism can be marshalled to moral and political purposes. *Imán* ('Magnet', 1930, published in English as *Earmarked for Hell*), still considered one of Sender's best novels, combines poetic imagery with a vivid account of the disastrous Spanish colonial campaigns in Morocco in the early 1920s. *Siete domingos rojos* (*Seven Red Sundays*, 1932) chronicles the social unrest, especially the proletarian uprisings, that contributed to the pre-Civil War climate of the Second Republic. The loose structure, a series of incidents narrated from a variety of viewpoints (even that of the moon), is reminiscent of the narratives of Salinas and Jarnés, but the prevalence of blood and the color red carries a much more serious message about Spain's growing political crisis.

Francisco Ayala began his career in a vanguard mode tinged with surrealism in five short narrations collected as *El boxeador y un ángel* ('The Boxer and an Angel', 1929). In "Cazador en el alba" ('Hunter at Dawn') the protagonist experiences a series of oneiric visions, narrated in a densely metaphorical style, that recall images from silent films. Ayala published a number of essays after his early narrative work, but returned to fiction only after the Civil War, when he introduced a profoundly moral content into his complexly layered prose. *Los usurpadores* (*Usurpers*, 1949) and *La cabeza del cordero* (*The Lamb's Head*, 1949) are collections of short novels that represent the best of Ayala's narrative art. "El inquisidor" ('The Inquisitor'), published the following year but now included in *Los usurpadores*, focuses on the soul-searching of a Jewish-convert inquisitor and the moral dilemma he faces when condemning those whose Christian loyalties are in doubt. "La cabeza del cordero" reveals the moral anguish of a man who denied his relationship to a family member killed during the Civil War in order to save himself from the same fate.

Whether you call the period from about 1900 until 1936 the Generations of '98, '14, and '27, the modernist/vanguard era, or, as José Carlos Mainer prefers, the Spanish Silver Age, it was an extraordinarily productive and innovative period in Spanish literature. Narrative was an important part of that exuberant artistic flowering, although it no longer dominated the literary world as in the late nineteenth century. In many ways, the new novelists sought to break with the realist-Naturalist tradition, although women novelists of the modernist era were less ready to abandon realist strategies that afforded means of addressing social problems. Novelists beginning their careers toward the end of the modernist/vanguard period, and who were caught up in the political chaos of the 1930s, returned to the social and moral issues we associate with Realism and Naturalism, incorporating the technical innovations of the modernist and vanguardist aesthetics. Some of these writers continued that fruitful marriage of style and social commitment in narratives produced in exile in the new world.

Younger writers who began their novelistic careers after the Civil War and expressed their reactions to Francisco Franco's repressive regime in a covert fashion inherited the legacy of modernist/vanguard writers. It is difficult to imagine Camilo José Cela's *La familia de Pascual Duarte* (*The Family of Pasual Duarte*, 1942), Carmen Laforet's *Nada* ('Nothing', 1945), Ana María Matute's *Primera memoria* ('First Memory', 1960, published in English as *Awakening*), Luis Martín Santos's *Tiempo de silencio* (*Time of Silence*, 1962), or Miguel Delibes's *Cinco horas con Mario* (*Five Hours with Mario*, 1966) without the context of pre-war narrative innovations. Each of these writers resisted the restraints placed on his or her artistic freedom by a strict censorship through elliptical plot structures, poetic language, and linguistic representation of thought processes they had learned from their early twentieth-century predecesors.

Guide to further reading

Johnson, Roberta, *Crossfire: Philosophy and the Novel in Spain, 1900–1934* (Lexington, KY: University Press of Kentucky, 1993).

Gender and Nation in the Spanish Modernist Model (Nashville, TN: Vanderbilt University Press, 2003).

Mainer, José Carlos, *La edad de plata* (Madrid: Cátedra, 1981).
Ortega y Gasset, José, *The Dehumanization of Art and Notes on the Novel*, tr. Helene Weye (Princeton University Press, 1948).
Pérez Firmat, Gustavo, *Idle Fictions: The Hispanic Vanguard Novel* (Durham, NC: Duke University Press, 1982).
Spires, Robert C., *Transparent Simulacra: Spanish Fiction 1902–1926* (Columbia, MO: University of Missouri Press, 1988).

11

GONZALO SOBEJANO
translated by CAROL ANNE TINKHAM AND HARRIET TURNER

The testimonial novel and the novel of memory

When placing works of prose fiction within the framework of modernity, critics find that diverse styles and trends tend to conform to a basic structure, which Nil Santiáñez-Tió has termed a "spectrum of possibilities":

> This spectrum has two poles: the realist pole (transparent language, tendency toward a transparent linguistic code, metonymical structure, unity of structure and subject, temporal organization, relation of subject to his/her biographic and social context, predominance of story over discourse, preference for unity and consistency, tendency to global visions, subordination to the principle of non-contradiction); the experimental, modernist pole (experimental and dislocated language, a dense linguistic code, metaphoric structure, dissolution of personal identity, spatial organization, predominance of fictional discourse over story, a narrative distanced from direct communication, rejection of global visions, epistemological doubt).[1]

In 1983 I proposed that a similar polarity existed between the testimonial novel, on the one hand, and the poetic novel, on the other. But whether one speaks of "realist" as opposed to "modernist" prose or of the testimonial as opposed to the poetic novel, it is certainly the case that the idea of literary polarity derives from what we consider "modern" literature. Both poles may be present at the same time, in the same writer, and even in the same work. These poles may exist in a relatively pure state or as subtle variations that combine the magnetic attraction of one to the other.[2]

The tendency in the modern Spanish novel toward the "realist" pole developed during the second half of the twentieth century. This period was characterized – at least in the political sphere – by two phases: the first takes

1 N. Santiáñez-Tió, "Temporalidad y discurso histórico. Propuesta de una renovación metodológica de la historia de la literatura española moderna," *Hispanic Review* 65 (1997), p. 279.

2 G. Sobejano, "Testimonio y poema en la novela española contemporanea," *Actas del VIII Congreso de la Asociación Internacional de Hispanistas*, vol. 1 (Madrid: Istmo, 1986), pp. 89–115.

place between the dates of the "victory" and the death of General Franco (1939–75); the second follows from 1975, after Franco's death, and encompasses the transition toward democracy and the nation's acceptance of a new democratic form of government. In the first phase, which was defined by the dictatorship, the predominant realist pole gives rise to the "testimonial novel," a genre that continues well into the 1960s. In the second phase, the "novel of memory" gains prominence. Though reflecting different circumstances, the "novel of memory" may be considered a literary successor to the "testimonial" novel. The purpose of this essay is not to recount the history of these two phases but to illustrate their salient features through reflections on certain key examples of this literary production.

The testimonial novel

In his presentation of the first edition of *La colmena* (*The Hive*), in 1951, Camilo José Cela declared that this novel was nothing but "a slice of life narrated step by step": "Its plot unfolds in Madrid – in 1942 – among a swarm or beehive of characters who are sometimes happy and other times not."[3] In an interview one year after the publication of *El Jarama* (*The One Day of the Week*, 1956), Rafael Sánchez Ferlosio clarified his principal aim in these words: "A delimited time and space. Showing simply what happens there."[4]

Narrating a slice of life or seeing what happens within a strictly limited time and space subordinates artistic construction to a series of reflections; these reflections simply bear witness to events. During the 1940s and 1950s readers and critics had become accustomed to escapist literature (generally in translation). Now they encountered a series of titles such as *Nada* (1945) ('Nothing') by Carmen Laforet, *La sombra del ciprés es alargada* ('Long is the Cypress's Shadow', 1948) by Miguel Delibes, José Suárez Carreño's *Las últimas horas* (*The Final Hours*, 1950); Cela's *La colmena* (1951), Ignacio Aldecoa's *El fulgor y la sangre* ('Lightning and Blood', 1954), *Los bravos* ('The Untamed', 1954) by Jesús Fernández Santos, *El Jarama* (1956), and *Nuevas amistades* ('New Friendships', 1959) by Juan García Hortelano. These titles and those of ensuing years – titles evocative of the world of work like *Central eléctrica* ('Power Plant', 1958), *La piqueta* ('The Pickaxe', 1959), *La mina* ('The Mine', 1960) *La zanja* ('The Trench', 1961) by Jesús López Pacheco, Antonio Ferres, Armando López Salinas and Alfonso Grosso

3 C. J. Cela, *La colmena* (Buenos Aires: Emecé, 1951). The quotation is taken from the jacket of this first edition.

4 D. Villanueva, *"El Jarama" de Rafael Sánchez Ferlosio. Su estructura y significado* (Santiago de Compostela: Universidad de Santiago de Compostela, 1973), p. 65.

respectively, convinced readers and critics alike that they were, in effect, witnessing the renaissance of an autochthonic novel of the "realist" type.

Thus from the 1940s to the 1960s, Spain's novelistic production offered a range of works that represented quite an innovation for their time. These novels had in common the conviction that writing should revolve around, and incorporate, historical events and social contexts. Writing should reflect what was real rather than display itself as an autonomous work of art, created simply to flaunt the genius of its maker. To understand how this change in literary direction occurred, we need to take into account several interrelated factors: not only the personality of each individual writer, but also the influence exerted by two basic constructs: the *historical climate*, experienced by authors and readers alike, and the *model* or generic idea of what constitutes a novel. The construct of "historical climate" refers to general, collective trends in thinking, feeling, and action that arise when people share a common set of experiences, bounded within a given time and place and marked, at beginning and end, by significant changes and events. The construct of a "model" arises from specific literary texts that are produced within a given historical climate. This model appears as a generic ideal and suggests literary possibilities that writers may either emulate or strive to exceed during a given period of time.

The end of the Civil War (1936–9), the events of the Second World War (1939–45), and the succeeding post-war years define what we may call the first "historical climate." In this climate, nationalist mythology and rhetoric no longer hold sway. Autarchic Spain, now isolated from Europe, moves from starvation to a prolonged scarcity. It is a time of repression, of the politics of purge, of isolation and misery. In schools and universities young people had to enroll for curricula consisting of thirteen years of religious education and five of a single party's political indoctrination. For the most part, orthodoxy and the traditional Catholic theology of Neo-Thomism precluded any echoes or parodies of the ideas of a now distant "Generación del '98" – a cultural and intellectual phenomenon that had gained greater prominence in the absence of more modern texts.

Soon after the end of the Second World War diverse ideas and feelings began filtering through existentialist themes: dereliction, nothingness, emptiness, the human condition, authenticity, risk and compromised circumstances. Poets invoked God. A few novelists indulged in the effects of violence (a trend occasionally called "tremendismo," marked by darkness, turbulence, and despair). The theatre cultivated entertainment. Cinematography promoted a kind of "heroic" nationalism. Journals, such as *Escorial*, *Índice*, *Ínsula* and the more traditional *Arbor*, all of which express a more liberal viewpoint, also began to appear. The philosopher Ortega y Gasset organized a lecture series in the Institute of the Humanities. Pedro Laín Entralgo's *España como problema* ('The Problem of Spain', 1949) was countered by Rafael Calvo Serer's *España sin problema* ('Spain Without Problems', 1949). Guided by the teachings of Ramón Menéndez Pidal, philologists devoted themselves to dialectology. It is a time of half-shuttered houses, slow trains, and reconstructed temples; full military barracks, brothels, tuberculosis, burials; the triumph and death of the bullfighter Manolete; segregated beaches, safe-conduct passes, droughts, stagnation.

Such were the "years of penance," as expressed in *Años de penitencia* (Carlos Barral) and of "infradevelopment" (Fernando Morán).[5] The government that saw itself as "partaking of neutrality and not belligerence" was followed, from 1945 to 1951, by a government "of autarchy" (Ramón Tamames).[6] The period between the Spanish Civil War and the Second World War also saw the transition from what had been a break in intellectual life before the Civil War to "the decline of an imperialist-totalitarian culture." From that time on, the "reconstruction of reason" and the "recovery of liberal thought" (Elías Díaz)[7] slowly gained ground. The semantic import of those times could be condensed into one word: anguish.

In those early years, the novelists who imparted privileged insights into their particular historical climate were Camilo José Cela, Carmen Laforet, and Miguel Delibes, all of whom saw the necessity for change. Wanting to shake off inertia with a flourish, Cela exposed the intractable roots of individual alienation in *La familia de Pascual Duarte* (*The Family of Pascual Duarte*, 1942) – the confession of a man condemned to death. In *Pabellón de reposo* (*Rest Home*, 1944) he reproduced diary entries of patients ill with tuberculosis, and in *La colmena* he presented a panorama of hunger. Carmen Laforet, in *Nada* (1945) and *La isla y los demonios* ('The Island and the Demons', 1952), traced the pathways of consciousness from illusion through disenchantment toward the necessity of a renewed enthusiasm for life. In his seclusion, Miguel Delibes probed the hidden power of fear and set for himself, time and again, the task of searching for a way that is his own, as in *La sombra del ciprés es alargada* (1947), *El camino* (*The Path*, 1950), *Diario de un cazador* ('Diary of a Hunter', 1955), *La hoja roja* ('The Red Leaf', 1959), and other novels.

Other writers kept pace, presenting human consciousness in conflict (Gonzalo Torrente Ballester, *Los gozos y las sombras* ['Pleasures and

5 F. Morán, *Novela y semidesarrollo* (Madrid: Taurus, 1971). The term "infradevelopment" comes from the word "semidesarrollo" in the title.

6 R. Tamames, *La República. La era de Franco*, 7th edn. (Madrid: Cupsa, 1978).

7 E. Díaz, *Pensamiento espanõl en la era de Franco (1939–1975)*, 2nd edn. (Madrid: Tecnos, 1992), Chapter II, pp. 42–61.

Shadows', 1957–62]), aspects of everyday life (Luis Romero, *La noria* ['The Waterwheel', 1952]), and abject failure (Suárez Carreño, *Las últimas horas*, 1950). According to Juan Benet's considered judgment, Suárez Carreño's novel

> already contained in embryonic form all the elements of condemnation that would nourish Spanish literary production over the following fifteen years: the existence of a people without a voice, who suffered but nonetheless emerged unscathed; the coarseness, bad taste, and debased culture of the nouveau riche; the equivocal and dramatic situation of woman, who lives with one leg bent in submission to ill-gotten gain, and the other almost up in the air, seeking the love of intransigent intellectuals; the aversion, boredom, and – abounding throughout, although never stated explicitly – the intractable malaise of inaction.[8]

A close reading of the early novels of Cela, Laforet, and Delibes, as well as of works by lesser-known writers, yields a model characterized by the following: the author assumes a narrator who, speaking in the first person or through focusing, either merges with the protagonist or identifies closely with him or her. Narration becomes a confessional discourse tending toward monologue. Thus, as Spires has observed, the implied reader, invested emotionally in the story, must now make a decision either in favor of the individual's role in society or against it. Time appears as a past sealed off from the present, over which the subject broods, yielding a retrospective view more linear than simultaneous. A past relived, framed by a broad evocative context, resounds within the consciousness of the main character, who chooses to recount several meaningful personal experiences. Space is experienced as a subtle state of being, delineated through atmospheric descriptions that focus on everyday objects. It is a reduced space, at times rigorously cellular.

Reflecting the coercions of an oppressive historical climate, the world of these novels revolves around an individual and his or her family, who form an isolated unit. Faced with an uncertain future, the protagonist gives vent to violence, suffers the emptiness of inner exile, or, paralyzed by indecision, becomes lost in monologues suffused with memory and endless waiting. Such early novels feature a person who, his or her development shaped by the interventions of those close to him or her, struggles to discover or attain an authentic self, a center toward which his or her desire for truth inevitably turns and through which he or she achieves a certain distance from a masked world. The main character lives through hollowness, repetition, nausea, guilt, struggle, agony. If and when they prevail, four solutions commonly occur: they die or simply close that painful chapter of their lives; their obsession burns out, or the deception that had blinded them is disclosed.

[8] Juan Benet, *En ciernes* (Madrid: Taurus, 1976), pp. 94–5.

If these novels appear as a cluster or cycle, their common axis turns on a fixed chronology of determining events. Titles may refer to the protagonist (e.g. *Pascual Duarte*), the particular situation (e.g. *Las últimas horas*), or an overwhelming negativity (e.g. *Nada*, *La sombra del ciprés es alargada*). They are melodic novels presented in a low-key manner. Narrative flow, paced through evenly divided chapters, is uniform. Filtered through the consciousness of the main character, words render a transparent image of reality. This image, though personal, is not unique but common to all, thereby inviting comparisons. Language itself projects the emotional resonance of inner voices. The image of the road, so often present, denotes uncertainty; the image of the island, another common trope, expresses an inability to communicate. The phenomenon of discontinuity, which marks the modern European novel, surfaces, in this fiction, more in the disconnection among people than in the rupture of the classical unities of time and space. The many individual destinies represented in these novels ultimately converge in the vision of a person withdrawn into loneliness.

This lyrical, emotional emphasis on withdrawal reflected the deprivations of war and isolation. Further, the aesthetic criteria proffered by the regime reinforced this withdrawal, engendering a collective psyche that gestured towards the image of an inward-turning individual, imprisoned within a close family circle and bereft of access to a wider community. Randolph Pope has identified the symptomatic frequency of common images, themes, motifs and fictional characters in the novel of the 1940s: the backward-looking glance, jail-school, marginality, and the cult of the family (the sense of clinging to the family despite a stifling domestic life); hunger and misery; the figures of the *indiano* (a newly rich Spanish emigrant returned from Latin America) and of the *inocente* ("simpleton").

The above characteristics defined the novelistic model of the 1940s and 1950s as a kind of existential confession, an existentialism "more vitalistic than philosophical,"[9] a phenomenon that G. Roberts and O. Barreiro Pérez have studied in depth. In that confessional novel, the "I" makes an effort to accept a fantasy world informed by illusory ideals (peace, family harmony, health, affection, or purity). Evoking such illusions, the novel may contain certain traits of romance, as in *Nada* or *Los Abel* ('The Abel Family', 1948) and *Pequeño teatro* ('Children's Theatre', 1954) by Ana María Matute, or tragic elements that degenerate into melodrama (*Pascual Duarte*). It is not a novel of lucidity but one imbued with illusionism. Traces of literary

[9] D. Villanueva, "La novela social. Apostillas a un estado de la cuestión," ed. Víctor García de la Concha *et al.*, *Literatura Contemporánea en Castilla y León* (Valladolid: Junta de Castilla y León, 1986, pp. 329–48), p. 338.

intertextuality are drawn from the picaresque genre and from writers like Baroja, Dostoievski, and Chekhov. Other traces derive from a scattering of foreign novels in translation (chosen by happenstance in an impoverished outdated market) and from influential films (*Rebecca*, *Wuthering Heights*).

If a novelist's persona can succeed in interpreting the underlying structures of a given historical climate in the throes of change, the novel itself shapes that change and communicates its message to a new climate. Memory, presented as a selective process, and the technique of expressing the narrator's own feelings of empathy through the consciousness of a naive, central character allowed *Nada* and *El camino* to forge the path to *neorrealismo*. *La colmena* bridged the gap between existential concerns and social realities. The image of the hive traced an underlying labyrinth of uncertainty, highlighted by its segmented design; glimpses of different lives exist juxtaposed yet without dialogue to connect them. *La colmena*'s narrative point of view, appearing "almost" objective, and its conversational technique were soon acclaimed and emulated. In some respects, Cela's novel became a model. It also proved so innovative as to open new literary vistas.

The publication of *La colmena* in 1951 coincided with a transition to another historical climate, one ending in 1962. Within this eleven-year period, Spain moved from a "government formed by treaties with the Vatican and the US" to a "government with a Plan of Stabilization" (1957) (Tamames, *La República*); the aim of both entities was to articulate Spain's position within Europe and her role as an anti-communist nation. A process of "intellectual liberalization and an international political opening, of dialogue with those in exile, of initiating ties between European thought, and of university crisis" also began to develop between 1951 and 1962. After 1956, "remnants of traditional *integrismo*" – a political affiliation advocating nationalistic goals – re-emerges as a viable voice, giving rise to "the technocratic ideology of economic development and the scientific criticism of ideological absolutism."[10]

These are "the years without excuse" (Barral) and of "partial development" (Morán), a time when poets, through their art, seek "communication," when poems speak of "solidarity." Sponsored by the Ministry of Education, writers produce essays on cultural liberalization; other thinkers look ahead to an economic liberalization supposedly divorced from ideology. While support from North America achieves positive results, increasing contact with Europe and America, entrenched mythologies and nationalist rhetoric betray their inner exhaustion. Scarcity yields to a relative solvency, facilitated by the emigration of workers, by tourism, and by the investment

[10] Díaz, *Pensamiento español*, Chapter IV, pp. 87–107.

of foreign capital. The Concordat with the Holy See (1953), an agreement that Spain signed with the Vatican, privileges canon law and thus almost erases civil law, consolidating the church's grip. Initial economic improvement and chronic political stagnation make social problems more evident. Movies and novels bring Italian *neorrealismo* to Spain; a literature of testimony, of condemnation, of censured protest, disseminates its message.

Change, conflict, and scarcity are the order of the day: exodus from the country to the city, workers migrating to urban suburbs, housing shortages, soccer triumphs, incursions of the super-conservative order of the Opus Dei, founded in 1928, vicissitudes of a handcuffed opposition, early dialogue with Spanish exiles and the student protest of 1956, which cracks the façade of the National Movement. More and more intellectuals and professionals leave the country. "Spain is in Europe," affirms Julián Marías, a little too optimistically, in 1952. Freedom should be a daily conquest, thinks José Luis Aranguren. Laín Entralgo publishes the book *La espera y la esperanza* ('Waiting and Hoping', 1957) and Antonio Buero Vallejo writes tragedies couched in a language of hope. In these years Ortega y Gasset, Pío Baroja, and Juan Ramón Jiménez all die. Enrique Tierno Galván's sociology and the economic history of Jaime Vicens Vives negotiate the passage from an existentialist stance based on "scarcity" to a neo-positivistic endorsement of "growth" (Díaz, *Pensamiento español*). Dionisio Ridruejo, a former Falangist, becomes one of the leaders of the opposition. Journals start to appear – *Papeles de Son Armadans* and *Boletín informativo de derecho político*, edited by Cela and Tierno Galván respectively. *Cuadernos del Congreso por la libertad de la cultura* comes out in Paris; also *Praxis*, a Marxist publication. In spite of rigid censorship, the editorial initiative becomes more and more vibrantly alive. Spain insists upon becoming part of Europe, culturally, and above all – economically – a project never fully brought to fruition ("nothing ever happens here" is a phrase that keeps cropping up in the literature of this period.)

In the work of novelists who reflect the new historical climate, we may note a rejection of Cela's sensationalism and a preference for Delibes's reclusiveness, even as Cela furnished younger writers with the format of the "travel book," a vehicle of first-hand knowledge of a now-forgotten Spain. Never were Spanish novelists less inclined to display genius or more seriously devoted to the representation of the real. Their gift to contemporary readers and writers is the unsparing apprehension of certain truths – social immobility (*El Jarama*); the widening gulf between social classes (*Los bravos*); the sense of belonging to, or alienation from, an inhospitable Spain (the first novels of Juan Goytisolo). These works define a new model – the "social" novel – also illustrated by the following contemporary texts: Aldecoa's novel about the fishing industry, *Gran Sol* ('Great Sole', 1957); *Las afueras* ('Beyond City Limits', 1958) by Luis Goytisolo; *Nuevas amistades* (1959) and *Tormenta de verano* ('Summer Storm', 1962) by García Hortelano. The social novel divides into three currents: a first wave of *neorrealismo* (more transcendent and of a more consciously crafted artistic density); a social realism (combining proletarian and anti-bourgeoisie strains); and the critical or dialectical realism that informs *Tiempo de silencio* (*Time of Silence*, 1962), a novel by Luis Martín Santos that establishes yet a different model.

In the social novel, broadly conceived, the novelist – tacitly a witness – lays out the inner life of the times for our contemplation; narration in the third person conveys both a limited point of view and an objective representation. The novelist may also structure narration so that multiple points of view become constitutive of a single event, rendered from several angles; or he or she may show us how different events define the same set of problems. Annotations, similar to stage directions, allow the narrator unobtrusively to construct scenes that develop through bits and pieces of conversation rather than dialogue. In this type of novel (according to R. Spires),[11] the implied reader begins to feel identified with the anonymous narrator and thus is able to distance himself from the stagnant society that stands exposed in the text.

Time – unique and irretrievable in its passing – is experienced, in these novels, as an open "present." A drawn-out circumspection results in extended scenes, either successive or simultaneous, and these approximate the feeling of real time. Scenic segments may last several hours, a day, or even a few days, time in which hardly anything (almost nothing) happens, and yet this "almost nothing" affects many. *El Jarama* succeeds in capturing the transient nature of life through the use of verifiable, palpably concrete nouns, appropriate to each person or thing. These nouns evoke, through that perfected sense of "yesterday will never return," a vividly felt recognition of what is most real, most present to us, and therefore most perishable. *El Jarama* conveys a renewed experience of our own mortality that, some time later, the author will attribute to certain stanzas of Jorge Manrique's medieval elegy of 1474. Space, concentrated in country, city, suburbs, places of work or leisure, usually emerges as reduced or confined within vast land- or city-scapes. Descriptions that focus obsessively upon objects, which acquire symbolic value, promote this sense of spatial reduction or confinement.

In the historical climate of the 1950s, contrasts marking the gulf between the "haves" and "have-nots" relegate the family unit to a secondary position, bringing forward the concerns of labor districts, economic groups, or

[11] R. Spires, *La novela española de postguerra* (Madrid: Cupsa, 1978).

social classes. The idea of a collective protagonist, conceived as the multitude in *La colmena*, now becomes the village community in *Los bravos* or groups based on age or neighborhood, as in *El Jarama*. In later novels, social class determines the collective identity of the protagonist. However, it is not yet the whole of the country represented through Madrid, as in *Tiempo de silencio*, nor is the collective protagonist emblematic of universal chaos, as in Juan Goytisolo's *Juan sin tierra* (*Juan the Landless*, 1975). As represented in these diverse social sectors, people endure a given state of affairs, try to escape, and in so doing attempt to come to some kind of decision. Since the group is the protagonist, people remain subsumed within the collective; character appears flat, not rounded, for individual consciousness gives way to a foregrounded social situation in which everyone takes part. Fenced in, as it were, by obstacles at every turn, these groups, afflicted by poverty and subject to oppression, decay, alienation, and a paralyzing isolation, engage in either endless work or mindless partying as they desperately search for some kind of solidarity.

In these novels, plot usually consists of a short succession of hours, days, or weeks in which nothing occurs; suddenly something happens, but in the end, the event does not alter (or hardly alters) the situation. Typical of the proletarian novel is the fatal accident: a gypsy kills a policeman (Aldecoa's *Con el viento solano* ['With the East Wind', 1957]); a girl drowns in a river (*El Jarama*); the village elder dies (*Los bravos*); the walls of a dam crumble (*Central eléctrica*); a net of fish crushes the owner of a fishing boat (*Gran sol*); the collapsing roof of a mine shaft buries a team of miners (*La mina*). Conversely, the police incident is typical of the anti-bourgeois novel, e.g. the apparent abortion of a young girl who thought she was pregnant (*Nuevas amistades*); the appearance of a dead, naked woman on the beach (*Tormenta de verano*). As a consequence of the police incident, a member of the idle rich does seem ready to change, but any inner recognition of wrongdoing dissipates as soon as the mystery clears up. In the proletarian novel, a fatal accident might provoke a change in the workers' conditions. Soon after, however, a surface calm reasserts itself and life goes on as before.

If there are cyclical novels, their construction is predominantly spatial: social zones are clearly marked, allowing certain living conditions to complement one another in significant ways. Examples of these juxtapositions occur in the trilogies of Aldecoa and Juan Goytisolo. Titles often flaunt a collective sign (*Los bravos*), or allude to a stationary mode (*Entre visillos* [*Behind the Curtains*, 1958] by Carmen Martín Gaite), or to the possibility of hope (*Central eléctrica*). These novels, rather extensive, graphically present a segmented story line: scenes occur without transitions. Language refers directly to what is real, avoids descriptions and summaries, and allows characters to express themselves in everyday speech. At the same time, the prose of Sánchez Ferlosio, Aldecoa, or Fernández Santos informs the text with a discernible poetic quality, one of transparent cogency, a quality seamlessly allied to the inherent force of testimonial expression. A common image – that of a redoubt (*reducto*), a military term for a final retreat – figures the theme of the fruitlessness of daily work; the theme of being lonely in a crowd surfaces in the image of the barrier. Such images trace out the idea of broken threads, of a distinctly spatial discontinuity that marks the divided nature of social sectors.

During these years the socialization of literature develops in opposition to the political aesthetics of the 1940s. Economic differences between classes become more obvious, while the presence of the individual person and of the family milieu gives way to group enclaves, leading the reader to contemplate not only what the press had kept intentionally from view but other facts and experiences omitted from the novel of previous generations. The new model, then, evolved as a primarily *testimonial* novel in which the world appears impervious to change, either by individuals or by isolated groups. This is the novel of disillusion, suffering, and patience. In the early 1950s intertextual traces stem from picaresque literature and the work of Pío Baroja. A renewed impetus regarding the testimonial novel comes from several other sources as well: the North American novel (Hemingway, Faulkner); Italian neorealism in narrative and cinematography (Zavattini); Marxist criticism (Marx and Lukács, Sartre and Brecht, Gramsci, now more frequently read); and from the Spanish novel of the preceding generation.

A focus on realism, either expressed or implied, marked the existential novel of the 1940s and the social novel of the 1950s. While the "structural" or "dialectical" novel of the 1960s maintained a realist orientation, these novels expanded the experiences of testimony, encompassing a broader social panorama and deepening the expression of personal consciousness. Writers like Luis Martín Santos (*Tiempo de silencio*) and Juan Goytisolo (*Señas de identidad* [*Marks of Identity*, 1966]) restored an acute, limitless elocutionary potential and variety to the art of the novel. Novels that followed, however, did not sustain the realist aim. Attention shifted either to the text itself – a preoccupation with language, metafiction, and the theory of the novel within the process of novel writing – or to the task of recovering an appropriate, amenable kind of narrativity, parodic in many cases, which many critics understood as constituting a kind of plural model of *post-modernity*. Only in the case of novels by younger writers in the 1990s (the so-called "Generation X") did people begin to speak again of neorealism. However, the task of tracing the causes of such a literary change goes beyond the confines of this chapter.

We may cite *El Jarama* as the best example of the testimonial novel. This text exhibits, in a highly developed form, the cluster of characteristics that constitute the model: exposition; vividly lived, inner experiences; prosaic daily routines; chronological time; concrete spaces; revelations of the way things are ("immobilism"); the representation of a world inscribed within the historical reality that contains it; successive or simultaneous scenes; the presence of objects, evoked in precise details; a condensed experience of time; actions that, appearing insignificant, nonetheless become charged with intensity, communicating symptomatic values; half-developed characters; a distant stance taken by a camera-like witness; transparent prose, colloquial speech, and poetry. Poetry infuses the text because the author of a good testimonial novel must be a poet, in the same way as the author of a good poetic novel – Juan Benet, for instance, in *Saúl ante Samuel* ('Saul Before Samuel', 1980) – must bear witness to his world, whether immediate or mediated.

El Jarama, a testimonial novel, is also a poem. Critics[12] have recognized its intrinsically poetic nature. Its symbolic qualities and values endow the text with a singular density, one enduring and inevitable in its expression. A poetic sensibility gives voice to those profound feelings that bear witness to a single moment in time – a unique, irrepeatable time, witnessed respectfully as truth. An honest respect for what is and what was, once upon a time, testifies as an act of love to the simple fact of life.[13]

The novel of memory

When General Franco died in November 1975, abrupt changes in politics were the order of the day, beginning with a period of transition. No perceptible break in literary production occurred, however. Faced with uncertainty, people suffered *desencanto*, a pervasive kind of "disenchantment." While "disenchantment" may have been experienced somewhat prematurely, that mood was the logical consequence of four decades of dictatorship. Turbulence marked the transitional years, yet the period conveyed a hope of new

[12] E. C. Riley, "Sobre el arte de Sánchez Ferlosio: Aspectos de *El Jarama*," *Filología* 9 (1963), pp. 201–21, corrected version in *Novelistas españoles de posguerra*, ed. Rodolfo Cardona (Madrid: Taurus, 1976), vol. 1, pp. 123–41; Villanueva, "*El Jarama*"; A. Risco, "Una relectura de *El Jarama*, de Sánchez Ferlosio," *Cuadernos hispanoamericanos* 288 (June 1974), pp. 700–11; R. Gullón, "Recapitulación de *El Jarama*", *Hispanic Review* 43 (1975), pp. 1–23; F. García Sarriá, "*El Jarama*. Muerte y merienda de Lucita," *Bulletin of Hispanic Studies* 53 (1976), pp. 323–37; G. Sobejano, "Retrovisión de *El Jarama*: el día habitado," in *Entre la cruz y la espada: en torno a la España de posguerra. Homenaje a Eugenio de Nora*, ed. J. M. López de Abiada (Madrid: Gredos, 1984), pp. 327–44.

[13] Sobejano, "Retrovisión."

horizons. In 1982 the triumph of social democracy brought many benefits, some of a contingent nature, others of lasting impact. Spain became more European.

The years of transition opened many pathways for the art of the narrative. A major development, arising from the legacy of the testimonial novel, was "the novel of memory," perhaps best illustrated by the work of Carmen Martín Gaite, particularly her novel *El cuarto de atrás* (*The Back Room*, 1978). Just as we spoke earlier of "the 'testimonial novel" and not of "testimony" per se, we refer now to the "novel of memory," not simply to "memoirs." Neither testimony nor memoir may assume per se the form of the novel. Testimonial writing captures a reality that the author has witnessed directly, while a book of memories represents, in writing, what the author recalls having experienced. The difference is instructive. If "history" is to be more than a catalogue of the facts of the past, the practice of New Historicism (Arthur Danto, Hayden White) is to construe historical writing as a "story." The idea of a "story" implies the selective and interpretive consciousness of a storyteller. Yet the new historicists would never claim that what such a "storyteller" offers is a "novel" or a "fiction." On the contrary, even new historicists present narrative as empirically grounded in fact. While imagination plays a role in interpreting facts, history, in their view, is not an imaginative art.

Travel books – Cela's *Viaje a la Alcarria* ('Journey to Alcarria', 1948) or Goytisolo's *Campos de Níjar* ('The Landscapes of Níjar', 1960) – are "testimonies." While they may be imaginative or emotional in tone, these books bear witness from the perspective of the traveler (Cela, Goytisolo) to the actual state of affairs at a given time and place. Conversely, *Memorias y olvidos* ('Remembering and Forgetting', 1982) by Francisco Ayala is a book of "memories." While it displays an imaginative writing style and records events – indispensable elements in any narrative – Ayala's book is not subtitled "novela" nor does it belong to the genre of the novel. His book is a narrative of remembering and forgetting; the memories, the forgotten things, belong not to an imaginary subject but to the Francisco Ayala who has written and published the book.

These cautionary comments help explain why, strictly speaking, "testimonies" and "memoirs" are not considered here: they are not "novels." From the 1940s to the 1960s the Spanish novel tended to bear witness to identifiable, contemporary realities; these realities called for close observation and criticism, hence the term *novela testimonial*. After a brief hiatus (1970–5), which featured a kind of exaggerated experimentalism, the novel recovered, in part, the "realist" accent of the testimonial novel. The aim of this new novel, however, was not to raise the reader's consciousness of life under a now defunct dictatorship but to revisit and reassess one's experience during that difficult time.

The novels appear within an historical climate characterized by obstructed beginnings and a transitional period of opportunity. As society manages to evade revolutionary change, transition itself becomes channeled into democratic reform. This climate gives rise to novels organized around remembering. Remembering often takes place through dialogue and finds expression in the self-reflexive act of writing, producing metafiction as well as incursions into a world of fantasy. Among these variants, our analysis will focus on the novel of memories – novels tilted, so to speak, in the direction of the "realist" pole – rather than on metafiction or fantasy, styles of writing that tend toward the "modernist" pole.

Autobiographical memory appears in dialogical form in *Diálogos del anochecer* ('Dialogues at Twilight', 1972) by José-María Vaz de Soto, *Retahílas* ('Endless Recitations', 1974) by Carmen Martín Gaite, *Las guerras de nuestros antepasados* (*The Wars of Our Ancestors*, 1975) by Miguel Delibes, *Luz de la memoria* ('Light of Memory', 1976) by Lourdes Ortiz, *Fabián* ('Fabian', 1977) by Vaz de Soto, *La muchacha de las bragas de oro* ('The Girl in Golden Panties', 1978) by Juan Marsé, and *El cuarto de atrás* (1978) by Martín Gaite, as well as others in the 1970s and beyond. The narrative of remembering informs amenable, impressionistic books like those of Francisco Umbral, as well as the fervent *Autobiografía de Federico Sánchez* ('The Autobiography of Federico Sánchez', 1977) by Jorge Semprún. The desire to recount one's life in relation to the death of Franco, which marked the end of an era, compels this retrospective mode of storytelling. The act of recalling one's personal history (evoking life as lived up to the moment the dictatorship ended or was about to end – a dictatorship, moreover, that had inscribed a writer's biography from childhood to adulthood) – expressed a will to distance oneself from those events, thereby achieving a clearer idea about the meaning of existence. The narrative of remembering also surfaces in debased forms: remembrances of things that never happened or the evocation of events supposedly occurring in an inconceivable future. Falsified accounts, promoted by people skilled in public relations, won prestigious prizes and gained easy sales.

Characteristic of the 1960s novel (whether seen as "dialectical" or "structural") was a self-dialogical mode of narrative discourse, articulated by the partial, even exclusive, use of the self-reflexive "you" (*tú*), equivalent to a split "I" (*yo*). In the 1970s writers divide this dual expression of the self into a dialogue between two different interlocutors. These interlocutors recall

Berganza and Cipión, characters in Cervantes's *Coloquio de los perros* ('The Dogs' Dialogue', 1613): one character assumes the role of a protagonist, similar to the autobiographical Berganza, while the other's parsimonious speech habits and supporting role remind us of Cipión. This "other" may shadow the protagonist, as it were, presenting attenuated versions of the protagonist's ideas; he may also contest the protagonist by presenting a problematic, a failed, or even a phantasmagoric identity.

In the case of Vaz de Soto's *Diálogos del anochecer* (1972), the first volume of a tetralogy, two friends, Fabián Azúa and Sabas Llorente, enact a dialogue in which each appears, at first, clearly differentiated from the other, each with a given name, marital status, biography, and distinct personality. At the same time, an ironic game of indistinction comes into play as the author shuffles and combines speech habits and psychological traits. As the novel progresses, one adopts the situation of the other, narrating his story as if he were the other. The second novel of the tetralogy, *Fabián* (1977), represents nothing more than the delayed publication of one day's worth of conversations between Fabián and Sabas, omitted from *Diálogos del anochecer* for fear of censorship. *Fabián* presents Fabián as character and Sabas as his psychotherapist and as the composer of the dialogical novel that the two friends gradually construct. As the novel *Fabián* appears to write itself through the dialogical exchanges of Fabián and Sabas, one as friend, the other as composer, both acquire a more acute awareness of themselves as people *and* as characters in the novel. Self-consciousness develops to the point where Fabián's story about personal communication and sexual fulfillment gives way to a series of digressions of every kind, mainly of a self-critical or metafictive nature.

In *Fabián*, Sabas seems to represent a constellation of interlocutive qualities and values. These values arise through questions and whatever else incites the speaker to continue his story, progressing through more or less extensive commentaries, finally resulting in momentary identification, productive discrepancies, corrective oppositions, and even contradictions. In sum, Vaz de Soto's novels present interlocutors each of whom may be an unknown person, a marginal or "sub" interlocutor, recalling Cipión. But on occasion a true interlocutor appears with as much right as the other to his own novel. This insistence on a rightful place for him finds expression in the two titles that complete the "tetralogy": *Fabián y Sabas* ('Fabian and Sabas', 1982) and *Diálogos de la alta noche* ('Dialogues Late at Night', 1982). In Carmen Martín Gaite's *Retahílas*, in which alternating chapters present the speeches of aunt and nephew through the duration of one night, Eulalia is the protagonist and Germán the secondary character who plays more the role of a catalyst than of an autonomous speaker. As we shall see, in *El cuarto de atrás* Martín Gaite creates the figure of "the man dressed in black," an intriguing example of an enigmatic being or the model of a phantom-like interlocutor.

No matter how shadowy the interlocutor may appear in the novel of memory, the impression persists that dialogue is always intended, even when unwitnessed. Matters of influence or first appearances have little bearing on the literary production of the novel of memory, for if *Diálogos al anochecer* precedes *Retahílas*, the theme of "the talking cure" already existed in Martín Gaite's *Ritmo lento* ('Slow Rhythm', 1963). Similarly, although *Fabián's* psychoanalytic dialogue was published two years later than Delibes's *Las guerras de nuestros antepasados*, Vaz de Soto's novel had been written at an earlier time. At issue is the collective will for self-expression, for dialogue, during the years of rupture and transition. This dialogue is not intellectual or contemplative: it is an emotional exchange, rendered through memory and realized dialectically between two speakers, each cognizant of past and future. It is a dialogue that uncovers religious anguish, deceptions that stem from an ideology in crisis, and palpable tensions between the individual and society. It is, in sum, a dialogue articulating a longing for communication and genuineness in the face of entrenched obligations imposed by the world's social codes. It is a dialogue between what could have been, given an atmosphere of freedom, and what now, after so many years of oppression, will never be. It is a dialogue whose temperature, responding to the incandescent quality of words, rises to a feverish pitch – that insomnia and intoxication captured so well in *Retahílas*, *Fabián*, *El cuarto de atrás*, or in the second half of *Luz de la memoria* – a choked succession of recitations that induce an ever-rising pulse rate.

Not all novels of memories are figured as dialogues. Rosa Chacel adopts a discourse that shares the qualities of essay and introspection in the trilogy *Escuela de Platón* ('Plato's School'), composed of *Barrio de Maravillas* (*The Maravillas District*, 1976), *Acrópolis* ('The Acropolis', 1984), and *Ciencias naturales* ('The Natural Sciences', 1988). The trilogy reconstructs, through reminiscences, the feelings and thoughts of a girl up to 1914, of a girl grown to womanhood during the Civil War, and later a girl in exile. A continuous, self-correcting discourse, marked by indeterminacy, distinguishes the novelistic art of this writer. She also reproduces certain unexpected moments of epiphany, reflecting upon them with a kind of inquisitive obstinacy.

Several of Francisco Umbral's novels evoke an individual and collective past, characterized by the drawn-out coercions of the Franco regime. Perhaps the best of these is his first, *Memorias de un niño de derechas* ('Memories of a Right-Wing Childhood', 1962) set in the 1940s and 1950s. Umbral's novels adapt the form of a series of fragments, each almost monological, which evolve as sketches of local customs, news commentaries, short essays, and poetry in prose. The form of the monologue defines the units that comprise José Luis Castillo-Puche's *Trilogía de la liberación*: *El libro de las visiones y las apariciones* ('The Book of Visions and Apparitions', 1977), *El amargo sabor de la retama* ('The Bitter Taste of Broom', 1979) and *Conocerás el poso de la nada* ('You'll Taste the Bitter Dregs of Nothingness', 1982). By construing writing and reading as a retrospective act of confession (the confession of a former anguish) Castillo-Puche's work explores further the theme of individual and general (Spanish) liberation in relation to the fanaticism and violence that provoked the outbreak of 1936 and its bloody consequences.

Other texts of reminiscence and reflection, composed during the years surrounding the disappearance of the dictatorship, take either a greater or lesser distance from the dictator's death, offering a variety of intriguing perspectives. Carlos Barral, a demanding poet and influential editor, is the author of some "memoirs" of superb critical-historical value. These are divided into three volumes: *Años de penitencia* ('Years of Penance', 1975), *Los años sin excusa* ('Years With No Excuse', 1978), and *Cuando las horas veloces* ('When Time Flies', 1988).[14] Before writing the third of these volumes, however, he published a first and only "novel," *Penúltimos castigos* ('Penultimate Punishments', 1983), defined by one critic as "a great fraud, based on the lure of a feigned autobiography, proffered to the reader by an artist who takes over narration, and who, as a narrative presence, can project himself upon the figure of both the author and the character named Carlos Barral, who dies at the end of the novel."[15]

In opposition to Carlos Barral, Juan Goytisolo, an apostate of testimonialism since 1975 (*Juan sin tierra*), published *Coto vedado* ('No Trespassing') in 1985 and in 1986 *En los reinos de taifa* (*Realms of Strife*). These form the first and second parts of an autobiography that adheres to the most established conventions of the genre. Recalling that Goytisolo, in the years between the publication of *Paisajes después de la batalla* ('Landscapes After the Battle', 1982) and *Las virtudes del pájaro solitario* ('Virtues of a Solitary Bird', 1988) – anti-novels of unrestrained vanguardism – had seemed to repudiate all forms of "realist" narrative, one critic expressed her bafflement in these words:

14 C. Barral, *Años de penitencia* (Madrid: Alianza, 1975); *Los años sin excusa* (Barcelona: Seix Barral, 1978); *Penúltimos castigos* (Barcelona: Seix Barral, 1983); *Cuando las horas veloces* (Barcelona: Tusquets, 1988).

15 Villanueva, "*El Jarama*", p. 55.

> While we have come to expect the unexpected, we find it quite disconcerting that this author now does what he had rejected originally for his own fiction since *Juan sin tierra. Coto vedado* and *En los reinos de taifa* may be considered autobiographies in every sense of the word: the writing focuses on tracing a life from its beginnings up to the present time of the story; the selection of certain episodes corresponds to whether or not each contributes to the understanding of a subject's will; Goytisolo locates himself in a chronological, historical reality, and through the operations of memory, brings his own past into the present.[16]

An even more paradoxical case is that of Luis Goytisolo in his book *Estatua con palomas* ('Doves By a Statue', 1992). The term "book" is necessary because this work has no subtitle referring to "memoirs" or "novel"; in fact, it does not belong to either of those literary categories. Goytisolo's work first appears to be an autobiography, in the form of memoirs: it tells of a reality that the author lived, an experience that is personal, familial, and above all fraternal, as well as socio-historical. But those memoirs, subject to the narrator's elaboration, suggest *novelization*, "having been made into a novel." The book consists of nine chapters and a total of forty-five segments. Beginning with fragment 13, part of Chapter IV, the "memories" that compose the first text alternate with a second text relating to Imperial Rome. This second text is clearly a text of "historical" fiction, based on the writings of Tacitus, an acute observer of character and destiny. Through Tacitus, Goytisolo highlights the "novelistic" quality of History itself. Autobiography now passes into the realm of history, and from fiction to the historical novel, all within the same volume.

Whether structured by monologue or dialogue, the novels of memory constituted the high point in Spain's literary production during the years immediately following Franco's death. Carmen Martín Gaite deserves special mention, for in *El cuarto de atrás* she discovered an ingenious way to blend memory, metafiction, and fantasy. In *Retahílas* (1974), she construed plot as dialogue and denouement as cessation of dialogue, creating the most perfected forms of expression. The author defines "retahílas" as long-winded, tiresome speeches. In fact, they are dialogical pieces, one linked to the other. As in her other novels, the writing in *Retahílas* has a tripartite format: "Preludio" (narrated in the third person), the spun-out speeches (*retahílas*) of Eulalia and of her nephew, Germán (two in each chapter, from Chapters I to V, plus one scatter-shot speech by Eulalia in Chapter VI), and an "Epílogo"

16 C. Moreiras-Menor, "Ficción y autobiografía en Juan Goytisolo: algunos apuntes," in *La autobiografía en la España contemporánea*, ed. Ángel Loureiro, *Anthropos* 125 (October 1991), pp. 71–6.

(narrated once again in the third person). The links, literal or semantic, operate without missing a beat from one "speech-string" to the other, emphasizing contact by words. The constant appeal to the person who listens (*tú*) exercises a conative function while the speaker's unburdening of thoughts and feelings performs an emotive function. Privileging the combination of the two processes creates a singular fluency and freedom of emission that approximates the text to a poem, a poem inspired by memory arising from familial relationships rather than from a nameless collective.

Conversely, a collective vision predominates in *El cuarto de atrás*. In that novel one feels more intensely than in *Retahílas* the loneliness that lies at the root of being, a loneliness that nurtures the desire for dialogical communication. Chapter I introduces the protagonist – Carmen Martín Gaite – in the solitude of insomnia; Chapters II to VI consist of dialogues; Chapter VII, the final one, returns to the protagonist, her solitude hardly interrupted. As in *Retahílas*, everything happens in one night. Unlike that novel, however, the interlocutors of *El cuarto de atrás* do not occupy the same space (the world of fiction), but exist in two distinct realms: Carmen in her own lived reality, and her visitor in Carmen's fantasy realm, each also existing in an intermediate zone between the bizarre and the marvelous (these distinctions assume, of course, that this "real" person and this "fantastic" entity each remain fictionalized as they establish relations with one another within the "novel").

El cuarto de atrás does not claim that a woman finds, by luck, a relative who adores her and in whom she confides (as in *Retahílas*); rather, the novel imagines that a woman receives an unexpected visit from a stranger. In spite of the indecisiveness with which everything is presented and the diverse roles attributed to him (interviewer, conjurer, adviser or collaborator in writing, intruder, dialogical "demon," psychiatrist), the "man dressed in black" represents an inner spirit or the hidden sounding board of her own consciousness. From the virtual reality of the state described at the beginning of the text – being able to fall asleep or not – the protagonist proceeds to engage in actions that appear to take place during either sleep or insomnia. This baffling experience leaves in its wake, as a kind of testimony, two cups on a tray and a little golden box of pills, and comes to an end in a mix of bewilderment, a flickering of hope, and the loneliness to which she returns.

In *El cuarto de atrás* the nocturnal visit of the man dressed in black does aid Carmen Martín Gaite. He helps her write this novel of memory, composed with the explicit aim of avoiding "the books of memoirs" so abundant since Franco's death and so bereft of imagination. In conversation with the visitor, as well as through intervals of monologue, Carmen Martín Gaite discloses in a vibrant and engagingly haphazard way memories of the war and the post-war period (forty years of her own life), availing herself of richly varied documentary evidence: songs and popular melodies, political allusions, observation of the habits and ways of romance, religion, public and private life, fashion, movies and literature, sports, trips, feminine writings, and a woman's illusions and disappointments. Much of what encompassed the uniformity of the Franco Regime during its long mandate finds expression in this novel, a text animated by the agile word of one who now knows she has been heard and thus feels encouraged to keep on speaking/writing.

El cuarto de atrás, which explicitly invokes Todorov's study of fantastic literature, proposes two principal ideas: dialogical relationships of one to an "other" can create viable connections, even though interlocutors may not exist ("You do not need the other to exist; if he doesn't exist, you'll invent him, and if he exists you'll transform him," says the visitor); secondly, invention constitutes the redemption of reality ("that capacity of Invention that makes us aware of being saved from death," says the visited one). Denouement occurs when dialogue ceases and Carmen returns to sleep or insomnia, a disjuncture that casts doubt upon the meaning of the denouement itself. At the end, the little golden box suggests the solution (the remedy) for the kind of memory that breathes new life into a sealed-off past, upsetting the so-called order of that past. Memory causes the story's conclusion to be inconclusive (imagination will reestablish the links). Memory retrospectively converts the epilogue into a potential prologue to new dialogical adventures. The book's dedication to Lewis Carroll, "who still relieves us from so much common sense, welcoming us to his upside-down universe," finds confirmation in the following reflection of the protagonist: "There is a point at which the literature of mystery crosses the threshold of the marvelous, and from there, everything is possible and believable; we fly through the air as in a fiction by Lewis Carroll..."

In the 1970s the "novel of memories" inherits the legacy of the "testimonial novel" of the 1940s to mid-1960s. Just as the testimonial novel trained its sights on the Spain of its day, the novel of memory sought to recover the inner lives of people who, in that recent past, had experienced the closure of a protracted process. Once completed, that past called for a kind of recapitulation, a view from a new vantage point, a view long desired and so patiently awaited. This sense of completion does not mean that the testimonial novel lacks continuity or that the novel of memories represents an inert prolongation of the testimonial novel. On the contrary, the potential that characterizes both the testimonial novel and the novel of memories opens the way to further innovation in the art of the Spanish contemporary novel.

Guide to further reading

Barriero Pérez, Oscar, *La novela existencial española de postguerra* (Madrid: Gredos, 1987).

Díaz, Elías, *Pensamiento español en la era de Franco (1939–1975)*, 2nd edn. (Madrid: Tecnos, 1992).

Herzberger, David K., *Narrating the Past. Fiction and Historiography in Postwar Spain* (Durham, NC: Duke University Press, 1995).

Mainer, José-Carlos, *De postguerra (1951–1990)* (Barcelona: Crítica, 1994).

Morán, Fernando, *Novela y semidesarrollo* (Madrid: Taurus, 1971).

Pope, Randolph, *Novela de emergencia, España 1939–1954* (Madrid: SGEL, 1984).

Roberts, Gemma. *Historia de la novela social española de postguerra*. 2nd edn. (Madrid: Gredos, 1978).

Sobejano, Gonzalo. *Novela española de nuestro tiempo*, 2nd edn. (Madrid: Epesa, 1975).

Soldevila, Ignacio, *La novela desde 1936* (Madrid: Alhambra, 1980).

Spires, Robert, *La novela española de postguerra* (Madrid: Cupsa, 1978).

Tamames, Ramón, *La República. La era de Franco*, 7th edn. (Madrid: Alfaguara, 1979).

Vilanova, Antonio. *Novela y sociedad en la España de la postguerra* (Barcelona: Lumen, 1995).

12

BRADLEY EPPS

Questioning the text

Sometime during the 1960s, the mirror breaks for Spanish narrative. Such works as Luis Martín Santos's *Tiempo de silencio* (*Time of Silence*, 1962), Juan Goytisolo's *Señas de identidad* (*Marks of Identity*, 1966), Miguel Delibes's *Cinco horas con Mario* ('Five Hours with Mario', 1966), José María Guelbenzu's *El mercurio* ('Mercury', 1968), Camilo José Cela's *Vísperas, festividad y octava de San Camilo del año 1936 en Madrid* (*San Camilo in 1936: The Eve, Feast, and Octave of St. Camillus of the Year 1936 in Madrid*, 1969) and, most radically, Juan Benet's *Volverás a Región* (*Return to Region*, 1967) wreak havoc on the reality, idea, and ideal of realism. To different degrees, and from often considerably different ideological positions, each of these works twists, blurs, stretches, smashes, or scoffs at mimetic representation, communicability, and referentiality. Language, turned into its own object, becomes opaque, restive, polyvalent, and at times even purposeless. The trend is solidified in the early 1970s with the publication of Goytisolo's *Reivindicación del conde don Julián* (*Count Julián*, 1970), Benet's *Una meditación* (*A Meditation*, 1970) and *Un viaje de invierno* ('A Winter's Journey', 1972), Gonzalo Torrente Ballester's *La saga/fuga de J. B.* ('The Saga/Fugue of J. B.', 1972), Juan Marsé's *Si te dicen que caí* (*The Fallen*, 1973), Luis Goytisolo's *Recuento* ('Recount', 1973), and Juan Goytisolo's *Juan sin tierra* (*Juan the Landless*, 1975).

Accordingly, the death of the dictator Franciso Franco in 1975 occurs after a generalized break with social realism, an influential doctrine of representation that – from the perspective of both its critics and many of its former practitioners – tended to limit creativity and to place few intellectual demands on its reader. While the demand placed by post- or anti-realist writers on themselves and their readers recalls one of the more select postures of José Ortega y Gasset, it also arises out of disillusionment with the transformative potential of the realist project itself. Once at the vanguard of the critique of Francoism, social realism, for all its worthy intentions, had revealed itself to be politically ineffective and artistically stagnant; most critically, it had underestimated the *mediating* role of language. As Juan Goytisolo put it in *El furgón de cola* ('Caboose', 1967), "the negation of an intellectually oppressive system necessarily begins with the negation of its semantic structure."[1] The critique of the establishment entailed, then, the critique of established forms of language and literature. That said, Goytisolo's idea of oppression is hardly the same as Cela's, for example, and his assessment must be nuanced. For there are other, less overtly political motives for the mirror's breakage, from Benet's grand defense of style to Torrente's recovery of play to a general refashioning of the literary market. To understand the breakage and the textual questioning of which it is a part, one needs to look back to when the mirror seemed whole.

By the 1950s, social realism, a more somber, less confident mode of socialist realism, had come to dominate virtually any narrative fiction in Spain that was critical of the status quo. While socialist realism – adopted as doctrine by the first Soviet Writers' Congress in the fall of 1934 – tended to present a positive picture of the heroic triumph of the proletariat, social realism (and neorealism) presented a decidedly less triumphant picture of oppression and resistance under capitalism. "Picture" is a crucial term, but only if it is taken as signifying an ostensibly faithful, even fastidious, reproduction of reality – more akin to photography or film than to painting – in which figuration and description continue to hold sway. Whatever its ties to the Spanish realist tradition, ostensibly running from the picaresque novel through nineteenth-century Realism and Naturalism, social realism is most closely associated with Marxism. Social realism has been called a realism of critical intention because it intends to criticize and denounce Francoist Spain by means of a seemingly transparent representation of it. Against art for art's sake, social realism advances art for society's sake, an art that strives to eschew artistry and artificiality, or at least to keep them in check, and to let the facts speak for themselves.

Such a doctrine requires, however, vigilance on the part of the author, who must take pains to keep from intruding, let alone interpreting. Social realism, like mid-twentieth-century Marxism, has scientific pretensions, and objectivity is again the order of the day. Subjectivity, in contrast, is saddled with suspicion, associated as it is with the ideology of individualism. This is not to say that subjectivity is discredited in its entirety, for its collective variants, still profoundly inflected by humanism, are fundamental to the critique of alienation and the promotion of solidarity. Indeed, it is in the reaction to, and rejection of, social realism that subjectivity, including that of the author, is most seriously questioned. For the author in social realism is

[1] J. Goytisolo, *El furgón de cola* (Barcelona: Seix Barral, 1976), p. 32, n. 2.

not so much "dead" as self-effacing, a figure who eludes the mirror in order to turn it elsewhere – as if its self-reflective glare were too troubling, or too inconsequential, to bear.

Jesús López Pacheco's *Central eléctrica* ('Power Plant', 1958), Armando López Salinas's *La mina* ('The Mine', 1960), and Alfonso Grosso's *La zanja* ('The Trench', 1961) chart the course of social realism, with places of labor explicitly identified in the titles. Like the society they relate, these texts are not generally rich in form, and if they play with language, it is typically in its colloquial, "degraded," serialized mode. There is more than a touch of the ethno-linguist or even neo-*costumbrista* in, for instance, Juan Goytisolo's use of argot in *La resaca* ('Undertow' or 'Hangover', 1958). Here, and elsewhere, the attempt to give an accurate account of the proletariat, including the lumpen proletariat, must deal with the bourgeois drag of the author and, realistically speaking, of most readers. Like a number of texts by other writers, *La resaca*, well-intentioned though it may be, can give the impression of "slumming," a pilfering of the lower depths for the edification and motivation, if not entertainment, of the less adventurous. Of course, almost any literary endeavor must contend with such problems. If *La resaca* recalls Goytisolo's earlier *Juegos de manos* ('Sleights of Hand', 1954), a text centered on the dangerous little games of privileged youth, it is perhaps because denouncing the bourgeoisie and laying bare the plight of the proletariat are two sides of the same critical coin. Goytisolo was not alone. Antonio Ferres focused on the working class in *La piqueta* ('The Pickaxe', 1959) and Juan García Hortelano on the bourgeoisie in *Tormenta de verano* (*Summer Storm*, 1962); together they attested to the complementary bipolarity of social realism. The denunciation of the power of one class goes hand in hand with the denunciation of the disenfranchisement of another. And yet, denunciation and critical intention, indeed *any* intention, fly in the face of neutrality, transparency, and objectivity. Social realism is thus caught in a double bind that helps bring about its dissolution but that makes it, almost despite itself, compelling.

The political bent of these texts produced in an era of scarcity and censorship derives from, and contributes to, contemporary debates on the role of the intellectual, so important and prevalent after Antonio Gramsci and Jean-Paul Sartre. Sartrean existentialism, especially as it bears on *engagement* (the idea that writing should strive to engage and transform reality), has an impact on Spanish narrative that is not limited to readings of so-called *tremendista* literature such as Cela's *La familia de Pascual Duarte* (*The Family of Pascual Duarte*, 1942). Indeed, Sartrean thought, with its emphasis on individual responsibility, freedom, and anguish, continues to have an impact, albeit weakened, on social realism itself, where the role of the engaged intellectual translates into an apparently disengaged author – disengaged, that is, from an intrusive, even dictatorial, telling of the tale. The avatars of the author tend to oscillate between extremes of presence (or omnipresence) and absence. The fact that "omniabsence" is a lexical curiosity gives a measure of what is at stake. For if it is generally accepted that the author can be everywhere, perhaps especially in a realist text, it is not generally accepted that the author, even in an anonymous or collective work, can be nowhere, *absolutely* nowhere. After all, the absence of the author by no means destroys the author's power. In fact, the author's absence can be one of the slyest exercises of authority, a ruse by which an *illusion of freedom* is at once generated and gainsaid. Absent from one space, the author yet lurks in another, out of sight but not out of work. The attempt to undo authority was often, however, an attempt to do it anew, to recast it in a more equitable and objective manner, to embody it not in a single man but collectively, in the people.

In the 1960s and 1970s, the authority of the author is disparaged, though not always in the manner suggested by the French critic Roland Barthes in his highly influential essay "The Death of the Author," first published in 1968. In Spain and Latin America, the authority of authoritarian regimes was not as metaphorical or academic as in the Western democracies. Objectivism, as a problem of authorship, was similarly implicated; the French *nouveau roman* of Alain Robbe-Grillet and Michel Butor had little in common, despite certain attempts at reconciliation, with Spanish social realism. Indeed, the promotion of interest in Spanish social realism and neorealism outside of Spain – pursued, for instance, by Goytisolo at the prestigious Parisian publishing house of Gallimard – is likely an effect of significant *differences* in the objective reality of authority on either side of the Pyrenees. Needless to say, objective reality has its subjective investments, its share of dreams and desires. Mario Santana cites the desire on the part of Western leftist intellectuals "to find a new historical hero in every Third-World country in turmoil, a role for which Franco's 'exotic' Spain easily qualified."[2] Santana further notes that once Spain attained a degree of economic success in the 1960s and became more fully integrated into a Western capitalist order, the interest of leftist intellectuals shifted to Latin America, with Castro's Cuba in the forefront. The questioning of authority entails the maintenance of a relatively unquestioning celebration of whatever resists authority.

In the historical period under consideration, such questioning and celebration typically assume the form of a quest: for authenticity, identity, and a true

[2] M. Santana, *Foreigners in the Homeland: The Spanish American New Novel in Spain, 1962–1974* (Lewisburg: Bucknell University Press, 2000), p. 54.

appreciation of reality, for *familiarity* with the "other." The quest can have, however, some uncanny effects. Spanish society, presumably represented by the social realists in its most down-to-earth form, at times appears almost too stilted and strange to be believed. Years later, Juan Goytisolo, in the significantly titled *La saga de los Marx* (*The Marx Family Saga*, 1993), struggles still with the specter of social realism and satirizes the editorial demand for "a novel as real as life itself" (p. 83). Goytisolo rather humorously holds Karl Marx and his followers "responsible" for the propagation of the realism that he judges to be so restrictive and unrealistic. What Goytisolo relates in the 1990s is not just his disenchanted recollection of social realism but also the persistence of its codes, if not its critical intention, in an age of multinational capitalism. Today, as Goytisolo suggests, the quest for transparency and accessibility sustains works that are quite at home in the established order. Others, including Torrente Ballester, Marsé, and Benet, also criticize the project of social realism by signaling its unreality, if not its absurdity. What they underscore is that the social realist texts, for all their documentary pretensions, are *fictional*, part of literature – even though Benet would classify them as part of sociology. Literary language, which the social realists understood and typically strove to reject as artificial, can become even more artificial the more artificiality is negated. In short, the quest for authenticity may take some very inauthentic turns.

The questioning of subjectivity, authority, and authorship that flecks social realism is accompanied by a questioning – or suspicion – of style, form, and literary language. The poverty of post-war Spain conditions the poverty, or economy, of verbal expression. Even Rafael Sánchez Ferlosio's *El Jarama* (*The One Day of the Week*, 1956), the one text affiliated with the social realist movement that has entered the canon, is laconic in its very garrulousness: in page after page of anodyne conversation, nothing "really" happens until one of the characters drowns. The accidental death is jolting because it issues from, and turns back to, a stream of petty, daily intercourse. Sánchez Ferlosio pens a powerful lesson in history and fiction. For the event that so marks *El Jarama* that it makes the page number of the first edition – 272 – memorable for some is bound to become as obscure as the bloody events of the Spanish Civil War that mark the river Jarama, also memorable for some. After all, the anodyne conversations take place by a river once, and not that long ago, bloodied by battle. The relation between the book and the world, textuality and topography, is fraught with oblivion. If a battle can be forgotten, so can a drowning, and one of the text's most devastating accomplishments is that it depicts reality as flowing beyond any firm and final recollection. One cannot go to the same river twice, and the Heraclitean message, in a country where tradition has been all but monumentalized, can be deeply upsetting.

Then again, it can also be upsetting for any project that would recover, let alone monumentalize, the memory or counter-memory of the oppressed. What Sánchez Ferlosio signals is thus the spuriousness of simple reflections, the ways the seemingly faithful rendering of everyday life can turn on itself and become unfaithful. Without the drowning, the story would sink into the anonymity of daily life. But with the drowning, literariness is retained, or rescued. Put bluntly, literature is purchased at the price of an imaginary sacrifice.

The preceding formulation is in line with what Darío Villanueva has called "the poetic and transcendent enrichment of daily reality."[3] For Villanueva, the dialogic objectivism of *El Jarama* actually preserves an authorial power that "is not bereft of those prerogatives of nineteenth-century omniscience, with the exception of access to the characters' thoughts, that may contribute to the expressive and poetic enrichment of the novel" (*Estructura y tiempo reducido*, p. 194). The insistence on the poetry of prose contributes decisively to the canonization of *El Jarama* and to the general eclipse of social realism and neorealism from literary studies. For if *El Jarama* is canonical, it is in large measure because it is *not* as transparent, straightforward, or prosaic as it may seem. Its status as a realist text is accordingly disturbed, maybe even set at naught, by the notion that prose, if it is to merit serious attention or praise, must be shot through with symbols and second meanings, and slip into poetry.

Such a bias, deeply entrenched in literary studies, "salvages" *El Jarama* from oblivion and brings it into contact with more openly "creative" texts that follow (and precede) it. Other texts, by Ferres, López Pacheco, Grosso, and López Salinas, do not fare so well. This may be because, as Gonzalo Navajas remarks, they "reflect [not just] the unyielding pressure of an external repressive force, but also a process of self-induced internal repression, whereby the free creativity of the author is arrested and subordinated to his political function."[4] Navajas's assessment is in line with that of such authors as Juan Goytisolo (from *Señas de identidad* on) and Benet, for whom "free creativity" is, in a sense, next to godliness. The coincidences are telling: despite all the twists and turns of the canon, Sánchez Ferlosio is brought into line with the "ambiguous" Goytisolo, the "playful" Torrente Ballester, the "enigmatic" Benet, and, for that matter, the "imaginative" Sánchez Ferlosio of *Industrias y andanzas de Alfanhuí* (*The Adventures of the*

[3] D. Villanueva, *Estructura y tiempo reducido en la novela* (Valencia: Bello, 1977), p. 198.

[4] G. Navajas, "The Derealization of the Text in Salinas's *La mina*," *South Central Review* 4.1 (1987), p. 123.

Ingenious Alfanhuí, 1951). It is clear that clarity is not generally valued, and that something else and extra is required, something that will keep readers busy, if not entertained. Mirroring Spanish society in the ever-receding wake of the Civil War, Sánchez Ferlosio shows how partial and inadequate the mirror is – and how poetic, and critically appealing, partiality and inadequacy can be. If there were no trouble with the mirror, there might be very little really to see.

As an image of realist representation, the mirror had been in trouble for some time, maybe ever since Stendhal, in *Le rouge et le noir* (Part II, Chapter 19), had it parade down a road, reflecting both blue sky and mud. In Spain, Valle-Inclán had deployed the mirror to grotesque effect in *Luces de Bohemia* (*Bohemian Lights*, 1920). The concave mirror that he locates in "el callejón del Gato" ('Cat's Alley') in Madrid returns a reflection whose adequacy is measured in terms of inadequacy. That is to say, a grotesque, distorted reality is reflected in a grotesque, distorted mirror. A principle of mimesis is still operative, but it disturbs rather than reassures. In a not-unrelated vein, Ortega y Gasset, in *La deshumanización del arte* ('The Dehumanization of Art', 1925), had questioned not just the reflective pretensions of the mirror but the transparent pretensions of the window as well. For Ortega, the tained glass of a mirror is as deceptive as the tainless glass of a window: both seduce the seer into turning a blind eye to the materiality of the glass itself. Ortega, in good avant-garde fashion, would turn our sights to the glass as glass, not to the human being reflected in the mirror or to the garden that lies beyond the window. In Ortega, however, the glass conserves a smooth integrity that is increasingly put to the test as the avant-garde lurches to an end. Marcel Duchamp's *Broken Glass* may be a felicitous accident, but in the realm of letters, the breakage of the (metaphorical) mirror appears a bit more deliberate. Mercè Rodoreda brings to the foreground the broken mirror in her epic of the rise and fall of a bourgeois family in *Mirall trencat* ('Broken Mirror', 1974). The title is appropriate because the modern doctrine of realist reflection has been wedded to the bourgeoisie. The point is important, for the turn away from the mirror, if not its distortion and breakage, is generally perceived as a turn away from bourgeois ideology.

Rodoreda's novel, published at the end of Francoism, closes with a rat's eye view of an empty, littered, destitute place of privilege and power: the house of an upper bourgeois family. The critique of the bourgeoisie in *Mirall trencat* is more fantastic and ambiguous than in Goytisolo's *La isla* ('The Island') or Marsé's *Últimas tardes con Teresa* ('Last Evenings with Teresa', 1966). A decade can make a difference, and a better indicator of the crisis of the mirror is Martín Santos's *Tiempo de silencio*, the text that initiates the break with social realism – its forms, if not its themes. The backwardness of scientific research; the provinciality of Madrid; the endurance of fanaticism, superstition, and illiteracy; the vacuity of thought (represented in a scathing parody of Ortega); police control, militarism, poverty, injustice, sordidness, resignation, frivolity, and alienation: the perceived reality of Spain is basically the same as in social realism. But the form in which it is rendered could scarcely be more different. Martín Santos employs virtually all of the tricks of classical rhetoric and modernist experimentation (stream of consciousness, defamiliarization, and demythification), of existential psychoanalysis and literary history, to represent reality as bound up in representation. The representational project, emphasizing form, has, however, its thematic anchor. The protagonist's attempt to prove that a certain kind of cancer is not hereditary but viral, and hence that it is susceptible to treatment and eradication, dovetails the novel's attempt to call into question literature as nothing but a reflection of reality. Without being beyond essentialism, particularly in its presentation of gender and race, *Tiempo de silencio* advances a sort of constructivist ethic; that is to say, it presents reality as made, or constructed, and not just as given. It is a quasi-subjectivist, formally experimental rendition of the "problem of Spain" that is also a heterogeneous collocation of elements from various genres, periods, languages, disciplines, and national traditions.

If in the 1960s the mirror breaks, it is also then, as Mario Santana remarks, "that the national conception of Spanish literature collapsed."[5] The "collapse" occurs under the combined pressure of "a reemergent pluricultural conception of the Spanish state" articulated primarily in Galicia, Euskadi, and Catalunya, and the extraordinary success of the aptly designated Latin American Boom (*Foreigners in the Homeland*, p. 18). While the terms "collapse" and indeed "breakage" may be too strong, they nonetheless point to a penchant for strong signifiers associated with modernism. The shock of the new, the rupture with the past, the cult of originality: so many modernist truisms are revamped in what can only with some temerity be called post-modernism. The term of preference was, of course, "magical realism," which, linked most notably to Gabriel García Márquez, proved eminently more enjoyable, entertaining, and profitable than social realism. Striking as the difference may be, the persistence of *something* realist is striking too. For what differs in the transatlantic passage is an adjective, "social" as opposed to "magical." From social realism to magical realism there is a shift of accent and form, though the critical intention and the commitment to society remain largely intact. There is also a shift from one "natural"

[5] Santana, *Foreigners in the Homeland*, p. 17.

reality to another. Much ink has been spilt over the exuberance of the Latin American landscape, the richness of its flora and fauna, its rhythms and music, the vibrant intensity of its people. Stereotypes abound here as they do about Iberia (austere and obscurantist), and many a person has fallen prey to the dubious pleasure of divisive evaluations. One thing is certain, however: *Tiempo de silencio* appears at practically the same time as Mario Vargas Llosa's *La ciudad y los perros* (*Time of the Hero*, 1963), and the novel in Spain is, in general, altered by both.

Along with something realist, there also persists in the Boom a quest for authenticity, truth, and justice, albeit with a more acute sense of irony and paradox. Rather predictably, the quest has heroic dimensions. The Boom was indeed characterized by heroic gestures, often as not manly or, to give a nod to Che Guevara, "newly" manly. Like so many artistic movements, the Boom was dominated by men, with hardly a woman penetrating the daunting upper echelons of experimentalism – or the publishing houses. Whether in Barcelona, Mexico City, Buenos Aires, or Madrid, the old boys' network was still more amenable to new boys than to women. García Márquez, Vargas Llosa, Julio Cortázar, Carlos Fuentes, Guillermo Cabrera Infante, and others set the stage for a reevaluation of literature in Spanish that generated a profound shift away from the Iberian Peninsula to Latin America.

The shift, however, from a male-dominated notion of culture to one more sexually equitable has been longer in coming. The few Spanish women who did manage to figure in critical overviews and editorial promotions – Carmen Laforet, Ana María Matute, Carmen Martín Gaite – were generally relegated to *particular* positions that figure only fitfully, if at all, in the male-dominated cultural debates of the day. For the questioning of the text in Spain is carried out most resoundingly by such men as Juan Goytisolo, Torrente Ballester, and Benet. However *particular* these writers are, each has been at the center of some controversy considered (but again, by whom?) to be of general cultural importance. Controversy may well be the "handmaid" of experimentation, the veritable proof of derring-do.

Goytisolo, Torrente, and Benet are caught in the sonic ripples of the Boom, though only Goytisolo throws himself into it with calculated abandon, managing to garner a chapter in Carlos Fuentes's *La nueva novela hispanoamericana* (1969). Torrente remains more guarded, while Benet waxes cantankerous. All three must contend with the notion that literary experimentation, like scientific research, is a foreign import (though they do not question whether or not it is a masculine prerogative): something from France, Colombia, Germany, Argentina, Mexico, or the United States. Goytisolo actually foments this notion, effecting in *Reivindicación del conde Julián* a deconstructive assault on Spain that pretends to reveal that what is authentically Spanish is nothing much at all. Goytisolo's contacts with Fuentes, Severo Sarduy, and other Latin Americans, even more than his contacts with Jean Genet and Simone de Beauvoir, secure him a relevance that might be qualified as enviable.

Torrente, older, more discreet, and haunted by youthful flirtations with fascism – most distinctly in *Javier Mariño* (1943), a work nonetheless quickly prohibited by Franco's censors – rockets to literary attention with *La saga/fuga de J.B.* after years of unobtrusive production. Though immersed in Galician and Spanish cultural history, *La saga/fuga* brings to mind the fabulative frenzy of García Márquez's *Cien años de soledad* (*One Hundred Years of Solitude*, 1967) and the inventive humor of Cabrera Infante's *Tres tristes tigres* (*Three Trapped Tigers*, 1967). Despite Torrente's repeated attempts to temper such comparisons, some sort of transatlantic relay is undeniable, though comparisons with fellow Galician Álvaro Cunqueiro also obtain. Benet, the cultivator of perhaps the most opaque literature in Spanish, is less marked by the Latin American Boom and derides its very existence. For Benet, the Boom is a commercial invention or, at most, a chance agglomeration of writers of widely dissimilar quality.[6] Still, there is little doubt that Benet benefits – however "vulgar" such an assertion might seem to him – from the questioning of realism that the Boom entails.

It would be foolhardy, however, to limit the web of contacts to the contemporary Spanish-speaking world or to reduce, as Benet fears, the literary to the socio-economic. The machinations of Carlos Barral, the influential editor involved in the promotion of both social realism and the Boom, do not account for the writing of the texts, which is necessarily overdetermined. Faulkner, Pessoa, Genet, Kafka, Unamuno, Cervantes, San Juan de la Cruz, the Bible, the Koran, and a lengthy if select "et cetera" punctuate the literary exercises of Benet, Goytisolo, and Torrente. That said, it would be equally foolhardy to collapse any one of these Spaniards into the other. All three writers, prolific and polemical, grappled with some mode of realism, Benet somewhat cavalierly from the outside (Benet's play *Max* [1953] is his most conventional work), Torrente and Goytisolo more tortuously from the inside. All three defended, or came to defend, some variant of literary autonomy, away from, beyond, or beside the realist mirror. Each one, however, writes in an unmistakably different manner; each one privileges a different idea of what writing is and should be.

For Benet a privileged term is style; for Torrente it is play, and for Goytisolo it is freedom. Three of their critical works – Benet's *La inspiración y el estilo* ('On Inspiration and Style', 1965), Torrente's *El Quijote como juego*

[6] J. Benet, *Cartografía personal* (Valladolid: Cuatro Ediciones, 1997), p. 48.

('*Don Quijote* as a Game', 1975), and Goytisolo's *Libertad, libertad, libertad* ('Freedom Freedom, Freedom', 1978) – make explicit what runs throughout much of their fiction. Style, play, and freedom are rather seriously bound to the perceived and professed lack of style of social realism, and this past seems to haunt these writers – haunts, but does not determine them. For while we might playfully conjecture that the social realists are the unwelcome ghostwriters of the highly stylized *Volverás a Región* or the seemingly loose and errant *Juan sin tierra*, we would not go so far as to make a case for a linear, genetic, teleological vision of literary history. Goytisolo, however, does go so far as to scorn some of his earlier texts and to parody almost all of them in his later texts. Even as he questions conventional chronologies, he writes, as in *En los reinos de taifa* (*Realms of Strife*, 1986), of his maturation and of "the conquest of a literary expression of [his] own, [his] subjective authenticity."[7] Benet, more consistently than Goytisolo, scorns an array of texts by *others*, from all of Galdós, Pereda, and Fuentes to most, if not all, of Nabokov, Joyce, Borges, and Martín Santos, his former friend. He does not, in general, refer to seeking or attaining authenticity, though he does make much of the impact that his "discovery" of Faulkner had on him and he does hold on to the value of rewriting. Torrente, for his part, is less scornful than mischievous, and parodies not just social realism but also the reaction against it, the metafictional experimentalism that he himself so brilliantly cultivates.

Benet and Goytisolo are men of strong opinions, perhaps especially when they touch on ambiguity, uncertainty, mystery, and other related terms that function almost fetishistically in their repertoire. They judge, extol, disqualify, and execrate with unswerving confidence, Benet more than Goytisolo, both more than Torrente. Comparisons can be odious, but anyone who has read the essays, interviews, and editorials of Benet and Goytisolo cannot but be struck by the passion of their convictions, the odiousness of *their* comparisons. But here, too, is a difference. Goytisolo, keeping his faith in the discourse of (personal) authenticity, does not abandon a notion of engagement and testimony, though it does become convoluted and introspective. Benet, in contrast, is adamant about never having had any inclination to "mix" or "confuse" literature and politics in the first place. For Benet, style is everything, and he manifests an almost slavish understanding of it, an understanding that fuels his desire to master it. Thus his trajectory is smoother than it might at first appear: an engineer by profession, he takes years to write his first works, years to find a publisher, and years to find a public, and never more than a small and select public at that. Benet puts up the money

[7] J. Goytisolo, *En los reinos de taifa* (Barcelona: Seix Barral, 1986), p. 153.

to publish 'Nunca llegarás a nada' ('You'll Never Get Anywhere', 1961), and enjoys nothing remotely like the contacts that Goytisolo enjoyed from a fairly young age. Benet's trajectory is smooth, however, because he does not seem to struggle with the contradictions between social commitment and aesthetic autonomy that make Goytisolo's later work so impressive; nor does he struggle with the specter of past political leanings that, however pale, makes Torrente's later comic work almost poignant. Benet does struggle with those who would take literature as a manifestation of politics, although again the struggle merely steels his resolve. For Benet, literature is, quite simply, only literature: and that is what makes it so difficult, so complex, so significant.

Accordingly, Benet debunks the mimetic imperative to advocate a more fractured, speculative approach. Specular representation had a tendency, from its inception, to be speculative, to give way to a theorization in which, as the dictionary puts it, "evidence is too slight for certainty to be reached." Of all the writers here considered, it is Benet who most unflinchingly mines the uncertainty that inhabits realist certainty, taking up many of the most trusted tools of realism (description of the natural environment, attention to detail, concern for time) and rendering them derelict. Examples abound. In *Volverás a Región*: "Why bother entering into details? Of what importance are people, names, places, dates, the type of error (or lack)?"[8] In *Un viaje de invierno*: "the enigma of destiny is produced back there, in forgetfulness, and [...] history is only the reproduction of the memory that dissolves it."[9] In *En la penumbra* ('In the Shadows', 1989): "silence is without a doubt what admits of most interpretations."[10] So many reflections on history, storytelling, and meaning constitute a sustained and supple *mise en cause* of the realist project.

Volverás a Región is the first text by Benet to merit serious attention. It opens with an unknown traveler's departure from Región – a place that, as critics have noted, could well be Spain – by way of an "antiguo camino real," an old royal, but also *real*, road. The traveler takes this road because the modern one is not passable. The traveler, rich in ancient symbolism, must traverse a desert that seems interminable and soon is lost. From the outset, *Volverás a Región* courts an allegorical reading that turns on its reader, likely lost as well in the poetic morass of Benetian prose. Loss, abandonment, inadequacy, deferral, decadence, and ruin are the signposts of a literary exercise where pleasure is meted out in frustration and illumination in obscurity. Sweet and

[8] J. Benet, *Volverás a Región* (Barcelona: Destino, 1981), p. 164.
[9] J. Benet, *Un viaje de invierno* (Madrid: Cátedra, 1980), p. 167.
[10] J. Benet, *En la penumbra* (Madrid: Alfaguara, 1989), p. 19.

useful instruction, *utile et dulce*, is all but wasted in Benet, and narration, as a mode of knowledge, let alone entertainment, is all but devastated. Which is perhaps a tortuous way of saying that they are saved, for Benet's work indicates that sweet instruction lies, if at all, in the heart of bitterness and pain, and that narrative knowledge lurks in the shadows, always out of our reach.

High-sounding stuff, but Benet is nothing if not high-sounding. He deplores what he calls the "entry into the tavern," the lowering of standards by which literature is rendered small and accessible.[11] Little wonder that he would have no truck with social, neo-, dialectical, or any other form of realism. At the same time, he also would have nothing to do with more sprightly modes of anti-realism along the lines of Julio Cortázar's *Rayuela* (*Hopscotch*, 1963) or Cabrera Infante's *Tres tristes tigres*. Railing against the vogue of the open book, the birth of the reader, and the pleasure of the text, Benet declares that "only an absolutely closed work can produce the maximum power of suggestion."[12] Closure, he asserts, is not dogmatism, but signifies instead the difficulty of knowledge, far removed from the seductive play and performativity that are, he intimates, the consolation of idiots. It is along these lines that Benet cultivates a difficult, demanding, solemn mode of writing. Even *El aire de un crimen* ('A Crime in the Air', 1980), a novel that Benet writes on the dare that he cannot write anything that is not demanding, is far from transparent. Some critics have described Benet's work as aristocratic, but Darío Villanueva describes it more convincingly as ascetic,[13] a description that Benet claimed, rather coyly, not to understand. Yet *Volverás* and, even more, *Una meditación* do suggest that there is something sacred in the cult of literature precisely because it no longer commands the respect it once did.

Secularization and socialization go hand in hand for Benet, and he would prefer to have nothing to do with either; however, this is not to say that he is a proponent of religious faith – far from it. For him, the ruin of religion, philosophy, and art is their finest token, and he is fond of quoting that "only ruin can save us from greater ruin."[14] Benet's disdain for communication, which he communicates in numerous interviews and essays and enacts in his fictional works, is intricately tied to his interest in the Spanish Civil War. Benet revisits the war in order not to clarify it but to delve its troubling

[11] Benet, *La inspiración*, p. 78.

[12] J. Benet, "Intervención de Juan Benet," in *Novela española actual*, ed. Andrés Amorós (Madrid: Cátedra/Fundación Juan March, 1977), p. 177.

[13] D. Villanueva, "Intervención de Darío Villanueva," in *Novela española actual*, p. 171.

[14] Benet, *Cartografía*, p. 61.

depths. Región itself is a bellicose scenario, one that does not admit of easy understanding. Against partisan presentations from both left and right, Benet offers an account in which right and wrong are much less clear-cut. What matters for Benet is not so much who did what to whom, where, and why, as that it all be rendered grandiloquently: truth lies in style, not in what others would take to be the verifiable presentation of facts. In Benet's fictionalized accounts of history, discourse reigns stylishly supreme.

Juan Goytisolo also abandons the realist road and finds himself in a world that could also be Spain, were Spain "true" to its heterogeneous past and hence "other" than it officially is. Influenced by such thinkers as Américo Castro, who challenged a purist conception of national history, Goytisolo embarks on a literary project that tends to eschew discrete boundaries, whether between nations, people, or cultural endeavors such as literature and politics. If Región is a realm unto itself that recalls not just the "reality" of Spain but also the fiction of Faulkner's Yoknapatawpha County, Goytisolo's is a realm that shifts from text to text, even within a given text. His scenarios are the real world – Paris, Pittsburgh, Barcelona, Tangiers, Marrakesh, Sarajevo, Cappadocia, and Cuba – rocked by desire, fantasy, and the imagination. *Señas de identidad* announces Goytisolo's break with the social realism that he had so fervently practiced. An autobiographically inflected story of a young intellectual's disenchanting coming of age, *Señas* presents a sobering picture of anti-fascist resistance (in exile) and ends with a view of Francoist Spain's incorporation into Europe through tourism. Goytisolo highlights subjective consciousness in a manner that conveys the gaps wrought by exile and time (generational difference) but that also conveys the fragility of consciousness, its imbrication in history, myth, and language itself. Whereas Benet's texts are distinguished by lengthy and involuted sentences, few if any paragraph breaks, a dearth of dialogue (the dialogues in *Volverás* function almost monologically), recondite vocabulary, and a profusion of parentheses, Goytisolo's later texts can be almost staccato in form. True, they also deploy a recondite vocabulary and parentheses, but Goytisolo's texts rely on fragmentation – with its cuts, breaks, and empty spaces – in a graphic fashion; the very *materiality* of the writing is distinct from Benet's.

It is with the publication of *Reivindicación del conde don Julián*, however, that Goytisolo breaks the mirror of representation or turns it intolerably inward. For Fuentes, *Conde Julián* is "the most monumental questioning of Spain, its history and culture, that has ever been written";[15] for Pere

[15] C. Fuentes, *La nueva novela hispanoamericana* (Mexico: Joaquín Mortiz, 1969), p. 83.

Gimferrer, it is "the most radically subversive masterpiece" of Spanish.[16] Such superlatives abound. Written in the wake of May 1968 and while Franco was still quite alive, *Conde Julián* is a virulent diatribe against the faded grandeur of Spain and an angry testimony to its resistance to change. A gruelingly passionate book, it draws on the history, myth, and legend of the Moorish invasion of Spain and champions the cause of the "traitor," Julián, who purportedly allowed the Moors entry into the Peninsula. Goytisolo grafts this national morality play, full of sex, violence, and intrigue, onto a contemporary story of anguished identity. The narrator-protagonist is alienated, sick, and given to drug-induced hallucinations, but he can also be identified – and that is perhaps the problem – as a Spaniard who hates being a Spaniard and who dreams of being otherwise. The dream leads to the imaginary destruction of "sacred Spain" and, by implication, of the recalcitrant narrator-protagonist himself. Identity and its marks are critical to Goytisolo's work, functioning as sources of play but more consistently of pain. In *Conde Julián*, Goytisolo figures the destruction of national identity as a sado-masochistic process that implicates the *linguistic* subject so thoroughly that no escape seems *completely* possible.

In *Juan sin tierra*, Goytisolo takes this insight to the limit, closing the text with the parodic disarticulation of Spanish and defiant articulation of Arabic. When *Juan sin tierra* first appeared, a number of critics read the last pages as a declaration of independence from the Spanish language, as if Goytisolo were to write henceforth only in Arabic. That was not the case, but both before and after Franco, the question of identity, linguistic and otherwise, remains tied to Goytisolo's major concern, freedom. Goytisolo's defense of literary freedom is always bound to his defense of a freedom beyond literature, a freedom not merely *from* but *of* particular identities. The shift in Goytisolo's corpus from a social-realist to an experimentalist aesthetic must be qualified. Goytisolo's language becomes more reticular and opaque; his frame of reference more global; his self-referential tricks more tenacious, but what does not shift is his commitment to the disenfranchised, marginalized, poor, and oppressed. His works, even at their most self-indulgent, relate an avid concern for justice, equality, peace, and freedom. In this, he could not be more different from Benet, who provocatively proclaimed that he was committed to himself.[17] Goytisolo's formal innovations, including his idiosyncratic use of punctuation (the colon), do not spell the disappearance of a testimonial or documentary ethic. However much Goytisolo celebrates ambiguity, it remains clear where his sympathies lie; however much he extols

[16] P. Gimferrer, "El nuevo Juan Goytisolo," *Revista de Occidente* 137 (1974), p. 22.

[17] Benet, *Cartografía*, p. 20.

aesthetic autonomy, it remains evident that his texts refer to a highly fraught political reality. And if he privileges a state of consciousness, it is a state under siege. His work, accordingly, is open to contradictions that, depending on one's perspective, can be riveting or tiring. Whatever the case, it nourishes and is nourished by a tension between art and society that Benet would resolve in favor of the former.

As important as Goytisolo's and Benet's endeavors are, the questioning of the text need not entail the abandonment of more established notions of storytelling. García Márquez and Günter Grass knew as much, and so did Torrente Ballester. The narrator of Goytisolo's *Makbara* (1980), inspired by *El libro de buen amor* (*The Book of Good Love*) and *The Arabian Nights*, may wax rapturous about storytelling, but it is a rapture that tends to remain at a remove. We are told that the storyteller is a magician and that narrative, particularly oral, is a delight, or even that it is "the necessary antidote for a miserable, barefoot existence, empty bellies, a reality that is cruelly unjust."[18] Torrente, in contrast, tells us about storytelling while telling us a story. True, in *La saga/fuga de J. B.* the story is extraordinarily intricate, abounding with characters that intersect, overlap, and may or may not be one and the same. Torrente's narrative games, full of comic verve, engage the oral traditions of Galicia, the Celtic cult of King Arthur, theology, detective stories, political history, Golden Age drama, high modernism, literary theory, and so on, in a swirling paean to the creative imagination. Goytisolo also casts a wide cultural net, drawing from literature high and low, and there is no doubt that his work, as well as Benet's, is richly imaginative. The difference is that Torrente's imagination is more unabashedly entertaining, not darkly comic or Kafkaesque. Castoforte del Baralla, the scenario of *La saga/fuga*, has little of the turgid darkness of *Región*, even though it is threatened with non-existence and figures on no official map. The title of Torrente's *opus* is well chosen, for it designates the flight – in an almost musical sense – of the great genealogical sagas of narrative (back) into the metamorphoses and adventures of yore. Lighthearted as this may be, the text touches on such weighty issues as censorship, governmental centralization, civil strife, rebellion, the manipulation of history, and the frailty of truth. Like his admired Cervantes, Torrente combines incisive cultural criticism with an appreciation of the insubstantiality of literature.

It is a lesson that Torrente learned after years of writing. His early works, including *Javier Mariño* and the trilogy *Los gozos y las sombras* ('Pleasures and Shadows', 1957–62), while certainly not assimilable to social realism, adhere to most of the tenets of mimetic narration, from chronological

[18] J. Goytisolo, *Makbara* (Barcelona: Seix Barral, 1980), p. 220.

development and well-rounded characters to attention to social history and reliance on dialogue. The result, for all its merits, is ponderous, far from the boisterous metafictional fantasies that, more or less from *Don Juan* (1963) on, would become Torrente's trademark. But there is no absolute break here either; *Don Juan* itself is born out of what the author describes as "a surfeit of realism" (p. 9). To say that *La saga/fuga* appears without warning or that it depends on *Cien años de soledad* is thus untenable. The self-referential ploys and abyssal moves of Torrente's later novels are evident even in *El señor llega* ('The Master Arrives'), the first installment of the aforementioned trilogy, where the title of the text that we read is the title of a text that one of the characters struggles to bring to light.

Torrente's metafictional bent has long been recognized, especially in the 1970s when metafiction was all the rage. Metafiction supposes not just an exteriority (a distancing from fiction) but also an interiority (an implication in fiction) and entails a constellation of concepts such as self-referentiality, self-consciousness, and self-reflexivity. It is typically avoided in realist fiction, because (or despite the fact that) one of its effects is to blur the boundaries between fiction and reality. The *Quijote* remains the model of all metafiction, and it comes as no surprise that Torrente takes Cervantes's masterpiece as an object of scholarly inquiry *and* imaginative recreation. Torrente is an insightful critic, and his painstaking analysis of parody as a comic imitation of a supposedly serious model in *El Quijote como juego* takes some delightful twists and turns. For one, it implicates social realism, an attempt at serious imitation, not of some fictional model but of a less than model world. For another, it implicates a good deal of so-called anti-realism, serious in its pretensions to ensure grandeur, attain authenticity, and preserve the mysterious truth of lying. For yet another, it implicates the criticism of realism and anti-realism, the generalized perception that the European novel was all but dead and that the only thing the questioning of the text had left unquestioned was the power of critique itself. It implicates or, better yet, *parodies* all of these modes of writing.

In *La saga/fuga*, *Fragmentos de Apocalipsis* ('Fragments of an Apocalypse', 1977), *La isla de los jacintos cortados* ('The Isle of Cut Hyacinths', 1980), and other novels, Torrente writes about writers who struggle to make sense of history, literature, the world, and themselves. Goytisolo does something similar, and many of his characters, as in *Las virtudes del pájaro solitario* ('The Virtues of a Solitary Bird', 1988) and *Las semanas del jardín: Un círculo de lectores* (*The Garden of Secrets*, 1997), are critics, students, translators, interpreters, and other subjects who wrestle with language and meaning. Both pay homage in various moments to Scherezade and Ariadne, and through them to the variations, labyrinthine constructions, and seductive poses of narration. If Goytisolo's characters are sketchier than Torrente's, it may be because his growing interest in Sufi mysticism, evident at least since *Paisajes después de la batalla* ('Landscapes After the Battle', 1982), has bestowed his suspicion of the existence of personality with an aura. After all, Sufi mysticism, which values illumination through darkness and ascent through debasement, seeks the devastation of personality (associated with individualism, selfishness, greed, jealousy, and so on). Torrente, less given to whirling dervishes and oriental gnosticism, also flirts with the nothingness of being, the masks of personality, but more in the line of Unamuno, the existentialists, and certain Catholic saints. And yet there is something rather than nothing.

Different as they are, Torrente and Goytisolo recognize that the transformative potential of the word is central to literature and that if it does not quite translate into the transformation of the world, that does not mean that the world is in no way implicated. The recognition that the world resists transformation or that rhetorical transformation is not *real*, or that the reality of rhetorical transformation is never the only reality, that there is a gap, a difference, may be the most worldly thing that these wordy endeavors accomplish. And it may be the most politically critical one, too. Even Benet, who underscores the gap between word and world, art and politics, might be said to do so out of respect for both. Literature does not mirror reality, or reality literature, without a gap. The mirror breaks, but it is quickly put back together, or its breakage is overstated, or it profits from the breakage and dazzles in all directions. Style, freedom, and play: the writers who question the text take the mirror as less than reliable, but take it, nonetheless, even if to break it. And so the mirror and its breakage become, if only for a period, a stylized and yet somewhat freewheeling game of mirrors. Then again, "perhaps what I have just said is too clear and thus rationalized and far from the truth": the quotation is from Torrente,[19] but it might have been from Benet or Goytisolo. At any rate, it has a way of snaking back and implicating the critic and literary historian, too.

Guide to further reading

Compitello, Malcolm Alan, *Ordering the Evidence: "Volverás a Región" and Civil War Fiction* (Barcelona: Puvill Libros, 1983).

Epps, Brad, *Significant Violence: Oppression and Resistance in the Narratives of Juan Goytisolo, 1970–1990* (Oxford University Press, 1996).

Manteiga Roberto C., David K. Herzberger, and Malcolm Alan Compitello (eds.), *Critical Approaches to the Writings of Juan Benet* (Hanover, NH: University Press of New England, 1984).

19 G. Torrente Ballester, *La saga fuga de J. B.* (Madrid: Alianza, 1998), p. 110.

Margenot, John B. III (ed.), *Juan Benet: A Critical Reappraisal of His Fiction* (West Cornwall, CT: Locust Hill Press, 1997).
Pérez, Janet and Stephen Miller (eds.), *Critical Studies on Gonzalo Torrente Ballester* (Boulder, CO: Society of Spanish and Spanish-American Studies, 1989).
Pope, Randolph D., *Understanding Juan Goytisolo* (Columbia: University of South Carolina Press, 1995).

13

AKIKO TSUCHIYA

Women and fiction in post-Franco Spain

When the Franco dictatorship ended in 1975, the time was ripe for the revitalization of women's literature in Spain. Spain's transition to democracy led to a so-called boom in women's narrative, with the emergence of a new group of women writers who began to publish at that time: among them are Rosa Montero, Lourdes Ortiz, Soledad Puértolas, Marina Mayoral, Cristina Fernández Cubas, Carme Riera, and Esther Tusquets. Still others such as Carmen Martín Gaite, Ana María Moix, and Montserrat Roig, who had already published during Francoism, started to write more self-consciously experimental works in the late 1970s, thus departing from the predominantly neorealist aesthetic of their own and other women's works in the earlier decades of the post-war period. Without attributing homogeneous characteristics to this group of women based on strictly chronological or historical criteria, it would not be inaccurate to claim that the literary techniques and preoccupations of post-Franco women writers generally constitute a break from the previous generation of writers.

A brief overview of women's social, political, and cultural history should serve to contextualize twentieth-century Spanish women's literature and literary history. In Spain, the women's movement not only arrived late, in comparison to other Western societies, but was also slow to develop within strictly women-centered, feminist organizations. The Napoleonic Civil Code of 1889, which prevailed until the Second Republic and was reinstated in March of 1938, legally imposed women's subordination to men in all spheres of life, denying the former their most basic rights and autonomy as individuals. Under the *patria potestad* clause of this law, women were considered to be minors under the guardianship of their husbands or fathers, who had exclusive authority and proprietary rights over them. Married women had no legal authority over their children, nor did they have equal rights to joint property. Within the marriage contract, only the wife had the obligation to maintain fidelity, and in the event of separation or abandonment by her husband, she was left without legal rights. Single women, for their part, could not leave their father's home and authority except to enter into marriage. In the working world, women were barred from practicing certain professions and were denied positions of authority in commerce. Above all, women's moral behavior was strictly legislated; therefore, if a single woman were to have a child out of wedlock, for example, the father of the child could legally deny her maternal rights.[1]

Some of the first organized feminist groups in Spain, which began to form well after the beginning of the twentieth century, failed to develop a truly progressive political agenda, since they were often unable to free themselves from the influence of the Catholic church and of other prevailing conservative ideological forces.[2] Other women, reluctant to be caught in the general conflict between the political right and the left, settled for a more centrist, purportedly apolitical stance that did little to produce social transformations. During the Second Republic (1931–6), feminists won significant legal rights for which they had been battling since the turn of the century, including the rights to vote and to divorce. Despite the presence of a small minority of committed feminist intellectuals and activists during the Republic, they were unable to win the general support of other women, who tended not to question their conservative, Catholic upbringing. The growing force of the Sección Femenina de la Falange, which launched a campaign against feminism and indoctrinated women into fascist ideology, attests to the predominantly anti-feminist climate in Spain during this period.

Before the end of the Civil War, the legal rights that women had won during the Second Republic were completely revoked. Once General Francisco Franco took power as dictator of Spain, the church and state combined their forces to establish official social organisms through which women were to be indoctrinated into fascist and patriarchal ideologies.[3] The government imprisoned feminist activists and intellectuals, such as Lidia Falcón and Eva Forest, and arbitrarily censored their writings. Although the Franco regime never succeeded in silencing completely the voices of individual feminists who continued to denounce women's oppression through the press, clandestine publications, and "public" appearances, it was not until after 1965

1 For a more extensive account of the legal position of women under the Civil Code, see G. Scanlon, *La polémica feminista en la España contemporánea 1868–1974* (Madrid: Akal, 1986), pp. 122–58. A more complete text of the 1889 Civil Code is provided in M. Nash, *Mujer, familia y trabajo en España, 1875–1936* (Barcelona: Antropos, 1983), pp. 159–93.

2 M. A. Durán, *Mujer y sociedad en España 1700–1975* (Madrid: Instituto de la Mujer, 1986), pp. 369–89; Scanlon, *La polémica feminista*, pp. 195–257.

3 Ibid., pp. 320–38.

that feminists were able to organize themselves collectively, most typically as concrete interest groups.[4]

A consciousness of the long legacy of women's political and social oppression in Spain finds expression, often through techniques of literary camouflage, in the works of early post-war writers such as Carmen Laforet, Ana María Matute, Mercè Rodoreda, and Carmen Martín Gaite. These writers faced an uphill struggle to find a voice within the constraints of external and internal censorship, including what one critic has called an unofficial "gender censorship."[5] Culturally imposed feminine passivity, solipsism, and silence are salient themes in many of the works of Laforet, Matute, Moix, and the early Martín Gaite, and female characters typically find themselves to be victims of the stifling, oppressive social atmosphere of Franco's Spain. In works such as *Nada* ('Nothing', 1944), *Entre visillos* (*Behind the Curtains*, 1958), *Primera memoria* (*Awakening*, 1960), and *Julia* (1968) there is a constant tension between a dominant discourse that entraps women in, and hence makes them implicitly complicitous with, the social status quo, and a muted discourse, often in camouflaged form, that represents possibilities of resistance to the repressive ideology of Francoism. Yet language and writing which, in theory, represent possibilities of opposition and of transformation often end up, albeit unintentionally, reaffirming the narrative of feminine defeat, despair, and guilt in these women's fiction.[6]

The proliferation of women's works during the post-Franco era and the new possibilities of political and aesthetic expression for women writers are manifestations of significant changes in the cultural climate of Spain.[7] Geraldine Nichols aptly characterizes the post-Franco women writers' relationship to the previous generation of female authors as that of "polemical dialogue."[8] Without denying their debts to their predecessors, post-Franco women write with an acute consciousness of their place within a new cultural context, addressing controversial issues that were treated only indirectly or guardedly by the early post-war writers. The works of Montserrat Roig and of the early Rosa Montero (*Crónica del desamor* [*Absent Love*, 1979]) and *La función Delta* [*The Delta Function*, 1981]), can be read as feminist documentaries on women's lives in Francoist and post-Francoist Spain,

4 A. González, *El feminismo en España, hoy* (Madrid: Zero, 1979), pp. 7–25; A. Moreno, *Mujeres en lucha: El movimiento feminista en España* (Barcelona: Anagrama, 1977).

5 J. Pérez, *Contemporary Women Writers of Spain* (Boston: Twayne, 1980), p. 11.

6 G. Nichols, *Des/cifrar la diferencia: Narrativa femenina de la España contemporánea* (Madrid: Siglo XXI, 1992), pp. 27–35.

7 E. Ordóñez, *Voices of Their Own: Contemporary Spanish Narrative by Women* (Lewisburg: Bucknell University Press, 1991), p. 127.

8 Nichols, *Des/cifrar la diferencia*, p. 28.

respectively. Montero's novels daringly broach the previously taboo subjects of menstruation, abortion, birth control, and sexual harassment, among others. Narratives by Esther Tusquets and Carme Riera, in a similar fashion, openly broach the issues of non-normative sexualities (such as lesbianism and male homosexuality) and of female eroticism.[9] Roig explores Catalan nationalism, class conflict, and female sexuality in her fiction. Literary forms and techniques no longer need to function, even implicitly, as a means of avoidance of either external or self-imposed censorship: instead, they serve to articulate openly each writer's unique voice, vision, or ideology.

Although their literary visions and ideological positions are diverse, a common characteristic of this new generation of women writers is their engagement with issues of gender and sexuality, which grew out of contemporary currents of feminist thought. Moreover, these writers work within the literary and theoretical milieu of the late 1970s and 1980s, in which accepted cultural codes and master narratives are being questioned. Whether or not these women acknowledge an explicit familiarity with contemporary (feminist) theories, each articulates textually the complex relationship between gender and representation, through the questioning of androcentric visions and discourses, the techniques of subversion and parody, or the construction and deconstruction of "feminine" (or gendered) identities and discourses. Although feminist criticism focuses on the literary constructions of gender, it is important not to view all women's writings of this period in Spain as representative of a single, totalizing female experience or worldview. The privileging of a stable category of "woman" – and, by extension, any essentialistic notion of women's writing – must be questioned in light of the diversity of voices and visions characterizing women of different cultural, ethnic, linguistic, and class origins, as well as sexualities, within Spain.

Spain's transition to democracy and the official abolition of censorship by the 1978 Constitution opened up new possibilities of expression and of overtly oppositional discourses for women and men alike. Yet the patriarchal legacy of Francoist culture continues to make its influence felt on women writers even today, although these women vary in their degree of awareness of the problem of gender oppression and discrimination. Despite the increasing visibility of women writers during the 1980s and 1990s, the

[9] Further discussion of the works of Tusquets, Riera, and Roig under analysis in this essay can be found, respectively, in my previous articles: "Theorizing the Feminine: Esther Tusquets's *El mismo mar de todos los veranos* and Hélène Cixous's *écriture féminine*," *Revista de Estudios Hispánicos* 26 (1992), pp. 183–99; "Seduction and Simulation in Carme Riera's *Una primavera per a Domenico Guarini*," in *Moveable Margins: The Narrative Art of Carme Riera*, ed. Kathleen M. Glenn, Mirella Servodidio, and Mary S. Vásquez (Lewisburg: Bucknell University Press, 1999), 83–103; "Reflections on Historiography in Montserrat Roig's *L'hora violeta*," *Arizona Journal of Hispanic Cultural Studies* 2 (1998), pp. 163–74.

critical establishment continues to underrate or, in some cases, even completely ignore women's literary achievements. When a woman writer does attain commercial success, critics often evaluate her works in a way that merely reinforces existing power structures, by gendering her writings and relegating them to a separate, less aesthetically valid discursive category.

The essays and interview statements of Spanish women writers reveal the cultural expectations that condition their attitudes toward gender and gendered writing, particularly the concept of women's writing. A rejection of the term "feminist," especially when applied to their writings, and their insistence on the separation between literature and (gender) politics, characterize their public statements. Montserrat Roig, for example, associates "feminist" literature negatively with political propaganda, in spite of the strong feminist subtext of her own novels, such as *L'hora violeta* ('The Violet Hour', 1980) and *L'òpera quotidiana* ('The Everyday Opera', 1982). Carme Riera, when asked about the influence of feminist thought on her writing, responds by acknowledging her familiarity with French feminism and even claims that she would not have written one of her novels, *Una primavera per a Domenico Guarini* ('Spring for Domenico Guarini', 1981), had she not read feminist theory.[10] Yet she, like Roig, insists on the separation between politics and literature, stating that "to write well" is independent of any ideological agenda and that her "feminist claims" will always remain "separate from literature."[11]

These women writers' desire to maintain a separation between literature and feminist politics results from the fear that any attention to gender difference might lead to a further marginalization of women's writing. What they deplore is their ghettoization within what Tusquets calls "the side room for women," a category understood to be separate from "serious" (read "men's") literature.[12] As Montserrat Roig notes with regard to the Catalan literary scene, even women writers (such as herself and Riera) who have

[10] By French feminism I refer to the new intellectual feminist movement that emerged in the wake of the student revolt of May 1968 in Paris. The feminists who were part of this movement, including Hélène Cixous, Luce Irigaray, and Julia Kristeva, wrote their most influential works in the 1970s, having received their grounding in two major currents of contemporary French theory: deconstruction and psychoanalysis. They revised from a feminist perspective the account of sexual identity formation, conceived by the psychoanalyst Jacques Lacan, in order to explore the relationships between gender, sexuality, and language. While some French feminists affirmed the specificity of feminine sexuality as a source of women's language and writing, others were inclined to dismantle the binary categories of gender ("feminine" vs. "masculine"), thus questioning the very notion of stable sexual identities.

[11] G. Nichols, *Escribir, espacio propio: Laforet, Matute, Moix, Tusquets, Riera y Roig por sí mismas* (Minneapolis: Institute for the Study of Ideologies and Literature, 1989), pp. 191–2.

[12] Ibid., p. 80.

enjoyed greater commercial success than their male counterparts are ignored by those critics who associate women's literature with a "lesser world," what Roig calls the world as seen through women's eyes. For the literary establishment, she continues, this "lesser world" is considered to be a distortion of "the world as it is," thus falsely implying the universality of the world as seen by men.[13]

In view of Roig's statements, the problem goes beyond privileging the "masculine" over the "feminine" perspective. The real problem is that only women's writing is perceived to be gendered, whereas men's writing can maintain the fiction of neutrality. True to the assertion of the French feminist Monique Wittig, there is only one gender: "the feminine, the 'masculine' not being a gender. For the masculine is not the masculine but the general. The result is that there are the general and the feminine, or rather, the general and the mark of the feminine."[14] In other words, women can never escape the mark of gender since men have always "appropriated the univeral for themselves."[15] Thus women's writing, which becomes identified with immanence and univocality, reinforces the myth of "woman" as an essentialist and homogeneous category, and ultimately leads to the literary segregation of women writers as a group. This segregation can take two interrelated forms. First, mainstream Spanish critics have tended to denigrate modes and genres that have been identified traditionally with women's writings, such as autobiography and confessional writing. Roig observes that critics have often singled out women by "accusing" them of writing autobiographical literature,[16] thus implying that autobiography is a woman's genre and, hence, a less serious one.

Such classifications of women's literature often become *prescriptive* as well. Roig recounts that, during a literary debate in which she and Montero once participated, a male critic "accused" the two women of not doing the same thing in their literary works,[17] thus assuming that all women should write in the same way or about the same issues. The fact that the critical establishment praises or condemns women writers according to their conformity to arbitrary, gender-inflected expectations becomes evident upon perusing book reviews in Spanish literary publications. Male critics frequently refer to women's writings as confessional, sentimental, hermetic, or narcissistic. One critic, for example, characterizes Tusquets's *El mismo mar de todos los*

[13] Ibid., p. 150.
[14] M. Wittig, *The Straight Mind and Other Essays* (Boston: Beacon Press, 1992), p. 60.
[15] Ibid., p. 80.
[16] M. Roig, *Dime que me quieres aunque sea mentira: sobre el placer solitario de escribir y el vicio compartido de leer* (Barcelona: Edicions 62, 1993), p. 71.
[17] Nichols, *Escribir, espacio propio*, p. 180.

veranos (*The Same Sea as Every Summer*, 1978) as a narcissistic reflection of the author's private "closed universe," all but ignoring the novel's highly stylized discourse, intertextual play, and theoretical self-consciousness.[18] A reviewer of Soledad Puértolas's *Queda la noche* ('The Night Remains', 1989) criticizes what he considers to be the novel's "desire for intimacy" based on its first-person point of view and concludes condescendingly that: "The gentle tone, in a minor key, evades contradictions to capture all tastes."[19] One could argue precisely the opposite: that Puértolas's work strives for distance, ellipticism, enigma, and ambiguity. Finally, in a review of the Spanish translation of Carme Riera's *Te dejo el mar* (*I Leave the Sea to You*), the reviewer calls attention to the "lyricism" and "eloquent intimacy" of the first book of the collection (*Te dejo, amor, en prenda el mar*, 'I Leave You, My Love, the Sea as a Token'), deploring that in the second (*Y pongo por testigo a las gaviotas*, 'And Let Seagulls be My Witnesses') "an element of distance appears that diminishes the freshness and passion of the earlier work."[20] Riera herself surmises that her short stories, particularly the earlier ones, have enjoyed a positive critical reception precisely because they conform to stereotypical notions of what women's literature should be: "sweet," "tender," and "lyrical." These are, ironically, qualities that she considers to be defects in her adolescent work.[21] The identification of women's writing with the personal and the private, in contrast to the supposedly transcendent and universal nature of men's writing, is not surprising in light of the culturally determined notion of separate, gendered spheres.

Given these critical reactions to a homogenizing vision of "women's writing," it is not altogether surprising that women writers perceive feminists' attention to gender as yet another way of ghettoizing their literature. As Soledad Puértolas decries: "What's troubling is the expectation that women ought to display a particular feminine point of view. Isn't it odd that we think ours can't be as broad and diverse as the masculine point of view? Because men are of all types. Writers are of all types. Why should it be that women, and within this category, women writers, are condemned to sameness?"[22] Since the challenge of the writer, in Puértolas's view, is to create a work of art that transcends cultural conditioning, including that of gender, it is

[18] L. Suñen, "El mito en el espejo," *Ínsula* 382 (1987), p. 5.

[19] M. J. Navarro, "Queda la noche: Conformarse con poco," *Reseña* 202 (January 1990), p. 28.

[20] S. Alonso, "*Te dejo el mar*: Elogio del sentimiento," *Reseña* 222 (November 1991), p. 31.

[21] Nichols, *Escribir, espacio propio*, pp. 197, 200.

[22] S. Puértolas, *La vida oculta* (Barcelona: Anagrama, 1993), p. 61.

necessary to resist the critics' tendency always to reduce women's works to "the supposedly feminine world."[23] Puértolas's paradigmatically modernist vision of literature is not unlike that of Wittig, who deplores the fact that the texts of "minority writers," such as women and homosexuals, are denied universality by being reduced to univocal symbols of the political concerns of a *particular* group (*The Straight Mind*, pp. 59–67). As writers, according to Wittig, both groups aspire to universalize the "minority point of view" (p. 64), while recognizing that universality is accorded only to members of the dominant culture.

Despite their seemingly naive adherence to the myth of a culturally and politically neutral conception of aesthetic value and transcendence, the position taken by both Puértolas and Wittig is understandable if we consider their desire to appropriate this myth to overcome their marginalization by the literary establishment. Yet women who seek literary "transcendence" in this way inevitably find themselves in a double bind. Any attempt to achieve "universality" according to the aesthetic criteria set by the male literary establishment is made impossible by this very establishment, which always ends up by segregating their writing under the rubric of the "feminine." If, on the other hand, they seek to produce a more overtly feminist work (however this term is to be understood), or one that centers concretely on women's issues, critics still evaluate their work according to the dominant culture's view of what women's literature is and should be. Many women writers in Spain have acknowledged experiencing this second form of discrimination.

Another negative consequence of this gender-based critical bias is the gendering of the reading public itself, which is evident in the case of contemporary Spain. The idea of "a literature by women for women"[24] has become a critical commonplace that has contributed to the gendering of the reading public for women's literature. Many Spanish women writers lament the fact that men generally do not read their works, due to the widely accepted presumption that women's literature can be of interest only to women. Tusquets and Riera, on the other hand, deplore the fact that women readers respond to their novels only through identification with their characters, whereas men seem to be able to appreciate their works for "more literary reasons."[25] For both Riera and Tusquets, the reaction of their female reading public only seems to confirm the assumption that women are naive and passive

[23] L. Talbot, "Entrevista con Soledad Puértolas," *Hispania* 71 (1988), p. 882.

[24] Nichols, *Escribir, espacio propio*, p. 193; Roig, *Dime que me quieres*, p. 77.

[25] Nichols, *Escribir, espacio propio*, p. 95.

consumers of literary texts, whereas men's readings constitute more sophisticated critical acts.

The above analysis is not intended to minimize the importance of the new market for women's literature that was created after Franco's death as a result of an expanded (female) readership and an increased public awareness about women's issues. Nor is it our intent to privilege a high modernist vision of literature above the perceived needs of a reading public in a moment of cultural transformation when issues of gender and sexuality were coming to the forefront. Instead, a critical examination of these women writers' rhetorical stances in a public forum aims to explain the gap between an apparently naive theoretical posture and a literary practice that reveals a sophisticated consciousness of the relationship between gender/sexualities and writing.

Jo Labanyi divides recent Spanish women's writings into two basic tendencies, "essentialism" and "postmodernism," which are in tension.[26] According to this critic, the first category includes those writers "concerned with specifically feminine forms of experience" (i.e. those "trying to create an identity for themselves"), whereas the second consists of "those interested in the falsity or instablity of identity" with the purpose of undermining the notion of fixed gender roles ("Postmodernism," p. 403). Although Labanyi suggests that these tendencies generally correspond to "successive stages" in the construction of identity, she also notes rightly that "both tendencies continue to be found" in recent women's writings (p. 404). In fact, the second tendency predominates in women's fiction of the post-Franco era, since very few of their works fail to question in some fashion the notion of stable identity, even when the search for an alternative female/gender identity appears to be the agenda of the work.

The problem of (female/gender) identity, in its multiple versions, is a central preoccupation in all of these works by post-Franco women. Notions of identity are typically renegotiated in moments of social, political, and cultural transformation, of which the end of the Franco dictatorship is emblematic. As the nation emerged from totalitarianism, homogeneous and hegemonic ideas of identity, including those of gendered subjects, gave way to the possibility of alternative constructions that allowed for plurality and difference. For women in particular, who had been denied subjectivity under the dictatorship, there was an urgency to refigure their identities as they witnessed the gradual destabilization and decomposition of the identity that

[26] J. Labanyi, "Postmodernism and the Problem of Cultural Identity," in *Spanish Cultural Studies: An Introduction*, ed. Helen Graham and Jo Labanyi (New York: Oxford University Press, 1995), p. 403.

had been imposed on them by the dominant discourses of the dictatorial regime. Therefore, at this juncture in Spanish history, the search for identity or, more accurately, the possibility of its renegotiation became central to women's writings.

Esther Tusquets's first novel, *El mismo mar de todos los veranos* (1978), published during the early years of the post-Franco era, exemplifies a work whose construction of a specifically "feminine" sexuality and mode of discourse is paralleled by a questioning of the essentialist, totalizing, and utopian premises of such a project. *El mismo mar* represents an attempt to inscribe theories of the "feminine" (in particular, French feminists' notion of *écriture féminine*) into discourse.[27] The central paradigm of the novel is the personal and narrative quest of the female narrator-protagonist, who undertakes a journey into her past in search of a union with her absent mother, a figure that represents an alternative, utopian space of feminine presence antithetical to the phallocentric logic of the masculine Symbolic.[28] A proliferation of metaphors that evoke maternal presence – in particular, the narrator's descent into the humid "wells" and "grottos," metaphors for the woman's vagina, and the sea that surrounds her childhood home, suggestive of an all-encompassing Mother Nature that erases all boundaries between past and present, mother and daughter, self and other – provides the setting for the protagonist's journey.

In her quest for a feminine utopia, the protagonist is accompanied by her lover and companion, Clara, who is both a part of herself and an Other with whom she wishes to fuse. Clara, who represents all that is foreign, exotic, and unfathomable, guides the protagonist in her journey to an idealized past and to the long-lost magical world of childhood literature and dreams. As Clara becomes the embodiment of such literary and mythical archetypes as the Little Mermaid and Ariadne, and narrative time virtually comes to a standstill, the two women participate in a symbolic ritual, diving naked into the sea with another lesbian couple, in the hope of relinquishing the

[27] *Ecriture féminine* is a term coined by the French feminist Hélène Cixous to conceptualize a (utopian) mode of writing that has its source in feminine sexuality and therefore defies masculine logic and signifying practices. See H. Cixous, "The Laugh of the Medusa," tr. K. Cohen and P. Cohen, *Signs* 1 (1976), pp. 875–93.

[28] "Phallocentrism" denotes a "system that privileges the phallus as the symbol or source of power" (T. Moi, *Sexual/Texual Politics: Feminist Literary Theory* [New York: Methuen, 1985], p. 179). According to the French psychoanalyst Lacan, the subject comes into being through a "repression of the desire for the lost mother" as s/he enters into the Symbolic order: "To enter into the Symbolic order means to accept the phallus as the representation of the Law of the Father" (ibid., pp. 99–100). That is, only by undergoing the Oedipal crisis and entering into the Symbolic can the child acquire language and subjectivity.

Symbolic world and of returning to an idealized, prelapsarian world of the *mother/sea*.

The narrator's quest culminates in her sexual union with Clara, whose body represents a utopian space, at the center of all other spaces, where difference between the self and the other has been abolished and desire for unity has been realized. The protagonist seeks to begin a new life in a utopian feminine world with her lover/mother Clara, who represents the origin of truth, identification, and unity, which have been lost in the Symbolic order. Significantly, for Tusquets's narrator the recovery of this utopian myth occurs within the realm of lesbian desire, idealized in the figure of Clara. What at first appears to be an alternative vision of a feminine desire that lies outside of the Symbolic, however, gradually becomes dismantled and, in the end, exposed as an impossible myth: the Symbolic order (i.e. language itself), and the structures of power that it generates, entrap the protagonist and ultimately impose a distance between her and the object of her desire (i.e. Clara and the prelapsarian world of presence and unity that she represents). Significantly, by employing the rhetoric of colonization to describe her "conquest" of Clara, who is both her student and a native of Colombia, the narrator transforms Clara into the colonized other, rather than creating a utopian space of feminine desire where differences and hierarchies are erased.

The multiple structures of power (of patriarchal, heterosexual, colonizing systems) that end up by entrapping the protagonist are reflected discursively in the complex fabric of words and (inter) texts that inscribes her existence. The mythological tale of Theseus and Ariadne constitutes a central literary paradigm through which the protagonist recreates the episodes of love and betrayal in her own life, beginning with her former lover's suicide and, hence, his abandonment of her. Rather than rewriting this myth and reinventing herself and her world according to her desire for a feminine utopia, the protagonist ends up by reenacting the plot of the Theseus–Ariadne myth: at the end of the novel, she allows herself to be seduced by her estranged husband Julio, thus betraying Clara and undermining the possibility of a utopia that she believes she has achieved with her lover.

Notwithstanding the apparent foreclosure of the text, the very nature of the narrator's discourse, infinitely contradictory and self-reflexive, reveals a "desire to communicate difference, differently."[29] In the narrator's imagination, Clara will remain a force that has disrupted masculine history and its phallocentric discursive system, by allowing her to discover her lesbian

[29] G. Nichols, "The Prison-House (and Beyond): *El mismo mar de todos los veranos*," *Romanic Review* 75 (1984), p. 383.

sexuality and by guiding her in a search for a language that inscribes a different kind of female desire. The concluding words of the novel, "And Wendy grew up" (p. 229), which refer intertextually to *Peter Pan* and project the narrator's quest into the future, question the seemingly unambiguous narrative of inevitable defeat, represented by the fate of the protagonist. Thus, in *El mismo mar*, the utopian myth of an alternative "feminine" desire, sexuality, or discourse, is simultaneously affirmed and questioned, as the novel proposes new possibilities of (re)formulating identities and discourses, while reminding us that each of these identities and discourses constitutes yet another construct, which can lead either to strategic empowerment or to an ideological impasse.

As in Tusquets's novel, the search for (female) identity is a central preoccupation in Carme Riera's first novel, *Una primavera per a Domenico Guarini* (1981). Riera's novel consists of two fundamental plotlines: the first is a narrative account of the female protagonist Clara's quest for identity at a moment of personal crisis; the second, which parallels the first, is a detective story centered on the resolution of the mystery that surrounds Domenico Guarini's vandalizing of Botticelli's *Primavera* ('Spring'). Clara's personal journey (both literal and metaphorical, as it begins on a train journey from Barcelona to Florence) to self-discovery is thus inseparable from her narrative quest for truth and veiled meanings in her role as journalist-detective whose task is to discover the motive behind Guarini's destructive act.

Part I of the novel, which focuses on Clara's personal reflections during her train journey from Barcelona to Florence, is narrated by the protagonist to herself in second person. Like Tusquets's narrator-protagonist, Clara interprets her entire life through literature, a tendency that is reflected in the literary nature of the journalistic account that she constructs around the Guarini case. In Part II, Clara (re)writes the story of Guarini's life by imagining his point of view, alternately in first- and third-person forms: in her version of Guarini's story, art mediates his quest for the object of his desire, as he confuses Flora, the central figure of the *Primavera*, with his supposed lover Laura. Laura/Flora is an artistic ideal, a literary archetype that he has invented through his literary imagination; in essence she is also the object of the male gaze and of the discourse of masculine desire. Ironically, it is a man, Clara's former lover Alberto, who questions the phallocentric vision implicit in Clara's textual rendition of Guarini's life, as well as her identification with the patriarchal ideology that underlies her vision of Guarini.

What is certain is that two works of art, Botticelli's *Primavera* and Petrarch's *Canzoniere*, play a central role in the development of the detective story in which Guarini figures as a protagonist. These artistic texts, and their respective representations of Flora and of Laura, circumscribe Guarini's life and actions, thereby diverting Clara's search for truth as a journalist. The copy of the *Canzoniere*, which is found under a laurel tree where Guarini claims to have buried his lover Laura's remains, acts as a metonymic link to the figure of Petrarch's beloved and evokes the myth of Daphne's rape by Apollo. Both archetypes, in turn, provide a link between Guarini's self-textualization and the *Primavera*, which glorifies the mythological Zephyr's rape of the nymph Chloris.

Part III of the novel juxtaposes two narratives: first, Clara's autobiographical narration that chronicles her struggle to come to terms with her gender role and identity; second, an art professor's academic exegesis of Botticelli's *Primavera* based on the phallocentric and homosocial premises of Renaissance Neoplatonism. This narrative strategy serves to highlight the analogy between Clara's role as woman in the "text" that she has written of her life in post-Civil War Spain, on the one hand, and the social and discursive position afforded women in the foundational texts of Western culture, on the other. The professor's glorification of Chloris's rape, for example, frames in a parallel fashion Clara's memories of sexual abuse and harassment during her childhood and adolescence. In the present, her narrative self-creation allows her to continue in her quest for self-understanding as she faces the dilemma of being an unmarried, pregnant woman with a fragile sense of identity. In her quest, she discovers the extent to which her own life has been shaped according to models that are alienating to women, including the traditional discourses of religion, mythology, and art, as well as the alternative ones of revolutionary politics, hippie culture, and even mainstream feminism. Surrounded by these alienating discourses, Clara redoubles her search for an identity that continually eludes her. The increasing fragmentation of Clara's narrative in this section of the novel mirrors the instability of her identity.

At the conclusion of Part III, Clara's personal journey leads her back, once again, to the central text of the *Primavera*. The painting, which has mediated her interpretive quest throughout the novel, becomes a locus where various other texts – Clara's autobiographical narration, her journalistic report on the Guarini case, and the professor's artistic exegesis – converge. Yet as she continues to struggle for self-definition through these texts, she recognizes that any sense of stable identity escapes her, just as Guarini's case and the meaning of the *Primavera* elude definitive interpretation. Although she perceives the *Primavera* to be a metaphorical mirror through which she recaptures the imaginary unity of her fragmented subjectivity, the novel exposes her newly discovered identity – bound up with a particular interpretation of the *Primavera* – to be a provisional and eternally unstable construct, subject to constant transformations through discourse. The epilogue of the novel, in which Clara finds herself on her train journey back to Barcelona, highlights the circularity of her quest for identity. Rather than ending her trajectory toward self-discovery, the future that she projects for herself, through images of the childbirth scene, launches her on yet another journey in search of her identity as a woman and a mother. Like Tusquets, Riera constructs, through the symbolic journey of a female protagonist, a version of feminine identity that appears to elude existing social and linguistic codes, while simultaneously exposing the constructedness and contingency of all identities.

In Montserrat Roig's *L'hora violeta* (1980), a "critique of historiography" predominates over the search for "a more accurate alternative to traditional top-down or androcentric accounts" that presupposes a somehow more authentic version of feminine identity.[30] The novel chronicles the transition between dictatorship and democracy through the *intrahistoria* of three women, which focuses on their experiences in the private sphere of home and family. The first section of the novel, entitled "Spring of 1979," frames the novel that Norma, an alter ego of the author, writes about the friendship between Judit (the mother of her friend Natàlia) and Judit's friend Kati during the Civil War years. Natàlia, who asks Norma to write the novel, provides her friend with various texts – among them, Judit's diary and Kati's letters – with the hope of recovering, through Norma's narrative account, the yet unwritten history of two women who existed on the margins of official history (i.e. history by and about men). Through this framing technique, Roig calls attention to the function of memory in reconfiguring identities, as well as the subject's relationship to history. In the second section of the novel ("The Lost Hour"), as Natàlia comments on Norma's literary project in first-person form, the former arrives at a realization that history – and identity – can acquire meaning only through the mediating consciousness of the remembering/narrating self.

In Roig's novel, the consciousness of a fragmented (female) subject mediates the telling of the women's "stories," both past and present, contained in the five principal sections. The stories of Norma, Natàlia and Agnes in the years immediately following the end of the Franco dictatorship in the "outer" frame of the novel are juxtaposed with that of Judit and Kati during the Civil War in the "inner" frame. Despite Norma's presence as a writer figure who authors the novel within the novel (in the third section aptly entitled "The Novel of the Violet Hour"), the lack of a single unifying perspective reflects the absence of a stable subject position from which literary discourse originates in the work. Natàlia, whose story is told in the section "The Lost Hour," calls attention to the fractured nature of her identity, which seems to be a vacuum that words cannot adequately represent. Her story traces a

30 A. B. Jones, *Women in Contemporary Spain* (Manchester University Press, 1997), p. 167.

circular pattern, as the novel begins and ends with the image of her reading *The Odyssey* on a Mediterranean island, reflecting the fact that she is trapped in the circular time of myth, unable to move forward in historical time. Her fate is to wait like Penelope: to wait for a man, for a purpose, for a historical destiny that exists only in the language of myth. The title of the section itself, "The Lost Hour," calls attention to the idea of loss or absence.

Likewise, the identities of Judit and Kati in "The Novel of the Violet Hour," the interior novel written by Norma, are ultimately unrepresentable. Their stories, consisting of textual fragments (even though these fragments are mostly first-person entries from Judit's diary), leave many hermeneutic gaps in Norma's novel, making the truth about the two women's identities difficult to grasp. A coherent narrative of experience becomes an impossible goal, due to the instability of the narrative fragments through which the characters' subjectivities are constituted. Norma herself, by the end of the novel, is conscious of her own disintegration as a subject. The elusive identities of Judit and Kati are products not only of Norma and Judit's unstable positions as writing subjects, but also of the contradictory discourses of gender, class, and nationality in which the two women are interpellated.[31]

The fourth section of the novel, entitled "The Dispersed Hour," set once again in the present of Norma and Natàlia (spring of 1979), focuses on Norma in the process of writing the story of Judit and Kati, at the same time as she is writing a journalistic report on Catalans in Nazi concentration camps. Through the conflation of these two narrative modes, the one predominantly fictional, and the other based on testimony and ostensibly historical, Roig's novel prompts a self-critical reflection on the process of signification whereby subjective experience acquires historical meaning. Norma's interaction with a survivor of a concentration camp ultimately reveals the impossiblity of recovering a totalizing and totalizable account of the original event, precisely because the integrity of the moment of witnessing the event is forever lost unless it is captured and transformed through discourse. This inability ever to know and to recover the truth leads to a schism in the ex-deportee's identity as witness (as one who supposedly knows his own life and history), just as Norma's ideal of journalistic objectivity is undermined by her status as a bourgeoise, Catalan female subject who has never personally known the horrors of the war or the atrocities committed in its aftermath.

[31] G. Nichols, "The Construction of Subjectivity in Contemporary Women Writers of Catalonia," in *Spain Today: Essays on Literature, Culture, and Society*, ed. José Colmeiro *et al.* (Hanover, NH: Dartmouth College, 1995), pp. 114–15.

Similarly, she must confront her ambiguous status as the author of Kati and Judit's (hi)story. Norma, on the one hand, questions her ability to represent, even in fictional form, an experience that she herself has never lived and identities that she has never shared. On the other hand, she is aware that these women's subjectivities can come to life only when they are rendered into narrative form. In the end, she can do little more than to (re)invent the (hi)stories of the two women, just as, in her journalistic report, she can only hope to give realization to the ex-deportee's promise of testimony by transforming this testimony into discourse. Roig's critique of historiography, then, problematizes any essentialist or totalizing notion of subjectivity and exposes the nature of identities as "a contested terrain, the site of multiple and conflicting claims" produced by competing discourses.[32]

Whereas Tusquets, Riera, and Roig posit alternative versions of "feminine" identities and discourses, in order ultimately to question them, other writers, such as Cristina Fernández Cubas, present a radical critique of subjectivity. Fernández Cubas's short stories in *Mi hermana Elba* ('My Sister Elba', 1980), *Los altillos de Brumal* ('Brumal Heights', 1983), *El ángulo del horror* ('The Angle of Horror', 1990), as well as her enigmatic novel, *El columpio* ('The Swing', 1995), show an obsessive preoccupation with the problem of subjectivity and its relationship to gender and writing. The short story "En el hemisferio sur" ('In the Southern Hemisphere'), published in *Los altillos de Brumal*, which dramatizes the crisis of subjectivity, is paradigmatic of many of her fantastic tales in that it tests the limits of established literary, social, and cultural conventions. If fantasy creates a space for unconscious desire, as psychoanalytic critics have claimed, it thus gives expression to an (impossible) attempt to recapture the ideal state of undifferentiation (what Lacan calls the imaginary) between self and other, subject and object, before loss and separation occur in the process of subject formation.

"En el hemisferio sur," like many other tales by Fernández Cubas, represents precisely such an attempt to reverse the process of the subject's formation. In this story, the female protagonist Clara, a writer, suddenly finds herself to be pursued by a mysterious Voice that, as the source of her creative activity, appears to be linked to the realm of the imaginary. Clara's desire to reenter the imaginary leads to her fragmentation as a subject, which takes the form of a doubling between her and another writer, Sonia Kraskowa, who is identified with a fantasized undifferentiated self. Clara's gradual fusion with her double, who seems to control her writing (everything that Clara writes has already been written by Sonia), and her inability to reconcile

[32] J. Scott, "Experience," in *Feminists Theorize the Political*, ed. Judith Butler and Joan W. Scott (New York: Routledge, 1992), pp. 31–2.

her two selves, ultimately reduce her to a state of madness and lead to her self-destruction through suicide. Significantly, Clara's story is told from the perspective of a masculine narrator, himself an unsuccessful writer. As Clara recounts her experience with the Voice to him, he is forced to confront his repressed desire for the imaginary and, hence, the instablity of his own (gender) identity. After Clara's death, he decides to write a novel about her experience, only to discover that her posthumous work contains her own version of the novel, with Clara casting him in the role of an emasculated, impotent subject of discourse. The male character's failure to achieve mastery over discourse, then, leads to his crisis of subjectivity. Thus Fernández Cubas's narrations radically undermine fixed gender roles and categories, through a deconstruction of the very notion of subjectivity.

"En el hemisferio sur" is paradigmatic of Fernández Cubas's fiction in its representation of the crisis of subjectivity. Her 1995 novel *El columpio* also explores this problem. As in her short stories, the female protagonist embarks on a journey – both literal and metaphorical – in search of her origins and identity. The novel opens as the unnamed narrator-protagonist travels alone to an abandoned region of the Pyrenees to visit her deceased mother's estranged relatives, who live in isolation in a proverbial Gothic tower. Soon after her arrival, she is overtaken by the enigmatic and the uncanny as she gradually discovers that the space she has entered is a hermetic world of the past, which her uncle and cousin have never abandoned. In this world, the adult protagonist becomes identified with her mother Eloísa, that is, the child Eloísa who spent her days swinging on her swing and playing with her diabolo, and even imagines that she hears her mother's voice. Like Clara in "En el hemisferio sur," the narrator of *El columpio* undergoes an experience of near madness and disintegration as a subject after reentering the realm of the imaginary, represented by her identification with the absent mother. Significantly, her male relatives are the ones who ultimately expel her from this world, leaving her to reconstruct her identity, once again, in real "life." Thus do issues of gender and subjectivity remain at the core of Fernández Cubas's fiction.

At the end of the millennium, yet another new crop of women writers – including Nuria Amat, Lucía Extebarria, Laura Freixas, Belén Gopegui, and Almudena Grandes – has emerged. While some writers, such as Gopegui, focus on the social relations of both genders in light of the ethical bankuptcy and general disillusionment of the generation of the late 1980s and 1990s, others, such as Amat, Extebarria, Freixas, and Grandes, continue to center their works on female subjectivity and on women's issues, including feminist issues. Furthermore, while some, such as Amat, address a predominantly highbrow, literary audience in their representations of female subjectivity, others, such as Extebarria and Grandes, cater more directly to the mass market in their treatment of gender and sexuality.

These writers maintain radically divergent attitudes toward the problem of (female) identity. Nuria Amat in her recent novel *La intimidad* ('Intimacy', 1997), for instance, tests the limits of female subjectivity by blurring the boundaries of the physical, psychic, and literary spaces that circumscribe the female narrator-protagonist's identity. At first, the protagonist is defined by the space of her room of her house of Pedralbes, from whose window she has a view of a psychiatric clinic. Her increasing identification with one of the psychiatric patients, who appears in the window of the tower of the clinic (evocative of Bronte's "madwoman in the attic") and commits suicide one day, inspires the protagonist to write an unreadable novel that permits her to transgress the boundaries of the physical and symbolic spaces that confine her. A voice, identified with her absent mother, motivates her writing and takes her to the "other side" of the limit, where she enters the ambiguous realms of literature, madness, and silence (i.e. metaphorical death). The novel subverts any notion of a boundary that delimits the (female) subject, as the protagonist embraces the identities of both her mother and the psychiatric patient, representations of otherness.

In contrast, Lucía Extebarria's novels, such as *Amor, curiosidad, prozac y dudas* ('Love, Curiosity, Prozac, Doubts', 1997) and *Beatriz y los cuerpos celeste*s ('Beatriz and the Heavenly Bodies', 1998) are more direct products of the consumer era: while claiming to question traditional gender roles and categories, these novels end up by reaffirming them through the deliberate commodification of socially marginal identities for a fundamentally conservative mass market. In spite of the apparently transgressive lifestyles and ideologies of her female characters (many of whom are lesbians, bisexuals, "feminists," or otherwise marginalized by society) and their awareness of the arbitrariness of gender roles, the novels' failure to question existing social structures in a profound way or to create alternative ways of conceptualizing female identities that are ultimately empowering for women, undermines their subversive potential. Moreover, the conventional and clichéd endings of Extebarria's novels leave little room for difference or complexity in the construction of a new female subject.

In sum, the contrary tendencies of aesthetic innovation and the forces of the mass market continue to exert their influence on contemporary writers, women and men alike. Although it is still difficult to predict the future direction(s) of Spanish women's fiction at the turn of the twenty-first century, the issue of (female) subjectivity, which is in a process of constant (re)definition and (re)negotiation, continues to occupy a prominent place in these women's works.

Guide to further reading

Brown, Joan L. (ed.), *Women Writers of Contemporary Spain: Exiles in the Homeland* (Newark: University of Delware Press, 1991).

Davies, Catherine, *Spanish Women's Writing 1840–1996* (London and Atlantic Highlands: Athlone, 1998).

Levine, Linda Gould, and Gloria Waldman (eds.), *Feminismo ante el franquismo: Entrevistas con feministas de España* (Miami: Ediciones Universal, 1980).

Levine, Linda Gould, Ellen Engelson Marson, and Gloria Feiman Waldman (eds.), *Spanish Women Writers: A Bio-Bibliographical Source Book* (Westport, CT: Greenwood Press, 1993).

Servodidio, Mirella (ed.), *Reading for Difference: Feminist Perspectives on Women Novelists of Contemporary Spain.* Special Issue of *Anales de la Literatura Española Contemporánea* 12 (1987).

14

ISOLINA BALLESTEROS

Cultural alliances: film and literature in the socialist period, 1982–1995

Literature and film have established an interdependent relationship since the beginning of the film industry at the turn of the twentieth century. From the first silent films, which the brothers Lumière and Georges Méliès made and which followed theatre's spatial laws and dramatic structure, to the innovations introduced by David Griffith, which turned cinema into a narrative language structured according to the models of the nineteenth-century novel,[1] cinema invariably appears as a mechanical form of reproducing a story.[2]

Cinema flirted with poetry for a short, intense period of time. The artistic avant-garde discovered film's potential to break with the old order and "dehumanize art," as well as its power to express political ideologies. Cinema could summon and mobilize an essentially popular audience through a new medium of mass communication. Cinema also articulated in images the ruptures produced in aesthetics or ideology in the first third of the century, and while continuing to be linked intrinsically to literature, it emerged, as

[1] P. Gimferrer, *Cine y literatura* (Barcelona: Planeta, 1985), p. 11.

[2] Georges Méliès (1861–1938) was one of the most important pioneers of early cinema. A successful magician and owner of the Théâtre Robert-Houdin in Paris, Méliès attended the first screening of the Lumière Cinématographe on 28 December 1895. That same year he started making films, using a home-made camera and projector. Méliès established basic techniques for the special effects of most modern films (stop motion, dissolve, fading, masking, etc.). He painted all his stage settings himself and was also the main actor in most of his works. Méliès's best-known film, *A Trip to the Moon* (1902), was one of the longest and most elaborate of his trick film epics. David W. Griffith (1875–1948) is considered the pioneer of American silent film. Actor, screenwriter, producer, and director, he is best known for exploiting the potential of film as an expressive medium and for his controversial perceptions of race and class in American society. Griffith's best-known and most controversial film is *Birth of a Nation* (1915).

Further to this note, I wish to thank Sean McNeal for his collaboration in the translation of the present essay from Spanish into English and Harriet Turner and Adelaida López de Martínez for their rigorous editing. A version in Spanish appears as a chapter titled "Convergencias y alianzas culturales: las adaptaciones fílmicas de obras literarias en el período socialista" in my book *Cine (ins)urgente: Textos fílmicos y contextos culturales de la España postfranquista* (Madrid: Fundamentos, 2001), pp. 153–74.

Peña-Ardid writes, as a necessary life raft if one were to "abandon rancid realism." Thus cinema became a powerful instrument "for expressing the imaginary, the unreal, or the dreamed."[3]

The surrealists saw cinema as an instrument of provocation, one promoting intellectual and artistic ruptures with the Western capitalist tradition. *Un chien andalou* (1929) and *L'âge d'or* (1930) by Luis Buñuel and Salvador Dalí are two prime examples of the early, brief convergence between film and surrealist poetry, considered to be, in the words of Octavio Paz, "a place of generic intersection between film and poetry,"[4] and whose scripts were constructed as the product of automatic writing.[5] In the same way *Viaje a la luna*, Lorca's film script written during his stay in New York in 1929, must be interpreted as a filmic poem or a poetic film, that is, as "a poetic discourse that draws support from the very organizational structures it explores."[6]

Years later, when literature and film severed their lyrical ties and again converged along a realist vein, Buñuel, in 1958, yearned for the cinematic experiments of the avant-garde:

> For many years now, because of the economic risks involved, cinematographic art seems to have renounced its immense creative possibilities, which currently move in only one direction: that of the strictest realism. [...] As [...] a marvelous instrument for the expression of poetry and dreams – of the subconscious – cinema is confined to the role of being simply a REPEATER of stories, already expressed by other art forms [...] Our age is one of uncertainty and the conscious man longs, albeit only in the imagination, to flee the agonizing reality that surrounds him [...] Isn't a work of art, a film, for example, which reflects the concerns and hopes of present-day humanity, the least he can ask for? The POETIC FILM, which would be at the same time the NEW FILM, sought so enthusiastically by today's producers, can fulfill that desire better than any other.[7]

When film resumed its role as "repeater of stories," literary works were the principal source of inspiration for filmic creation. Via a process of reciprocal interests, literature was adapted to film to popularize the former and dignify the latter. As Rafael Utrera points out, "literature is offered as a synonym of

[3] C. Peña-Ardid, *Literatura y cine. Una aproximación comparativa* (Madrid: Cátedra, 1992), p. 58.

[4] Quoted in J. Talens, *El ojo tachado* (Madrid: Catédra, 1986), p. 48.

[5] L. Buñuel, *Mi último suspiro* (Madrid: Plaza y Janés, 1992), p. 126.

[6] A. Monegal (ed.), *Viaje a la luna (guión cinematográfico)* by Federico García Lorca (Valencia: Pre-Textos, 1995), p. 37.

[7] A. Sánchez Vidal, *Vida y opiniones de Luis Buñuel* (Teruel: Instituto de Estudios Turolenses, 1985), pp. 33–4.

a guarantee for an expressive medium [cinema], which seeks prestige among the most educated classes."[8] The potential of cinema to become literature's new "printing press" – had been discovered.

The most explicit filmic reference/reverence to literature comes in the form of cinematographic adaptations of dramatic works and, above all, novels. The cinema of adaptations, notes Francisco Ayala, introduced literature to the wider field of collective representation.[9] The alliance between the two media and the convergence of their narrative patterns took place for two major reasons: film became a useful instrument to "illustrate, serve, and propagate" literary texts,[10] and was seen as a potential medium for the expression of culture, also as a political, economic, and social arm.[11]

Cinema participates in the culturally significant act of disseminating ideology, which the Marxist philosopher Louis Althusser defines as "the representation of the imaginary relationship of individuals to their real conditions of existence."[12] According to Althusser, the state uses a series of ideological apparatuses to constitute and affirm its legitimacy; among these are culture, including the arts, literature, cinema, and even sports, and the systems of mass media (press, radio, and television). These apparatuses share their status with a series of other institutions, whether political, legal, educational, or religious. In line with these ideas, Mas'Ud Zavarzadeh reinterprets Althusser's theories. In *Seeing Films Politically* he writes that "films [...] do not so much 'report', 'reflect' or even 'interpret' (in the conventional sense of the word) the world 'out there' or 'in there' as they do in fact 'produce' it and produce it historically; that is to say, within the frames of intelligibility available to a culture at a particular moment."[13] In this sense, Zavarzadeh sees cinema as a cultural vehicle "through which the dominant ideology attempts to maintain its authority over the affairs of society [...]"; cinema is also used as a guide to show the viewer "how to recognize, and, above all, 'experience' the real in culture" (p. 77).

The explicit "literaturization" of cinema – the transfer to images of a text that forms part of a literary canon, previously classified as part of an artistic heritage – reinforces cinema's potential to "produce" cultural and ideological

[8] Quoted in Peña-Ardid, *Literatura y cine*, p. 35.

[9] F. Ayala, *El escritor y el cine* (Madrid: Aguilar, 1988), p. 162.

[10] V. Molina Fox, "El mirón literario (el cine de Jean Genet, Samuel Beckett y Eugene Ionesco)," *Revista de Occidente* 40 (September 1984), p. 34.

[11] J. Urrutia, *Imago Litterae/Cine. Literatura* (Seville: Ediciones Alfar, 1984), p. 17.

[12] L. Althusser, "Ideology and Ideological State Apparatuses," in *Lenin and Philosophy and Other Essays*, tr. Ben Brewster (New York: Monthly Review Press, 1971), p. 162.

[13] M. Zavarzadeh, *Seeing Films Politically* (Albany: State University of New York Press, 1991), p. 92.

discourses. Within the Spanish cinematographic context, the adaptation of literature to film operates as a cultural referent enjoined to produce a national identity through the rewriting/reviewing of the past in various historical moments of the twentieth century. The initial moment corresponds to the first decades of official Francoist cinematography, whose goals included the reenactment of the imperial past through the rescue of literary master works and the reification of the concept of Spanishness through traditional popular genres like *sainete* (light musical comedy) and *zarzuela* (traditional Spanish operetta). In the 1940s, coexisting with historical, folkloric, and religious dramas, literary texts identified with imperial splendor and the Spanish tradition were adapted to film, as were texts by authors whose political proximity to the regime garnered respect (e.g. Blasco Ibáñez, Pedro Antonio de Alarcón, José María Pemán, Armando Palacio Valdés, Jacinto Benavente, and the Álvarez Quintero brothers).[14]

In 1942 the playwright Joaquín Álvarez Quintero, a faithful representative of the precepts of the Francoist regime, declared to the magazine *Primer Plano* (an ideological tool of the Falange) that the "rising" (*naciente*) and "stammering" (*balbuceante*) new art would only triumph if it drew support from what was exclusive and essential to the race: "our way of feeling, our idiosyncracy, our accent, our nationality, rich and picturesque [...] our Spanishness!"[15] Urrutia points out that such attitudes caused the "literary" cinema of the immediate post-war period to draw largely on the Andalusian-flavored dramatic works by the Álvarez Quintero brothers; between 1939 and 1957, nineteen filmic adaptations of works by these playwrights were made (*Imago Litterae*, pp. 25–6). With the help of the theater, especially the national genres of *zarzuela* and *sainete*, the cinema of the 1940s appropriated certain defining elements: "recognizability" (*reconocibilidad*), produced through the cultivation of *costumbrismo* or the picturesque, and "unlikeliness" (*inverosimilitud*), a quality involved in figuring spaces, characters, and situations. Through the effects of "unlikeliness," playwrights sought to manipulate an audience, promoting a kind of escapism from the social and political reality of post-war Spain.[16]

14 See, for example, S. Zunzunegui, "El cine español en la época del socialismo," in *Cuatro años de cine español (1983–1986)*, ed. Francisco Llinás, IMAGFIC VIII (Festival de cine de Madrid: Discrefilm, 1987), p. 179; also the films of Rafael Gil: *Don Quijote de la Mancha* (1947); *El clavo* (1944), and *La pródiga* (1946), based on texts by Alarcón; *La fe* (1947), an adaptation of a text by Palacio Valdés; and *El fantasma de Doña Juanita* (1944), an adaptation of a text by José María Pemán (J. E. Monterde, *Veinte años de cine (1973–1992). Un cine bajo paradoja* [Barcelona: Paidós, 1993], pp. 225–6).

15 Cited in Urrutia, *Imago Litterae/Cine*, p. 23.

16 Ibid., p. 27; Álvaro del Amo, *Comedia cinematográfica española* (Madrid: Cuadernos para el diálogo, 1975), p. 18.

A second moment of political and cultural reconstruction of the nation, styled as an ideological inversion of the Francoist initiative of the 1940s and 1950s, occurs during the years of the transition to democracy (1975–82). This movement maintains its hegemony in the socialist period (1982–95), primarily in the 1980s. From 1982 on, socialist policy generated a system of protection for the cinema. This system sustained the anti-Francoist policy initiated in the transition, and attempted to readjust production via certain criteria related to the questions of quality and competitiveness.[17]

In order to promote cultural patronage and regenerate the cinematographic industry, Pilar Miró was placed in charge of promulgating a new law that supported Spanish cinema. This "Miró Law" put into practice a series of measures that included the following: the creation of a system of subsidies comparable to those of other European countries; strict government control of coproductions; the creation of categories to control the quality of the product; promotion of films in international festivals and the consolidation of relations between the cinematographic industry and Televisión Española, which brought about the showing of Spanish films on television. This system of subsidies, maintained throughout the socialist period, sustained a political ideology that considered cinema fundamental to the nation's cultural development; thus protection by the state was absolutely necessary. As John Hopewell points out in the Spanish edition of *Out of the Past*, "if heritage is in danger it must be protected," and such protection is a political issue: "If Spaniards consider the ostentatious practice of recreational activities to be the decisive aspect of their lives, to provide for such activities with similar ostentation has to become the decisive aspect of the political practice of a party. A cinema directed by the state is a noticeable announcement of a State directed by a party."[18] This notion received immediate support from institutions of regional governments, which began to subsidize a large percentage of all the films produced in their regions with themes related to their culture, and which incorporated autochthonous language and local actors. Nevertheless, the critics of the Miró Law alleged that the system of subsidies favored the production of a cinema that turned its back on the spectators. The law was criticized for cultural elitism and excessive protectionism, for raising the cost of productions without assuring box-office results, fomenting inefficiency, favoritism, and lack of interest in market strategies, all of which led Pilar Miró to resign from her position in 1985; however, she had installed a system that for the first time promoted the quality of the national

[17] Monterde, *Veinte años de cine*, p. 101.

[18] J. Hopewell, *El cine español después de Franco* (Madrid: El Arquero, 1989), p. 400. Originally published as *Out of the Past. Spanish Cinema after Franco* (London: British Film Institute, 1986).

film industry.[19] According to Peter Besas, with the goal of raising cinematographic quality, support was directed toward those firms considered "artistic" to the detriment of those labeled "for entertainment" or "commercial." "In effect," writes Besas, "the Miró Law decimated the ranks of those not within the inner circle of 'serious' production. It lavished money on new 'talent' and on the by-now aging anti-Franco centurions with their penchants for politics, the Spanish Civil War, and 'educating' audiences."[20]

Reinterpreting the historical and cultural heritage became a priority for undoing the secrecy and manipulation of the Francoist past, while making evident the need for the socialist present and its expediency. With ideological and economic aid from the state, cinema began deconstructing the national-Catholic mythology, preparing to rescue myths either forgotten or distorted by the regime. Cinema applied its art to the redefinition of genres, such as historical cinema or the filmic adaptation of literary works, once appropriated by Francoism to aggrandize national values. Cinema also focused on the reevaluation of popular traditions and the reinscription of a cultural identity distanced from stereotypes. An important part of this project was the rescue of certain canonical literary texts which, in their day and despite censorship, had exposed the social conditions of those dark years. Thus the two-fold goal involved in the recuperation of culture marked the developing relationship between Spanish cinema and literary texts. Through the patronage of the state, an effort was made, using all the resources at hand, to acculturate a population that had suffered nearly four decades of repression. At the same time there was a desire to lend prestige to a cultural apparatus discredited as much for the mediocrity of the official Francoist commercial product as for the inaccessibility of the independent product, relegated to "art" circles (cinemas of *arte y ensayo*).

Across different genres and periods, the most successful literary adaptations of the 1980s shared two principal motives: an urgent need to make cultural icons out of the works of writers who had been ignored or victimized by the Franco regime, as in the case of poet and playwright Federico García Lorca, and to expose the situation of those defeated in the Civil War who survived the post-war period. These literary adaptations function simultaneously as an historical testimony of Francoism and as a symbolic

[19] See P. Miró, "Ten Years of Spanish Cinema," in *Literature, the Arts, and Democracy. Spain in the Eighties*, tr. Alma Amell, ed. Samuel Amell (London and Toronto: Associated University Presses, 1990), pp. 38–46, and J. Hopewell, "'Art and Lack of Money': the Crises of the Spanish Film Industry, 1977–1990," *Quarterly Review of Film and Video* 13:4 (1991), pp. 113–22.

[20] P. Besas, "The Finance Structure of Spanish Cinema," in *Refiguring Spain. Cinema / Media. Representation*, ed. Marsha Kinder (Durham, NC: Duke University Press, 1997), p. 247.

discourse of post-Francoism. Some of the most successful are adaptations of García Lorca's dramas – *Bodas de sangre* ('Blood Wedding', 1981) by Carlos Saura and *La casa de Bernarda Alba* ('The House of Bernarda Alba', 1987) by Mario Camús; adaptations of Camilo José Cela's social novels – *Pascual Duarte* (1979) by Ricardo Franco and *La colmena* ('The Hive', 1982) by Mario Camús; *Tiempo de silencio* (*Time* of *Silence*, 1986) and *Si te dicen que caí* (*The Fallen*, 1989) by Vicente Aranda, based on the novels by Luis Martín Santos and Juan Marsé, respectively; *La Plaza del Diamante* (*Time of the Doves*, 1982), first released as a four-episode series for Televisión Española and then as a shortened version for the big screen, and *Requiem por un campesino español* (*Requiem for a Spanish Peasant*, 1985), by Francesc Betriu, films based on the novels by Mercè Rodoreda and Ramón J. Sender, respectively; *Los santos inocentes* ('Holy Innocents', 1984) by Mario Camús, based on Miguel Delibes's novel; *Las bicicletas son para el verano* ('Bicycles Are for Summertime', 1983) by Jaime Chávarri, based on the play written by Fernando Fernán Gómez; and *El sur* (*The South*, 1983) by Víctor Erice, based on a story by Adelaida García Morales.

Some film critics and historians criticized the recuperative policy of the socialist government for being excessively formulaic and homogenous, both aesthetically and ideologically. Estève Riambau refers to the socialist cinema as a "polyvalent cinema," designed to achieve several specific goals by means of a series of standard formulas.[21] In the treatment of "rescued" themes and genres John Hopewell finds a certain manicheism that at times reduces and simplifies the history of Spanish cinema to an opposition between Francoist regression and censorship, on the one hand, and socialist ideas of progress and freedom, on the other. Moreover, he writes, "Spanish films (under socialist patronage) steer clear of contemporary problems [unemployment, ETA] and attack, somewhat superficially, the supposedly unequivocal target of Francoism in the past."[22] Santos Zunzunegui, in particular, points to the political servitude and lack of creativity that characterize transpositions into film of the 1980s, comparing these to adaptations carried out in the 1940s. In each case, a film was merely "an operation that consisted of changing names while serving ancient rhetorical discourses" ("El cine español," p. 179).

Leaving aside any judgment about the propagandistic nature of the socialist project of cultural recuperation, I will discuss some of the aforementioned adaptations, selecting films that best represent the fusion of literary text and cinema, culture and ideology; these films today define the canon and

[21] E. Riambau, "La década 'socialista' (1982–1992)," in *Historia del cine español*, ed. Román Gubern *et al.* (Madrid: Cátedra, 1995), p. 421.

[22] Hopewell, *Out of the Past*, p. 241.

cultural identity of that period. Alterations in the text that result from the transposition of one medium to the other constitute a set of strategies for the transmission or suppression of ideological and cultural values. Thus these films exhibit the hagiographic tribute paid to the intellectuals and artists of the Republic who suffered under the Franco regime, epitomized by Federico García Lorca and achieved through adaptations of works such as *Bodas de sangre* (1981), *La casa de Bernarda Alba* (1987), and *El balcón abierto* ('The Open Balcony', 1984). Other features include the adaptation of texts written in the "other languages," once silenced by the Franco regime, which stand as symbols of the cultural resistance of the autonomous regions to the nation-state. *La Plaza del Diamante* (1982) by Betriu is an example. Variations on this theme include pedagogically minded popularizations of experimental narrative through films intended to "acculturate" audiences by making the original text easier to understand; this is a trend that finds expression in Aranda's version of *Tiempo de silencio* (1986). These are strategies that promote a new reading of the literary text in light of the optimistic impulses of the socialist era. Another notable example is *Los santos inocentes* (1984) by Camús.

Federico García Lorca's recovery and reevaluation of traditional forms of popular culture in music and in verse, as well as the incorporation of these to his own poetic and dramatic art, had profiled him as a pivotal figure in the 1920s and 1930s. His work had to be recognized by the socialist government, now aspiring to continue the cultural projects initiated by the Republic and to return Spain to its proper place within the international sphere. In 1922 Lorca had collaborated with Manuel de Falla in the organization of a Festival of *Cante Jondo*. Their objective was, in Lorca's own words, "to save the *cante jondo* [flamenco 'deep song'] from the trash of *cuplés* [Spanish variety song] and *flamenquerías* [clichéd flamenco styles]"[23] and to destroy the stereotypical concept of *la españolada*, the false image of Spanish culture.[24] The *cuplé* and the *flamenquería* to which Lorca refers made their appearance later in the cinema of the Republic. The genre of the "españolada," already developed by directors such as Florián Rey, Benito Perojo, Edgar Neville, and Saénz de Heredia, reached its apogee in the official Francoist cinema that proliferated in the 1950s and 1960s. This genre represented an ideology characterized by folkloric reductionism, xenophobic nationalism, anti-feminist

[23] This sentence by Lorca comes from the paper he read in 1922 at the Artistic Center of Granada: "The Historical and Artistic Importance of the Primitive Andalusian Song Known as *Cante Jondo*," included in *Manuel de Falla y el 'Cante Jondo'*, ed. E. Molina Fajardo (Universidad de Granada, 1962), pp. 117–208.

[24] A. Soria Ortega, "Notas sobre el andalucismo de Lorca," in *Valoración actual de la obra de García Lorca* (Madrid: Universidad Complutense, 1988), pp. 195–6.

machismo, and ultra-conservative religious views.[25] As a representative of the extensive project of socialist cultural recuperation and with the same objective of saving Spanish cultural identity from stereotype, Carlos Saura first rescued three of the classics that had been, in one way or another, associated with Spanishness – Lorca's *Bodas de sangre*, *Carmen*, by Merimée or by Bizet, and Manuel de Falla's ballet *El amor brujo* ('Love the Magician') – reinterpreting them within the tradition of flamenco. Later Saura recovered classical and popular forms of flamenco from the cultural ghetto of the *españolada* and from the touristic *tablao*-style show in the subsequent films *Sevillanas* and *Flamenco*, produced in the 1990s.[26]

The project of dignifying flamenco and stylizing popular elements began in 1981 with the adaptation of *Bodas de sangre*, produced in cooperation with Antonio Gades, dancer and director of the Spanish National Ballet. The originality of Saura's film resides in its condition as a double adaptation of Lorca's work, carried out through two representations: Gades's choreography for his own dance company and a simulated general rehearsal filmed by Saura in the dance studio. To emphasize the documentary quality of the film and its nature as a work in progress, Saura introduces the performance with prior images of dressing rooms where dancers get ready and talk about their origins and artistic careers. This strategy shows a social commitment to the art of flamenco musicians and dancers, generally gypsies, an ethnic group that had experienced racial and social discrimination in Spain. In this way Saura continued the work begun by Lorca.

Saura's *Bodas de sangre* achieves the dramatic tension of Lorca's work through a fusion of choreography and cinematographic technique. The cinematographic medium serves dance: it adjusts to the dancers' steps, captures their gestures and expressions in close-ups, and creates contrasts between their movements and pauses.[27] For example, in the wedding dance the technique of the classic shot/reverse shot captures the sexual desire of the bride and Leonardo and the impossibility of expressing that desire openly.[28] At the same time, Gades's choreography adjusts itself to the cinematographic medium.[29] In the final duel between Leonardo and the groom, music is

[25] R. Gubern, *El cine sonoro en la II República (1929–36)* (Barcelona: Lumen, 1977), pp. 126–7.

[26] B. Jordan and R. Morgan-Tamosunas, *Contemporary Spanish Cinema* (Manchester University Press, 1998), p. 28.

[27] A. Sánchez Vidal, "*Bodas de sangre*," *El Cine de Carlos Saura* (Zaragoza: Caja de Ahorros de la Inmaculada, 1988), p. 157.

[28] Most commonly used for dialogue, shot/reverse angle-shot (shot/counter-shot) is a set of two alternative shots, generally in a medium close-up (frames a character from the waist, hips, or knees, up or down), that frame in turn the two speakers.

[29] Vidal, "*Bodas de sangre*," p. 155.

eliminated and dancers simulate slow motion with their steps and symmetrical movements, thus recognizing and incorporating into their representation the technical elements of the medium used to take the performance to completion. Gades and Saura eliminate language but provide Lorquian rituals and rhythms via flamenco and the cinematographic set.[30]

In 1987 Mario Camús completed the filmic adaptation of *La casa de Bernarda Alba* with a sober, realist production that established once again the connection between Lorca's work and flamenco. This connection reflected the commitment of the socialist government to the celebration of cultural heritage, emphasizing, above all, the allegorical tone of the house and the mother figure, symbolic foreshadowers of Spain under the authoritarian regimen of the dictatorship. María Dolores Perea notes that the adaptation is framed by *cante jondo* music, which announces and closes the pathos of the drama with its wrenching cry.[31] The film establishes a greater visual and auditory contrast between the masculine exterior (luminous and noisy) and the feminine interior (dark and silent) via the staging and the movement of a camera that breaks the boundaries of the theatre stage and moves freely through rooms and garden, church and streets, reinforcing the sensation of enclosure.[32]

Paul Julian Smith finds that Camús's adaptation maintains academic rigor but neglects to incorporate the most avant-garde and lyrical aspects of Lorca's work, choosing a purely documentary setting and placing dramatic emphasis on the authoritarianism of the mother:

> Camus's film lacks almost completely the spiralling dramatic intensity of García Lorca's original [...]. It is a style typical of Camus's literary adaptations, a style promoted as exemplary by Pilar Miró [...]. The hidden history of Camus's *Bernarda Alba* is that of a Socialist government which sponsored a cinema intended to mirror its own consensus politics, a cinema specializing in adaptations of literary classics with unimpeachable anti-authoritarian credentials [...]. The glossy production values of Camus's *Bernarda Alba* are thus not merely the result of an individual director's artistic temperament, they also betray the ideological commitment of the Spanish government to the celebration of a certain cultural heritage.[33]

30 See also Marvin D'Lugo's analysis of the film in his book *The Films of Carlos Saura. The Practice of Seeing* (Princeton University Press, 1991), pp. 193–201.

31 M. D. Perea Barberá, "*La casa de Bernarda Alba*: Lorca y Camús," *Anuario de Cine y Literatura en Español* 1 (1995), p. 85.

32 Perea Barberá, "*La casa de Bernarda Alba*," p. 95.

33 P. J. Smith, "García Lorca / Almodóvar: Gender, Nationality and the Limits of the Visible," in *Vision Machines. Cinema, Literature and Sexuality in Spain and Cuba, 1983–1993* (London and New York: Verso, 1996), pp. 24–5.

In 1989 Jaime Camino, who had achieved great success and recognition for *La vieja memoria* ('The Old Memory', 1977), a documentary about the Republic and the Civil War, endeavored to find a visual equivalent for Lorca's poetic images in *El balcón abierto*. Years later Frédéric Amat achieved this goal in his artistic adaptation of Lorca's cinematographic script *Viaje a la luna* ('Journey to the Moon', 1998). *El balcón abierto* is a visual, lyrical exercise whose narrative is made up entirely of Lorca's texts: letters, essays, poems, and excerpts from some of his dramatic works. It can be considered an example of the film-poetry that Lorca envisioned in his script of *Viaje a la luna*, of what Buñuel sought in his surrealist collaborations with Salvador Dalí or to what Buñuel referred when he defended a poetic film that did more than "repeat stories." Similarly, Camino's film reproduces and illustrates Lorquian texts visually via the following techniques and materials: linking dislocated images that bear a surrealist stamp; emphasizing the presence and repetition of certain symbols, such as the horse, which are central to the Lorquian vision; incorporating excerpts from performances of plays like *Bodas de sangre* and *La casa de Bernarda Alba*, combining them with archival images of the period; using documentaries of the cityscape of New York and of the lives of underprivileged peoples; and the obligatory dramatization of the poet's murder in a ravine in Víznar.

However, Camino's film does not evade the didacticism characteristic of cinematic production during the socialist period. That didacticism became an accomplice to Lorca's own pedagogical project. Camino's visual exercise is framed within the context of a school in which students are preparing a homage to the poet. Among other activities, including cut-outs of photographs, conversations about the poet, a theatre performance, and a puppet show, the students see Jaime Camino's film, which inevitably begins and ends with the reproduction of Lorca's murder. Cinematic adaptations of García Lorca's life and work have been, and are, inseparable from pedagogical projects and commemorative events, emerging inextricably linked to the context of flamenco. Lorca's premature death made his life and works into icons of artistic, political, and sexual freedom. These iconic, didactic, and allegorical visions have prevailed up to the recent centenary (1998) of his birth.

From the first years of the transition to democracy, film played an important role in the process of recovering Catalan as well as other autochtonous languages, Basque and Galician, within the public space of the media. As a result, the screening of films made by Catalans, with Catalan themes, and/or spoken in Catalan became true political demonstrations. Some of the key titles of this first moment of nationalist restoration were the following: *La ciutat cremada* ('The City Burned', 1976), by Antoni Ribas; *Companys, procés a*

Catalunya ('Companys, Catalonia on Trial', 1979), by Josep Maria Forn, and *La Plaza del Diamante* (1982) by Francesc Betriu.

Betriu's adaptation of Rodoreda's novel exemplifies the fusion of the main cultural apparatuses in the multicultural definition of the socialist nation (literature, film, and television)[34] and of two social segments, women and Catalan linguistic and cultural autonomy, formerly marginalized by the unidimensional Francoist vision. Both segments were used to defend nationalist restoration. The alienation and the physical and linguistic oppression suffered by Natalia, the main character of the novel, become metaphors for Catalonia's alienation; the survival story of the former becomes an epic tale of the survival of the latter. Natalia's inability to express herself, manifested in the novel through the repetition of phrases like "I couldn't complain," "I couldn't tell him,"[35] metaphorically expresses in the film Catalonia's enforced silence. Natalia's final cry in the Plaza del Diamante is interpreted in the novel as a failed attempt at expression on the part of the female voice suffocated for years by patriarchal repression, while in the film it also expresses a lament for Catalan culture, silenced during forty years of political repression.

The film reinforces visually the political/nationalist symbolism of the novel. In the novel the pigeons represent Natalia's oppression. Like her, they live as prisoners in the dovecote built by Quimet, Natalia's husband, who calls her Colometa ('little pigeon'). The obsessive burden that the pigeons represent for Natalia in the novel is diminished in the film. Nonetheless the birds emphasize the symbolic nature of the oppression of the Catalan people, established in the novel by gesture – Quimet frees them on the day of the proclamation of the Second Republic – and by analogy: the birds are enclosed and sacrificed as was Quimet during the Civil War. According to the political reading favored by the film, the doves symbolize Catalonia's position within Republican Spain, invaded by Franco's nationalist forces.

As Juan Company notes, in Betriu's film the step from the individual to the collective is taken via a "metonymic figuration" so that "the most ideologically restorative aspects of the literary original [are made to] emerge."[36]

[34] The project for *La Plaza del Diamante* was chosen in a competition for best scripts, sponsored by Radio Televisión Española in 1979; it was made first for television in a four-hour series filmed entirely in Catalan, and was adapted later to a cinematographic version dubbed in Spanish by the same actors.

[35] See the chapter on *La Plaza del Diamante* in P. Rodríguez, *Vidas Im/Propias. Transformaciones del sujeto femenino en la narrativa española contemporánea* (West Lafayette: Purdue University Press, 2000).

[36] J. M. Company, "Variaciones sobre un oso de juguete (*La plaça del diamant*)," *Contracampo* 30 (August/September 1982), pp. 18, 19.

To that end, the film visually develops historical episodes and typical scenes of Catalonia, either absent or insignificantly portrayed in the novel. Some examples are the reactions of joy or hopelessness at the elections, the proclamation of the Republic, and the start of the Civil War (the front, the sirens, the bombardments, the refugees), as well as the representations of Catalonian high or popular culture (Gaudí's architecture in scenes filmed in Guell Park and the popular festivals with *sardana* music, *castellers* (human towers), and *gigantes* y *cabezudos* (elaborate giants and costumed "big-heads").[37] The film version of *La Plaza del Diamante* failed to convince members of feminist circles and certain nationalist sectors because of its emphasis on cultural restoration. Ultimately, the film diminishes the initiative of the female protagonist and uses the novel for what some critics see as an opportunistic, provincial, and utilitarian aim.[38]

Since one of the objectives of adaptations is to popularize literature not likely to penetrate the social corpus as effectively as cinema, most "literary" films are constructed as realist, documentary, mimetic texts; these tend to turn formal experimentation into conventional formats. In so doing, such films adapt original literary texts to more traditional visual and narrative patterns to facilitate the reception of a political message by a popular audience. This is precisely the case of Vicente Aranda's adaptation of the novel by Martín Santos. The film version of *Tiempo de silencio* favors the novel's neorealistic, existential tone over elements of formal experimentation. The film also eliminates the novel's mythical dimension and intellectual development. Aranda avoids the creation of a filmic language that incorporates such literary strategies as irony, parody, hyperbole, repetition, erudite expressions, neologisms, and interior monologue, so essential to the text of Martín Santos. The film version gives priority to the social context of the

37 Patricia Hart analyzes the details that speak of the oppression, division, and annulment of Natalia's identity in the novel and that are absent in the film: omission of problematic, disagreeable, or ambiguous scenes, and the correction and beautifying of characters and episodes; additions of images with political content; reordering of events; juxtaposition of the voice-over; and images that contradict the implicit message of the voice. See P. Hart, "More Heaven and Less Mud: The Precedence of Catalan Unity over Feminism in Françesc Betruiu's Filmic Vision of Merçé Rodoreda's *La plaça del diamant*," in *The Garden across the Border. Merçé Rodoreda's Fiction*, ed. Kethleen McNerney and Nancy Vosburg (Selingsgrove: Susquehanna University Press, 1994), pp. 42–60. See also P. Rodríguez, "Experiencia, literatura y cine: traducciones y traiciones en *La plaza del diamante*," *Anuario de Cine y Literatura en Español 1* (1995), pp. 111–120, and L. Ball, "El lenguaje de la división y el silencio en Rodoreda," in *Cine Lit. Essays on Peninsular Film and Fiction I*, ed. George Cabello Castellet, Jaime Martí-Olivella and Guy Wood (Portland State University, Oregon State University, Reed College, 1992), 92–8.

38 L. Miñarro Albero, "*La Plaça del diamant*," *Dirigido por 91* (March 1982), pp. 61–2.

novel – existential frustration, social misery, scientific backwardness in research, the weakness of the hero – and employs the novel's Marxist ideology and critique of the social differences that existed in the Madrid of the 1940s. Allegorical readings by critics of the Muecas family and their life in Madrid shanty towns are those that prevail in the film: "Muecas' family stands as a degraded image of the patriarchal authoritarianism of Franco's Spain";[39] "the book presents an allegorical picture of the family of Spain. The country is depicted as an organic community harboring apparently hereditary diseases which are spread across virtually the entire class spectrum, reaching into every national institution and affecting women [...] in a particularly insidious way."[40]

Ironically enough, *Tiempo de silencio* emerged in 1962 as a symptom of the intransigent reaction in intellectual circles against the artistic poverty of mid-century novels, perceived as stuck in social realism. With his novel Martín Santos had denounced his contemporary reality without limiting himself to telling the story; rather he transformed that story into a narrative discourse in which the action is seen from the realm of philosophy and conveyed through irony. While Aranda's film recovers the "socialization" of the literary product, it favors historic implications over discursive function. Aranda's adaptation, whose purpose is principally pedagogical or commercial, must be understood as a simplification of Martín Santos's text.

Los santos inocentes (1981) by Miguel Delibes expressed new narrative tendencies that coincided with political change. Post-modern Spanish literature offers reflections on central, cultural aspects of the country, representing them through an ironic, disenchanted filter. In a way similar to that of cinema, narrative fiction (testimonial novel and memoir) claimed as its own the restorative project of personal and historical memory; it recovered the pleasure of telling stories, of creating fictions. Narrative abandoned the dictatorship of experimental formalism, of the "technical pirouette"[41] that had marked the literature of the previous decade and gave preference to the traditional procedures of realism and to the preponderance of the environment. The projection of the past onto the present, the re-creation of the Spanish Civil War and of Francoism, appear frequently as themes in the historical

39 J. Labanyi, "Fiction as Mask: Tiempo de silencio," in *Myth and History in the Contemporary Spanish Novel* (Cambridge University Press, 1989), p. 71.

40 R. W. Fiddian and P. W. Evans, "*Tiempo de silencio*: 'Los españoles pintados por sí mismos,'" in *Challenges to Authority: Fiction and Film in Contemporary Spain* (London: Támesis, 1988), p. 39.

41 M. Vázquez Montalbán, "La novela española entre el postfranquismo y el postmodernismo," in *La renovation du roman espagnol depuis 1975*, ed. Y. Lissorgues (Toulouse: Presses Universitaires du Mirail, 1991), p. 24.

novel, while signs of identity, the shift in the role of the narrator vis à vis the reader, and oral discourse characterize the memoir.[42]

Delibes's text, written in 1981, returns to a rural and calculatedly timeless space to reproduce feudal hierarchy and the inherent inequities of lord and serf. The narrative mimics the simplicity of speech of the peasants, protagonists of the novel; at the same time, the complexity of a rural lexicon, based on the hunt, shapes a discourse utterly foreign to the majority of readers. The combination of an intensely regional setting, practice, and speech, seen nonetheless as a timeless mode of feudalism, expresses the attitudes of the two social segments represented in the novel, lords and serfs, and the impotence and immobility of the serfs under the dominance of the lords.

Delibes's novel belongs to a realist tradition of "sociological dependence," which, according to Mario Camús, for generations has defined the essence of Spanish literary production and enjoyed the preference of the public. In line with the cultural vision of the socialist era, after the film's premiere Camús declared that, when adapting literature to film, it is appropriate from a sociological and commercial point of view to choose the mode that tells the story of the country: "[C]inema has always achieved great success when it has dealt with Spanish themes or when it has adapted Spanish literary works."[43] Citing the example of *Los santos inocentes*, Camús insisted that "[t]he cinema of today must be related to reality, to a culture, to the knowledge of a country and its people" (p. 41). Favorable critiques and reviews praised the film (as well as the two previous films, *Fortunata y Jacinta* [1979–80], produced for television, and *La colmena* [1982]) for its origins in Spanish "tragedy," "history," and "tradition," also for its connection to "the hidden soul of this country."[44]

The preoccupation with the goal of creating a cinema that tells "Spanish stories" recalls, albeit from a different and more distant ideological perspective, the nationalistic enterprise of the Franco regime; further, as in the case of the other arts, to conceive of cinematographic production as bound to the eternal repetition of certain social and cultural patterns is reductive and produces a paradox: the effort to replace the stereotyping of cinema during the Franco regime with a project of cultural recuperation often results also in stereotypical tendencies. The inclination to reproduce tradition or, more accurately, the cultural clichés associated with Spain as seen from the outside persists into the 1990s, continuing to be the identifying sign that marks

42 See D. Villanueva, "La novela," in *Letras españolas 1976–1986*, ed. A. Amorós *et al.* (Madrid: Castalia, 1987), pp. 19–64.

43 J. Cobos and M. Rubio, "*Cinco horas con Mario*," *Casablanca* 42 (June 1984), p. 43.

44 P. M. Lamet, "*Los santos inocentes*. Gañanes y señoritos," *Reseña 151* (July/August 1984), pp. 29, 30.

every film aspiring to international recognition. Cinema appears incapable of erasing the impress of time-worn cultural clichés. In an article entitled "Lo que se espera de España" ('What is Expected of Spain'), published in 1996, Marvin D'Lugo rightly points out that the Spanish cinematic product that finds itself sustained by certain signs of national identity which for decades have helped create a kind of "black legend" of Spanishness – religious fanaticism, political and social intolerance, sexual repression – is precisely the kind of film that enjoys international acclaim. In D'Lugo's view, this fact applies as much to the filmic creations of Buñuel and Saura in the 1960s and 1970s as to films produced during the transition and socialist periods, such as *Furtivos* ('Poachers', 1975), *Los santos inocentes*, or even the recent films – *Matador* (1986) and *La flor de mi secreto* ('The Flower of My Secret', 1995) by Pedro Almodóvar, the representative par excellence of post-modern Spain. The success of these films is related intrinsically to the capacity of the director for maintaining "the cultural cliché" – a recognizable "familial and physical geography" – and for expressing "particular themes via a rhetoric of Spanishness."[45]

Unquestionably the retrieval of "signs of identity" not only attracted international audiences but also proved essential to the project of redefining the ideological and political character of cultural apparatuses during the socialist period. In this regard, *Los santos inocentes* achieves an almost exemplary status within the socialist political agenda as the film is seen as a politically correct reinterpretation of a dominant cliché: *Los santos inocentes* represents a literary adaptation in the service of historical restoration and social criticism, and as such achieved one of the most sensational successes at the box-office – nationally and internationally – in the entire history of Spanish film.[46]

Camús's film represents a continuation of the novel in two ways: it benefits from the cinematographic strategies inherent in Delibes's text while it complicates and captures the novel's sociological reality. As Patricia Santoro has noted, in many instances Delibes's novel can be read as cinematographic prose. Some features are: beginning and ending *in medias res*; the lack of punctuation; the use of temporal narrative links created to support oral

[45] M. D'Lugo, "Lo que se espera de España," *Academia* 15 (July 1996), p. 44.

[46] John Hopewell, in *El cine español despues de Franco*, views *Los santos inocentes* as the paradigm of a cinematographic policy based on the heritage of anti-Francoism. Nevertheless, he considers the liberal assumption permeating the film to be excessively transparent, and even "dangerously manichean" if compared with certain cinematographic classics by authors from the first stage of anti-Francoism, such as Bardem or Berlanga: "the film reveals socialist cinematography's basic liberal assumption: that repression is foreign to the Spanish people and that once eliminated, these people will reap the fruits of their own goodness," p. 412.

storytelling; a sense of timelessness; and a narrative style that "frequently includes descriptions of facial movements, body gestures, background noises, and voice inflection," similar to those of a film script.[47] Santoro finds that if Camús has based his adaptation upon the novel's own cinematographic character, emphasizing narrative objectivity with pictorial/photographic staging, some of the structural and spatial-temporal changes in the film also facilitate the interpretation of Camús's adaptation as an ideological (as well as artistic) rereading and re-creation of the master text (*Novel into Film*, p. 160).

The film is structured as a retrospective story told from the "present," which is some time in the 1960s. On the screen children appear, freed from the serfdom of the estate; now they are to benefit from the opportunities afforded by emigration to urban centers. Through the juxtaposition of images of the present and flashbacks of past time, the film depicts an exterior world beyond the estate. The novel, in turn, concentrates on the isolation of the estate to which social changes have not yet arrived. The filmic text emphasizes the dichotomies associated with the binomial structure of the lord/serf relationship, focusing on the character of *el señorito* ('mister') Iván in order to create in the spectator an identification with Azarías and thus justify his crime. The novel ends when Azarías murders Iván by hanging him from a tree. Patricia Santoro notes that Ivan "is the embodiment of all that is inherently evil in this pseudo-feudalistic society [...]. His death, therefore, [...] is more strongly advocated [...] by the film whose images have made his deeds more heinous to the viewer" (p. 167).

The film also depicts imaginatively the consequences of Azarías's crime to the family, consequences implied also in the novel: the children have been able to leave the estate and the parents are both punished by being expelled and returned to La Raya (the wretched shack on the outskirts of the estate where they had lived at the beginning of the novel/film), relieved of the burden of the two retarded (innocent) members – la Niña Chica dies and Azarías is placed in a mental institution. Santoro indicates that the role of la Niña Chica and Azarías, in the novel and in the film, is to "point to the retardation of the Spanish nation in relation to the rest of modern Europe" (p. 153). Santoro's view is that this new temporal dimension signifies an optimistic reading of the end of the novel:

> [T]he new, more liberal Spain of the mid-1960s has replaced the traditional, retrogressive ideology of the old Spain with a new set of progressive and more liberal values [...]. [T]he departure of Quirce and Nieves from the estate signifies that Spain's youth has recognized this potential for change. The new

47 P. Santoro, *Novel into Film. The Case of "La familia de Pascual Duarte" and "Los santos inocentes"* (Newark: University of Delaware Press, 1996), pp. 136, 135.

> generation has found its own voice, and it is one that rejects the oppresive social structures that have permanently damaged and closed off hope to their parents' generation. (ibid., p. 175)

The film version is rife with the optimism of the socialist era in deliberate contrast to the pessimism of the novel, a view more suited to the actual social conditions of the time. The view of new possibilities open to youth arises from the context of the economic miracle and the rural exodus of the 1960s; at the same time, this view anticipates the spirit of economic bonanza and political euphoria of the socialist present (1984) in which the film was made. To confine Azarías to a sanatorium robs his action – taking justice into his own hands to eliminate the principal representative of oppression – of its symbolic, revolutionary, and universal value, relegating it to madness.[48] His punishment is much less severe than is appropriate since his "crime was deemed that of an 'innocent' driven to murder by powerful social circumstances that were totally beyond his comprehension."[49]

A symbolic interpretation of this film ending – which undoes the uncertainty marking the end of the novel and depicts isolation for Azarías, degradation for Paco and Régula, and hope for Nieves and Quirce – suggests as well that "Cainite" Spain, of two opposing sides in which revenge and violence are the means for resolving differences, is no longer acceptable in the new, democratic Spain. Azarías's isolation in an asylum (the last thing that Régula would have allowed to happen to her brother in the novel) implies reconciliation. Punishment for his crime is meted out in exchange for the plan that allows the parents to dwell within the margins of the estate and, above all, for the freedom of youth and the betterment of their way of life. The past cannot be modified, once it has been registered in historical records (family photograph, film); the past must be left behind (on the estate/in the sanatorium) so that people may face the present and future with optimism – prospects of betterment for youth in the factory or urban center.

Regarding Camús's adaptation, Santos Zunzunegui denies the efficacy of the cultural vehicle that, in principle, motivated the film adaptations of the socialist years. He finds that these works, which insist on defining themselves as mere faithful reproductions, actually carry out an "implacable chore [...] of cultural deactivation," managing "to bury definitively the original work with the pretext of respecting it" ('El cine español', pp. 180, 181). What

[48] In an interview in *La Révue du Cinéma*, Camús makes clear that for him the most important, and most logical, rebellion is not that of Azarías, but rather that of the young people, who, as of the crime, will no longer live as before (C. De Béchade, "Entretien avec Mario Camus," *La Revue du Cinéma* 401 (January 1985), p. 58.

[49] Santoro, *Novel into Film*, p. 175.

Zunzunegui complains of in the "literary" filmic product is the inability to create a personal vision of a literary work, an inability arising from the goal of achieving homogenization both ideological and aesthetic. We may apply this view to the entire acculturation project of the early years of the socialist period, in which writers and directors espoused the project of reclaiming history according to the new democracy, globally characterized by "lightness" and an end to ideology. Cultural tradition, past and present, faced the challenge of constructing a new image, beginning in 1975 and culminating in 1992. The façade or simulacrum of democratic practice and cultural sophistication, developed programatically during the socialist decade, constitutes an essential element in the re-creation of Spanish cultural identity at the end of the twentieth century.

Since the means to knowledge in our time of post-modernity is the image, cultural and literary transmission becomes inseparable from the media of mass communication – cinema and its domestic reproducers, television and video. Relegating literature to visual representation may be seen as a process that empties culture, for the vision of literary works only reaches the public through the filter of the ideological apparatus in power. As Baudrillard shows, "mediators" (political, intellectual, technical, or operational apparatuses) are used to free the masses from "the obligation of being responsible, of enduring philosophical, moral, and political categories."[50] Mediators, by definition, adapt themselves to the purpose of managing, as Baudrillard says, "by delegation, by procuration, this tedious matter of power and of will, to unburden the masses of this transcendence for their great pleasure and to turn it into a show for their benefit" (*Selected Writings*, p. 216). Thus the general public of the post-Francoist era are progressively turned into voyeurs, spectators of their historical and literary past. Such a public has delegated to the cultural apparatuses of the state the task of choosing, mediating, and "turning into a show" the literary texts that best represent, according to the socialist ideological filter, the darkened Francoist past. For many spectators who did not experience either the war or post-war, the cinema of adaptations (historical or literary) is no longer a case of imitation or reduplication of a real or textual origin. Rather, as Baudrillard points out, cinema represents the visual substitution of the sign for the real or textual itself (p. 167).

Along the same lines, in *La cultura como espectáculo* ('Culture as Spectacle', 1988), Eduardo Subirats notes that in post-modernity, culture is produced as a technological simulacrum whose ultimate consequence is "the production of self-conscious and subjective [and collective] identity as a

50 M. Poster (ed.), *Jean Baudrillard. Selected Writings* (Palo Alto: Stanford University Press, 1988), p. 215.

virtual and fictitious reality: the self as the drama of the person, history as a show performed via the media, the subjective spirit as the unreality of a scenographic fiction."[51] The literary canon produced by and through the media becomes representation (simulacrum), its essence configured for the viewers exclusively through the image. In effect, the successful release of a film adaptation of a literary work is followed by a new edition of the book, which uses a photogram of the film to illustrate the cover and promote the sales of both book and film. The literary entity is replaced by its filmic replica and the reader by the spectator, who reveres this reproduction as the only way of achieving knowledge about reality. The socialist cultural product bears the post-modern stamp; therefore, one way to conceive the reinterpretation of history is necessarily via the filmic/visual mediation and simulation of the literary text.

Guide to further reading

Deveny, Thomas, *Contemporary Spanish Film From Fiction* (Lanham, MD: Scarecrow Press, 1999).

Jordan, Barry and Rikky Morgan-Tamosunas, *Contemporary Spanish Cinema* (Manchester University Press, 1998).

[51] E. Subirats, *La cultura como espectáculo* (México: Fondo de Cultura Económica, 1988), p. 94.

15

TERESA M. VILARÓS

The novel beyond modernity

When we look back at Spanish modern literary historiography it soon becomes evident that Spain's literary corpus as a whole was often and overly conceptualized as "different" in relation to the Western European canon. Inversely, when reviewing Spain's current literary critique on Spanish post-modern production – that is, from 1975 onwards – it is also strikingly evident that what is usually expressed is its "normalcy."

Spain's formerly assigned non-modern literary "difference" as well as its current post-modern "normalcy" cannot be understood as an isolated cultural phenomenon but, rather, as part of a broader constellation. Although profoundly cultural, the process-formation of "Spanish difference" or "Spanish normalcy," as conceptual designators for the non-modern and the post-modern respectively, widely surpasseses the literary. It ultimately relates to Spain's intervention vis à vis the history of capital development – Spain's initial and increasing estrangement from modernity starting with the shift in imperial economic power in the late seventeenth century from the Spanish via the Netherlands to the English and ultimately, to Anglo-America, and its final plunge into the new contemporary post-modern world economy after 1975.

During modernity, Spanish non-modern literary difference should be understood as akin to a political, cultural and economic configuration deeply and unavoidably linked to the realities of Western economic modernization and to its corollary of hegemonic cultural and political dominance. Through the eighteenth century to the 1960s, Spain experienced massive economic stagnation. Isolated from the centers of economic and political power, the period of modernity in Spain is marked by an uneven modernization and industrialization, steaming with social and political turmoil.

Modernity in Spain was a time of distress, a period when the perceived non-modern Spanish difference became the mold in which to shape a set of essentialist virtues symbolically and nostalgically representative of a heroic Spanish national character long gone. Emerging as an almost desperate response to the unfavorable economic and political reality of Spain during the period of Western modernization, heroic national difference was the discourse par excellence of an agonic and obsolete Spanish imperial state. With almost no interruption, and in order to counter the growing relegation of Spain to the margins of modernization, this was the main cultural discourse developed by the ruling aristocratic and military elites during the eighteenth and nineteenth centuries: a claim so pervasive that the literary production of the nineteenth and early twentieth century, mostly featured in the form of essays and novels, could not easily disregard it and to which that production had to respond either in allegiance or in opposition.

Representations of Spanish essentialist and heroic difference took the Imperial Catholic Spain of the sixteenth and seventeenth centuries as its model. It is of no surprise therefore that the dictatorial military regime of General Francisco Franco (1939–75), a period mistakenly characterized as profoundly non-modern for its imitative simulacrum of Imperial Spanish iconography, enthusiastically embraced the essentialist rhetoric and aesthetics of the national/imperial discourse based on Spanish heroic difference. Yet for all of the attacks on the Spanish differential as the non-Modern or anti-modern expression of an equally non-modern site, difference is in fact a wholly modernist construct. It is true that Spanish difference was harshly uttered during modernity as, precisely, its counter-expression; however, even though difference was mostly referred to as a collective heroic self, it was intended as a surrogate representation for each national individual self.

The much-mocked anti-modern Spanish difference in fact falls within the logic of modernity. Fredric Jameson has stressed that it is "a particular experience and ideology of the unique self what would be informing the stylistic practices of classical modernism."[1] That "unique self," in as much as it refers to an ideology or a set of ideologies, is tied to the constellation of singular experiences and practices reflecting a collective hegemonic abstraction termed "the modern Subject." Spanish difference, therefore, as a cultural construct acting as a surrogate for each individual self, is "organically linked to a unique self and private identity" (*The Cultural Turn*, p. 6), a structure described by Jameson as intrinsic to modernist aesthetics.

After the hiatus of the Second Republic (1931–6), which was a brief period in contemporary Spanish history indisputably accepted as modern, and following the economic and cultural backlash at the end of the Spanish Civil War, Franco's regime returned to former discourses on "Spanish heroic difference." However, once again Francoist reappropriation of former

[1] F. Jameson, *The Cultural Turn. Selected Writings on the Postmodern, 1983–1998* (London: Verso, 1998), p. 6.

representations of a heroic collective subject was, no matter how anti-modern or non-modern it seemed to be, very much a modern geopolitical and cultural process. Although it apparently pushed forward a paradoxical "non-Modern" heroic collective subject, Franco's populist cultural politics was investing *de facto* in grand meta-narratives of historical restoration.

The apparent Spanish "non-modern" heroic collective subject was a spectral, but ultimately very modern, grand narrative, a fact that allowed the Spanish social imaginary of the transitional period effectively and expeditiously to move away from its recent past. In consonance with the emerging global post-modern arena, the Spanish social and symbolic imaginary responded to the new economic geopolitical paradigm with the giving away of the meta-narratives of modernity.

Beyond modernity, local narratives of difference needed to be processed anew and the renarrativization of Spain as a decentralized nation began to take flight in a spectacular way. Historians, writers of fiction, and literary critics quickly moved away from the old discourses on Spanish non-modern differences,[2] embracing a global process described by Arif Dirlik as a "repudiation of the metanarratives of modernization."[3] After 1975, Spain became part of a new post-modern arena that renounced the old differentiation between the cultural, the economic, and the political. The novel offered itself as a smooth cultural artifact of mediation: one that could work as an interface between the symbolic and the economic, between the local and the global, between past and present; and, at the end, between the modern and the post-modern.

The new democratic state strove to relocate a significant measure of political power from the center to the periphery.[4] In tune with this, writers wanted to break loose from the historical entanglement created by the conflict between an emerging, new construct of Spanish difference and the spectral politics of the imperial state that had been maintained for so long by the Francoist regime. In a present now located beyond modernity Spain's past had to be re-imagined not as a non-modern burden, but as one of normalcy, beaming with a plethora of potentials that would ultimately lead to its accomplished post-modern reality. It is in that sense that a reconceptualization of nineteenth and twentieth-century Spain as a site of alternate modernity

[2] In the Spanish literary tradition, the term "modern" or "modernist" applied only to the arts, avoiding broader cultural, economic, and political connotations. For example, critics and scholars endowed the term "modernist" with specifically Spanish and Hispanic attributes.

[3] A. Dirlik, "The Global in the Local," in *Global / Local. Cultural Production and the Transnational Imaginary*, ed. Rob Wilson and Wismal Dissanayake (Durham, NC: Duke University Press, 1999), p. 25.

[4] See Michael Keating's article "Minority Nations of Spain and European Integration: A New Framework for Autonomy?" *Journal of Spanish Cultural Studies* 1.1 (2000), pp. 29–42.

took place. A most important strategy, since, as Jo Labanyi and Helen Graham have noted, it allowed for the uncovering of "the complex interaction of cultural, social, and political alternatives which competed in the past," revealing "not a 'single,' homogeneous 'modernity' but many potentials."[5]

The conceptualization of Spain as a historical site of uneven, intermittent, or alternate modernities proved to be the epistemological vehicle in which to navigate the rough waters of the modern Spanish experience of isolation and uniqueness. It enabled writers to deal with those historical tensions stemming, on the one hand, from isolation and, on the other, from counteracting peripheral narratives. At the symbolic level the conceptualization of Spain as a former site of uneven modernity reaffirmed a political, cultural, and economic relocation of Spain within an increasingly unionist Europe. Feeding on what could be called neo-memory, it stimulated and nourished a multiplicity of Spanish companion narratives, to be added without conflict to the Western, European literary and historical canon.

Following the general repudiation of the grand meta-narratives of the past that, according to Dirlik, at the global level "allowed greater visibility to local narratives" ("The Global in the Local," p. 25), in the new Spanish political democratic paradigm novels provided voices that spoke in new ways to the various emergent communities in the Spanish state. As part of the new geocultural and geopolitical system that produced them, novels became active participants in the building of local neohistorical narratives. Novels of the period were cultural artifacts that, functioning in an adaptive mode, were able to negotiate the drastic economic and political changes undergone by Spain at the end of the Francoist regime.

Novels of the democratic state negotiated the rift between the two former, antagonistic constructs of Spanish difference by wiping them out. Emerging as wholly post-modern cultural constructs, they are part and fabric of our present moment, defined by Rob Wilson and Wismal Dissanayake as the period that produces "the dissoluting global and the resisting local."[6] They engaged in the production of neo-historical narratives valid to explain a former "Spanish" history as well as its peripheral counterparts.

As Wilson and Dissanayake observe, within the new world order discourses no longer revolve around "an 'imagined community' of coherent modern identity [shaped] through warfare, religion, blood, patriotic symbology, and language" (*Global / Local*, p. 3). Founded upon this post-modern contract, the new novel turns the formerly confined, local-national binary

[5] Helen Graham and Jo Labanyi, *Spanish Cultural Studies. An Introduction: The Struggle for Modernity* (Oxford University Press, 1995), p. 18.

[6] Wilson and Dissanayake, *Global / Local*, pp. 2–3.

into local-supranational sites. Accordingly, the novel began to function as a kind of mediating interface between history and memory. Occupied with the revision of the nation's past, novels and narratives often argue for "the dissolution and disinvention of '*e pluribus unum narratives*' ['one from many narratives'] of modernity" (p. 3). Against the former modern, totalizing push that sought to convert the plural into one, they now allow us to witness "the rehabilitation, affirmation and renewal" of "local cultural originality" (ibid.) by offering themselves as the post-national – or supranational – sites of the new world order. It is in that sense that these texts become major producers of neo-memory discourses. Neatly following these symbolic processes, and entangled within the new global market economy, the novel of democratic Spain would soon participate in the boom of the neo-historical novel, with works like Miguel Delibes's *El hereje* ('The Heretic', 2000) or Carme Riera's *Dins el darer blau* ('Beyond the Last Blue', 1996) as two among many examples.

Interpreting the cultural logic of post-modernism that emerged during the mid-1970s and early 1980s, according to Jameson, "the end of individualism as such" (*The Cultural Turn*, p. 6) becomes a new factor. In the post-modern period, then, literature, like other cultural products, became involved in processes of de-subjectivization and de-historicization, processes that would ultimately make possible the abandonment of the "Spanish differential" construct. After the death of General Francisco Franco, Spain moved beyond its own particular ideology of difference and national uniqueness. Thus after 1975, especially during the transitional period (1975–82), the processes of de-historicization and de-subjectivization dominated literary and cultural discourses. What writers and artists enacted and celebrated was not only the reality of the dictator's death, signaling the end of his regime, but also, in symbolic ways, the death of an iconic representation of the Spanish people as a distinctive subject, one linked to the military dictatorship. As resurgent capitalism accelerated the tendency toward de-subjectivization on the global stage, in Spain the dynamic interplay between de-historization and de-subjectivization may be interpreted as the local performance of a world-wide phenomenon.

Today however, even though the death of individualism – the modern subject, so defined – continues to permeate cultural and literary spheres, the former concept of Spanish difference pervasively and stubbornly bespeaks still an essentialist construct of identity. As Elena Delgado observes in "Prozaic Fissures," a random compilation of recent writing on contemporary Spain by Spanish intellectuals and scholars from Juan Pablo Fusi to Javier Tusell, from Xavier Rubert de Ventós to Mikel Arzumendi, from Jon Juaristi to Javier Varela, articulates a peculiar dialectic embedded in denial:

"[N]ational difference is not invoked [...] except to negate it [...]. [T]he rhetoric used in the titles [...] to describe the 'Spanish non-problem' is that same [rhetoric] which, according to [Eduardo] Subirats, has been displaced: labyrinths, tragedies, anguish, struggle." Further, "it is somewhat incongruent to devote the majority of their pages to analyzing a problem, which has supposedly been resolved, while relegating the discussion of the Europeanized and normalized status of Spain to the last few pages, in the manner of an epilogue."[7]

The post-modern novel, like the post-modern essay, is also haunted by what could be termed as a writing-in-denial. At the beginning of the political transition from 1975 to 1982, such denial, however, is not immediately present. Many novels appeared in the mode of 'lite' or sub-genre writing, including the enormously successful products delivered by the neo-thriller (Manuel Vázquez Montalbán, Lourdes Ortiz) and the neo-erotica (María Jaén and, later, Almudena Grandes). Romance, detective fiction, adventure, and erotica all seem to put their emphasis on "normalcy." Often offering a vast, de-subjectivized, de-nationalized landscape, they apparently aim at erasing any residue of the old "Spanish difference." The same may be said of many novels published after 1982. Departing from the 'lite' sub-genre novels, they could perhaps still be strategically and safely positioned as late "modernist" fiction: especially Miguel Espinosa's *Tribada. Theologiae Tractatus* (1982), but also Antonio Muñoz Molina's *Beatus Ille* (1986), Soledad Puértolas's *Burdeos* (*Bordeaux*, 1986), Jesús Ferrero's *Belver-Yin* (1981), and even Rosa Montero's *Amado amo* ('My Dear Boss', 1988). Nevertheless, they, too, reflect the new processes of de-historicization, de-nationalization, and de-subjectivization at work at the global level. They are truly post-modern texts, part and parcel of a process of symbolic and economic de-territorialization.

It is not until the Spanish democratic state is consolidated and the political sites of the peripheral nationalities are negotiated in the mid-1980s that we find a new textual tension in the novel that also refers to this writing-in-denial. The peripheral novel will depict "the convergence of predicament and promise introduced by all things local in the postmodern, globalized age."[8] However, the novels of the new post-nationalist sites also voice awareness of a precarious equilibrium vis à vis the global capitalist map. They show

7 E. Delgado, "Prozaic Fissures," paper read at the conference "Brokering Spanish Postnational Culture: Globalization, Critical Regionalism, and the Role of the Intellectual," Duke University, November 1999. Forthcoming in the *Arizona Journal of Hispanic Cultural Studies*, 2003.3.

8 G. Arrighi, B. J. Silver, and Iftikhar Ahmad, *Chaos and Governance in the Modern Worker System* (Minneapolis: University of Minnesota Press, 1999), p. 1.

both renewed local strength and vulnerability, being very much aware that, as Dirlik says, "from the perspective of global capitalism" the local can become "a site not of liberation but of manipulation" ("The Global in the Local," p. 10). In this sense, many of the peripheral novels can be thought of as *textos de la raya* ("borderline texts"), as Cristina Moreiras-Menor suggests in her reading of "Arraianos," a short story by Xosé Lluis Méndez-Ferrín.[9] Bernardo Atxaga's seminal novel *Obabakoak* (1988) as well as Manuel Rivas's short stories, Souso de Toro's *Tic Tac* (1993) and *Calzados Lola* ('Lola's Shoe Store', 1998), Luisa Castro's *El somier* ('Bedsprings', 1990) or Quim Monzó's *Vuitante-sis contes* ('Twenty-Six or So Stories', 1999), among many others, are also examples of *textos rayados* – scarred texts that show how their locality has been, in Dirlik's words, "worked over by modernity" (p. 35).

Not only the peripheral novel of the period can be conceptualized as *textos rayados*. Many novels kept arising in the mid-1980s in a "spectacular" mode. Entangled in the post-modern logic that does not differentiate between market and culture, they can also, however, be conceptualized as a marked, scarred corpus. They were the spectacular 'lites', massively successful in the new market of mass consumption. Yet an encrypted discourse comes into play in them. Emerging as new post-modern urban narratives, they offer themselves as a tensed, and often violent, spectacle implicated in the negation of difference. In most of the new urban (or, better, post-urban) spectacular "lite" novels of the period, an unexpected spectral negativity is often at stake. In many of the novels published between the mid-1980s and mid-1990s (by Lucía Extebarria, Ray Loriga, and Juan Manuel Mañas, among others), a shadowy struggle violently disrupts the newly constructed post-modern narrative of "normalcy." Performing in the negative, these novels point to the fissures and ripples appearing in the seemingly harmonious relation between Spain's new collective image of itself as a cosmopolitan nation, and an image of Europe as a whole, coherent community.[10] On the one hand, the strong negation of difference detected in the post-modern Spanish novel

[9] X. L. Méndez-Ferrín, "Medias azules" ('Blue Stockings'), in *Arraianos*, tr. Luisa Castro (Barcelona: Ronsel, 1991); Cristina Moreiras-Menor, "Arraianos: Notas para una arqueología posnacional," paper read at the conference "Brokering Spanish Postnational Culture." Forthcoming in the *Arizona Journal of Hispanic Cultural Studies*, 2003.3.

[10] The majority of post-national narratives followed the non-revolutionary, emancipatory mode articulated by Gianni Vattimo a decade later in his introduction to the Spanish edition of his seminal book *La sociedad transparente* (Barcelona: Ediciones Paidós. ICE de la Universidad de Barcelona, 1990). We have to note, however, after 1978 the unresolved articulation of the Basque Country within the new democratic state. See, for example, Begoña Aretxagas's article "Playing Terrorist: Ghastly Plots and Ghostly States," *Journal of Spanish Cultural Studies* 1.1 (2000), pp. 43–58.

signals a developing awareness that Spain, as a nation, is not geopolitically located on the margin; on the contrary, it stands integrated within the European Union, a hegemonic site of the world system. On the other, however, a special tension arises: 'Lite' fiction persists in negating the experience of isolation and difference that had marked Spanish culture for centuries; and yet, in so doing, this negation has somehow kept difference alive, albeit in an encrypted form, while at the same time such fiction detaches itself from negativity by embracing the concept of the spectacular. Writing that goes "beyond modernity" – that is, fiction published in the 1970s and 1980s – participates in what the French theorist Guy Débord defines as "the society of the spectacle."[11] Cristina Moreiras-Menor explains how, after 1975, "Spain unreservedly embraces the culture of spectacle, while focusing on a de-historicized present. In an ideological move to eliminate a past that situated Spain in a position of inferiority with respect to the rest of the world, new models of identification – signs of identity – are adopted for the newly established democracy."[12]

At the same time, however, in post-modern Spanish fiction significant qualitative differences arise in the various modes of denial that materialize through the development of the spectacular. As we have seen, since 1975 the Spanish essay has continued to struggle – in a still-in-mourning mode – with the experience of "difference." Although spectacle informs its melancholy, the essay wavers between an empty site or a sense of emptiness of place, bound up with an invocation of normalcy and a recurrent negation of difference. Conversely, we find no mourning, no melancholia in novels of the mid-1980s and 1990s, which engage in the spectacular in an entirely different way.

In a dazzlingly 'lite' mode, the novel showers the reader with a kaleidoscopic spectrum of de-subjectivization, recording what was lived intensely during and after the years of the transitional period. As narrated, this experience evolves within the mechanism of the "double-take" common to cinema: while texts remain partly haunted by the Francoist ideology of Spanish difference, they also express the current global ideology of de-subjectivization more appropriate to a post-modern, corporate state than to a modern nation-state.[13]

[11] G. Débord, *The Society of the Spectacle* (New York: Zone Books, 1995).

[12] C. Moreiras-Menor, "Spectacle, Trauma and Violence in Contemporary Spain," in *Contemporary Spanish Cultural Studies*, ed. Barry Jordan and Rikki Morgan-Tamosunas (London: Arnold Publishers, 2000), p. 135.

[13] Michael Hardt and Toni Negri have recently defined the sovereignty of a new globalized corporate state as a new Empire, "composed of a series of national and supranational organisms united under a single logic of rule": *Empire* (Cambridge, MA/London: Harvard University Press, 2000), p. xii.

In retrospect, we see that after Franco's death the post-modern novel intuitively grasped the spectacle produced by new global powers. In various ways, texts registered the paradigmatic cultural/political/economic de-differentiation that was already taking place in Spanish culture as one of the new sites of the post-modern paradigm. That mode contrasts with the social realist novel of the pre-democratic era (1939–75), texts structured and sustained by a social imaginary based on subject-difference.[14] Once this collective perception of difference had been erased, traces of "Spanish national difference" dissolved into the concept of European/global "de-differentiation." The heavy burden of "national" difference, emblematic of highly politicized social realist novels and lowbrow literature, suddenly mutated into a spectacular mode of writing set in local venues.

After the demise of the social realist novel, the spectacular boom of "lite" fiction during the late 1980s and 1990s came quite unexpectedly, especially as it occurred after the cultural cacophony now widely known as *La Movida*, a moment when, ironically enough, the novel itself was being mourned as a dead form. Indeed, the novel of democratic Spain experienced a market expansion of tremendous proportions that today continues to generate huge sales. This boom corresponds to the process of de-differentiation that reflected the political, cultural, and economic developments of the new global paradigm, and writers like Almudena Grandes, Lucía Extebarria, Arturo Pérez-Reverte, and Manuel Vázquez Montalbán found an avid national, as well as international, readership.

However, not all novels, not even all novels authored by a particular writer, work in the same way. Caught between the spectral politics of social realist novels and the erasure of politics initiated by the new paradigm, in post-modern fiction certain novels may be seen as trying to fill empty spaces. These are texts that, like Vázquez Montalbán's early Carvalho series, mask ghostly traces of prior preoccupations still discernible in the wake of the erasure of the historical/political subject. Filling and masking are accomplished through a detached and politically disenchanted point of view. For example, responding to the post-modern paradigm, in Vázquez Montalbán's *Tatuaje* ('Tattoo', 1974), *La soledad del manager* (*The Angst-ridden Executive*, 1977), and *Los mares del sur* (*Southern Seas*, 1979), a triad of novels of the early transitional years, the protagonist Carvalho, acting as a private investigator, explores a cold, non-melancholic contemporary scene. Vázquez Montalbán, with his successful adaptation of the thriller genre to the new

[14] From Camilo José Cela's *La familia de Pascual Duarte* (*The Family of Pascual Duarte*, 1942) to Juan Goytisolo's *Señas de identidad* (*Marks of Identity*, 1966), most novels published during the Franco years belong to social realism. Notable exceptions are the work of the Galician authors Álvaro Cunqueiro and Gonzalo Torrente Ballester.

Spanish concept of the local, communicates what María Paz Balibrea terms "a critical chronicle of the transition" or, more specifically, "what Vázquez Montalbán reconstructs in his early novels is the transformation-capitulation of the left-wing Spanish parliament."[15]

The vanishing of the political and its disenchanted aftermath comes up also in other novels as a nihilist, violent "lite" mode, popular in the 1990s and represented by Ray Loriga's *Días extraños* ('Strange Days', 1994) or by Juan Antonio Mañas's *Historias del Kronen* ('Kronen Stories', 1971). As Cristina Moreiras points out, such novels confirm "the absence of an explicit motivating desire or object" in our times, an absence that prevents "the subject from 'speaking,' or from even producing meaning" ("Spectacle, Trauma and Violence," p. 140). After 1975 the Spanish novel, whether nostalgic for the lost voice or the lost subject, whether coldly detached or even muted, finds itself at the heart of the social structure of a self-reflexive spectacle. In Débord's view, always mediated by the virtual eye, it is a virtual eye itself (*Society of the Spectacle*, p. 10).

The need for re-telling finds, in the post-modern novel, a most appropriate vehicle through which to reimagine and reprocess recent history. The boom of the historical novel exemplifies this trend. Aware of the uncanniness of the Spanish past, novelists of the neohistorical often elect to bypass the gaps and silences caused by Francoist repression, invoking instead a pre-Columbian, pre-national, pre-imperial epoch. From documentary novels to the fiction of pure entertainment, the neohistorical novel aims to establish a historical narrative that would allow for an uninterrupted – invented – positive reading of the Spanish past. This does not mean, as Dirlik has said in another context, that the present "is immune to the burden of the past; only that the burden itself is restructured in the course of the present activity" ("The Global in the Local," p. 39).

This development is not unique to the Spanish novel, nor to a particular field or genre or even to a particular national history. Its claim for re-narrativization is part and parcel of the global post-modern repositioning. As Immanuel Wallerstein has observed, "a civilization refers to a contemporary claim about the past in terms of its use in the present to justify heritage, separateness, rights [and therefore such] claims cannot be located in what happened in the past but in what is happening in the present."[16] Novelists seized upon this proposition, construing it as a tool with which

[15] M. P. Balibrea Enríquez, *En la tierra baldía: Manuel Vázquez Montalbán y la izquierda española en la postmodernidad* (Barcelona: El viejo topo, 1999), pp. 68–9.

[16] I. Wallerstein, *Geopolitics and Geoculture: Essays on the Changing World System* (Cambridge University Press, 1991), p. 236.

to construct a new social imagination. The notion of a past at further removes, which can be reconfigured to mirror obliquely the present, becomes a field in which the enterprise of rewriting history, as one would desire it to have been, is projected, commodified, and disseminated. Impelled by formidable corporate mergers, in which transnational giants took over national publishing houses, the market could now deliver to a voracious reading public the product most desired: the telling anew of past history, stripped of inconvenient historically accurate data. Hence an impressive corpus of 'lite' historical, pseudo-historical, and fictional-historical novels occupied the literary scene. In a work-frenzied melee, the post-modern historical novel now forms a tapestry of texts that aims to placate Spain's desire for hegemony.

It is no coincidence that the boom of the post-modern historical novel began not in the transitional period but after the 1982 elections that ushered in the socialist government of Felipe González. The move toward implementing a solid Spanish European political agenda, accomplished during this regime, incited the development of a pastiche narrative that led to a reformulation of Spanish difference while constructing a new set of de-nationalized virtues. It was then, in politics as well as in the cultural arena at large, that old experiences of difference were recycled and retold in order to create a new (post)national identity, one that could easily become commodified through the existing ideologies of a post-modern global market.

In 1985 Wallerstein pointed to the relations that obtain between national and world identities: "[P]eoples of the modern world have not always been there" and "even less have states always been there" (*Geopolitics*, p. 141). Thus we may understand how, after the death of the dictator, Spain's wish to be European represented a kind of "coming out," articulating a (post) national desire engendered, on the one hand, by Spanish history, and on the other by an exuberance, a kind of desire unlimited, to become a player in global economics and politics. In response to the isolation imposed by the Francoist regime, the transitional period was a time of immense supranational desire, a tsunami that swept away any obstacles standing between desire and its object.[17]

While particular in expression, the Spanish transitional period was one among many geopolitical and geocultural reconfigurations in Europe. From the May 1968 student uprising in Paris to the September 1974 Portuguese

[17] The wave almost crashed on 21 February 1981 in an unsuccessful military coup that sought the restoration of the military dictatorship. Eduardo Mendicutti's *Una mala noche la tiene cualquiera* ('One Hell of a Night', Barbastro: Unali, 1982) offers a hilarious and acid account of that infamous night.

Revolution to the fall of the Berlin Wall in 1989, Europe experienced liberation and economic unification. The phenomena of local re-positioning during the 1970s and 80s, either peaceful as in Spain or traumatic as in the Balkans, were responses to a new global paradigm. This period is characterized by changes so broad that Giovanni Arrighi, Beverly J. Silver, and Iftikhar Ahmad refer to "a sea change of major proportions" (*Chaos and Governance*, p. 1). Eric Hobsbawm designates these years as "decades of universal or global crisis;"[18] and a year before the fall of the Berlin Wall, Immanuel Wallerstein writes: "The 1970s and the 1980s mark the period in which considerable reshuffling – of location of economic activity, of sectoral profitability, of world economic structures – is occurring. The real question, however, is where this reshuffling is going to come out in the 1990's and beyond" (*Geopolitics*, p. 55).

The post-modern Spanish novel is a product of such reshuffling, which opened up new correlations between the symbolic and the real, the cultural and the political. Spectacle informs the correlations – of excess or celebration – that characterize *La Movida*, a youthful phenomenon depicted variously as "lite," "excessive," "unaccountable," and which – precisely in such unaccountability – manifested the destabilizing power of an economic system producing the unexpected surplus that allowed it to flourish in the 1980s. *La Movida* – that effervescent, engorged, popular youth movement generated by spectacle, surplus, and the idiosyncratic moves of a mixed cultural and political upheaval – also signaled major realignments taking place in Europe at the time. "La Movida de la transición" gestures toward the untranslatable underside of the political and economic reshuffling – *movida* – of Spain's transition into the global arena.

If Spain at the end of the Francoist regime engaged in a spectacular reshuffling and re-sifting at all levels, so did literature – and within it, the novel. As a cultural artifact deeply entangled in a global economic, political and cultural web, during the last quarter of the twentieth century Spanish writing reached back and imagined a new cultural lineage. Effectively erasing the former dichotomy established between the modern and the non-modern, it disposed of its national history as a form of repudiation of grand metanarratives. At the end of history, whether a pastiche or a tale of violence, haunted or neo-utopian, global or local, wounded or in a 'lite' mode, the Spanish novel beyond modernity performed as a spectacular site for such re-imagining. A spectacle itself, the novel cleared the way for the new virtual beginning to follow.

[18] E. Hobsbawm, *The Ages of Extremes: A History of the World, 1914–1991* (New York: Pantheon, 1994), p. 9.

Guide to further reading

Brownlow, Jeanne P. and John W. Kronik (eds.), *Intertextual Pursuits: Literary Mediations in Modern Spanish Narrative* (Lewisburg: Bucknell University Press, 1988).

Cruz, Anne J. and Carroll B. Johnson, *Cervantes and his Postmodern Constituencies* (New York: Garland, 1999).

Natoli, Joseph and Linda Hutcheon (eds.), *A Postmodern Reader* (Albany: State University of New York Press, 1993).

Rico, Francisco, *Historia y crítica de la literatura española. Los nuevos nombres: 1975–2000*, ed. Jordi García, vol. 9/1, *Primer suplemento* (Madrid: Crítica, 2000).

Vilarós, Teresa M., *El mono del desencanto. Una crítica parcial de la transición* (Madrid: Siglo Veintiuno, 1998).

16

RANDOLPH D. POPE

Writing about writing

Readers gain a rare and privileged glimpse into the extended, yet implicit, dialogue that all texts possess when writing becomes the object of description, commentary, or meditation in a novel or essay. While commentary by critics and self-reflexive allusions to writing, embedded in the fiction itself, often aspire to the authority of scientific assertions, such reflections form part of complex cultural debates in which good taste, common sense, truth, verisimilitude, and originality are affirmed rather than questioned. As literature evolves, we can easily recognize that the periods of Romanticism and Realism are different; criticism also evolves, reflecting changing cultural perspectives and styles. When Juan Goytisolo writes in *Reivindicación del Conde don Julián* (*Count Julian*, 1970) that "erudition deceives,"[1] he alludes to scientific imperturbability and detachment, a view held by certain critics. Criticism's desire for Olympian stability, demonstrated by Menéndez y Pelayo in the nineteenth century and José Montesinos in the twentieth – each convinced of the propriety of his own values – was seen as opposed to the flux of the novel. In recent decades, concepts steeped in relativity recognize that the vantage point from which we are observing is also in motion and fully engaged with its own time. A close look at how books are represented within novels as well as at the opinions expressed about writing in novels and essays during the modern period will explore this deep commonality between creation and criticism.

The invention of modernity in the late seventeenth and early eighteenth centuries produced a clean break with the past; previous ages had located authority in classical tradition and mythical reiteration. Rousseau, who uncomfortably straddles an aristocratic past and a democratic future, still speaks of the revival of the old, while Condillac, coming later with greater confidence, sees the new period as superior to the past and inferior to the future, the

[1] J. Goytisolo, *Revindicación del conde don Julián*, 2nd edn. (Barcelona: Seix Barral, 1976), p. 26.

characteristic attitude that defines progress. The "new" was produced and marketed during the industrial revolution with the same profusion as mass-produced shoes or machine-made china are today. Spain, however, presents a significant difficulty, since there is little doubt that the first modern novel and one of the most meta-fictional of all times is *Don Quijote*. Cervantes's novel, published in two parts in 1605 and 1615, appeared at a time when Quevedo, Zayas, and Lope were writing texts that still interest us today but which can hardly be called modern. These authors found few imitators in the eighteenth and nineteenth centuries, while Cervantes's traces could be found everywhere. For example, two of the most committed cultivators of personal writing characteristic of the modern are Unamuno and Juan Goytisolo. Both are deeply steeped in Cervantes and many of their most acute meditations about writing are motivated by *Don Quijote*.

Cervantes developed a strategy that consisted in dividing the modern from the obsolete. Cadalso, in his *Cartas marruecas* ('Letters from Morocco'), observed how this attitude had become pervasive and commonplace in eighteenth-century Europe:

> In our present century Europeans have become unbearable in the flattery they heap upon the age in which they were born. If you were to believe them, according to their new chronology, you would say that human nature brought about a prodigious and incredible crisis precisely around the year 1700. Each individual attaches enormous personal vanity to having had many ancestors not only as good as he but much better, and yet a whole generation abhors those that came before. I don't understand it.[2]

Therefore, in reading any text about writing, a reader should be alert to the rhetoric of progress, invoked to push the writing of previous generations into the background. Such rhetoric either declares former authors to be less aware than contemporary readers of the underlying biases and assumptions of texts or considers those authors less sophisticated regarding the problematic issue of representation.

Ortega's *Meditaciones del Quijote* ('Meditations on the *Quijote*', 1914), which occupies a privileged place in reflection about the modern novel, offers a telling example of the rhetoric of progress. His essay includes a denunciation of the period previous to his: "Greatness did not see itself as so; purity hardly struck the heart. The quality of perfection and of the supremely excellent were invisible to those people, like ultraviolet light."[3] The beauty of Ortega's prose cannot hide the unconvincing nature of his sweeping

[2] J. Cadalso, *Cartas marruecas. Noches lúgubres*, ed. J. Arce (Madrid: Cátedra, 1990), p. 90.

[3] J. M. Ortega y Gasset, *Meditaciones del Quijote e Ideas sobre la novela*, 8th edn. (Madrid: Revista de Occidente, 1970), p. 55.

assertion. We may ask: for half a century was it possible that all human beings in a country could have lost their feelings, intelligence, and ambition? And how would a country recover from such collective blindness? We are reading not a statement of fact but a rhetorical erasure of the forefathers meant to increase the stature of present-day culture in Ortega's time. Skipping over several centuries to find a viable and recognizable ancestor is Ortega's way of stressing the novelty of the present, its changed nature amid progress. For Ortega, then, *Don Quijote* is "the first novel in time and in value" (*Meditaciones*, p. 95) in which he finds the congenial whiff of modernity: "Scanning those old pages, [the contemporary reader] finds a modern tone that draws this venerable book closer to our hearts: we feel it to be as close to our most profound sensibilities as Balzac, Dickens, Flaubert, Dostoievsky, makers of the contemporary novel" (ibid.). *Our* sensibility is tacitly opposed to *theirs* – that of our recent ancestors, blind to the light of greatness. This paradox of finding modernity before the modern period cannot be easily dismissed: nineteenth- and twentieth-century novelists learned their most valuable lessons from the *Quijote*, written two centuries earlier. Appropriately, but also symptomatically, the first chapter of the present volume, which deals with the novel from the sixteenth century to the present, is dedicated to Cervantes and the genre of the picaresque novel.

In the *Quijote*, Cervantes created the semblance of the new by incorporating and transforming old genres – novels of chivalry, sentimental and pastoral novels – within his own text. Ironically enough, often he points out the shortcomings of this incorporated literature as he describes the actual life of his readers. Don Quijote, by putting to the test the books he has read, proves in a peculiarly warped and cautious way their inadequacy as guidelines for daily life. The long-lasting discussion about the madness and wisdom of reading books attests to the complexity and ambiguity of literary tradition. Following the *Quijote*, the lesson frequently echoed is that the novel must debunk illusion and offer insight into the real state of society. In a hermeneutical orientation that has its roots in the Enlightenment, *Don Quijote* and later novels celebrated in the canon are highlighted because they convey truth. Their continued use as a pedagogical tool, in our times when humanism often has been declared to be in crisis, is related to this thread of thought: fiction conveys truth even when it shows us how difficult truth is to attain. Novels like Galdós's *La desheredada* (*The Disinherited Lady*, 1881) and Clarín's *La Regenta* ('The Judge's Wife', 1884–5) exploit this interaction of reading and reality, showing us characters led astray by books. These texts write off a whole category of writing, while at the same time, in a literary *trompe l'oeil*, they smuggle in another form of writing – their own – presented as pure transparency. Since the Cervantine lesson has been well learned, savvy readers also become privy to the secret that the author of a realist novel is aware that in fact there exists nothing but writing. In novels like *El amigo Manso* (*Our Friend Manso*, 1882) and *Misericordia* ('Compassion', 1897) Galdós provides the most salient examples of the technique of flaunting illusion in the guise of realism.

The ambiguous relation between authors, texts, and readers can be found at the very beginning of Spain's early, albeit uneven, modernity. An assiduous reviewer, Mariano José de Larra wrote extensively about other writers. He often lamented the servile imitation of the foreign in the form of translations and second-rate adaptations, and the retrograde nature of Madrid's culture. While he could not embrace modernity completely – his pervasive irony bleeds even into his images of progress – he understood the inevitability and the necessity of change. His novel *El doncel de don Enrique el Doliente* ('Henry the Infirm's Page', 1834) begins with an ironic paragraph that expresses his detachment from the nineteenth century's claims of progress:

> Readers are well advised to travel with us to remote ages and centuries in order to live, one might say, in another social order not at all like ours – today's nineteenth century – which marks the most advanced civilization of a sophisticated Europe. Whether living in happy or unhappy times, neither the beauty of our cities nor the ease of communication among people of faraway countries nor the individual security that our up-to-date, enlightened legislation almost guarantees, nor, in sum, that multitude of refined, exquisite necessities – fictional all – enjoined to satisfy our desires could ever convince a Christian man or woman of that bygone era that we pass through this life but once, as dogma teaches, on our way to a better life in another world.[4]

Literature is conceived as a time-machine, and the journey of reading as an instructive experience. The late medieval world, viewed through the Romantic prism, works as a corrosive contrast to the "advanced civilization of a sophisticated Europe." Larra continues his ironic counterpoint by introducing a reference to another sort of writing – legislation – insinuating that it contains a utopian strain that reflects more the expression of wishful thinking than an accurate mapping of the real. His last critical barb against the proliferation of desire generated by commerce and publicity (another form of competitive writing that shared the same page in the newspaper as Larra's reviews) evokes the nostalgic echo of religious dogma and mythic and ritual writing dismantled by the Enlightenment. That his nostalgia is not for the transcendent is soon evident in the novel, concerned with private heroism

[4] M. José de Larra, *Obras completas de Fígaro*, 2nd edn., 2 vols. (Paris: Vve Baudry, Librería Europea, 1857), p. 101.

and worldly love. As much as Larra appears to reverse the wheel of progress, valuing the past over the present, the final madness of one of the protagonists in *El doncel de don Enrique el doliente* shows the world ruled by the medieval sword to be inhospitable.

Nonetheless Larra's novel casts a dubious light upon the values brought about by modern science, transmitted in books of scientific discovery. Don Enrique de Villena, a character based on a historical figure and the villain of the novel, is distinguished by his erudition, for he has dedicated his time to "languages, poetry, history, and the natural sciences" (*El doncel*, p. 115). According to Larra, literature at that time was not highly esteemed: "songs and poems by troubadors served only momentarily to kill boredom during a banquet for ladies and courtiers while a well-handled lance brought down an enemy – in those warring times, there was more to fear from enemies than from boredom" (p. 204). Here Larra expresses a preoccupation about the diminished role of literature in a utilitarian society. He also shows a strong Romantic fascination with heroic deeds, with epic themes more than he does with the quality of the text. In order to emphasize action rather than literariness, he describes a knight who can hardly read, who makes his points with his lance, and who is, therefore, "a man of action [...] who would not have played a bad role in the nineteenth century" (p. 205). Writing in the early nineteenth century carries for Larra a double burden, since the country revels in repetitive and derivative texts. The virtues Larra values – freedom, imagination, feeling – have shriveled away. In a review of a French history of Spanish literature, he expresses his disillusion brilliantly:

> Times and tastes follow one another in rapid succession and people should recall that they were not born only to live a bitter, desiccated reality; daring writers tried to shake off the yoke imposed by instructors; in the end, everyone should find, in politics as in literature, the freedom for which they are born; from this moment on, Spanish literature should arise more radiant than ever before, shining like an immense globe of light, obscured for so long by a thickening mist.[5]

This reinvigorated literature remains only a wish, conceived in terms of *light*, the traditional emblem of the Enlightenment. Yet only a few lines earlier he had criticized the desiccated world of pure reason, which the previous century had seen as a liberating capacity. In his review of a book of poems, Larra wrote these lines, following his assertion that there was no one seriously dedicated to literature in Spain:

[5] M. José de Larra, "Espagne poétique," in *Obras completas de Fígaro*, p. 436.

> These bleak reflections respond to what happens whenever an original, published piece of writing gingerly raises its head among us. It is like a voice crying in the wilderness: no echo ensues, no ear shelters it, no people listen. Only heaps of sand, here today, blown thither tomorrow – and a violent hurricane. Nothing more.
>
> While from time to time some genius shines forth, our literature is only a heap of dead ashes in a brazier wherein a hidden spark still glows, pale and wavering. Our golden age has already passed and our own nineteenth century has hardly arrived.[6]

Whereas in the previous quotation Larra evokes the image of a lantern or beacon, shining over open seas, that image recurs now scaled down as the lowly domestic brazier. The hurricane puffs in vain, shifting aimlessly mountains of sand: time upon time, the weight of a dead tradition. Stranded in a wretched epoch, writing remains a memory and a wish but not a reality. As the title of one of his essays states, "What one cannot say is better left unsaid." For Larra, too many limitations have been placed by official and unofficial censorship, by public apathy, and by the narrow-mindedness of the Spanish intellectual establishment, reluctant to believe that true writing can exist. The Romantic critic sees lack and loss even in what he praises, and invites us to imagine a superior literature, one that is sublime, beyond the limitations of the present age.

Thinking they had responded to Larra's lament, Realists believed they had created at long last a literature for their time. Galdós wrote in 1882 an encomiastic prologue to Pereda's *El sabor de la tierruca* ('The Taste of One's Homeland', 1882) in which he portrays himself in a scene of revelation:

> I met Pereda eleven years ago, when he had written *Escenas montañesas* ['Mountain Scenes'] and *Tipos y paisajes* ['Local Types and Landscapes'] Reading this second collection of picturesque sketches made an intensely lively, indelible impression on me. It felt like the discovery of unknown, unseen regions of which one had not even dreamed. Sensing in myself a modest aptitude for such writing, for the skills to reproduce what was natural, Pereda's marvelous ability to combine truth and fantasy in a vigorous, bewitching style, revealed to me a new direction in narrative art, a direction that later became assured and affirmed, in the end a triumph, in which he [Pereda] who began the process played a major role.[7]

6 M. José de Larra, "Literatura: Poesías de don Juan Bautista Alonso," in *Obras completas de Fígaro*, p. 511.

7 J. María de Pereda, *Obras completas*, 5th edn., 2 vols. (Madrid: Aguilar, 1948), vol. 1, p. 1354.

While Galdós may be politely exaggerating what he owes Pereda, the dramatic scene of reading he presents is unmistakably a foundational myth similar to St. Augustine's conversion: Galdós describes a timid search for a language that could reproduce the landscape and the speech of Spain, a revelation, a change of approach, and the triumphant access to truth. Progress gains the day. Once again, precursors are thrown into the region of the blind. Galdós, like Cervantes, incorporates into his novels all forms of writing that circulated in his time, deploying the same ambiguous strategy. On the one hand, these genres are devalued and shown to be distorted, exaggerated, trivial, and deceitful in comparison to the novel that encompasses them. Once appropriated, however, these "other" kinds of writing reappear transmuted and transformed in the main body of the novel. *Tormento* (*Inferno*, 1884), for example, presents Agustín Caballero, an *indiano* who has made his fortune in America and returns to his native country to construct a house with a library in Madrid, now a city entering the European mainstream. It is the very moment "when the modern capital began to arise above the commonness of its lowly origins as an overgrown village."[8] Along with the comfortable furniture, the large kitchen, the gas lights, Galdós includes "two shelves, one full of books about commerce, the other of books about literature, which set off nicely the display of figurines, for his literary collection consisted entirely of decorative works, as remarkable for their content as for their bindings" (*Tormento*, p. 69). Juxtaposed to the *chinoiserie*, the French decorative objects of Egyptian design, and other proliferations of bourgeois respectable exoticism, the books divide into the useful – commercial texts – and the entertaining – literary texts.

The description of the library and its furnishings is a way of graphically writing about reading. Galdós was, of course, aware of the imbrications between literature and commerce, of the marketability of novels, and the fact that reading involved a money transaction. In the above instance, however, it is rather the collapse into the decorative and frivolous that he laments, creating, in a very Cervantine fashion, an ironic distance that both includes and relegates at the same time. The realist novel takes for granted the fundamental economic underpinnings of society. The fluff of fashion, bric-à-brac, and ostentatious trophies of the well to do, while tenderly described, simultaneously convey the anxious message, tinged with Romantic ambition, that this text, dear reader, that you hold in your hands is, above all, austere, insightful, detached, based as it is upon the disinterestedness of pure science. Writing must be rescued from indifferent consumption and the threat

[8] B. Pérez Galdós, *Obras completas*, 6 vols. (Madrid: Aguilar, 1973), vol. II, p. 68.

of reduction to one more commodity, as had occurred with the delightful and non-nourishing *bodegones* (still life paintings) that enlivened the dining rooms of merchants, bankers, and politicians described in Galdós's novels.

In *Tormento* the wonderfully named Ido del Sagrario is "a former teacher of writing" (p. 984) whose novels do not sell. He is reduced to a sort of *escribidor* – a hack writer – rejected from Parnassus, expelled from the *sagrario* or inner circle (as his name implies), now selling only a few handwritten pages from his latest novel. He pathetically offers these as a model of penmanship. In *Fortunata y Jacinta* Ido reappears, selling from door to door such books as *Mujeres célebres* ('Famous Women'), *Cortesanas célebres* ('Famous Courtesans'), *Hijos del trabajo* ('Sons of Labor'), and similar editorial concoctions aimed at an undiscriminating public. Peering over the shoulders of Juanito Santa Cruz and his wife Jacinta, as they entertain with mixed emotions this demented representative of the fringes of respectable society, the reader immediately understands that what Ido offers is inferior forms of literature, and that the exemplary and fallen women of Galdós's own novel, *Fortunata y Jacinta*, compared to Ido's *Mujeres célebres*, are of a more refined and complex nature – that is, they are more real.

In the late eighteenth century, the notion that had presided over the nature of the novel – that the novel can and should be useful – is simultaneously mocked and reinforced by Galdós and other contemporary authors. Only the right books – their own – map out society and its tangle of emotions. *Madame Bovary* provides the most salient modern example of this strategy that I call *backgrounding and relegation*. As stated earlier, this strategy finds its model in *Don Quijote*. For example, in *Fortunata y Jacinta* we read that Maximiliano Rubín, Fortunata's not-too-bright and cuckholded husband, "devoured *Faust* and Heine's poems."[9] This is a cruel joke: while the reader can perceive how Goethe's drama offers a mirror in which Maximiliano could see his own pact with the devil and the destructive, yet also redeeming, power of love, this perception completely goes over Maximiliano's feverish head. Equally ambiguous is the commentary by Maximiliano's brother, Nicolás Rubín, as he seeks to persuade Fortunata to marry: "Women today let themselves be perverted by novels and by those false ideas about love that other women put into their heads. What bald-faced lies and indecent propaganda Satan makes through the mediation of poets, novelists, and other lazy bums!" (*Fortunata y Jacinta*, p. 649). While the priest Rubín's conclusion – that only spiritual love matters – is proven untenable for Fortunata, the series

[9] Ibid., vol. v, p. 613.

of practical arrangements she will enter into later, counseled by her lover and mentor Feijoo, are also inconceivable in the still-Romantic models of Goethe or Heine. That was then, this is now. Those models are literature, this is life. Just as Cervantes brings in a *canónigo* – a high ranking priest – to show how a novel written according to the standards of the period would be very different from the novel Cervantes himself is writing and we are reading, Galdós also brings in, rather abruptly, a literary critic after Fortunata's burial. Once he hears her story, this critic concludes:

> The high-flown pronouncer of literary works said that [in Fortunata's story] there were, indeed, dramatic or novelesque elements, although, in his opinion, the artistic weave wouldn't turn out to be showy enough without introducing certain strands, which were absolutely necessary for transforming the commonplaces of life into aesthetic material. He couldn't stand the idea that life as it is could be transferred to art without being garnished, seasoned with fragrant spices, and placed on the stove until it had been well cooked. (p. 977)

What matters here, as the critic and his friend come to agree, is not that "raw fruit, well-ripened," is as good a thing as "stewed fruit" but that the whole novel itself be set against a backdrop of other novels less faithful to reality, cooked up with traditional recipes, and therefore not truly contemporary, not representing life *as it really is*.

In *Fortunata y Jacinta*, Galdós affirms that for the character Estupiñá "his library was the social scene, his texts, the lively words of real people" (p. 475). "Reading" – in the opinion of another character, Juanito – "is artificial, borrowed from life; it is an enjoyment that takes place through the mental operation of appropriating the ideas and sensations of others; it is only the acquisition of treasured human truths through purchase or swindle, not from work" (p. 450). Jacinta, we are specifically told, "had no kind of learning. She had read hardly any books" (p. 488). One should not set aside these observations as idle commentary. They go to the core of modernity: truth, reality, democracy, progress, and the sciences endanger the privileged activity of literature, which will have to be reasserted through the claims of art as scientific observation or through art for art's sake. Literature seems threatened, becoming at the same time one more piece of merchandise and a frivolous decoration.

In authors such as Pereda, Valle-Inclán, and Gabriel Miró, who describe the declining grandeur of a landed gentry, the references to books are surrounded by a halo of reverence and nostalgia, with mentions of religious and history books that contain the spirit of a vanishing time. When Fernando, the agnostic anti-hero of Pereda's *De tal palo, tal astilla* ('A Chip Off the Old Block', 1880), arrives to visit the good priest who may help him to recover his faith, thus enabling him to marry his beloved who is fervently religious, the reader is provided with a description of the priest's house that includes "three shelves of books in Latin." The priest "had open on the table the *Flos Sanctorum* and was reading the life of the saint of that day."[10] Instead of reading these ancient books, the fact that Fernando has dabbled in "the roiling seas of [today's] ruling ideas" (p. 1155) is suggested as the reason for his rejection by the town and his subsequent suicide.

This novel of 1880 can easily be seen as Pereda's response to Galdós's *Doña Perfecta* (1876), since these two novels offer clearly diverging views on the same topic, the difficulty of bringing progress to a country mired in traditional ideas. Books carry either the seeds of a healthy growth into modernity or the virus of decay, depending on the reader, but in both cases the importance of these foreign ideas, imported by travel and the circulation of printed matter, is unmistakably stressed. In a vignette included by Pereda in *Tipos trashumantes* ('Transhumant Types') and ironically entitled "Un sabio" ('A Wise Man'), he rails against the nineteenth century, "a legitimate son of the glacial philosophy of the eighteenth century" (p. 1740), and concludes with a warning to his readers:

> This is so, reader: in no other age, since the world has been the world, have such major efforts been made to drag human reason to extremes that reason itself abhors; never has one seen such a heap of nonsense presented as seductive lures – in religion, in philosophy, in politics, while it seems useless to point out that such clusters, differing widely among themselves, coincide on one point: a declared hatred of older institutions and beliefs.[11]

Gabriel Miró, who peppers his texts with Latin words as if they were gold doubloons (an ancient currency no longer in circulation but of high value) describes in *El obispo leproso* ('The Leprous Bishop', 1926), the conversation of a missionary with a group of teachers who praise their own library:

> "Oh, Monseignor! I've had the glory of finding in my hands the *editio princeps*!"
> "Princeps? How fine!"
> "It's Ratdolt's. The edition in roman type, with the *Elementos*, the *Specularia* and *Perspectiva*. The volume *Fenómenos* is lost."
> "What a shame! Books . . ."[12]

This loss and lamentation makes a larger point than the literary gulf between the active missionary and the bookish instructors. It is not clear if the Monseignor laments the missing book or the fact that these teachers have

10 Pereda, *Obras completas*, vol. 1, p. 1554. 11 Ibid., p. 740.
12 G. Miró, *Obras completas*, 2nd edn. (Madrid: Biblioteca Nueva, 1953), p. 1003.

lost their apostolic fervor and become sensuous erudites versed in books that distract from faith. In either case, however, the named texts remain indexes of changing and disquieting times encrusted in the polished modernist surface of Miró's rich prose. In a similar vein, Valle-Inclán, in *Sonata de otoño* (*Autumn Sonata*, 1902) shows his Marqués de Bradomín, the suave seducer and decadent Don Juan, reading the *Florilegio de Nuestra Señora,* a book of sermons written by the bishop who founded the palace where the Marquis now finds himself. The description emphasizes the ancient and protected nature of the library by stressing the inclemency of the outside weather as opposed to the calm that radiates from the books:

> At times, listening to the roar of the wind in the garden and the rustle of dry leaves scattering across the path lined by century-old myrtles would distract my attention. Bare branches brushed against leaden window panes. A monastic quiet invaded the library, a dreamy silence like that of canons engrossed in study. The atmosphere breathed ancient folios bound in parchment, humanist and theological books studied by a Bishop.[13]

This literary cocoon is disrupted by the entrance of Don Juan Manuel, the uncle of the Marquis's lover, who comes in from the outside, drenched by rain, thirsty for good wine, and with plans to affirm the privileges of the family in a forthcoming legal challenge. The following lines could not express more clearly his opinion of reading:

> "Nephew, are you shut up in here, reading? You'll go blind!"
> He approached the hearth and spread his hands toward the flames.
> "It's snowing outside!"
> Then he turned his back to the fire and, drawing himself up before me, he exclaimed in his emblazoned voice of a great lord:
> "Nephew, you've inherited the mania of your grandfather who also spent the days reading. It drove him crazy! . . . And what kind of huge book is that?"
> His sunken, green eyes threw a scornful look at the *Florilegio de Nuestra Señora*.
> He moved away from the fire and paced about the library, spurs clinking.
> (*Sonata de otoño*, p. 69)

The clinking noise seems intended as a reminder that the family did not win its spurs through reading or womanly virtues. Since the Marquis can hardly be considered truly religious, the book he reads, at one time associated with a family legacy of warriors and priests, is now merely an entertainment for the bon-vivant aristocrat as well as an object of derision for the retired soldier

[13] R. del Valle-Inclán, *Sonata de otoño*; *Sonata de invierno*, 20th edn. (Madrid: Espasa Calpe, 1995), p. 68.

Don Juan Manuel. As with most of what is touched by the modern spirit, the split between past and present splinters further into different forms of alienation and loss.

In a slightly different manner, in *Los pazos de Ulloa* (*The House of Ulloa*, 1886), Pardo Bazán also writes about the physical repositories of writing in the old manors of Galicia. The priest Julián is confronted with a ruined library. Its chaotic disorder represents not only the disintegration of the family that owns it but also their incapacity to read any of the volumes. While the priest dusts and arranges these volumes, he chances upon traces of the old splendor:

> All was placed in order now except one shelf of the bookcase; there Julián glimpsed the dark spines, edged in gold, of some ancient volumes. It was the library of an Ulloa from the beginning of the century. Julián stretched forth a hand, grasped a volume at random, opened it, and read the cover... *The Henriad, a Poem in French, Translated into Spanish; the Author, Monsieur Voltaire*. He returned the volume to its place, compressing his lips and lowering his eyes as he always did whenever something hurt or scandalized him; he was not an intolerant person, not at all extreme, but Voltaire... he'd crush him as he would a cockroach. However, he limited himself to condemning the library, not wiping the books with so much as a rag so that termites, worms, and spiders, ambushed everywhere, would find refuge in the smiling Arouet and his enemy Jean-Jacques, who also had slept on peacefully since around 1816.[14]

Few quotations better convey the power attributed to books by conservatives and liberals during the Spanish nineteenth century. Writing could never be simply writing, for it was always an interloper in a vehemently conflictive political life. While Julián looks away and condemns the enlightened library to decay, the reader cannot help but be reminded of the alternative that such books represented to the primitive society of the Ulloa manor house, a primitivism to which a noble family had degenerated. Those insects and worms persecuted by Julián's cleansing zeal find a refuge next to Voltaire and Rousseau. The smiling, sentimental glow of these writers continues to protect the lowest forms. This library is not forgotten in Pardo Bazán's second novel *La madre naturaleza* ('Mother Nature', 1887), centered in the same house. Gabriel Pardo, sophisticated and well read, comes from the city to the manor and searches for some intellectual entertainment in the old library that Julián had abandoned. In Pardo Bazán's view, this library is a splendid emblem of the bleak fortunes of progressive ideas in the Galician region of Spain:

[14] E. Pardo Bazán, *Obras completas*, vol. 1 (Madrid: Aguilar, 1973), p. 178.

> Upon opening the fronted shelves, casements lined with a wire screen instead of glass, a dusty cloud of musty, humid air escaped; ashen-colored termites scattered quickly from their preferred refuge. But, undaunted, he kept on pulling out volumes. Every book opened was a nest of larvae, a network of tunnels bored through by book-loving insects, and the cadaver of the eighteenth century, devoured by worms, arose from the grave.[15]

We already have seen how Larra described writing as a time-machine. Here Pardo Bazán sees books as a tunnel through which the spirit of the past can still become present. Yet in a characteristic strategy of modernity, those same books that are slyly invoked are at the same time shown to be weighed down by their foreignness to the present time, a period adequately described only by the novel in hand.

From a slightly different perspective, Unamuno made a similar point in an essay called "Examen de conciencia" ('Examination of one's conscience'): "And so literature lives on badly because it doesn't respond to the naturally felt needs of the people. It doesn't stem from life's flowering nor is it a reserve of vital energies. This can only exist as an imitation."[16] For Unamuno, the novel, as he perceived it, was insufficient, lost in description, flat in emotion, and ultimately trivial. Typically, his opinion becomes a judgment, asserting the importance of his own feeling as a decisive tool for determining truth, an authority based on the individual that developed fully with modernity: "I've forgotten almost all the novels I've ever read in my life, and these haven't been many; I only have a scant memory of a few, even less, any feeling at all" (I: 219). Writing becomes erasure, a willful clearing of the decks in order to start anew; out with novels, bring in the new, the *nivola*. Seen in this light, the apparently light-hearted discussion in *Niebla* (*Mist*, 1914) about the genre to which it belongs is the ultimate modern gesture: there is nothing that can contain Unamuno's writing as it breaks away from all traditional molds; it is so *new* it merits the coining of a new designation. Unamuno never tires of repeating that the past, save for a few exceptional individuals, is unsatisfactory. In "Examen de conciencia" he affirms that the literature of the period immediately preceding his "was, in general, one of nonsense and fatigue for Spain; literature lacked liveliness.... [Novels] that once were hailed as daring fall from our hands today" (I: 282).

Given this opinion, it is not surprising that he remembers how "we all felt ourselves to be iconoclasts" (I: 325). Unamuno is too shrewd not to understand where this frenzy of the new will lead him: into the scrap heap of

[15] Ibid., p. 345.
[16] M. de Unamuno, *De esto y de aquello*, vol. I (Buenos Aires: Sudamericana, 1950), pp. 27–8.

history, once his own work becomes part of the tradition that must be continually overcome. In *Niebla*, it is no accident that the final encounter with his character, Augusto Pérez, takes place in the library. Usually this scene is read at face value: Augusto, the character, tells Unamuno, the author, that a book will survive the writer, that a character is endlessly reborn in each reader's imagination. By including in the text three images of his own self – one, as the author Unamuno who receives his character in his Salamanca house, another, as a portrait that hangs in the imaginary library where Unamuno welcomes Augusto Pérez, and a third, his own books included in this library – the text splinters the individual and anticipates his ultimate fall into mortality, not only as a physical body but also as a series of deceptive reproductions. They are deceptive because they can only allude to a life gone and relegated to the past.

However, backgrounding whole genres and modes of writing presents the considerable difficulty of also allowing them to persist, creating the plurality of voices that Bakhtin first accurately described as being the core of the modern novel. It is easier to declare the obsolescence of a book than actually to be assured of it. Thus the library becomes an oppressive place for writers who want to stake their own claim to a territory already occupied, to speak where so much has already been said. No one has captured better this fatigue with the weight of the past than Juan Goytisolo in a famous scene of *Reivindicación*. The main character (who only tenuously holds to this title in a text pervaded by self-doubt and the ironic hesitation between fiction and essay) visits a library described as "a rather shabby building" (p. 31), "a vast pantheon for learning" (p. 37). He has come armed with dead flies that he proceeds to squash within the pages of the Spanish classics, describing this action as a futile gesture of rebellion against the "exemplary weight of its [the library's] heroism, its piety, its knowledge, its conduct, its glory" (p. 33). The lack of continuity between the pollution of the pages and the untouchable quality of the text, of which the book is only a version, reveals the impossible nature of this endeavor, similar to Don Quijote's ill-fated charge against the windmills.

At the turn of the century some of the most distinguished literary critics were also writers: Valera, Unamuno, Ortega, Azorín. These authors seek for literature a unique space beyond the marketplace, distinct from science and insulated from progress. Yet they remain alert to new trends, sensitive to Spain's marginalization from Europe's intellectual center as they attempt to integrate the past. Valera values the aesthetic, elegant, and classical, claiming for literature a place of beauty and enjoyment. Unamuno transforms his literary criticism into polemics, intricate thought, and religious meditation, but clearly his topic is always the drama of the individual who is thrust into the whirlwind of the modern amid the obsolete bearings of the past. Azorín will empty out the narrative line of his novels to leave only atmosphere and feeling, so his criticism will also concentrate on texture and color, as if all texts were films, the visual taking precedence over the word. But his descriptions involve a criticism that Ortega points out:

> Azorín has seen this radical fact that encompasses all others: Spain doesn't live in the present – Spain's current reality is the persistence of the past. Aristotle says that life is made up of transformation amid change. Well and good: Spain neither changes nor alters; nothing new begins, nothing old ever dies. Spain doesn't change, Spain keeps on repeating herself, reiterating today what was yesterday and tomorrow, what was today. To live here is to keep on doing the same thing.[17]

What matters about this quotation is that one author reading another sees in the text not a description of towns or the story of a woman waiting for her lover but a diagnostic allegory of the country's immobility. The lack of dynamic storylines, which Ortega would submit as the defining element of the contemporary novel, corresponds to Spain's own stagnation. High literature and its criticism were involved in a national debate about the country's soul, or what could be so imagined. Every text became the possible map for the soul of the nation. There is more to writing about writing than discussions about the novelistic craft. In fact, Ortega makes numerous disparaging comments about Baroja's novelistic composition, characters, and language, including his mangled syntax, but still he finds in Baroja's pages a vibrancy and verisimilitude that evoke life, especially a new sensibility for which usefulness is unimportant.[18] The reader of these critics should be aware of the many hidden agendas that drive them as they comment upon each other's work.

In an essay about modernity written in 1916 ("Nada 'Moderno' y 'muy siglo XX'"), Ortega identifies the unease that the nineteenth century causes him when he writes and tries to be contemporary, that is, a writer of the twentieth century. How can one go beyond a century that has defined itself as progressive? To declare the nineteenth century superseded because we have progressed would be simply to imitate and prolong the previous century's defining gesture. And yet Ortega introduces a wedge of dissent when he identifies a certain rigidity in progressive thought. In a sentence worthy of consideration, he observes: "Thus it is precisely that period which lays claim to progressive changes in ideas, in institutions, in human life as a whole that turns out to be the one that, ever so effectively, lends a semblance of eternity,

[17] J. M. Ortega y Gasset, "Azorín, o primores de lo vulgar," in *El espectador*, 4th edn. (Madrid: Biblioteca Nueva, 1966), p. 271.

[18] J. M. Ortega y Gasset, "Ideas sobre Pío Baroja," ibid., pp. 99–157.

of immutability, to its genuinely transitory behavior."[19] Yet modernity was not eternal, and it did change.

Of subsequent developments of the theme of writing about writing I can only give a glimpse, but the emerging contrast will allow a better understanding of what that phenomenon represented during modernity. It took at least fifty years, two world wars, a civil war, and other horrors of the twentieth century for the belief in progress to collapse into post-modernism. Along the way, writers and critics saw writing as an exploration of the self and its tragic existence, a denunciation of repression and class injustices, and an ironic purging of the accumulated evils of culture. Texts were declared revolutionary, contestatory, and subversive. Yet seen from today's vantage point, these claims seem excessive. Most have been easily absorbed by the marketplace and the academic industry, and few, if any, have shaken the basis of society or affected the behavior of institutions.

In a collection of essays entitled *¿Por qué no es útil la literatura?* ('Why Isn't Literature Useful?'), a contemporary novelist, Antonio Muñoz Molina, begins his contribution entitled "Las hogueras sin fuego" ('Bonfires without Fire'), recalling Don Quijote's love of books. Muñoz Molina reveals that he is a fellow enthusiast for reading and that his memory is also inhabited by literary creations: Homer's, Quevedo's, Flaubert's, and Kafka's, among others. He laments all that has been lost, whether by natural catastrophe or censorship. He has created his own memory informed by the solitary act of reading, a free and private choice he associates with modernity: "The modern world arose from the individual act of reading, promoted by the prestige of the press, which, for the first time, multiplied indefinitely the possibility of access to books."[20] This claim is not surprising, although on closer scrutiny one observes that the argument is based on the pleasure of reading, not on knowledge produced or an accurate description of reality, criticism of society, or even narrative innovation. The final image with which Muñoz Molina closes the lecture is an allusion to a painting, a silencing of the text in order to reflect on the reader, on his enjoyment:

> Recall Holbein's painting in which we see a humanist reading: he's alone, attentive, absorbed, with a tranquil expression of happiness in his eyes, on his lips, which seem to be smiling. That man is any one of us when for a moment we break the bonds of reality and alight upon the pages of a book. I know no better paradise. Now, as we go out into the street, we'll discover it on this May afternoon, in the open light of the street. (*¿Por qué...?*, p. 76)

[19] J. M. Ortega y Gasset, "Nada 'Moderno' y 'muy siglo xx'", pp. 29–30.
[20] L. García Montero and A. Muñoz Molina, *¿Por qué no es útil la literatura?* (Madrid: Hiperión, 1993), p. 75.

The final lines refer not to life going on in the streets but to the books for sale in Granada's Eleventh Book Fair (1992) at which the lecture was delivered. A democratic society has promoted easy access to books, which Muñoz Molina celebrates; this access, however, would probably have been rejected by the founders of modernity, who proposed a strenuous and selective path to enlightenment. The Romantics and Realists also would have distrusted such ecumenism for reasons based on the idea of writing as exclusive to people of exquisite emotion, in the first case, and of true insight, in the second. And was the result of reading to be happiness, paradise? Unamuno would disagree, as would Juan Goytisolo. The point is not to deny that pleasure has accompanied the history of writing, which it obviously has, but to remind ourselves that other questions, other issues, generally prevail at times when writers feel compelled to write about writing.

Some contemporary examples will confirm the value of Muñoz Molina's insight into the pleasure of reading. In Lucía Extebarria's *Beatriz y los cuerpos celestes* (*Beatriz and the Heavenly Bodies*), which won the 1998 Premio Nadal, the opening sentence finds the main character, Beatriz, rebuking her lover, Mónica, for what she reads. Mónica defends her rights to privacy, freedom, and pleasure:

> "I can't understand why you read that garbage," I told her, piqued not because I wanted to censure her taste in reading but because I wanted to get her attention....
>
> She looked up, pushed her glasses to the bridge of her nose as if she were a teacher, and gave me a glance of amused superiority.
>
> "Come on, don't bug me by being a cultural fascist. Do you mean I'm supposed to spend the whole day reading Dostoevski or something like that?"[21]

Freedom from the canon is based not only on skepticism about universal values but also on another impulse of modernity: the erasure of a strong sense of history. The characters in *Beatriz y los cuerpos celestes* live in a world of simultaneity and reiteration where writing is so saturated with writing that originality is not possible. Beatriz expresses this idea not as a malaise but as a matter of fact:

> There's no new world nor new ocean, in life whatever you've screwed up stays that way wherever you are. I'm twenty-two years old and I speak for others.
>
> These very same words have been said elsewhere. I've read them in books. Some were written a thousand years ago, others were published only in the last

[21] L. Extebarria, *Beatriz y los cuerpos celestes* (Barcelona: Destino de bolsillo, 2000), p. 13.

> two years. It turns out that everything written ends up being only a footnote to something written before. There's only one theme – life itself – and life is always the same. (pp. 19–20)

If there is an echo of Nietzsche's theory of eternal return, it is without the strain he imposes on his readers to overcome time and self with the creation of a superior man. The protagonist goes abroad, studies literature without much conviction, and falls in love several times. The narrative line is blurred, unaccented, ultimately unimportant. Moments of emotion, instants of happiness, illuminate the story. It is not surprising that in the concluding pages of the novel we find another meditation on writing: the need to free it from interpretation and the rigors of judgment. Beatriz has just told a friend that she studies English literature, and he responds:

> "English literature . . . Shoot. In the first place, I can't understand how anyone can study literature: you read books or you don't, that's all. You don't *study* them. As for me, I've never understood this stuff about literary criticism. If someone has to explain it to you, you haven't felt a thing when you read it. Bad news."
>
> "That's debatable," I contradicted him. "A text can't be understood out of context – society, history, psychology, the degree of freedom . . ."
>
> "Oh, knock it off. A text ought to lend itself to understanding, or at least each reader ought to understand it in his or her own way. But to give a text a context, an explanation, is to impose a limit, construe a definitive meaning for it, close it down.
>
> "That is, each time sacrosanct criticism dictates an opinion, the text is interpreted. Victory for the critic, who controls the reader, not allowing that person to make up his or her own mind." (pp. 300–1)

It would be tempting to discard this opinion as naive. After all, any critic knows that control is impossible, that there is always another critic who comes up with a new, definitive interpretation. But the defense of the reader's independence from an authoritative external opinion fits well with the dispersion of authority experienced in the contemporary world, a profusion of information that makes each voice or byte less final, more transient and partial. Muñoz Molina's smiling reader, immersed in his own paradise, removed from reality, is part of the breakdown of the grand old narrative. Beatriz's friends are representatives of a brave world that does not need to call itself new.

A second example is Luis Goytisolo's novel *Mzungo* (1996). The narration itself is unremarkable, much less dense and meta-fictional than his previous texts. The story follows several Spaniards who travel in a ship to Africa and encounter all sorts of catastropic events. More significant is that the book includes a CD-ROM with a game loosely based on the characters and situations of the novel. The linear quality of writing becomes the random access of the hard disk. The written is now visual and whatever intellectual challenge the novel presented has now been shifted to the skills needed to transverse a set of tunnels in a small car liable to explode as it hits the walls of the labyrinth, or help a man walk along a road while a rain of coconuts threatens to knock him cold – unless a snake bites him first. On the CD-ROM sleeve we are told that the characters have escaped from the author and prefer solidarity with the reader. But more than this escape has happened: the shifts from author to reader, from truth to pleasure, from linearity to simultaneity, and from canonicity to plurality and freedom have slowly but inevitably created a different concept of writing from the one that existed at the beginning of the modern era.

Guide to further reading

Flitter, Derek, *Spanish Romantic Literary Theory and Criticism* (Cambridge University Press, 1992).

Navajas, Gonzalo, *Teoría y práctica de la novela española posmoderna*, (Barcelona: Ediciones del Mall, 1987).

Sieburth, Stephanie, *Inventing High and Low: Literature, Mass Culture, and Uneven Modernity in Spain* (Durham, NC: Duke University Press, 1994).

Spires, Robert C., *Transparent Simulacra* (Columbia, MO: University of Missouri Press, 1988).

BIBLIOGRAPHY

Novels only.

Agustí, Ignacio. *La ceniza que fue árbol* ('Tree into Ashes'): title of a series that includes *Mariona Rebull* (Barcelona: Destino, 1944), *El viudo Rius* (1945), *Desiderio* (Barcelona: Planeta, 1957); and *19 de julio* (Barcelona: Planeta 1966).

Alarcón, Pedro Antonio de. *El sombrero de tres picos* (1874), in *Novelas completas. Prólogo de Jorge Campos*. Madrid: Aguilar, 1974. *The Three-Cornered Hat*, tr. Alexander E. Tulloch, ed. A. E. Tulloch and Malveena McKendrick. London: J.M. Dent, 1995.

Alas, Leopoldo ('Clarín'). *La Regenta*, 2 vols., ed. Gonzalo Sobejano. Madrid: Castalia, 1981. *La Regenta*, tr. John Rutherford. Athens: University of Georgia Press, 1984.

Su único hijo, ed. Juan Oleza. Madrid: Cátedra, 1998. *His Only Son*, tr. Julie Jones. Baton Rouge: Louisiana University Press, 1981.

Aldecoa, Ignacio. *El fulgor y la sangre*. Barcelona: Planeta, 1954.

Con el viento solano. Barcelona: Planeta, 1956. "Critical Essays and a Translation of Aldecoa's *Con el viento solano*," tr. Chester Hope Mills, PhD thesis, Washington State University, 1982.

Gran Sol. Barcelona: Noguer, 1957.

Alemán, Mateo. *Guzmán de Alfarache*, ed. S. Gili Gaya, 5 vols. Madrid: Espasa-Calpe, 1972. *The Rogue; Or, the Life of Guzmán de Alfarache*, tr. James Mabbe, introduction by James Fitzmaurice-Kelly. New York: AMS Press, 1967 (reprint of 1924 translation).

Amat, Nuria. *La intimidad*. Madrid: Alfaguara, 1997.

Angelón y Broquetas, Manuel. *El pendón de Santa Eulalia o los fueros de Cataluña*. Madrid: Salvador Montserrat, 1858.

Anónimo. *Lazarillo de Tormes*, ed. J. Cejador y Frauca. Madrid: Espasa-Calpe, 1969. *The Life of Lazarillo de Tormes*, tr. David Rowland, introduction and notes by Kevin Whitlock. Warmister: Arise Philips, 2000.

Anónimo. *Los misterios de Córdoba*. Córdoba, 1845.

Anónimo. *Madrid y sus misterios*. Madrid: Sánchez, 1844.

Atxaga, Bernardo. *Obabakoak*. Donostia: Erein, 1988. *Obabakoak: A Novel*, tr. Margaret Jull Costa. New York: Vintage Books, 1994.

Aub, Max. *Laberinto mágico*, 6 vols. 1943–82: *Campo cerrado*. México: Tezontle, 1943. *Field of Honour*, tr. Gerard Martin. New York: Verso, 1988. *Campo de sangre*. México: Tezontle, 1945. *Campo abierto*. México: Tezontle, 1951. *Campo de Moro*. México: Joaquín Mortiz, 1963. *Campo de los almendros*. Mexico: Joaquín Mortiz. *Campo francés*. Paris: Ruedo ibérico, 1965.

Ayala, Francisco. *El boxeador y un ángel* (1929). Madrid: Cuadernos Literarios, 1929.

La cabeza del cordero (1949), ed. Keith Ellis. Englewood Cliffs, NJ: Prentice Hall, 1968. *The Lamb's Head: A Translation and Critical Study*, tr. Cecile Craig Fitzgibbons Wiseman. PhD thesis, University of Texas at Austin (1979).

Los usurpadores (1949). Madrid: Alianza, 1988. *Usurpers*, tr. Carolyn Richmond. New York: Schocken Books, 1987.

Ayguals de Izco, Wenceslao. *María o La hija de un jornalero*, 2 vols. Madrid: Ayguals de Izco, 1845–6.

Azorín. *Doña Inés*, ed. Elena Catena. Madrid: Castalia, 1975.

La voluntad (1902), ed. E. Inman Fox. Madrid: Castalia, 1982.

Baroja, Pío. *El árbol de la ciencia* (1911), ed. Pío Caro Baroja. Madrid: Caro Raggio/Cátedra, 1985. *The Tree of Knowledge*, tr. Aubrey F. G. Bell. New York: H. Fertig, 1974.

Camino de perfección (1902). New York: Las Américas, n.d.

El mundo es ansí (1912), ed. José Antonio Pérez Bosnic. Madrid: Espasa-Calpe, 1990.

Obras completas, 8 vols. Madrid: Biblioteca Nueva, 1946–52.

Benet, Juan. *El aire de un crimen*. Barcelona: Planeta, 1980.

En la penumbra. Madrid: Alfaguara, 1989.

Nunca Llegarás a nada. Madrid: Tebas, 1961.

Saúl ante Samuel. Barcelona: La Gaya Ciencia, 1980.

Una meditación. Barcelona: Seix Barral, 1970. *A Meditation: A Novel*, tr. Gregory Rabassa. New York: Persea Books, 1982.

Un viaje de invierno. Madrid: Cátedra, 1980.

Volverás a Región. Barcelona: Destino, 1981. *Return to Region*, tr. Gregory Rabassa. New York: Columbia University Press, 1985.

Blasco Ibáñez, Vicente. *Flor de mayo* (1895), ed. José Mas and María Teresa Mateu. Madrid: Cátedra, 1999. *The Mayflower: A Tale of the Valencian Seashore*, tr. Arthur Livingston. London: Unwin Hyman, 1922.

La barraca (1898), ed. José Mas and María Teresa Mateu. Madrid: Cátedra, 1998. *The Holding*, tr. Lester Clarke and Eric Farrington Birchall. Warminster: Arise Philips, 1993.

Brayer de Saint-Léon, Louise. *Maclovia y Federico o las minas del Tirol. Anécdota verdadera traducida del francés*. Valencia: Miguel Domingo, 1814.

Burgos, Carmen de. 'El abogado', *Los contemporáneos*, no. 340, 1915. *La entrometida*, *La novela corta*, vol. VI, no. 292, 1924.

La flor de la playa y otras novelas cortas (1989), ed. Concepción Núñez Rey. Includes *El veneno del arte* (1910). Madrid: Castalia, 1989.

La rampa (1917). Madrid: Renacimiento, 1917.

Caballero, Fernán. *La gaviota* (1849), ed. Julio Rodríguez Luis. Barcelona: Labor, 1972. *La gaviota: A Spanish novel*, tr. J. Leander Starr. New York: J. Bradburn, 1996.

Cadalso, José. *Cartas marruecas. Noches lúgubres*, ed. Joaquín Arce. Madrid: Cátedra, 1990.

Castillo-Puche, José Luis. *El libro de las visiones y las apariciones*. Barcelona: Destino, 1977.

El amargo sabor de la retama. Barcelona: Destino, 1979.

Conocerás el poso de la nada. Barcelona: Destino, 1982.

Castillo, Rafael del. *Misterios catalanes o el obrero de Barcelona*. Madrid: Librería Española de E. Font, 1862.

Castro, Luisa. *El somier*. Barcelona: Anagrama, 1990.

Castro, Rosalía de. *El caballero de las botas azules*, ed. Ana Rodríguez-Fisher. Madrid: Cátedra, 1995.

La hija del mar, ed. Mauro Armiño, in *Obra completa*, vol. II. Madrid: Ediciones Akal, 1992. *Daughter of the Sea*, tr. Kathleen N. March. New York: Peter Lang, 1995.

La familia de Pascual Duarte. Madrid: Aldecoa, 1942. *The Family of Pascual Duarte*, tr. Anthony Kerrigan. Boston: Little, Brown, & Co., 1999.

Pabellón de reposo. Madrid: Afrodisio Aguado, 1944. *Rest Home*, tr. Herma Briffault. New York: Las Americas, 1999.

La colmena. Buenos Aires: Emece, 1951. *The Hive*, tr. J. M. Cohen and Arturo Barea. Normal, IL: Dalkey Archive Press, 2001.

Vísperas, festividad y octava de san Camilo del año 1936 en Madrid. Madrid: Alfaguara, 1969. *San Camilo, 1936: The Eve, Feast, and Octave of St. Camillus of the Year 1936 in Madrid*, tr. J. H. R. Polt. Durham, NC: Duke University Press, 1991.

Cervantes Saavedra, Miguel de. *Don Quijote*, ed. L. A. Murillo, 2 vols. Madrid: Castalia, 1978. *Don Quijote: A New Translation, Background and Contexts, Criticism*, tr. Burton Raffel, ed. Diana de Armas Wilson, Norton Critical Edition. New York: W.W. Norton, 1999.

Chacel, Rosa. *Acrópolis*. Barcelona: Seix Barral, 1984.

Barrio de Maravillas. Barcelona: Seix Barral, 1976. *The Maravillas District*, tr. D. A. Démers. Lincoln: University of Nebraska Press, 1992.

Ciencias naturales. Barcelona: Seix Barral, 1988.

Estación. Ida y Vuelta (1930). Barcelona: Bruguera, 1980.

Memorias de Leticia Valle (1945). Barcelona: Bruguera, 1981. *Memoirs of Leticia Valle*, tr. Carol Maier. Lincoln: University of Nebraska Press, 1994.

La sinrazón (1970). Barcelona: Bruguera, 1981.

Delibes, Miguel. *La sombra del ciprés es alargada*. Barcelona: Destino, 1948.

El camino. Barcelona: Destino, 1950. *The Path*, tr. John and Brita Haycraft. London: Hamish Hamilton, 1961.

Cinco horas con Mario (1966). Barcelona: Destino, 1967. *Five Hours with Mario*, tr. Frances M. López-Morillas. New York: Columbia University Press, 1988.

Diario de un cazador. Barcelona: Destino, 1955.

El hereje. Barcelona: Destino, 2000.

La hoja roja. Barcelona: Destino, 1959.

Las guerras de nuestros antepasados. Barcelona: Destino, 1975. *The Wars of Our Ancestors*, tr. Agnes Moncy. Athens: University of Goergia Press, 1992.

Los santos inocentes. Barcelona: Planeta, 1981.

Díaz Fernández, José. *El blocao* (1928), ed. Víctor Fuentes. Madrid: Turner, 1976.
El nuevo romanticismo (1930). Madrid: Zeus, 1930.
La Venus mecánica (1929). Madrid: Renacimiento, 1929.
Espina, Concha. *La esfinge maragata* (1914), ed. Carmen Díaz Castañón. Madrid: Castalia, 1989. *Mariflor*, tr. Frances Douglas. New York: Macmillan, 1924.
Espinosa, Miguel. *Tríbada. Theologiae Tractatus*. Murcia: Editora Regional, 1986.
Extebarria, Lucía. *Amor, curiosidad, prozac y dudas*. Barcelona: Plaza & Janés, 1997.
Beatriz y los cuerpos celestes. Barcelona: Destino, 1998.
Fernández Cubas, Cristina. *Mi hermana Elba*. Barcelona: Tusquets, 1980.
Los altillos de Brumal. Barcelona: Tusquets, 1983.
El ángulo del horror. Barcelona: Tusquets, 1990.
El columpio. Barcelona: Tusquets, 1995.
Fernández Santos, Jesús. *Los bravos*. Valencia: Castalia, 1954.
Ferrero, Jesús. *Belver Yin*. Barcelona: Bruguera, 1981.
Ferres, Antonio. *La piqueta*. Barcelona: Destino, 1959.
García Hortelano, Juan. *Nuevas amistades*. Barcelona: Seix Barral, 1959.
Tormenta de verano. Barcelona: Seix Barral, 1962. *Summer Storm*, tr. Ilsa Barea. New York: Grove Press, 1962.
García Malo, Ignacio. *Flavio e Irene*, in *Voz de la naturaleza*, ed. Guillermo Carnero. Madrid: Támesis, 1995.
La desventurada Margarita, in *Voz de la naturaleza*.
García Morales, Adelaida. *El sur; seguido de Bene*. Barcelona: Anagrama, 1998. *The South and Bene*, tr. Thomas G. Deveny. Lincoln: The University of Nebraska Press, 1999.
Gil y Carrasco, Enrique. *El Señor de Bembibre* (1844), ed. Enrique Rubio. Madrid: Cátedra, 1986.
Gironella, José María. *Los cipreses creen en Dios*. Barcelona: Planeta, 1953. *The Cypresses Believe in God*, tr. Harriet de Onís. New York: Knopf, 1969.
Un millón de muertos. Barcelona: Planeta, 1961.
Ha estallado la paz. Barcelona: Planeta, 1966.
Gómez de Avellaneda, Gertrudis. *Sab*, ed. José Servera. Madrid: Cátedra, 1997. *Sab; and Autobiography*, ed. and tr. Nina M. Scott. Austin: University of Texas Press, 1993.
Gómez de la Serna, Ramón. *Greguerías. Selección 1910–1960*. Madrid: Espasa-Calpe, 1968. *Aphorisms*, tr. Miguel González-Gerth. Pittsburgh: Latin American Literary Review Press, 1989.
El novelista (1923). Madrid: Espasa-Calpe, 1973.
El secreto del acueducto (1921), ed. Carolyn Richmond. Madrid: Cátedra, 1986.
Goytisolo, Juan. *Coto vedado*. Barcelona: Seix Barral, 1985. *Forbidden Territory: The Memoirs of Juan Goytisolo, 1931–1956*, tr. Peter Bush. San Francisco: North Point Press, 1989.
Juan sin tierra. Barcelona: Seix Barral, 1975. *Juan the Landless*, tr. Helen R. Lane. London: Serpent's Tail, 1990.
Juegos de manos. Barcelona: Destino, 1954.
La isla. Barcelona: Seix Barral, 1961.
La resaca (1958). Mexico: Joaquín Mortiz, 1977.
La saga de los Marx. Barcelona: Mondadori, 1993. *The Marx Family Saga*, tr. Peter Bush. London: Faber, 1996.

Las semanas del jardín. Madrid: Alfaguara, 1997. *The Garden of Secrets*, tr. Peter Bush. London: Serpent's Tail, 2000.
Las virtudes del pájaro solitario. Barcelona: Seix Barral, 1988.
Makbara. Barcelona: Seix Barral, 1980. *Makbara*, tr. Helen R. Lane. London: Seaver Books, 1981.
Paisajes despvés de la batalla. Barcelona: Montesinos, 1982.
Reivindicación del conde don Julián. Mexico: Joaquín Mortiz, 1970. *Count Julian*, tr. Helen R. Lane. New York: Viking Press, 1974.
Señas de identidad. México: Joaquín Mortiz, 1966. *Marks of Identity*, tr. Gregory Rabassa. London: Serpent's Tail, 1988 (1969).
Goytisolo, Luis. *Las afueras*. Barcelona: Seix Barral, 1958.
Estatua con palomas. Barcelona: Destino, 1992.
Mzungo. Barcelona: Grijalbo Mondadori, 1996.
Recuento. Madrid: Alianza, 1987.
Grandes, Almudena. *Las edades de Lulú*. Barcelona: Tusquets, 1989. *The Ages of Lulu*, tr. Sonia Soto. London: Abacus, 1994.
Grosso, Alfonso. *La zanja*. Barcelona: Destino, 1961.
Guelbenzu, José Maria. *El mercurio*. Barcelona: Destino, 1968.
Isla, José Francisco de. *Fray Gerundio de Campazas*, 4 vols., ed. Russell P. Sebold. Madrid: Espasa-Calpe, 1969. *The History of the Famous Preacher Friar Gerund de Campazas, Otherwise Gerund Zofes*, tr. Thomas Nugent. London: T. Davies, 1772.
Jaén, María. *Amorrada al piló*. Barcelona: Columna, 1986.
Sauna. Barcelona: Columna, 1987.
Jarnés, Benjamín. *El profesor inútil* (1926). Madrid: Revista de Occidente, 1926.
El convidado de papel (1928). Madrid: Historia Nueva, 1928.
Locura y muerte de nadie (1929). Madrid: Revista de Occidente, 1929.
Lo rojo y lo azul (1932). Madrid: Espasa-Calpe, 1932.
Paula y Paulita (1929). Madrid: Revista de Occidente, 1929.
Teoría del zumbel (1930). Madrid: Espasa-Calpe, 1930.
Laforet, Carmen. *La isla y los demonios*. Barcelona: Destino, 1952. "Introductory Notes and the Translation of *La isla y los demonios*," tr. Carolyn V. Bell, PhD thesis, University of Pennsylvania (Kutztown) (1974).
Nada (1945). Barcelona: Destino, 1955. *Nada*, tr. Galfyra Ennis. New York: Peter Lang, 1993.
Larra, Mariano José de. *El doncel de don Enrique el Doliente* (1834), ed. José María Varela. Madrid: Cátedra, 1978.
López Pacheco, Jesús. *Central eléctrica*. Barcelona: Destino, 1958.
López Salinas, Armando. *La mina*. Barcelona: Destino, 1960.
Loriga, Ray. *Días extraños*. Madrid: El Europeo & la Tripulación, 1994.
Mañas, José María. *Historias del Kronen*. Barcelona: Destino, 1971.
Marsé, Juan. *La muchacha de las bragas de oro*. Barcelona: Planeta, 1978.
Si te dicen que caí. Barcelona: Planeta, 1973. *The Fallen*, tr. Helen R. Lane. Boston: Little, Brown, 1979.
Últimas tardes con Teresa. Barcelona: Seix Barral, 1966. Video: *Last Evenings with Teresa*. Media Home Entertainment, 1998.
Martín Gaite, Carmen. *Entre visillos*. Barcelona: Destino, 1958. *Behind the Curtains*, tr. Frances López-Morillas. New York: Columbia University Press, 1990.

Ritmo lento. Barcelona: Seix Barral, 1963.
Retahílas. Barcelona: Destino, 1974.
El cuarto de atrás. Barcelona: Destino, 1978. *The Back Room*, tr. Helen Lane. San Francisco: City Lights Books, 2000.
Martín Santos, Luis. *Tiempo de silencio*. Barcelona: Seix Barral, 1962. *Time of Silence*, tr. George Leeson. London: J. Calder, 1965.
Martínez Colomer, Vicente. *El Valdemaro* (1792), ed. Guillermo Carnero. Alicante: Instituto de Estudios "Juan Gil-Albert," 1985.
Martínez Villergas, Juan. *Los misterios de Madrid*. Madrid: Manini, 1844–5.
Matute, Ana María. *Los Abel*. Barcelona: Destino, 1948.
Pequeño teatro. Barcelona: Planeta, 1954.
Primera memoria (1960). Barcelona: Destino, 1984. *Awakening*, tr. James Holman Mason. London: Hutchinson, 1963.
Méndez-Ferrín, Xosé Lluis. "Medias azules," in *Arraianos*, tr. Luisa Castro. Barcelona: Ronsel, 1991.
Mendicutti, Eduardo. *Una mala noche la tiene cualquiera*. Barbastro: Unali, 1982.
Mendoza, Eduardo. *La ciudad de los prodigios*. Barcelona: Seix Barral, 1986.
Milá de la Roca, José Nicasio. *Los misterios de Barcelona*. Barcelona: Imprenta y Librería Española y Extranjera, 1844.
Miró, Gabriel. *Obras completas*. Madrid: Biblioteca Nueva, 1961. Includes: *Años y leguas* (1928). "The Years and the Leagues," tr. Marcus Parr, PhD thesis, University of Utah, 1958. *Las cerezas del cementerio* (1910). *Del vivir* (1904). *El humo dormido* (1914). *El libro de Sigüenza* (1917). *Nuestro padre San Daniel* (1921). *Our Father San Daniel*, tr. Charlotte Remfry-Kidd. London: E. Benn, 1930. *El obispo leproso* (1926).
Moix, Ana María. *Julia*. Barcelona: Seix Barral, 1972.
Montengón, Pedro. *El Eusebio*, ed. Fernando García Lara. Madrid: Editora Nacional, 1984.
Montero, Rosa. *Amado amo*. Madrid: Debate, 1988. *Amado amo* (English version by Rosa Montero). Madrid: Debate, 1988.
Crónica del desamor. Madrid: Debate, 1979. *Absent Love: A Chronicle*, tr. Cristina de la Torre and Diana Glad. Lincoln: University of Nebraska Press, 1998.
La función Delta. Madrid: Debate, 1981. *The Delta Function*, tr. Kari Easton and Yolanda Molina Gavilán. Lincoln: University of Nebraska Press, 1991.
Montseny, Federica. *La indomable* (1928). Madrid: Castalia, 1991.
Monzó Quim. *Vuitanta sis contes*. Barcelona: Quaderns Crema, 1999.
Muñoz Molina, Antonio. *Beatus Ille*. Barcelona: Seix Barral, 1986.
Nelken, Margarita. *La trampa del arenal* (1923). Madrid: Librería de los Sucesores de Hernando, 1923.
Oller, Narcís. *La bogeria* (1899), ed. Sergio Beser. Barcelona: Laia, 1980.
Ortiz, Lourdes. *Luz de la memoria*. Madrid: Akal, 1976.
Pardo Bazán, Emilia. *El cisne de Vilamorta*, ed. Carlos Sainz de Robles, *Obras completas*, 3rd edn, vol. II. Madrid: Aguilar, 1973. *The Swan of Vilamorta*, tr. Mary J. Serrano. New York: Cassell Publishing Co., 1891.
La madre Naturaleza (1887), ed. Ignacio Javiero López. Madrid: Cátedra, 1999.
Memorias de un solterón, ed. Carlos Sainz de Robles, in *Obras completas*, 3rd edn., vol. II. Madrid: Aguilar, 1973.

Los pazos de Ulloa (1886), ed. Marina Mayoral Madrid: Castalia, 1987. *The House of Ulloa: A Novel*, tr. Roser Caminals-Heath. Athens: University of Georgia Press, 1991.

La piedra angular, ed. Carlos Sainz de Robles, in *Obras completas*, 3rd edn., vol. II. Madrid: Aguilar, 1973.

La tribuna, ed. Benito Varela Jácome. Madrid: Cátedra, 1975. *Tribune of the People*, tr. Walter Borenstein. Lewisburg: Bucknell University Press, 1999.

Pereda, José María de. *Obras completas*, 5th edn., 2 vols. Madrid: Aguilar, 1948.

Peñas arriba, ed. Antonio Rey. Madrid: Cátedra, 1988.

Sotileza, ed. Anthony H. Clarke, notes by Francisco Caudet. Santander: Tantin, 1996. *Sotileza: A Novel*, tr. Glenn Barr. New York: H. Fertig, 1976.

Pérez de Ayala, Ramón. *A.M.G.D.* (1910). Madrid: Mundo Latino, 1923.

Belarmino y Apolonio (1921), ed. Andrés Amorós. Madrid: Cátedra, 1982. *Belarmino and Apolonio*, tr. Murray Baumgarten and Gabriel Berns. Berkeley: University of California Press, 1971.

La pata de la raposa, in *Obras completas*, vol. I, ed. José García Mercadal. Madrid: Aguilar, 1963. *The Fox's Paw*, tr. Thomas Walsh. New York: E.P. Dutton, 1924.

Tigre Juan y *El curandero de su honra*, ed. Miguel Ángel Lozano Marco. Madrid: Espasa-Calpe, 1990.

Tinieblas en las cumbres, in *Obras completas*, vol. I. Madrid: Aguilar, 1963.

Troteras y danzaderas, in *Obras completas*, vol. I.

Pérez Galdós, Benito. *Fortunata y Jacinta. Dos historias de casadas*, 2 vols., ed. Francisco Caudet. Madrid: Cátedra, 1983, 1985. *Fortunata and Jacinta: Two Stories of Married Women*, tr. Agnes Moncy Gullón. London: Penguin Books, 1988.

Obras completas, ed. Federico Carlos Robles, 6 vols. Madrid: Aguilar, 1966. Includes:

Vols. I–III: *Episodios nacionales: Memorias de un cortesano de 1815* (1875), *Los cien mil hijos de San Luis* (1877), *Un faccioso más y algunos frailes menos* (1879), *Mendizábal* (1898), *La estafeta romántica* (1899), *Luchana* (1899), *Vergara* (1899), *Los ayacuchos* (1900), *Bodas reales* (1900), *Las tormentas del '48* (1902), *Narváez* (1902), *Los duendes de la camarilla* (1903), *La revolución de julio* (1904), *Prim* (1906), *La de los tristes destinos* (1907), *España sin rey* (1907–8), *España trágica* (1909), *Amadeo I* (1910), *La primera República* (1911), *De Cartago a Sagunto* (1911), *Cánovas* (1912).

Vol. IV: *La fontana de oro* (1867–8). *The Golden Fountain Café*, tr. Walter Rubin. Pittsburgh: Latin American Literary Review Press, 1989. *La sombra* (1870). *The Shadow*, tr. Karen Austin. Athens: Ohio University Press, 1980. *El audaz* (1871), *Doña Perfecta* (1876). Tr. Alexander R. Tolloch. London: Phoenix House, 1999. *Gloria*, *La familia de León Roch* (1878), *La desheredada* (1881). *The Disinherited Lady*, tr. Guy E. Smith. New York: Exposition Press, 1957. *El amigo Manso* (1882). *Our Friend Manso*, tr. Robert Russell. New York: Columbia University Press, 1987. *Tormento* (1884). *Inferno*, tr. Abigail Lee Six. London: Phoenix House, 1998. *La de Bringas* (1884). *That Bringas Woman*, tr. Catherine Jagoe. Rutland, VT: C.E. Tuttle, 1996.

Vol. V: *Miau* (1888). Tr. J. M. Cohen. Harmondsworth: Penguin Books, 1966. *La incógnita* (1888–9). *The Unknown*, tr. Karen O. Austin. Lewiston, NY: E. Mellen Press, 1991. *Realidad* (1889). *Reality*, tr. Karen O. Austin. Lewiston,

NY: E. Mellen Press, 1992. *Torquemada en la hoguera* (1889); *Torquemada en la Cruz* (1893); *Torquemada en el purgatorio* (1894); *Torquemada y San Pedro* (1895). *Torquemada* [a tetralogy], tr. Frances López Morillas. New York: Columbia University Press, 1986. *Ángel Guerra*, tr. Karen O. Austin. Lewiston NY: E. Mellen Press, 1990. *Misericordia* (1897). *Compassion*, tr. Toby Talbot. New York: F. Ungar, 1989.

Puértolas, Soledad. *Burdeos*. Barcelona: Anagrama, 1986. *Bordeaux*, tr. Francisca González Arias. Lincoln: University of Nebraska Press, 1998.

Queda la noche. Barcelona: Planeta, 1989.

La vida oculta. Barcelona: Anagrama, 1993.

Riera, Carme. *En el último azul* (Spanish version of *Dins el darrer blau*). Madrid: Alfaguara, 1996.

Una primavera per a Domenico Guarini. Barcelona: Edicions 62, 1981.

Te deix, amor, la mar can a penyora. Barcelona: Laia, 1975. *Te dejo el mar*, Spanish tr. by Luisa Cotoner. Madrid: Espasa-Calpe, 1991.

Rodoreda, Mercè. *Mirall trencat*. Barcelona: Club Editor, 1974.

La plaza del diamante. Barcelona: Edhasa, 1994. *The Time of the Doves*, tr. David H. Rosenthal. St. Paul, MN: Greywolf Press, 1986.

Roig, Montserrat. *Dime que me quieres aunque sea mentira: sobre el placer solitario de escribir y el vicio compartido de leer*, Spanish tr. by Antonia Picazo. Barcelona: Edicions 62, 1993.

L'hora violeta. Barcelona: Edicions 62, 1980.

L'opera quotidiana. Barcelona: Planeta, 1982.

Romero, Luis. *La noria*. Barcelona: Destino, 1952.

Salinas, Pedro. "*Prelude to Pleasure*." *A Bilingual Edition of* "*Víspera del gozo*", tr. Noël Valis. Lewisburg: Bucknell University Press, 1993.

Sánchez Ferlosio, Rafael. *El Jarama*. Barcelona: Destino, 1956. *The One Day of the Week*, tr. J. M. Cohen. London: Abelard-Schuman, 1962.

Industrias y andanzas de Alfanhuí. Madrid: Gráficas CIES, 1951. *The Adventures of the Ingenious Alfanhuí*, tr. Margaret Jull Costa. Sawtry: Dedalus, 2000.

Semprún, Jorge. *Autobiografía de Federico Sánchez*. Barcelona: Planeta, 1977. *Communism in Spain of the Franco Era: The Autobiography of Federico Sánchez*, tr. Helen R. Lane. Brighton: Harvester Press, 1980.

Sender, Ramón. *Imán* (1930). Madrid: Cenit, 1930. *Earmarked for Hell*, tr. James Cleugh. London: Wishart, 1934.

Mister Witt, en el cantón, ed. José María Jover. Madrid: Castalia, 1987.

Requiem por un campesino español. New York: St. Martin's Press, 1991. *Requiem for Spanish Peasant*, tr. Eleanor Randall. New York: Las Américas, 1960.

Siete domingos rojos. Barcelona: Balqué, 1932. *Seven Red Sundays*, tr. Sir Peter Chalmers Mitchell. Chicago: Elephant Paperbacks, 1990.

Sinués de Marco, María del Pilar. *Celeste*. Madrid: Imprenta la Española, 1863.

La senda de la Gloria, 2nd edn. Madrid: La Moda Elegante Ilustrada, 1880.

Suárez, Francisco. *Los demócratas o El ángel de la libertad*. El Ferrol: N. Taxonera, 1863.

Suárez Carreño, José. *Las últimas horas*. Barcelona: Destino, 1950. *The Final Hours*, tr. Anthony Kerrigan. New York: New American Library, 1955 (1953).

Sue, Eugène. *Les mystères de Paris*, in *Le journal des débats*, 19 June 1842–15 October 1843. *The Mysteries of Paris*, tr. Eugène Sue. Sawtry: Dedalus, 1989.

Toro, Souso de. *Tic-tac*. Barcelona: Ediciones B, 1993.
Calzados Lola. Barcelona: Ediciones B.
Torrente Ballester, Gonzalo. *Don Juan*. Barcelona: Destino, 1975. *Don Juan*, tr. Bernard Molloy. Madrid: Iberia, 1986.
El señor llega. Madrid: Arión, 1960.
Los gozos y las sombras (trilogy). Madrid: Arión, 1957–62.
Fragmentos de Apocalipsis. Barcelona: Destino, 1977.
Javier Mariño, historia de una conversación. Madrid: Editorial Nacional, 1943.
La isla de los jacintos cortados: carta de amor con interpolaciones mágicas. Barcelona: Destino, 1980.
La saga/fuga de J. B. Madrid: Alianza, 1998.
Torres Villarroel, Diego de. *Los desahuciados del mundo y de la gloria*, ed. Manuel María Pérez. Madrid: Editora Nacional, 1979.
Vida, ed. Dámaso Chicharro. Madrid: Cátedra, 1984. *The Remarkable Life of Don Diego, Being the Autobiography of Diego de Torres Villarroel*, tr. William C. Atkinson. London: Folio Society, 1958.
Tressera, Ceferino. *Los misterios del Saladero*. Madrid: A. de San Martín, 1860.
Tusquets, Esther. *El mismo mar de todos los veranos*. Barcelona: Lumen, 1978. *The Same Sea as Every Summer*, tr. Margaret E. W. Jones. Lincoln: University of Nebraska Press, 1990.
Umbral, Francisco. *Memorias de un niño de derechas*. Barcelona: Destino, 1972.
Unamuno, Miguel de. *Abel Sánchez* (1917), ed. Ángel and Amelia Del Río. New York: Holt, Rinehart, and Winston, 1947. *Abel Sánchez*, tr. Anthony Kerrigan. Washington, DC: Regnery Gateway, 1992.
Amor y pedagogía (1902). Barcelona: Bruguera, 1986. *Love and Pedagogy*, tr. Michael Bande Berg. New York: Peter Lang, 1996.
Niebla, ed. Harriet S. Stevens and Ricardo Gullón. Madrid: Taurus, 1982. *Mist*, tr. Warner Fite. Urbana: University of Illinois Press, 2000.
Paz en la guerra (1897). Madrid: Espasa-Calpe, 1964. *Peace in War*, tr. Allen Lacy and Martin Nozick with Anthony Kerrigan. Princeton University Press, 1983.
San Manuel Bueno, mártir (1933). Madrid: Alianza, 1978. *Comparative and Critical Edition of "San Manuel Bueno, mártir"*, ed. María Elena de Valdés. Chapel Hill: University of North Carolina, 1973.
La tía Tula (1921), ed. Carlos A. Longhurst Madrid: Cátedra, 1990.
Valera, Juan. *Juanita la Larga* (1895), ed. Jaime Vidal Alcover. Barcelona: Planeta, 1988.
Pepita Jiménez (1874), ed. Leopoldo Romero. Madrid: Cátedra, 1988. *Pepita Jiménez*, tr. Harriet de Onís. Great Neck, NY: Barron's Educational Series, 1970.
Valladares de Sotomayor, Antonio. *La Leandra*, 2 vols. Madrid: Antonio Ulloa, 1797.
Valle-Inclán, Ramón María del. *Femeninas. Epitalamio*. Madrid: Espasa-Calpe, 1978.
Obras completas, 3rd edn, 2 vols. Madrid: Plenitud, 1954. Includes: trilogy entitled *La guerra carlista* (1908–9), comprising *Los cruzados de la causa* (1908–9), *El resplandor de la hoguera* (1908–9), *Gerifaltes de antaño* (1908–9). Unfinished series entitled *Ruedo Ibérico* that includes two completed novels, *La corte de los milagros* (1927) and *Viva mi dueño* (1928), and a portion of *Baza de espadas* (posthumously published in 1958).

Sonata de otoño. Sonata de invierno. Madrid: Espasa-Calpe, 1985. *Autumn and Winter Sonatas*, tr. Margaret Jull Costa. Sawtry, Cambs: Dedalus, 1998.
Sonata de primavera. Sonata de estío. Madrid: Espasa-Calpe, 1984. *Spring and Summer Sonatas*, tr. Margaret Jull Costa. Sawtry, Cambs: Dedalus, 1997.
Tirano Banderas, ed. Alonso Zamora Vicente. Madrid: Espasa-Calpe, 1978. *The Tyrant: A Novel of Warm Lands*, tr. Margarita Pavitt. New York: H. Holt, 1929.
Vaz de Soto, José María. *Diálogos del anochecer*. Barcelona: Planeta, 1972.
Diálogos de la alta noche. Barcelona: Argos Vergara, 1982.
Fabián. Madrid: Akal, 1977.
Fabián y Sabas. Barcelona: Argos Vergara, 1982.
Vázquez Montalbán, Manuel. *La soledad del manager*. Barcelona: Planeta, 1977. *The Angst-Ridden Executive*, tr. E. Emery. London: Serpent's Tail, 1990.
Los mares del sur. Barcelona: Planeta, 1979. *Southern Seas*, tr. Patrick Camiller. London: Serpent's Tail, 1999.
Tatuaje. Barcelona: J. Batlló, 1974.
Vernes, François. *El viajador sensible*, Spanish tr. by Bernardo María de Calzada. Madrid: Imprenta Real, 1791.
Zavala y Zamora, Gaspar. *La Eumenia*, in *Obras narrativas*, ed. Guillermo Carnero. Barcelona: Sirmio-Quaderns Crema, 1992.

INDEX

CAMBRIDGE COMPANIONS TO LITERATURE

The Cambridge Companion to Greek Tragedy
edited by P. E. Easterling

The Cambridge Companion to Old English Literature
edited by Malcolm Godden and Michael Lapidge

The Cambridge Companion to Medieval Romance
edited by Roberta L. Krueger

The Cambridge Companion to Medieval English Theatre
edited by Richard Beadle

The Cambridge Companion to English Renaissance Drama, 2nd edn
edited by A. R. Braunmuller and Michael Hattaway

The Cambridge Companion to Renaissance Humanism
edited by Jill Kraye

The Cambridge Companion to English Poetry, Donne to Marvell
edited by Thomas N. Corns

The Cambridge Companion to English Literature, 1500–1600
edited by Arthur F. Kinney

The Cambridge Companion to English Literature, 1650–1740
edited by Steven N. Zwicker

The Cambridge Companion to Writing of the English Revolution
edited by N. H. Keeble

The Cambridge Companion to English Restoration Theatre
edited by Deborah C. Payne Fisk

The Cambridge Companion to British Romanticism
edited by Stuart Curran

The Cambridge Companion to Eighteenth-Century Poetry
edited by John Sitter

The Cambridge Companion to the Eighteenth-Century Novel
edited by John Richetti

The Cambridge Companion to the Gothic Novel
edited by Jerrold E. Hogle

The Cambridge Companion to Victorian Poetry
edited by Joseph Bristow

The Cambridge Companion to the Victorian Novel
edited by Deirdre David

The Cambridge Companion to Travel Writing
edited by Peter Hulme and Tim Youngs

The Cambridge Companion to American Realism and Naturalism
edited by Donald Pizer

The Cambridge Companion to Nineteenth-Century American Women's Writing
edited by Dale M. Bauer and Philip Gould

The Cambridge Companion to the Classic Russian Novel
edited by Malcolm V. Jones and Robin Feuer Miller

The Cambridge Companion to the French Novel: from 1800 to the Present
edited by Timothy Unwin

The Cambridge Companion to the Spanish Novel: from 1600 to the Present
edited by Harriet Turner and Adelaida López de Martínez

The Cambridge Companion to Jewish American Literature
edited by Hana Wirth-Nesher and Michael P. Kramer

The Cambridge Companion to Modernism
edited by Michael Levenson

The Cambridge Companion to Australian Literature
edited by Elizabeth Webby

The Cambridge Companion to American Women Playwrights
edited by Brenda Murphy

The Cambridge Companion to Modern British Women Playwrights
edited by Elaine Aston and Janelle Reinelt

The Cambridge Companion to Virgil
edited by Charles Martindale

The Cambridge Companion to Ovid
edited by Philip Hardie

The Cambridge Companion to Dante
edited by Rachel Jacoff

The Cambridge Companion to Cervantes
edited by Anthony J. Cascardi

The Cambridge Companion to Goethe
edited by Lesley Sharpe

The Cambridge Companion to Dostoevskii
edited by W. J. Leatherbarrow

The Cambridge Companion to Tolstoy
edited by Donna Tussing Orwin

The Cambridge Companion to Proust
edited by Ricahrd Bales

The Cambridge Companion to Thomas Mann
edited by Ritchie Robertson

The Cambridge Companion to Lacan
edited by Jean-Michel Rabaté

The Cambridge Companion to Chekhov
edited by Vera Gottlieb and Paul Allain

The Cambridge Companion to Ibsen
edited by James McFarlane

The Cambridge Companion to Brecht
edited by Peter Thomson and Glendyr Sacks

The Cambridge Chaucer Companion
edited by Piero Boitani and Jill Mann

The Cambridge Companion to Shakespeare
edited by Margareta de Grazia and Stanley Wells

The Cambridge Companion to Shakespeare on Film
edited by Russell Jackson

The Cambridge Companion to Shakespeare Comedy
edited by Alexander Leggatt

The Cambridge Companion to Shakespearean Tragedy
edited by Claire McEachern

The Cambridge Companion to Shakespeare on Stage
edited by Stanley Wells and Sarah Stanton

The Cambridge Companion to Shakespeare's History Plays
edited by Michael Hattaway

The Cambridge Companion to Spenser
edited by Andrew Hadfield

The Cambridge Companion to Ben Jonson
edited by Richard Harp and Stanley Stewart

The Cambridge Companion to Milton, 2nd edn
edited by Dennis Danielson

The Cambridge Companion to Samuel Johnson
edited by Greg Clingham

The Cambridge Companion to Jonathan Swift
edited by Christopher Fox

The Cambridge Companion to Mary Wollstonecraft
edited by Claudia L. Johnson

The Cambridge Companion to William Blake
edited by Morris Eaves

The Cambridge Companion to Wordsworth
edited by Stephen Gill

The Cambridge Companion to Coleridge
edited by Lucy Newlyn

The Cambridge Companion to Keats
edited by Susan J. Wolfson

The Cambridge Companion to Jane Austen
edited by Edward Copeland and Juliet McMaster

The Cambridge Companion to the Brontës
edited by Heather Glen

The Cambridge Companion to Charles Dickens
edited by John O. Jordan

The Cambridge Companion to George Eliot
edited by George Levine

The Cambridge Companion to Thomas Hardy
edited by Dale Kramer

The Cambridge Companion to Oscar Wilde
edited by Peter Raby

The Cambridge Companion to George Bernard Shaw
edited by Christopher Innes

The Cambridge Companion to Joseph Conrad
edited by J. H. Stape

The Cambridge Companion to D. H. Lawrence
edited by Anne Fernihough

The Cambridge Companion to Virginia Woolf
edited by Sue Roe and Susan Sellers

The Cambridge Companion to James Joyce
edited by Derek Attridge

The Cambridge Companion to T. S. Eliot
edited by A. David Moody

The Cambridge Companion to Ezra Pound
edited by Ira B. Nadel

The Cambridge Companion to Beckett
edited by John Pilling

The Cambridge Companion to Harold Pinter
edited by Peter Raby

The Cambridge Companion to Tom Stoppard
edited by Katherine E. Kelly

The Cambridge Companion to Herman Melville
edited by Robert S. Levine

The Cambridge Companion to Edith Wharton
edited by Millicent Bell

The Cambridge Companion to Henry James
edited by Jonathan Freedman

The Cambridge Companion to Walt Whitman
edited by Ezra Greenspan

The Cambridge Companion to Henry David Thoreau
edited by Joel Myerson

The Cambridge Companion to Mark Twain
edited by Forrest G. Robinson

The Cambridge Companion to Edgar Allan Poe
edited by Kevin J. Hayes

The Cambridge Companion to Emily Dickinson
edited by Wendy Martin

The Cambridge Companion to William Faulkner
edited by Philip M. Weinstein

The Cambridge Companion to Ernest Hemingway
edited by Scott Donaldson

The Cambridge Companion to F. Scott Fitzgerald
edited by Ruth Prigozy

The Cambridge Companion to Robert Frost
edited by Robert Faggen

The Cambridge Companion to Eugene O'Neill
edited by Michael Manheim

The Cambridge Companion to Tennessee Williams
edited by Matthew C. Roudané

The Cambridge Companion to Arthur Miller
edited by Christopher Bigsby

The Cambridge Companion to Sam Shepard
edited by Matthew C. Roudané

CAMBRIDGE COMPANIONS TO CULTURE

The Cambridge Companion to Modern German Culture
edited by Eva Kolinsky and Wilfried van der Will

The Cambridge Companion to Modern Russian Culture
edited by Nicholas Rzhevsky

The Cambridge Companion to Modern Spanish Culture
edited by David T. Gies

The Cambridge Companion to Modern Italian Culture
edited by Zygmunt G. Barański and Rebecca J. West